Lecture Notes in Artificial Intellig

Edited by J. G. Carbonell and J. Siekmann

Subseries of Lecture Notes in Computer Science

Jürgen Dix   João Leite (Eds.)

Computational Logic in Multi-Agent Systems

4th International Workshop, CLIMA IV
Fort Lauderdale, FL, USA, January 6-7, 2004
Revised Selected and Invited Papers

 Springer

Series Editors

Jaime G. Carbonell, Carnegie Mellon University, Pittsburgh, PA, USA
Jörg Siekmann, University of Saarland, Saarbrücken, Germany

Volume Editors

Jürgen Dix
Technische Universität Clausthal
Lehrstuhl für Computational Intelligence, Dept. CS
Julia-Albert-Str. 4, 38678 Clausthal, Germany
E-mail: dix@tu-clausthal.de

João Leite
Universidade Nova de Lisboa
Faculdade de Ciências e Tecnologia
Departmento de Informática, 2829-516 Caparica, Portugal
E-mail: jleite@di.fct.unl.pt

Library of Congress Control Number: 2004115978

CR Subject Classification (1998): I.2.11, I.2, C.2.4, F.4

ISSN 0302-9743
ISBN 3-540-24010-1 Springer Berlin Heidelberg New York

Springer is a part of Springer Science+Business Media

springeronline.com

© Springer-Verlag Berlin Heidelberg 2004
Printed in Germany

Typesetting: Camera-ready by author, data conversion by Scientific Publishing Services, Chennai, India
Printed on acid-free paper   SPIN: 11363989   06/3142   5 4 3 2 1 0

Preface

Over recent years, the notion of agency has claimed a major role in defining the trends of modern research. Influencing a broad spectrum of disciplines such as sociology, psychology, philosophy and many more, the agent paradigm virtually invaded every subfield of computer science, because of its promising applications for the Internet and in robotics.

Multi-agent systems (MAS) are communities of problem-solving entities that can perceive and act upon their environments to achieve their individual goals as well as joint goals. The work on such systems integrates many technologies and concepts in artificial intelligence and other areas of computing. There is a full spectrum of MAS applications that have been and are being developed: from search engines to educational aids to electronic commerce and trade.

Although commonly implemented by means of imperative languages, mainly for reasons of efficiency, the agent concept has recently increased its influence in the research and development of computational logic-based systems.

Computational logic, by virtue of its nature both in substance and method, provides a well-defined, general, and rigorous framework for systematically studying computation, be it syntax, semantics, and procedures, or implementations, environments, tools, and standards. Computational logic approaches problems, and provides solutions, at a sufficient level of abstraction so that they generalize from problem domain to problem domain, afforded by the nature of its very foundation in logic, both in substance and method, which constitutes one of its major assets.

The purpose of the Computational Logic and Multi-agent Systems (CLIMA) series of workshops is to discuss techniques, based on computational logic, for representing, programming, and reasoning about multi-agent systems in a formal way. This is clearly a major challenge for computational logic, to deal with real-world issues and applications.

The first workshop in this series took place in Las Cruces, New Mexico, USA, in 1999, under the designation Multi-agent Systems in Logic Programming (MASLP 1999), and affiliated with ICLP 1999. In the following year, the name of the workshop changed to Computational Logic in Multi-agent Systems (CLIMA 2000), taking place in London, UK, and affiliated with CL 2000. The subsequent edition, CLIMA 2001, took place in Paphos, Cyprus, affiliated with ICLP 2001. CLIMA 2002, took place in Copenhagen, Denmark, on August 1st, 2002, and was affiliated with ICLP 2002 and was part of FLOC 2002.

The 4th International Workshop on Computational Logic in Multi-agent Systems, CLIMA IV (renamed because it took place in 2004 instead of 2003), was co-located with the 7th International Conference on Logic Programming and Nonmonotonic Reasoning (LPNMR-7) and with the 8th International Symposium on Artificial Intelligence and Mathematics, and was held on January 6–7 in Fort Lauderdale, Florida, USA.

For CLIMA IV, we received 25 submissions of which 13 were selected for presentation, after a careful review process where each paper was independently reviewed by three members of the Program Committee. After the workshop, authors were invited to resubmit revised and extended versions of their papers. After a second round of reviewing, 11 papers were finally selected for publication.

This book contains such revised and extended papers together with two invited contributions coauthored by the CLIMA IV invited speakers: V.S. Subrahmanian from the University of Maryland and Michael Fisher from the University of Liverpool. It is composed of five parts: (i) invited papers, (ii) negotiation in multi-agent systems, (iii) planning in multi-agent systems, (iv) knowledge revision and update in multi-agent systems, and (v) learning in multi-agent systems. There follows a brief overview of the book.

Invited Papers

In *Distributed Algorithms for Dynamic Survivability of Multi-agent Systems,* *V.S. Subrahmanian, S. Kraus, and Y. Zhang* address the problem of survivability of a multi-agent system. They present three distributed algorithms that ensure that a multi-agent system will survive with maximal probability. Such algorithms extend existing centralized algorithms for survivability but are completely distributed and are adaptive in the sense that they can dynamically adapt to changes in the probability with which nodes will survive.

M. Fisher, C. Ghidini, and B. Hirsch, in their paper on *Programming Groups of Rational Agents*, develop a programming language to deal with agents that cooperate with each other and build teams and organizations. They suggest an executable temporal logic, augmented by the concepts of capabilities, beliefs, and confidence. An implementation in Java is described and illustrated by various examples.

Negotiation in Multi-agent Systems

M. Gavanelli, E. Lamma, P. Mello, and P. Torroni present *An Abductive Framework for Information Exchange in Multi-agent Systems*. They propose a framework for information sharing among abductive agents whose local knowledge bases are enlarged with a set of abduced hypotheses.

In *Fault Tolerant and Fixed Scalable Structure of Middle Agents* by *P. Tichý*, the design and implementation of a structure of middle-agents called dynamic hierarchical teamworks is described. This structure has a user-defined level of fault-tolerance and is scalable.

An approach to negotiation using linear logic (LL) is introduced by *P. Küngas and M. Matskin* in the paper *Symbolic Negotiation with Linear Logic*. This paper extends their previous work by taking advantage of a richer fragment of LL and introducing two sorts of nondeterministic choices into negotiation. This allows agents to reason and negotiate under certain degrees of uncertainty.

Planning in Multi-agent Systems

S. Costantini and A. Tocchio, in *Planning Experiments in the DALI Logic Programming Language*, discuss how some features of the new logic programming language DALI for agents and multi-agent systems are suitable for programming agents equipped with planning capabilities.

In *A New HTN Planning Framework for Agents in Dynamic Environments*, *H. Hayashi, K. Cho, and A. Ohsuga* extend previous work where they presented an agent life cycle that interleaves HTN planning, action execution, knowledge updates, and plan modification. The agent life cycle is extended so that the agent can handle partial-order plans.

Knowledge Revision and Update in Multi-agent Systems

In the paper *Revising Knowledge in Multi-agent Systems Using Revision Programming with Preferences*, *I. Pivkina, E. Pontelli, and T.C. Son* extend *Marek and Truszczyński's* framework of *Revision Programming* to allow for the specification of preferences, thus allowing users to introduce a bias in the way agents select one between alternative feasible ways of updating their knowledge. An answer set-based computation methodology is presented.

A. Bracciali and P. Torroni, in their preliminary report *A New Framework for Knowledge Revision of Abductive Agents Through Their Interaction*, describe a multi-agent framework for revising agents' knowledge through cooperation with other agents, where abduction and a constraint relaxation algorithm play the central role.

P. Dell'Acqua in his paper *Weighted Multi-dimensional Logic Programs*, extends *Leite et al.*'s framework of *Multi-dimensional Dynamic Logic Programs* by adding weights to the acyclic digraph that defines agent relationships in a multi-agent setting, thus allowing the addition of a measure of strength to the knowledge relationships represented by the edges.

In the paper *(Dis)Belief Change Based on Messages Processing*, *L. Perrussel and J.-M. Thévenin* explore a belief revision framework where agents have to deal with information received from other agents. A preference relation over the agents embedded in the multi-agent system is specified and agents' epistemic states are modelled by keeping track of current (consistent) beliefs, current disbeliefs, and potential beliefs.

Learning in Multi-agent Systems

A.G. Hernandez, A. El Fallah-Seghrouchni, and H. Soldano address the issue of *Learning in BDI Multi-agent Systems*. Their implementation enables multiple agents executed as parallel functions in a single Lisp image. In addition, their approach keeps consistency between learning and the theory of practical reasoning.

C. Child and K. Stathis define *The Apriori Stochastic Dependency Detection (ASDD) Algorithm for Learning Stochastic Logic Rules*. They show that stochastic rules produced by their algorithm are capable of reproducing an accurate world model in a simple predator-prey environment, and that a model can be produced with less experience than is required by a brute force method which records relative frequencies of state, action, and next state.

We would like to take this opportunity to thank the authors who answered our call with very good quality contributions, the invited speakers, and all workshop attendants. We would also like to thank the members of the Program Committee for ensuring the high quality of CLIMA IV by giving their time and expertise so that each paper could undergo two rounds of reviewing.

July 2004   Jürgen Dix
                                                                    João Leite

Workshop Organization

Workshop Organizers

Jürgen Dix   Technical University of Clausthal, Germany
João Leite   New University of Lisbon, Portugal

Program Committee

Chitta Baral   Arizona State University, USA
Gerd Brewka   University of Leipzig, Germany
Jürgen Dix   Technical University of Clausthal, Germany
Thomas Eiter   Vienna University of Technology, Austria
Klaus Fischer   DFKI, Germany
Michael Fisher   University of Liverpool, UK
James Harland   Royal Melbourne Institute of Technology, Australia
Katsumi Inoue   Kobe University, Japan
Gerhard Lakemeyer   Aachen University of Technology, Germany
João Leite   New University of Lisbon, Portugal
Yves Lespérance   York University, Canada
John Jules Ch. Meyer   University of Utrecht, The Netherlands
Leora Morgenstern   IBM, USA
Luís Moniz Pereira   New University of Lisbon, Portugal
Fariba Sadri   Imperial College London, UK
Ken Satoh   National Institute of Informatics, Japan
Renate Schmidt   University of Manchester, UK
Guillermo Simari   Universidad Nacional del Sur, Argentina
V.S. Subrahmanian   University of Maryland, USA
Francesca Toni   Imperial College London, UK
Paolo Torroni   University of Bologna, Italy
Wiebe van der Hoek   University of Liverpool, UK
Cees Witteveen   Delft University of Technology, The Netherlands

CLIMA Steering Committee

Jürgen Dix   Technical University of Clausthal, Germany
João Leite   New University of Lisbon, Portugal
Fariba Sadri   Imperial College London, UK
Ken Satoh   National Institute of Informatics, Japan
Francesca Toni   Imperial College London, UK
Paolo Torroni   University of Bologna, Italy

Additional Reviewers

Marcela Capobianco	Koji Iwanuma	Sebastian Sardina
James Delgrand	Antonis C. Kakas	Dmitry Tishkovsky
Marcelo Falappa	Robert Kowalski	Gregory Wheeler
Marco Gavanelli	Maurice Pagnucco	
Ullrich Hustadt	Chiaki Sakama	

Sponsoring Institutions

We gratefully acknowledge CoLogNET, the European Network of Excellence in Computational Logic, which financially helped us to support one of the two distinguished invited speakers.

Table of Contents

Learning in BDI Multi-agent Systems

Distributed Algorithms for Dynamic Survivability of Multiagent Systems[*]

V.S. Subrahmanian[1], Sarit Kraus[2], and Yingqian Zhang[3]

[1] Dept. of Computer Science, University of Maryland, College Park, MD 20742
vs@cs.umd.edu
[2] Dept. of Computer Science, Bar-Ilan University, Ramat Gan, 52900 Israel
sarit@cs.biu.ac.il
[3] Dept. of Computer Science, University of Manchester, M13 9PL, UK
zhangy@cs.man.ac.uk

Abstract. Though multiagent systems (MASs) are being increasingly used, few methods exist to ensure survivability of MASs. All existing methods suffer from two flaws. First, a centralized survivability algorithm (CSA) ensures survivability of the MAS - unfortunately, if the node on which the CSA exists goes down, the survivability of the MAS is questionable. Second, no mechanism exists to change how the MAS is deployed when external factors trigger a re-evaluation of the survivability of the MAS. In this paper, we present three algorithms to address these two important problems. Our algorithms can be built on top of *any* CSA. Our algorithms are completely distributed and can handle external triggers to compute a new deployment. We report on experiments assessing the efficiency of these algorithms.

1 Introduction

Though multiagent systems are rapidly growing in importance, there has been little work to date on ensuring the survivability of multiagent systems (MASs for short). As more and more MASs are deployed in applications ranging from auctions for critical commodities like electricity to monitoring of nuclear plants and computer networks, there is a growing need to ensure that these MASs are robust and resilient in the face of network outages and server down times.

To date, there has been relatively little work on survivability of MASs. Most approaches to ensuring survivability of MASs are based on the idea of replicating or cloning agents so that if a node hosting that agent goes down, a copy of the agent residing on another network location will still be functioning. This paper falls within this category of work. However, existing replication based approaches suffer from two major flaws.

---

[*] Sarit Kraus is also affiliated with University of Maryland. This work was supported in part by the Army Research Lab under contract DAAD19-03-2-0026, the CTA on Advanced Decision Architectures, by ARO contract DAAD190010484, by NSF grants 0205489, IIS0329851 and IIS0222914.

J. Dix and J. Leite (Eds.): CLIMA IV, LNAI 3259, pp. 1–15, 2004.

The first major flaw is that the survivability algorithms themselves are *centralized*. In other words, even though the agents in the MAS may themselves be distributed across the network, the survivability algorithm itself resides on a single node. Thus, if the node hosting the survivability algorithm goes down along with all nodes containing some agent in the MAS, then the system is compromised. This way of "attacking" the MAS can be easily accomplished by a competent hacker.

The second major flaw is that the survivability algorithms do not *adapt* to changes that affect the survivability of the MAS. Most algorithms assume that once the survivability algorithm tells us where to replicate agents, we just replicate the agents at the appropriate nodes and then ignore survivability issues altogether. It is clearly desirable to continuously (or at least regularly) monitor how well the MAS is "surviving" and to respond to changes in this quantity by redeploying the agent replicas to appropriate new locations.

We present three *distributed* algorithms to ensure that a multiagent system will survive with maximal probability. These algorithms *extend centralized algorithms for survivability* such as those developed by [1] but are completely distributed and are adaptive in the sense that they can dynamically adapt to changes in the probability with which nodes will survive. The algorithms are shown to achieve a new deployment that preserves whatever properties the centralized algorithm has. For example, in a recent paper on survivability, Kraus et al. [1] develop a centralized algorithm called COD for computing deployments of MASs that maximize the probability of survival of the deployment. If our distributed algorithms were built on top of COD, the resulting deployments created by our system would also maximize probability of survival.

We have also developed a prototype implementation of our algorithms and conducted detailed experiments to assess how good the algorithms are from three points of view: (i) what is the CPU time taken to find a deployment, (ii) what is the amount of network time used up in redeploying agents, and (iii) what is the survivability of deployments.

2   Assumptions

Throughout this paper, we assume that an *agent* is a program that provides one or more services. Our framework for survivability is independent of the specific agent programming language used to program the agent. In addition, we assume that a *multiagent application* is a finite set of agents. We will develop the concept of a *deployment agent* introduced in the next section that can be used by the MAS to ensure its own survivability.

We assume that a network is a fully connected graph $G = (V, E)$, i.e. $E = V \times V$. In addition, we assume that each node $n \in V$ has some memory, denoted $space(n)$, that it makes available for hosting agents in a given multiagent system. We also use $space(a)$ to denote the space requirements of an agent a. If A is a set of agents, $space(A)$ is used to denote $\sum_{a \in A} space(a)$.

When a set D of nodes in a network $G = (V, E)$ *goes down*, the resulting network is the graph $G' = (V - D, E - \{(v_1, v_2) \mid (v_1, v_2) \in E$ and either $v_1 \in D$ or $v_2 \in D\})$.

A *deployment* of a MAS $\{a_1, \ldots, a_n\}$ w.r.t. a network $G = (V, E)$ is a mapping $\mu : V \to 2^{MAS}$ such that for all $1 \leq i \leq n$, there exists a $v \in V$ such that $a_i \in \mu(v)$.

Suppose μ is a deployment of $\{a_1, \ldots, a_n\}$ w.r.t. a network G and suppose $G' = (V', E')$ is the resulting network when some set D of nodes goes down. μ *survives the loss of* D iff the restriction μ' of μ to $V - D$ is a deployment w.r.t. G'. Intuitively, this definition merely says that a MAS survives when a set of nodes goes down if and only if at least one copy of each agent in the MAS is still present on at least one node that did not go down. We demonstrate our problem using the following example.

Example 1. Suppose $V = \{n_1, n_2, n_3, n_4\}$ and $MAS = \{a, b, c, d\}$. A current deployment is given by: $\mu_{old}(n_1) = \{a\}, \mu_{old}(n_2) = \{b, d\}, \mu_{old}(n_3) = \{a, b\}, \mu_{old}(n_4) = \{b, c\}$.

Suppose the system administrator of node n_4 announces that this node will go down in an hour in order to perform an urgent maintenance task. It is easy to see that μ_{old} will not survive this event as agent c will not be present in any of the nodes. Thus, μ_{old} should be changed: a copy of agent c should be deployed on one of the nodes $n_1, \ldots, n_3$ and additional copy of b may also be deployed in $n_1, \ldots, n_3$. Space restrictions of these nodes may lead to additional changes in the deployment, e.g., a copy of d may be moved from node n_2 to node n_3.

3 Distributed Multiagent Survivability

In this section, we provide three alternative algorithms to ensure the survivability of a MAS. As mentioned above, we assume that our distributed survivability algorithms build on top of some arbitrary, but fixed centralized survivability algorithm CSA. Several such algorithms exist such as those in [1]. We now describe each of these three algorithms. **Note that all copies of the deployment agent perform the actions here, not just one copy** (if only one copy performed the computations, then we would just have a centralized algorithm).

As mentioned earlier, our algorithms will use a *deployment agent* (*da* for short) which will ensure survivability. *da* is added to the MAS as an additional survivability agent.

Definition 1. *Suppose MAS is a multi-agent application. The* survivability enhancement *of MAS, denoted* MAS^*, *is the set* $MAS \cup \{da\}$ *where da is a special agent called* deployment agent.

The rest of this section focuses on different ways of designing and implementing the deployment agent *da*.

3.1 The ASA1 Algorithm

The ASA1 algorithm deploys a copy of *da* in every node of the network. We make the following assumptions about *da*: (i) *da* knows the current deployment, (ii) whenever a new deployment needs to be computed, *da* is triggered, (iii) *da* is built on top of any arbitrary centralized survivability algorithm CSA.

As *da* is located in each node, we will assume that for any $n \in V$, $space(n)$ is the available memory on n excluding the space for *da*.

Whenever the *da* agents are notified that a new deployment needs to be computed, each copy of the *da* agent performs the following steps:

1. It examines the current deployment μ_{old};
2. Once da is told to redeploy by an external process, it uses the CSA algorithm to compute a new deployment μ_{new};
3. da stores the difference between μ_{old} and μ_{new} in a special data structure called a *difference table*. The difference table dif has the following schema:
    - Node (*string*): node id for all $n \in V$;
    - Deploy (set of *string*): agents' current deployments μ_{old};
    - Insrt (set of *string*): agents that are presently not located in the node but need to be allocated according to the new deployment μ_{new};
    - Remv (set of *string*): agents that are presently located in the node but need to be deleted from it according to the new deployment μ_{new};
4. Each copy of da at each node looks at its *Insrt* and *Remv* columns and makes a decision on how to delete and/or add agents from its node.

Notice that at any given instance in time, all the deployment agents on all nodes have the same difference table. Our key task is to design step 4. Before doing this, we present an example of a difference table.

Example 2. Consider the MAS and μ_{old} of Example 1. Consider a new deployment: $\mu_{new}(n_1) = \{a, b\}$, $\mu_{new}(n_2) = \{b, c\}$, $\mu_{new}(n_3) = \{a, d\}$, and $\mu_{new}(n_4) = \{d\}$. In this case, the difference table between μ_{old} and μ_{new} is given by Table 1.

Table 1. A difference table generated by *deployment agent*

Node	Insrt	Remv	Deploy
n_1	b		a
n_2	c	d	b, d
n_3	d	b	a, b
n_4	d	b, c	b, c

Adding and/or deleting agents to/from nodes can be performed according to the difference table. However, these operations should be handled very carefully as there are two constraints that must be satisfied during the whole re-deployment process:

- *space*: while these operations are being performed, the space constraint on each node must be satisfied;
- *copies of agents*: at any point in time during step (4), there must exist at least one copy for each agent $a \in MAS$ in the network.

Example 3. To see why Step 4 is complex, consider the difference table in Table 1. One may be tempted to say that we can implement the insertions and deletions as follows: (i) Insert c on n_2. (ii) Delete d from n_2. Notice however that we can insert c on n_2 only if there is enough space on n_2 to accommodate b, c, d simultaneously (as otherwise the host node n_2 may reject the insertion of c) for space violations. Alternatively, one may be tempted to first delete d from node n_2 to free space to insert c - but this means that agent d has disappeared from all nodes and is hence lost for ever!

Before presenting our algorithm for deleting/adding agents, we first present a few definitions of concepts that will be used in the algorithm.

Definition 2. *An agent a can be safely deleted from node n (denoted by $safeDel(a, n)$) if the number of copies of agent a in the* Deploy *column of the difference table is larger than the number of copies of agent a in the* Remv *column.*

When an agent can be *safely deleted*, we are guaranteed that at least one copy of the agent is present elsewhere on the network. In our running example (Table 1), the only agent that can be safely deleted is agent b at node n_3.

We use $Insrt(n)$, $Remv(n)$ and $Deploy(n)$ to denote the insert list, the remove list and the deploy list of node $n \in V$ in the difference table. The implementation of da in **ASA1** algorithm is based on a set of logical rules governing the operations of da. We first present these rules before describing the algorithm in detail. The rules use the following action predicates (predicates representing actions are used in much the same way as in Kowalski's and Green's formulations of planning, cf. [2]).

- $ADD(a, n)$: Add agent $a \in MAS$ to node $n \in V$;
- $DEL(A, n)$: Delete a set of agents $A \subseteq MAS$ from node $n \in V$;
- $SWITCH(A, n, A', n')$: Switch two sets of agents $A \subseteq MAS$ and $A' \subseteq MAS$ that are located on nodes n and n' respectively;
- remdif(A, L, n) and insdif(A, L, n): Suppose A is a set of agents, L is a string in $\{Remv, Insrt, Deploy\}$, and n is a node. remdif(A, L, n) removes all nodes in the L-list of node n in the difference table. Likewise, insdif(A, L, n) inserts all nodes in A into the L list of node n's entry in the difference table.

Note that $Insrt(n)$ represents the $Insrt$ field of node n in the difference table. It specifies what new agents must be inserted into node n. In contrast, insdif$(A, Insrt, n)$ specifies that $Insrt(n)$ must be updated to $Insrt(n) \cup A$, i.e. it refers to an update of the difference table itself. In the example of Table 1, remdif$(\{b\}, Deploy, n_2)$ causes the deploy field associated with n_2 to be reset to just $\{d\}$ instead of $\{b, d\}$.

We now introduce the rules governing the execution of these actions.

Rule 1. *The first rule says that if A is a set of agents each of which can be safely deleted from node n, then A can be removed from node n.*
$DEL(A, n) \leftarrow (\forall a \in A) safeDel(a, n)$

Rule 2. *This rule says that if a set A of agents is deleted from node n, we need to update the difference table by removing A from the remove and deploy lists of node n.*
remdif$(A, Remv, n) \wedge$ remdif$(A, Deploy, n) \leftarrow DEL(A, n)$

Rule 3. *This rule says that an agent a can be added to node n if there is sufficient space on node n to accommodate a's memory needs.*
$ADD(a, n) \leftarrow (space(n) - space(Deploy(n))) \geq space(a)$

Rule 4. *If agent a is added to node n, we must remove its id from the insert column and add it to the deploy column of node n.*
remdif$(\{a\}, Insrt, n) \wedge$ insdif$(\{a\}, Deploy(n)) \leftarrow ADD(a, n)$

Rule 5. *These rules says that two sets of agents, A deployed on node n and A' on node n', can be switched if: A' is a subset of the insert set on node n as well as A' is in the deleted set of node n'; A is a subset of the remove set on node n and it is also in the added list of node n'; furthermore, the space constraints on switching A and A' between n and n' must be satisfied.*

$SWITCH(A, n, A', n') \leftarrow$
$\quad A' \subseteq Remv(n') \wedge A' \subseteq Insrt(n) \wedge A \subseteq Remv(n) \wedge A \subseteq Insrt(n') \wedge$
$\quad CHKSWITCH(A, n, A', n').$
$CHKSWITCH(A, n, A', n') \leftarrow$
$\quad (Space(n) - space(Deploy(n)) + space(A) \geq space(A')) \wedge$
$\quad (space(n') - space(Deploy(n')) + space(A') \geq space(A)).$

$SWITCH(A, n, A', n')$ *performs appropriate* ADD *and* DEL *actions on agents at the appropriate nodes.*

$(\forall a \in A')ADD(a, n) \wedge (\forall a \in A)ADD(a, n') \wedge DEL(A', n') \wedge DEL(A, n)$
$\quad \leftarrow SWITCH(A, n, A', n')$

Rule 6. *This rule says when* $SWITCH(A, n, A', n')$ *is performed, we must update the difference table.*

remdif(A, Remv, n) $\wedge$ remdif(A', Remv, n') $\wedge$ remdif(A', Insrt, n)
$\wedge$remdif(A, Insrt, n') $\wedge$ remdif(A, Deploy, n) $\wedge$ insdif(A', Deploy, n)
$\wedge$remdif(A', Deploy, n') $\wedge$ insdif(A, Deploy, n')
$\quad \leftarrow SWITCH(A, n, A', n').$

Rule 7. *The rules below deal with the case where there is no agent that can be safely deleted from node n (the case shown in rule 1) and there is no current available space for adding an agent (as described in rule 3) and there is no direct switch that could be performed (the case of rule 5). That is, when more than two nodes are involved with switch, we need the following rules.*

$SWITCH(A, n, A', n') \leftarrow$
$\quad A' \subseteq Remv(n') \wedge A \subseteq Remv(n) \wedge (\exists B \subseteq A')B \subseteq Insrt(n) \wedge$
$\quad CHKSWITCH(A, n, A', n').$
$(\forall a \in A')ADD(a, n) \wedge (\forall a \in A)ADD(a, n') \wedge DEL(A', n') \wedge DEL(A, n)$
$\quad \leftarrow SWITCH(A, n, A', n')$

When switching A and A', if we move an agent b to a node where b is not the desired agent in the new deployment, we should delete b from that node in the future process, that is, we should add b to the delete list of the node.

remdif(A, Remv, n) $\wedge$ remdif(A', Remv, n') $\wedge$ remdif(A, Deploy, n)$\wedge$
$\quad$ insdif(A', Deploy, n) $\wedge$ remdif(A', Deploy, n') $\wedge$ insdif(A, Deploy, n')
$\quad \leftarrow SWITCH(A, n, A', n')$
insdif($\{b\}$, Remv, n) $\leftarrow (\forall b \in A')b \notin Insrt(n) \wedge SWITCH(A, n, A', n').$
remdif($\{b\}$, Insrt, n) $\leftarrow (\forall b \in A')b \in Insrt(n) \wedge SWITCH(A, n, A', n').$
insdif($\{b\}$, Remv, n') $\leftarrow (\forall b \in A)b \notin Insrt(n') \wedge SWITCH(A, n, A', n').$
remdif($\{b\}$, Insrt, n') $\leftarrow (\forall b \in A)b \in Insrt(n') \wedge SWITCH(A, n, A', n').$

Our algorithm to redeploy a MAS is based on the above set of rules.

Algorithm 1. ASA1(Ne, MAS, dif)
$(\star$ *Input:* (1) *network* $Ne = (V, E)$ $\star)$
$(\star$ (2) *multiagent application* MAS $\star)$
$(\star$ (3) *current difference table* dif $\star)$

1. $flag_1 = true$
2. **while** $flag_1$ **do** (* *changes are needed by diff table* *)
    – **if** (*for all* $n \in V$, $Remv(n) = \emptyset$ **and** $Insrt(n) = \emptyset$), **then** $flag_1 = false;$
    – **else, do**
        (1) $flag_2 = true, flag_3 = true$
        (2) **while** $flag_2$, **do** (* *do updates; diff table updated* *)
            (a) $flag_2 = false$
            (b) **for** *each* $n \in V$, **do**
                A. $A = Remv(n)$ (* *do all possible deletions* *)
                B. **if** $A \neq \emptyset$, **then**
                    $(dif, flag_2) = DEL(A, n, dif, flag_2)$
            (c) **for** *each* $n \in V$ **do**
                A. $A = Insrt(n)$
                B. **if** $A \neq \emptyset$, **then** (* *add all agents you can* *)
                    $(dif, flag_2) = ADD(A, MAS, n, dif, flag_2)$
        (3) **for each** $n \in V$, **do**
            if $flag_3$, **then**
                i. $A = Insrt(n)$
                ii. **if** $A \neq \emptyset$, **then** (* *switch agents that could not be added before* *)
                    $(dif, flag_3) = SWITCH(A, MAS, n, dif, flag_3)$

The function DEL$(A, n, dif, flag)$ receives as input: (1) a set of agents A, (2) a node n (3) a current difference table dif and (4) a flag. For each agent in A, the algorithm checks if it can safely delete the agent; if so it deletes the agent from n and updates the dif table. It returns the updated dif table and sets the flag to be true if any agent was deleted. The function ADD(A, MAS, n, dif) receives as an input (1) a set of agents A, (2) a multiagent application MAS, (3) a node n, (4) the current difference table dif, and (5) a flag. For each agent $a \in A$ if there is enough space on n to deploy a, i.e., $space(n) - space(Deploy(n)) \geq space(a)$, it adds a to n, updates the dif table and changes $flag$ to indicate an agent has been added to n. It returns: (1) the dif table, and (2) the flag.

The $SWITCH$ function uses a subroutine called $CHKSWITCH(A, n, A', n', dif, MAS)$. This function checks to see if any space overflows occur when exchanging a set A of agents current on node n with a set of agents A' currently on node n'. If no space overflow occurs, it returns true - otherwise it returns false.

Algorithm 2. $SWITCH(R, MAS, n, dif, flag)$
$(\star$ *Input:* (1) *a set of agents* R $\star)$
$(\star$ (2) *multiagent application* MAS $\star)$
$(\star$ (3) *node id* n $\star)$
$(\star$ (4) *current difference table* dif $\star)$
$(\star$ (5) $flag$ $\star)$
$(\star$ *Output* (1) *updated difference table* dif $\star)$
$(\star$ (2) $flag$ $\star)$

1. **for** *each agent* $a \in R$, **if** *(flag)*, **do**
   if *there exists a set* $A \subseteq Remv(n)$, $n' \in V$ *and a set* $A' \subseteq Remv(n')$ *such that*
   a. $a \in A'$, **and**
   b. $CHKSWITCH(A, n, A', n', dif, MAS) = true$
   then
   a. *switch* A *and* A' *between nodes* n *and* n'
   b. $Remv(n) = Remv(n) \setminus A$, $Remv(n') = Remv(n') \setminus A'$,
       $Deploy(n) = Deploy(n) \cup A' \setminus A$,
       $Deploy(n') = Deploy(n') \cup A \setminus A'$
   c. **for** *each* $b \in A'$, **do**
       if $b \notin Insrt(n)$ **then** $Remv(n) = Remv(n) \cup \{b\}$
       else $Insrt(n) = Insrt(n) \setminus \{b\}$
   d. **for** *each* $b \in A$, **do**
       if $b \notin Insrt(n')$ **then** $Remv(n') = Remv(n') \cup \{b\}$
       else $Insrt(n') = Insrt(n') \setminus \{b\}$
   e. *update* dif
   f. $flag = false$
2. *return* dif *and* $flag$

The following lemmas are needed to prove that **ASA1** is correct.

Lemma 1. *Each execution of action DEL, ADD, and $SWITCH$ always results in a decrease on the number of agents in column $Remv$ or $Insrt$.*

Proof. Rules 2 and 4 clearly show that the actions $DEL(A, n)$ and $ADD(a, n)$ remove agents from $Remv(n)$ and $Insrt(n)$ respectively. Now consider the $SWITCH$ action. When switching agents between two nodes only (Rule 5), $SWITCH(A, n, A', n')$ removes A from $Remv(n)$, A from $Insrt(n')$, A' from $Remv(n')$, and A' from $Insrt(n)$, as shown in Rule 6. In the case of Rule 7, where more than two nodes are involved in the switch, action $SWITCH(A, n, A', n')$ adds at most $A + A' - 1$ agents in $Remv(n)$ and $Remv(n')$, while removing at least $A + A' + 1$ agents from $Remv$ and $Insrt$ of node n and n'. This shows that performing each action must reduce the number of agents in the $Remv$ or $Insrt$ columns.   □

Lemma 2. *In each iteration of the while loop shown in Step 2 of algorithm $\mathsf{ASA1}$, at least one action (DEL, ADD, or $SWITCH$) must be executed.*

Proof. In Step (b) of the while loop (2), all possible deletions DEL will be performed if agents in $Remv$ can be safely deleted according to Rule 1. In the loop of Step (c), all possible additions ADD will be done based on constraints shown in Rule 3. Even if no action is performed in the while loop (2), in Step (3), according to Rule 5 and Rule 7, there must exist two sets of agents on two different nodes such that action $SWITCH(A, n, A', n')$ can be performed. This shows that for each while loop in Step 2, at least one action on agents will be executed.   □

Theorem 3 (Correctness). *Suppose the rules (Rule 1 - 7) are applied according to the order listed. Then the sequence of actions performed by Algorithm $\mathsf{ASA1}$ is the one performed by the rules. $\mathsf{ASA1}$ always terminates.*

Proof. In **ASA1**, the execution of actions is determined by the rules. With the assumption that the actions of the rules are taken according to their order, actions executed by the algorithm are those entailed by the rules.

In Algorithm **ASA1**, the while loop of Step (2) makes sure that no more agents can be safely deleted and no more agents can be added to the nodes, i.e. $flag_2 = false$. Thus, the loop in Step (2) terminates after some iterations.

For each execution of the while loop in Step 2, according to Lemma 2, there must execute at least one action on some agent at some nodes. Moreover each action must reduce the size of $Remv(n)$ or $Insrt(n)$ as explained in Lemma 1. Thus the size of $Remv$ and $Insrt$ decreases monotonically with each iteration of the while loop. Therefore the algorithm must reach a step where for all n in the network, $Remv(n) = \emptyset$ and $Insrt(n) = \emptyset$, which make $flag_1$ false, and the algorithm terminates. □

Example 4. Consider the network and the deployment of example 1. Suppose each node in the network can store a deployment agent da and two regular agents. Suppose that da were triggered and suppose they computed a new deployment as specified in example 2. Then, each copy of da computes the dif table as listed in Table 1. According to algorithm **ASA1**, b is first deleted from node n_3 by da located on that node and b and c are deleted from node n_4 by its deployment agent. d is not deleted in the first round because it is not safe to delete it at that stage. b is then inserted into node n_1 (copied from n_2) and d is inserted into node n_3 and n_4. d is then removed from n_2, and finally c is inserted into node n_2.

3.2 The ASA2 Algorithm

In this algorithm the deployment agent da is not located at each node. Instead, we add da to a multiagent system MAS to get an updated multiagent system MAS^* and apply the centralized algorithm on MAS^*. This returns a new deployment μ_{new} which is then executed by the deployment agent. In this case, the programming of da is somewhat different from the programming of it in **ASA1** because there is no guarantee that every node has a copy of da.

Algorithm **ASA2** assumes that each agent has a mobility capability, i.e., it can obtain a movement instruction from a da and perform it. In addition, each agent can delete itself. In addition, all agents in MAS as well as da satisfy the condition that whenever it receives a message from *any* da to move to another location, it does so. After performing the move, it sends a message to all deployment agents saying it has moved.

Once μ_{new} is computed by **CSA**, each copy of da executes an algorithm called $DELETECOPY$ that deletes all but one copy of all agents in MAS. All copies of da send messages to the agent copies to be deleted telling them to delete themselves. da copies create a plan to move and/or copy the one remaining copy of each agent to the nodes specified by μ_{new}. Note that all copies of da perform the same actions at the same time.

Algorithm 4. ASA2($Ne, MAS^*, \mu_{\blacksquare\square\square}, \mu_{\square\blacksquare\square}$)
($\star$ *Input:* (1) *network* $Ne = (V, E)$ $\star$)
($\star$ (2) *multiagent application* MAS^* $\star$)
($\star$ (3) *current deployment* $\mu_{\blacksquare\square\square}$ $\star$)
($\star$ (4) *new deployment* $\mu_{\square\blacksquare\square}$ $\star$)

1. **for** *each* $a \in MAS^*$, **do** *DELETECOPY*$(a, \mu_{\blacksquare\blacksquare\blacksquare})$;
2. $flag = true$;
3. **while** $flag$, **do**
    - **if** (*for all* $n \in V$, $\mu_{\blacksquare\blacksquare\blacksquare}(n) = \mu_{\blacksquare\square\blacksquare}(n)$), **then** $flag = false$
    - **else, do**
        (a) $flag2 = false$, $flag3 = true$
        (b) *for all* $n \in V$, *do*
            i. $A = \mu_{\blacksquare\square\blacksquare}(n)$
            ii. $flag2 = ADDCOPY(A, \mu_{\blacksquare\blacksquare\blacksquare}, \mu_{\blacksquare\square\blacksquare}, n)$
        (c) *if*$(flag2 = false)$, *then*
            for each $n \in V$, *do*
            if flag3, then
            i. $A = \mu_{\blacksquare\blacksquare\blacksquare}(n)$
            ii. $flag3 = SWITCHCOPY(A, \mu_{\blacksquare\blacksquare\blacksquare}, \mu_{\blacksquare\square\blacksquare})$

The above algorithm uses $DELETECOPY$ (not specified explicitly due to space constraints) which uses a deterministic algorithm to delete all but one copy of each agent (e.g. via a lexicographic order on nodes). It is important that all copies of da use the same $DELETECOPY$ algorithm so that they all agree on what nodes each agent should be deleted from. Likewise $ADDCOPY(a, \mu_{old}, \mu_{new}, n)$ adds a copy of agent a to node n if there is space on node n and if the new deployment μ_{new} requires a to be in n - it does this by asking a node currently hosting a to clone and move such a copy of n. Details of $ADDCOPY$ are suppressed due to space constraints. All these algorithms update μ_{old}.

Algorithm 5. *SWITCHCOPY*$(A, \mu_{\blacksquare\blacksquare\blacksquare}, \mu_{\blacksquare\square\blacksquare})$
(*   Input: (1) a set agents A *)
(*   (2) old deployment $\mu_{\blacksquare\blacksquare\blacksquare}$ *)
(*   (3) new deployment $\mu_{\blacksquare\square\blacksquare}$ *)
(* Output: (1) flag   *)

1. **for** *each agent* $a \in A$, **do**
        if *there exists a set* A' *on* n' *such that*
    (a) $a \in \mu_{\blacksquare\blacksquare\blacksquare}(n')$, *and*
    (b) $CHKSWITCH(A, n, A', n') = true$
    then
    (a) *switch* A *and* A' *between nodes* n *and* n' *and update* $\mu_{\blacksquare\blacksquare\blacksquare}$;
    (b) $flag = false$;
2. *return* $flag$

Example 5. Suppose nodes n_1 and n_3 of the network of Example 1 can store a da agent and two other agents. Suppose n_2 and n_4 can store only two regular agents. First, agents a,b and da are removed from node n_3. Then, agent b is removed from node n_4. The deployment agent da in node n_1 is responsible for all these deletions and for further updates. It also updates μ_{old} accordingly. b is then added to node n_1, and d and da are added to nodes n_3 and n_4. Only then is d deleted from n_2. c is then added to n_2 and then deleted from n_4.

3.3   The ASA3 Algorithm

Just as in algorithm **ASA2**, the deployment agent used in Algorithm **ASA3** is not located on each node. Instead it is treated just like any other agent and deployed using the CSA. However, the procedure to decide on the order of deletion and adding copies of agents to nodes is that of algorithm **ASA1**. The behavior of the deployment agent is as follows.

> Originally, it is deployed (along with other agents) using the CSA algorithm. When survivability of one or more nodes changes, each da computes the difference table (as in the **ASA1**). Each da then sends a message to all agents that can be safely deleted (including, possibly a deployment agent da) telling them to delete themselves and send a message just when they are about to finish the operation. After this, they send "move" or "exchange" messages to agents one at a time. When they get an acknowledgment that the move has been performed, they send a move message to the next agent, and so on until they are done. Note that while in Algorithm **ASA1**, agents can be moved/copied to other nodes simultaneously, in algorithm **ASA3** this is done sequentially.

The correctness proof of **ASA3** is similar to the one done for **ASA1**. The details of the proof are omitted in the paper due to space constraints.

4   Implementation and Experimental Results

We developed a prototype implementation of all the above algorithms in Java and tested them out on a Linux PC. We used a sample of 31 existing agents to determine a distribution of agent sizes (in the 0 to 250 KB range). We ran experiments with varying network bandwidths - for space reasons we only report on experiments where the bandwidth was 100 KB/s (this is twice the bandwidth of a dial-in model, but much smaller than the bandwidth of broadband connections that may exceed 100 MB/s). The centralized survivability algorithm we used for our experiments was COD [1].

Figure 1 shows the effect of problem size on the CPU time required by the algorithms as well as the network time required to move the agents around. We used various measures of "problem size" in our experiments (such as sum of numbers of agents and nodes, ratio of number of agents to the number of nodes, etc.). Only the first is reported in figure 1 due to space constraints. The markings such as $n : 5, a : 4$ refer to a MAS of 4 agents deployed over 5 nodes. We made the following observations:

1. CPU Time: **ASA1** and **ASA3** always outperform **ASA2** w.r.t CPU time. **ASA1** and **ASA3** are more or less incomparable.
2. Network Time: Again, **ASA1** and **ASA3** always outperform **ASA2**. As the problem size gets larger, **ASA1** outperforms **ASA3**.

Due to space constraints, we are unable to present full details of all our experiments. However, the above experiments imply that **ASA1** is preferable to both **ASA2** and **ASA3** as far as time is concerned.

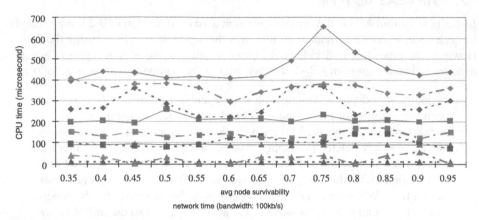

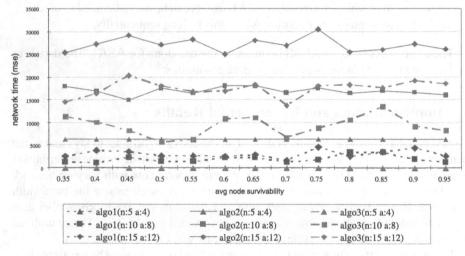

Fig. 1. CPU and Network Times of the Three Algorithms

Figure 2 reports some results on survivability of deployments using the three algorithms described in this paper. In the first set of experiments, we fix the size of *da* agent but vary the problem size, while in the second set of experiments, we change the ratio of *da* size to the average agent's size. As shown in Figure 2, when the problem size increases or the size of the *da* agent increases, the survivability of the deployments identified by ASA3 becomes higher than the survivability of deployments identified by ASA1 (note ASA2 has the same survivability as ASA3). The results demonstrate the effect of *da* agents on survivability of deployment. Compared with ASA2 and ASA3, ASA1 deploy more *da* agents in the network, and hence, the amount of available space for adding regular agents is decreased.

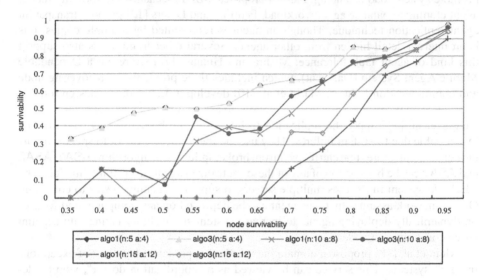

Survivability of deployments (Algorithm 1 and 3)

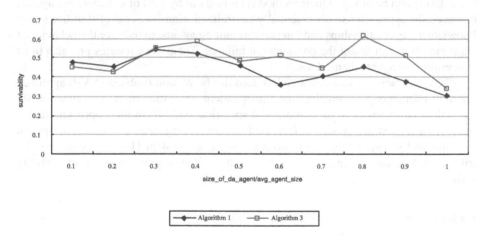

Fig. 2. Survivability of deployments by ASA1and ASA3when the problem size increases and when the size of da increases

5   Related Work and Conclusions

To our knowledge, there are no distributed probabilistic models of survivability of a MAS. In addition, there are no works we are aware of that allow for redeployment of agents when there are changes that trigger the need to examine if a redeployment is needed. [7, 6] use agent-cloning and agent-merging techniques to mitigate agent over-loading and promote system load balancing. Fan [8] proposes a BDI mechanism to formally model agent cloning to balance agent workload. Fedoruk and Deters [12] propose transparent agent replication technique. Though an agent is represented by multiple copies, this is an internal detail hidden from other agents. Several other frameworks also support this kind of agent fault tolerance. Mishra and Huang [17, 13] present a Dependable Mobile Agent System (DaAgent), which includes three protocols for recovering node and communication failures. Marin et al. [10] develop a framework to design reliable distributed applications. They use simulations to assess migration and replication costs. Kumar et al. [11] apply the replication technique to the broker agents who may be inaccessible due to system failures. They use the theory of teamwork to specify robust brokered architectures that can recover from broker failure. Our algorithms ASA1, ASA2 and ASA3 can be built on top of any of these centralized agent survivability models. The RECoMa system in [3] uses multiple servers to support matching agents to computer. Our framework assumes that any agent can be deployed on any computer, and focuses on dynamically deploying agents to increase system survivability taking into account space constraints on nodes.

Klein et al. [18] propose a domain independent approach to handling of exceptions in agent systems. This service can be viewed as a "coordination doctor", who predefines several typical abnormal situations that may arise in the system. Based on that, they monitor agent's behaviors, diagnose problematic situations and take recovery actions. Exception handling in their method is carried out by a set of collaborative agents, however, the approach itself is essentially centralized. Kaminka et al [19] utilize social knowledge, i.e. relationships and interactions among agents, to monitor the behavior of team members and detect the coordination failures. Their work focuses on exceptions concerning the agents themselves.

The fault-tolerance research area has used the N-Version Problem (NVP) approach for fault tolerance. NVP involves the "independent generation of $N \geq 2$ functionally equivalent programs from the same initial specification" [4]. In this approach, the reliability of a software system is increased by developing several versions of special modules and incorporating them into a fault-tolerant system [14]. However, no distributed architecture for ensuring the survivability of the program ensuring survivability is discussed.

References

1. S. Kraus, V.S. Subrahmanian and N. Cihan Tacs: Probabilistically Survivable MASs. Proc. of IJCAI-03. (2003) 789-795
2. N. J. Nilsson: Artificial Intelligence: A New Synthesis. Morgan Kaufmann Publishers. San Mateo, CA, USA. 1998
3. J. A. Giampapa, O. H. Juarez-Espinosa and K. P. Sycara: Configuration management for multi-agent systems. Proc. of AGENTS-01. (2001) 230–231
4. M. Lyu and Y. He: Improving the N-Version Programming Process Through the Evolution of a Design Paradigm. IEEE Trans. Reliability. 42(2), (1993) 179-189
5. T. H. Cormen, C. E. Leiserson and R. L. Rivest: Introduction to Algorithms. MIT Press. 1990. Cambridge, MA
6. O. Shehory, K. P. Sycara, P. Chalasani and S. Jha: Increasing Resource Utilization and Task Performance by Agent Cloning. Proc. of ATAL-98.(1998) 413-426

7. K. S. Decker, K. Sycara and M. Williamson: Cloning in Intelligent, Adaptive Information Agents. In: C. Zhang and D. Lukose (eds.): Multi-Agent Systems: Methodologies and Applications. Springer-Verlag. (1997) 63-75
8. X. Fan: On splitting and Cloning Agents. Turku Center for Computer Science, Tech. Reports 407. 2001
9. D. B. Shmoys, E. Tardos and K. Aardal: Approximation algorithms for facility location problems. Proc. of STOC-97. (1997) 265–274
10. O. Marin, P. Sens, J. Briot, and Z. Guessoum: Towards Adaptive Fault Tolerance for Distributed Multi-Agent Systems. Proc. of ERSADS. (2001) 195-201
11. S. Kumar, P.R. Cohen, and H.J. Levesque: The adaptive agent architecture: achieving fault-tolerance using persistent broker teams. Proc. of ICMAS. (2002) 159-166
12. A. Fedoruk, R. Deters: Improving fault-tolerance by replicating agents. Proceedings AAMAS-02, Bologna, Italy, (2002) 737–744
13. S. Mishra: Agent Fault Tolerance Using Group Communication. Proc. of PDPTA-01, NV. 2001
14. W. J. Gutjahr: Reliability Optimization of Redundant Software with Correlate Failures. The 9th Int. Symp. on Software Reliability Engineering, 1998
15. S. Pleisch and A. Schiper: FATOMAS - A Fault-Tolerant Mobile Agent System Based on the Agent-Dependent Approach. Proc. of the DSN-01, IEEE Computer Society, (2001) 215-224
16. C. Basile: Active replication of multithreaded applications. CRHC-02-01, Univ. of Illinois at Urbana-Champaign, 2002
17. S. Mishra, Y. Huang: Fault Tolerance in Agent-Based Computing Systems. Proc. of the 13th ISCA, 2000
18. M. Klein and C. Dallarocas: Exception handling in agent systems. Proceedings of the Third International Conference on Autonomous Agents (Agents'99), (1999) 62-68
19. G. A. Kaminka and M. Tambe: Robust agent teams via socially-attentive monitoring. Journal of Artificial Intelligence Research, 12:105–147, 2000

Programming Groups of Rational Agents

Michael Fisher[1], Chiara Ghidini[2], and Benjamin Hirsch[1]

[1] Department of Computer Science, University of Liverpool, United Kingdom
{M.Fisher, B.Hirsch}@csc.liv.ac.uk
[2] Automated Reasoning Systems Division, ITC-IRST, Trento, Italy
ghidini@itc.it

Abstract. In this paper, we consider the problem of effectively programming groups of agents. These groups should capture structuring mechanisms common in multi-agent systems, such as teams, cooperative groups, and organisations. Not only should individual agents be dynamic and evolving, but the groups in which the agents occur must be open, flexible and capable of similar evolution and restructuring. We enable the description and implementation of such groups by providing an extension to our previous work on programming languages for agent-based systems based on executable temporal and modal logics. With such formalism as a basis, we consider the grouping aspects within multi-agent systems. In particular, we describe how this logic-based approach to grouping has been implemented in Java and consider how this language can be used for developing multi-agent systems.

1 Introduction

Computational power is increasing, and increasingly available, for example via the development of ubiquitous computing. Once large numbers of computational elements can communicate with each other, via wireless networks or the INTERNET, then new problems arise in engineering software for such systems. By representing these computational elements as agents, we can provide a simple and intuitive metaphor for both individual computation and that within multi-agent systems. However, software designers need to have appropriate, and semantically clear, mechanisms for controlling not only how individual agents adapt and evolve, but also how agents interact and combine to form new systems. Without this control not only will the practical development of complex multi-agent systems remain difficult, but agents themselves will not be trusted for use in critical applications.

In our work, we are concerned with the development of a set of appropriate logic-based abstractions that can allow us to program both individual rational agents and more complex fluid organisational structures, and their encapsulation within an agent-based programming language. In previous papers we have started our investigation on the basic abstractions that can allow us to program agent-based systems. In particular, we have based the programming of individual agents, their dynamic behaviour and the evolution of their knowledge and

J. Dix and J. Leite (Eds.): CLIMA IV, LNAI 3259, pp. 16–33, 2004.

goals on the framework of executable temporal logic [7, 10], recently augmented with the concepts of ability, belief, and confidence [11]. This framework provides high-level descriptions of the concepts we are interested in, while having clearly defined semantics.

The first contribution of this paper is to set the scene for our approach to developing agent programming languages based upon computational logic by outlining:

1. The implementation of individual agents through the direct execution of a formal description of individual (rational) agent behaviour given using a combination of temporal logic and logics concerning belief and ability.

This summarises work carried out over a number of years, where we have attempted to use intuitive logical aspects to provide a simple, but effective, mechanism for describing agent computation. It is our assertion that computational logic in general (and executable temporal logics in particular) can provide an appropriate tool for studying not only verifiable agent descriptions, but also novel concepts that can form the basis for the future programming of agent-based systems.

We will then describe recent work extending the above framework, in particular:

2. The core notion of agent groups and how such groups contrast with individual agents; and
3. The ways in which multi-agent applications might be developed, by utilising the combination of executable logic (as in 1) and group evolution (as in 2).

The work described in (1) and, partially, (2) above can be traced back to previous work produced with a number of co-authors on executable temporal logics [6, 2] and programming rational agents [9, 10]. However, our more recent work has tackled the problem of organising agents within multi-agent systems, not just programming individual agents. To some extent, such organisational aspects are independent of the language used in each agent. Yet, we have shown how, by again using executable temporal and modal logics, a high-level language for developing multi-agent structures can be developed [15]. This is eased by the fact that we treat group structures within multi-agent systems in *exactly* the same way as individual agents [12]. Thus, the work tackling (3) covers more recent work concerning grouping [12], group evolution [11] and construction [15]. In particular, this combination of executable temporal and modal logics, together with a flexible agent grouping mechanism, has now been implemented in Java. Thus, we provide examples based on this system in the paper.

To sum up, in this paper we will review the logic-based abstractions that we have identified to program both individual rational agents and more complex fluid organisational structures, and we will take a step forward by showing how these abstractions can be encapsulated (implemented) within an agent-based programming language. The structure of the paper is as follows. In §2 we outline the logical framework we have developed to program individual agents. In §3 and

§3.3 we consider the basic concepts and mechanisms that allow us to organise and communicate between agents in a multi-agent space. In §4, we will describe the implementation of the framework described in §2 and §3. In §5 and §6, we conclude by showing an example of how to program group computation and provide concluding remarks and future work.

2   Programming Individual Agents

There are many rational agent theories, and agent programming languages. However, the two rarely match. Our approach is to attempt to directly execute rational agent specifications — in this way, we can be more confident that the required behaviour is being exhibited. This not only provides a close link between the theory and implementation, but also provides high-level concepts within the programming language.

In [11] we introduced a logical model of rational agency incorporating the key notions of *ability*, *belief*, and *confidence*, the last of these capturing a flexible motivational attitude. This logical model is built upon the METATEM [1, 6] language, a language that has been developed as a high-level mechanism for specifying and executing simple individual agents. This approach is based upon the principle of specifying an agent using temporal logic, and then *directly executing* [7] this specification in order to provide the agent's behaviour. It provides a high-level programming notation, maintaining a close link between program and specification. With temporal logic as a basis, METATEM is able to describe the dynamic behaviour of an agent and the evolution of its knowledge and goals. The extensions introduced in [10, 11] provide the basic METATEM language with the capability of expressing also abilities of agents, their belief, and their confidence.

We briefly review here the approach, starting by the original METATEM and then illustrating the additional concepts of ability, belief and confidence. For lack of space we only provide an intuitive description of the approach and do not consider the logical basis for this agent programming language in any great detail. The interested reader can refer to [7, 10, 11] for a better description of the METATEM framework.

2.1   Programming Using Temporal Logics

Temporal logic is an extension of classical logic with the notion of temporal order built in. With such logics we can describe many dynamic properties, but they all boil down to describing

- what we must do *now*,
- what we must do *next*, and
- what we guarantee to do at *some* point in the future.

This, seemingly simple, view gives us the flexibility to represent a wide range of computational activities.

The syntax of the temporal logic used here to specify an agent's behaviour is formally defined as the smallest set of formulae containing: a set, $\mathcal{P}$, of propositional constants, the symbols **true**, **false**, and **start**, and being closed under propositional connectives $\neg$, $\vee$, $\wedge$, $\Rightarrow$ and temporal operators $\bigcirc$, $\Diamond$, $\square$.

As usual, the semantics of this logic is defined via the satisfiability relation on a discrete linear temporal model of time, m, with finite past and infinite future [5]. Thus, m is a sequence of states $s_0, s_1, s_2, s_3, \ldots$ which can be thought of as 'moments' in time. Associated with each of these moments in time, represented by a temporal index $u \in \mathbb{N}$, is a valuation π for the propositional part of the language. Intuitively, the temporal formula '$\bigcirc A$' is satisfied at a given moment in time if A is satisfied at the *next* moment in time, '$\Diamond A$' is satisfied if A is satisfied at *some* future moment in time, and '$\square A$' is satisfied if A is satisfied at *all* future moments in time. We also use a special propositional constant **start**, which is only satisfied at the initial moment in time. Formally, the semantics of the temporal language used here is defined in Fig. 1. Satisfiability and validity are defined in the usual way.

$$
\begin{array}{lll}
\langle m, 0 \rangle \models \textbf{start} & & \\
\langle m, u \rangle \models \textbf{true} & & \\
\langle m, u \rangle \models p & \text{iff} & \pi(u, p) = T \text{ (where } p \in \mathcal{P}) \\
\langle m, u \rangle \models \neg A & \text{iff} & \langle m, u \rangle \not\models A \\
\langle m, u \rangle \models A \vee B & \text{iff} & \langle m, u \rangle \models A \text{ or } \langle m, u \rangle \models B \\
\langle m, u \rangle \models \bigcirc A & \text{iff} & \langle m, u+1 \rangle \models A \\
\langle m, u \rangle \models \square A & \text{iff} & \forall u' \in \mathbb{N}. \text{ if } (u \leq u') \text{ then } \langle m, u' \rangle \models A \\
\langle m, u \rangle \models \Diamond A & \text{iff} & \exists u' \in \mathbb{N}. (u < u') \text{ and } \langle m, u' \rangle \models A
\end{array}
$$

Fig. 1. Formal Semantics of the temporal language

A close link between theory and implementation is maintained by directly executing the specification of the behaviour of an agent, represented by a temporal formula [1]. The execution process first transforms the temporal specification into a specific normal form, SNF [8], then it attempts to build a model for the formula in a simple forward-chaining fashion, constraining the construction of the model by trying to satisfy goals, represented by eventualities of the form $\Diamond A$. This is extended, in [9], whereby the choice of which eventualities to satisfy is provided by user defined deliberation functions, rather than by a fixed ordering heuristic.

Instead of going into details we illustrate an example of how temporal logic can be used to specify an agent's behaviour. Imagine a 'car' agent which can be *go*, *turn* and *stop*, but can also run out of fuel (*empty*) and *overheat*. We can specify the behaviour and goals of the 'car' agent with the following set of temporal formulae

$$\mathbf{start} \Rightarrow \neg moving$$
$$go \Rightarrow \Diamond moving$$
$$(moving \wedge go) \Rightarrow \bigcirc(overheat \vee empty)$$

Thus, *moving* is false at the beginning of time; whenever *go* is true, a commitment to eventually make *moving* true is given; and whenever both *go* and *moving* are true, then either *overheat* or *empty* will be made true in the next moment in time.

By executing the temporal specification directly, particularly using a forward chaining approach, we are carrying out gradual model construction; this corresponds to our (usual) notion of execution.

2.2   Adding Ability, Belief and Confidence

An extension of the approach presented above is introduced in [10, 11], where the propositional linear temporal logic is combined with a multi-context belief logic [13], a simple notion of ability, and a notion of confidence obtained as a combination of belief and eventualities.

Adding Belief. The main idea is to add to the language a set of belief predicates, $B_1, \ldots, B_n$, where formulae of the form '$B_i\phi$' mean "agent i believes that ϕ", and to structure the belief of an agent ϵ about a set $I = \{1, \ldots, n\}$ of agents, into a structure of *belief contexts* (see [10] for further details).

Adding belief gives the specification language the capability of expressing facts like:

$$B_{me}\Diamond B_{you} attack(you, me) \Rightarrow B_{me}\bigcirc attack(me, you)$$

that is,

> *if I believe that, in the future, you believe you will attack me, then I believe that I will attack you next*

Adding Ability. Here we add to the language a set of ability predicates, $A_1, \ldots, A_n$, where formulae of the form '$A_i\phi$' mean "agent i is able to do ϕ". Abilities in our formalism are not very sophisticated. In particular they are constant over time, that is if agent i is able to do ϕ now, it was, and will be, able to do ϕ always in time. While this confirms the fact that this version of our formalism is only appropriate for situations where agents never gain or loose the ability to achieve something, it does simplify the formal framework required. As we will see later, our typical examples of agent reasoning are not affected by this hypothesis. On the contrary, this assumption seems appropriate every time we wish to enforce that, if an agent is confident about something and has the ability to achieve it, then that thing will eventually occur.

Adding ability gives the specification language the capability of expressing facts like:

$$A_{me}attack(me, you) \Rightarrow \bigcirc attack(me, you)$$

that is,

if I'm able to attack you, then I will attack you at the next moment in time

Adding Confidence. The concept of confidence is defined in terms of the logic we already have. Thus, if we were to introduce a new logical operator to represent confidence, we would in fact define it exactly as $B_i \Diamond \varphi$. That is, an agent being confident about something is defined as meaning that the agent believes that thing will occur at some point in the future. Confidence helps during the deliberation process. In particular confidence seems appropriate every time we wish to enforce that, if an agent is confident about something and has the ability to achieve it, then that thing will eventually occur. In logical terms, this means that agent i satisfies

$$B_i \Diamond \varphi \wedge A_i \varphi \Rightarrow \Diamond \varphi \qquad (1)$$

which is an important property showing that if agent i is able to perform φ, and also believes that φ will occur sometime in the future, then it will effectively try to actively make φ happen.

Finally, we note that the underlying logic is a combination of linear-time temporal logic and several modal dimensions. Since we do not have complex interaction axioms between the modal and temporal dimensions, then this logical basis remains decidable.

3 Grouping Logic-Based Agents

3.1 Agents in Groups

Agents, encapsulating state and behaviour, are the basic entities within our framework. By default, the description of each agent's behaviour is based on the logic described in §2. Individual agents only act depending on their state which can be altered through identified messages (modelled as predicates) received from their execution environment. Agents are concurrently active, in particular they are asynchronously executing; and communicate via message-passing. Specifically, the basic communication mechanism between elements is *broadcast* message-passing. Thus, when an agent sends a message it does not necessarily send it to a specified *destination*, it merely sends it to its environment, where it can be received by *all* other agents within the environment. Although broadcast is the basic mechanism, both multicast and point-to-point message-passing can be implemented on top of this.

The default behaviour for a message is that if it is broadcast, then it will *eventually* be received by all possible receivers. Note that, by default, the order of messages is not preserved, though such a constraint can be added if necessary. Individual elements only act upon certain identified messages. Thus, an element is able to filter out messages that it wishes to recognise, ignoring all others.

We could simply define a multi-agent system as a collection of agents, and define the semantics of the entire system as a suitable combination of the semantics of the individual agents. This choice would lead us to an unstructured agent space. While there are multi-agent systems of this form, the majority involve highly structured agents spaces. Thus, our aim is to be able to model both simple, unstructured, multi-agent systems and complex multi-agent systems which can benefit from high-level structuring abstractions.

In order to give structure to the agent space, we allow agents to occur in groups. Groups are dynamic and open, groups may contain different elements (agents or sub-groups), and each agent can be a member of several groups. Groups are used in our framework both for structuring the agent space and for restricting the extent of broadcast within the system. Groups must understand certain messages, in particular those relating to group manipulation, such as adding, deleting, and so on.

While the basic purpose of groups is to restrict the set of receivers for broadcast messages, and thus provide finer structure within the element space, more complex applications can be envisaged. For example, the group element might enforce a different model of communication within that group. Thus, groups can effectively enforce their own 'meta-level' constraints on message-passing between elements, for example specifying that the order of messages is preserved.

3.2   Agents as Groups

Recent work has shown that agent groups can productively be treated in a similar way to agents [12]. Thus, in our framework, groups and agents are basically the same entities, avoiding the need to introduce separate mechanisms and entities dealing with the agent structuring and organisation. Thus, groups are also agents. More surprisingly, perhaps, agents are also groups. In fact, basic agents are simply groups with no content. One of the values of identifying these two concepts is that any message that can be sent to an agent, can be sent to a group (concerning cloning, termination, activation, etc) and vice versa (concerning group membership, addition to groups, etc). Thus, not only can agents be members of one or more groups, but they can also serve as groups for other agents. Further advantages of this approach are:

- communication (which, in our approach, is based on broadcasting) can be limited to particular networks of groups;
- since agents have behaviour, and groups are also agents, groups can also have internal policies and rules. Therefore groups are much more powerful than mere "containers"[1];
- the inherent structure can be exploited to group agents based on different aspects such as problem structure, abilities, and even meta-information such as owner, physical location etc; and

---

[1] As an example, in [15] we showed how simple rules could be used to formulate different behaviours of agents, and how those behaviours influence the resulting group structures.

– groups can capture key computational information. For example groups can be transient, can be passed between agents, can evolve, while long-lived groups may also capture the idea of "patterns of activity".

Thus, from the different behaviours of agents, different group behaviours can follow. And vice versa.

In order to realise the equivalence between agents and groups, the core components of an agent[2] is now be defined as:

$$Agent ::= Behaviour : \ Logical\_Specification$$
$$Contents : \mathcal{P}(Agent)$$
$$Context : \mathcal{P}(Agent)$$

Thus, a very simple agent can be defined with $Contents = \emptyset$, a very simple group can have $Behaviour = \emptyset$, while more complex entities can be obtained adding elements to $Contents$ and $Behaviour$. Notationally, we sometimes use CN and CX to denote $Content$ and $Context$, respectively.

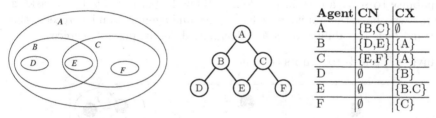

Agent	CN	CX
A	{B,C}	$\emptyset$
B	{D,E}	{A}
C	{E,F}	{A}
D	$\emptyset$	{B}
E	$\emptyset$	{B.C}
F	$\emptyset$	{C}

Fig. 2. The agents' structure - three different representations

3.3   Structuring the Agent Space

Using groups as the basic components of an agent space, and the notions of content and context, makes us able to structure this space in a very flexible way. Fig. 2 shows a simple example of an agent space and its description using different notations.

The agent space is obviously dynamic, and agents can be organised, and reorganised, in some collections according to the specific scenarios we have to model or to the actual needs of the agents themselves. We consider here three simple, yet very common, examples of behaviour involving agents belonging to some sort of collections, and we illustrate how to represent these behaviours in our framework.

Point-to-Point Communication. In order for agent E1 to communicate directly to (and only with) agent E2, E1 may

---

[2] In the following, the terms 'agent' and 'group' mean the same thing. Which one we use depends on the intuitive role that the entity plays in the system.

1. make a new group, called G,
2. add both itself and E2 to G,
3. then broadcast a message, m, within G.

Filtering. Agent E is a member of both F and G. When F broadcasts messages to its contents, E will receive these and can pass on selected messages to G. Thus, E acts as an intermediary between F and G.

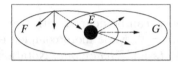

Ability Groups. Agent E wishes to collect together all those elements that have the capability to solve a certain problem ϕ. Thus E can broadcast $A?\phi$ asking for agents who have the ability to solve ϕ. Assume agents F and P receive the request and have the ability to do ϕ. E has now different possible choices:

– E invites F and P to join its content

– E creates a new dedicated element, G, and asks F and P to join G. G will serve as a container for agents having the ability to solve ϕ.

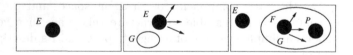

– E creates a new dedicated element, G, joins G and asks F and P to join G.

Depending on the choice, agent E has different forms of control, visibility and knowledge over the activities and the communication between agents F and P. For instance E has a strict control over F and P in the case they join its content, while these agents remain more autonomous if they join an "ad hoc" group G. On the other hand E becomes more complex and may be involved in more "administrative" activities in the first case, especially if it starts collecting more and more sets of agents having certain abilities, while it can maintain a more agile structure if it creates external groups able to provide the required abilities. A better analysis of the different group policies that agents can implement is contained in [16].

In order to make the agent space dynamic and make the examples above possible, agents need to exchange an appropriate set of message, which will trigger, in the implementation of the system, the corresponding appropriate actions. As we already said, agents and groups must understand certain messages, in particular those relating to group manipulation, such as adding, deleting, etc. Thus, the basic properties we require of agents is that they should be able to

- **send** a message to a group,
- **receive** a message,
- send a message to the entire agent space (**sendAll**),
- add an agent to the content or context (**addToContent/addToContext**),
- **disconnect** an agent from its content or context,
- **create** a new group,
- move an agent 'up' in the hierarchy. We envisage two different "move up" actions: **moveUp** and **goUp**. While **moveUp** is initiated by the element that moves, **goUp** would be sent to an element by one of the elements in its context. Fig. 3 illustrates the difference between the two actions. The figures on the top represent the group structure before the composite actions are executed, while the bottom part represent the new group structures after the execution of the composite actions.
- move an agent down in the hierarchy. We envisage two different move down actions: **moveInto** and **goInto**. Again, **moveInto** is initiated by the moving element, while **goInto** is initiated by the one that will receive the moving element (see Fig. 3),
- **die**, that is, stop the computation of the agent gracefully, **merge** and **clone**. The modification of these actions to the agent space is shown in Fig. 4. The actions are initiated by the agent(s) represented as an empty circle.

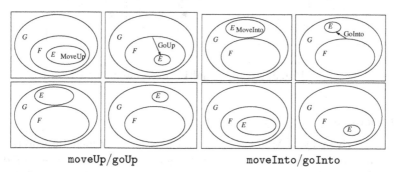

moveUp/goUp   moveInto/goInto

Fig. 3. Changing the agent space: movement

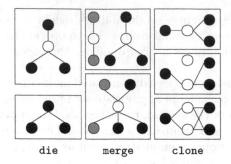

die merge clone

Fig. 4. Changing the agent space: restructuring

4 Implementing the System

The current implementation is based on Java. Agents are represented by threads, and communicate via shared objects, so-called MessageBuffers. Each agent has one Inbox, and two lists of references to other agent's Inboxes, the Content and the Context, as depicted in Fig. 5.

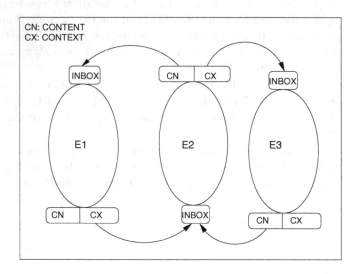

Fig. 5. A simple multi agent system

4.1 Execution

Execution is driven by a METATEM engine (see §2.1), which interprets a set of rules that describe the behaviour of the agent, which constructs a model in a forward-chaining fashion. At each cycle, the agent first checks its Inbox for new messages. The METATEM engine then uses the predicates contained in the messages just received, predicates that were made true from the last state, and eventualities that need to be honored still, to create a new state for the agent execution. If the created state turns out to be consistent, the cycle is repeated with the newly created state, otherwise, backtracking occurs, firstly within the state (by making a different set of predicates true) and if that fails by rolling back states. Again METATEM tries to resolve the contradiction by assigning different truth values to predicates within the state. Note that we allow an agent only to backtrack to the point where it interacted with its environment, by sending messages or executing side effects connected with certain predicates[3]. This is due to the inability of agents to un-do effects on the environment. (Part of our future work is to examine alternative approaches providing possible (partial) solutions involving Nested Transactions [3].)

4.2   Side Effects

As mentioned above, certain predicates can have side-effects. That is, the role of certain predicates is not only to describe a certain behaviour (and thus to be true or false), but also to "make things happen". We distinguish between two types of side effects. First, we have the, so-called, internal side effects. These are side effects connected to predicates provided by the system, and that cannot be changed or adapted by the programmer. Examples of currently implemented internal side effects are: send(Set,Message), doAddToContent(Agent), and doRemoveFromContent(Agent). Similar internal side effects allow to manipulate Context, while further internal side effects concern the creation and deletion of new agents.

The other set of side effects is connected with the, so-called, external abilities. External abilities can consist of (i) a set of SNF rules, (ii) a Java class (which implements a certain interface), or (iii) a combination of both. External abilities can be described as external predicates, which are then represented as normal Java objects. They can be used by an agent to manipulate its environment, from printing status information on the screen to accessing external databases.

4.3   Rule-Based System

Agents are programmed using temporal formulae in SNF form. It may be clear to the reader that while an arbitrary temporal formula can be transformed into SNF, it will often be transformed into a set of several smaller formulae. Therefore an agent program will be often composed of many small SNF formulae, where blocks of SNF formulae may describe a certain behaviour that could be represented in a more compact way as a single complex temporal formula. While SNF formulae are good for execution they are not as good for structuring and representation of code. In order to overcome this problem we have introduced the possibility of tagging rules. The reason for this is twofold. Firstly, it allows the programmer to better structure her code. More importantly, it allows for sets

---

[3] Reading messages is not direct interaction, as the agents keeps track of messages read during each cycle, and re-reads them in case of backtracking.

of formulae which describe a complex behaviour to be identified, and possibly modified (to modify the complex behaviour) within an agent.

We provide a (simple) implementation of most of the behaviours depicted in Fig. 3 as a file which agents can load. However, in order to allow the programmers to devise their own behaviours, and overwrite the default implementations, they can re-define groups of rules and this will completely overwrite the default behaviour. To give an example, Fig. 6 illustrates two sets of tagged rules. These tagged rules contain a simple definition for moveInto and addToContent . In more complex agents, moveInto and addToContent will most probably need to be adapted/rewritten to, e.g., only allow certain agents to join the group.

Note also the use of $Self in Fig 6. $Self refers to the agent interpreting the rules. In the example of addToContent, only the agent mentioned as first argument will match a given addToContent message and execute the rules associated with it.

```
addToContent: {
  addToContent($SELF,Sender)   =>
        NEXT doAddToContent(Sender).
  addToContent($SELF,Sender)   =>
        NEXT send(Sender, addedToContent($SELF,Sender)).
  addedToContent(Sender,$Self) =>
        NEXT doAddToContext(Sender).
}


moveInto: {
  moveInto($Self, FromGroup, TargetAgent) =>
        NEXT removeFromContext($Self,FromGroup).
  moveInto($Self, FromGroup, TargetAgent) =>
        NEXT removeFromContext($Self,TargetAgent).
  moveInto($Self, FromGroup, TargetAgent) =>
        NEXT addToContext($Self,TargetAgent).
}
```

Fig. 6. Code to implement addToContent and moveInto

5   Practical Examples

In order to show the versatility and general usage of the agent programming language, we will present here two short examples, including some code fragments. Due to space constraints we will not include the entire code. Instead we will show and comment in detail on relevant parts of the implementation of the examples.

The first example concerns a coffee delivering agent and is used to show how the structure of the agent space can be used to encode information, such as the information about the physical space, that usually has to reside within the agents. The second example, which is a typical example of a travel agent, explains how the dynamics of the agent space structure can be used to solve problems.

5.1   The Coffee Agent

Suppose we have an office building, with an arbitrary number of rooms, attached to corridors, which may also connect to other floors. Suppose furthermore that we want to create a system that lets users order a coffee agent to bring coffee to their desks.

We represent rooms and corridors as agents. Each corridor agent contains all the room agents that it connects to. Note that room agents can be member of more than one corridor agent if, for instance, they have doors leading to different corridors.

```
agent room1: room1.agent;
agent room2: room2.agent;
agent room3: room3.agent;
agent room4: room4.agent;
agent corr1: corr1.agent;
agent corr2: corr2.agent;
agent coffeerobot: coffeerobot.agent;
...
room1: { context: corr1; content: coffeerobot; }
coor1: { content: room1, room2, room3}
coor2: { content: room4}
...
```

Fig. 7. An example of an environment definition

The system is initialised by defining the initial structure of agents and groups using a simple language. This structure reflects the structure of the building. To define two corridors, one with 3 rooms and another with 1 room, we could use a definition like the one in Fig. 7. The first part defines the agents and their definition files, while the second part defines the relation between the agents.

A user now sends a request for coffee (needcoffee(X)) to its room agent (the variable X represents a number to distinguish between different requests). The definition file of a room can contain a piece of code similar to the one depicted in Fig. 8, while a coffee robot agent can be defined by the code shown in Fig. 9. Note the external ability of the coffee robot to move. The room agents, upon receiving a request, store that request (as execution consists of building new states, we need to ensure that predicates that have to "live" for more than one state are made true in following states), and forward it to their Content. If no answer arrives after a given time, they assume that there is no robot in their room and forward the request to their Context (the corridor, which in turn forwards it to the other rooms connected to it). The forwarded request is adapted to reflect the

```
name room1;

coffee: {
    receive(needCoffee(From, User)) =>
        NEXT rememberQuery(needCoffee(From, User)).
    receive(needCoffee(From,User)) =>
        NEXT send({content},
            needCoffee($Self, needCoffee(From, User))),
            wait(30,needCoffee(From, User)).
    waited(needCoffee(From, User)),needCoffee(From,User) =>
        NEXT send({context},
                needCoffee($Self,
                    needCoffee(From, User))).
    rememberQuery(X), not(delivered(X)) =>
        NEXT rememberQuery(X).
    receive(delivering(Robot, User)),
    rememberQuery(needCoffee(From,User)) =>
        NEXT send(Robot, move($Self, From)), delivered(X).
}
```

Fig. 8. An example file for a room agent

path that the message took - this allows the robot to follow the message path to its origin.

```
name coffeerobot;

ability move: Move;

receive(needCoffee(From,User)),not(delivering(_)) =>
    NEXT send(delivering($Self, User)),
        delivering(User).
receive(addedToContent(Room)), delivering(X) =>
    NEXT send(Room, delivering($Self, X)).
delivering(X), not(delivered(X)) => NEXT delivering(X).
```

Fig. 9. An example file for a coffee robot

The above example is obviously a simplification. For example, we do not deal with the situation where more than one coffee agent exists. We also assume that there won't be more than one request at a time (as a request now would not be answered by the agent, and get therefore lost eventually). However, one can see that neither the robot nor the rooms have any explicit knowledge about their location. In fact, the latter does not even know the number of rooms / corridors they are connected to. Yet the robot will move through the space without difficulty.

5.2   The Travel Agent

The final example we provide concerns a common (at least in research papers) agent scenario. For this example, we will describe, informally, how the agents will work, rather than giving detailed code. This agent based system consists of a Personal Agent (PA) which is asked to organise a holiday, and is given certain dates and preferences to guide this choice. The PA knows that a holiday consists of booking a flight, an hotel, and entertainment, but it does not have the abilities to do either.

A possible way of reaching its goal is to create a new vacation agent within its Content, which it seeds with the rules it has about organising the holiday. The PA then has no further interaction with the holiday planning.

The vacation agent itself creates three new groups/agents in its Context, (one with the ability of booking flight, one for booking hotels, and one for organising entertainment) as in the third option of the Ability Groups described in §3.3, and invites appropriate agents to join. It then sends its requests to these agents. By being a member of the three different groups, the vacation agent will listen to offers of the different groups, and will be able to fine-tune the negotiation. In this case, the system's ability to dynamically change the agent space is exploited. Different ways to interact with groups can be deployed depending on the circumstances.

Although we have not provided explicit code here, this type of example combining rational behaviour in individual agents, together with organisational grouping, is just the type of scenario our language was designed for.

6   Conclusions

Agent-based systems are clearly important within both Computer Science research and the software industry. They are used in many areas, including e-commerce [14], industrial process control [4], web services [17] and autonomous vehicles [18]. Moreover, as computational platforms and wireless networking becomes ubiquitous, and software artifacts will increasingly be able to migrate through large physical/virtual distances, access vast amounts of information, spawn new computations on a wide variety of platforms, and so on, so agent-based techniques for mobile and ubiquitous systems will provide such software artifacts with autonomous and 'intelligent' behaviour to cater for their dynamic environment, requirements and knowledge.

We have based the programming of individual agents, their dynamic behaviour and the evolution of their knowledge and goals on the framework of executable temporal logic [7, 10], augmented with the concepts of ability, belief, and confidence [11]. This framework provides high-level descriptions of the concepts we are interested in, while having clearly defined semantics. The system implemented incorporates more recent work on the problem of organising agents within multi-agent systems, not just programming individual agents. Although we have shown that organisational aspects are independent of the language used in each agent, we believe that, by again using executable temporal and modal logics, a high-level language for developing multi-agent structures can be developed [15]. This combination of executable temporal and modal logics, together with a flexible agent grouping mechanism, has now been implemented in Java. It is this that we have described in this paper.

Acknowledgements

The research of the second author is partially supported by MIUR under FIRB RBNE0195K5 contract.

References

1. H. Barringer, M. Fisher, D. Gabbay, G. Gough, and R. Owens. METATEM: An Introduction. *Formal Aspects of Computing*, 7(5):533–549, 1995.
2. H. Barringer, M. Fisher, D. Gabbay, R. Owens, and M. Reynolds, editors. *The Imperative Future: Principles of Executable Temporal Logics*. Research Studies Press, Chichester, United Kingdom, 1996.
3. P. Busetta. A Transaction Based Multi-Agent System. Master's thesis, Department of Computer Science, University of Melbourne, 1999.
4. S. Bussmann and K. Schild. Self-Organizing Manufacturing Control: An Industrial Application of Agent Technology. In *Proc. Fourth Int. Conf. on Multi-Agent Systems*, pages 87–94, Boston, MA, USA., 2000.
5. E. A. Emerson. Temporal and Modal Logic. In J. van Leeuwen, editor, *Handbook of Theoretical Computer Science*, pages 996–1072. Elsevier, 1990.
6. M. Fisher. Representing and Executing Agent-Based Systems. In *Intelligent Agents*. Springer-Verlag, 1995.
7. M. Fisher. An Introduction to Executable Temporal Logics. *Knowledge Engineering Review*, 11(1):43–56, March 1996.
8. M. Fisher. A Normal Form for Temporal Logic and its Application in Theorem-Proving and Execution. *Journal of Logic and Computation*, 7(4):429–456, August 1997.
9. M. Fisher. Implementing BDI-like Systems by Direct Execution. In *Proceedings of the Fifteenth International Joint Conference on Artificial Intelligence (IJCAI'97)*. Morgan-Kaufmann, 1997.
10. M. Fisher and C. Ghidini. Programming Resource-Bounded Deliberative Agents. In *Proceedings of International Joint Conference on Artificial Intelligence (IJCAI)*. Morgan Kaufmann, 1999.
11. M. Fisher and C. Ghidini. The ABC of Rational Agent modelling. In *Proceedings of the first international joint conference on autonomous agents and multiagent systems (AAMAS'02)*, Bologna, Italy, July 2002.
12. M. Fisher and T. Kakoudakis. Flexible Agent Grouping in Executable Temporal Logic. In *Proc. 12th International Symposium of Intensional Programming Languages*, 1999.
13. C. Ghidini and F. Giunchiglia. Local Models Semantics, or Contextual Reasoning = Locality + Compatibility. *Artificial Intelligence*, 127(2):221–259, April 2001.
14. R. J. Glushko, J. M. Tenenbaum, and B. Meltzer. An XML Framework for Agent-Based E-commerce. *Communications of the ACM*, 42(3), March 1999.

15. B. Hirsch, M. Fisher, and C. Ghidini. Organising Logic-Based Agents. In M.G. Hinchey, J.L. Rash, W.F. Truszkowski, C. Rouff, and D. Gordon-Spears, editors, *Formal Approaches to Agent-Based Systems. Second International Workshop, FAABS 2002*, volume 2699 of *LNAI*, pages 15–27. Springer, 2003.

16. B. Hirsch, M. Fisher, and C. Ghidini. Programming Group Computations. In *First European Workshop on Multi-Agent Systems (EUMAS 2003)*, December 2003.

17. Michael N. Huhns. Agents as Web Services. *IEEE Internet Computing*, 6(4):93–95, July/August 2002.

18. N. Muscettola, P. Pandurang Nayak, B. Pell, and B. Williams. Remote agent: To boldly go where no AI system has gone before. *Artificial Intelligence*, 103(1-2):5–48, 1998.

An Abductive Framework for Information Exchange in Multi-agent Systems

Marco Gavanelli[1], Evelina Lamma[1], Paola Mello[2], and Paolo Torroni[2]

[1] Dip. di Ingegneria - Università di Ferrara - Via Saragat, 1 - 44100 Ferrara, Italy
{mgavanelli, elamma}@ing.unife.it
[2] DEIS - Università di Bologna - Viale Risorgimento, 2 - 40136 Bologna, Italy
{pmello, ptorroni}@deis.unibo.it

Abstract. In this paper, we propose a framework for information exchange among abductive agents whose local knowledge bases are enlarged with a set of abduced hypotheses. We integrate the aspects of information exchange and abductive reasoning, and show theoretically the information inferred by the single abductive agent as a product of joint reasoning activity. We show examples, like dining philosophers, resource exchange and speculative computation, and give an implementation of the space of interactions based on $CLP(\mathcal{SET})$.

1 Introduction

In the past years, Computational Logics has proved itself to be a powerful tool for modelling and implementing many forms of reasoning of intelligent systems, such as deduction (the basic logic reasoning method), abduction (Abductive Logic Programming) for reasoning from effects to causes, machine learning (Inductive Logic Programming).

Traditionally, such techniques have been developed for monolithic systems, to solve problems such as diagnosis (expert systems) and learning by examples. More recently, following the development of multi-agent research, considerable effort has been done in exporting the technological achievements of Computational Logics into a multi-agent setting [1]. For instance, through abduction, an agent can make hypotheses on the outer world, and on causes of observable events, which is a natural extension of what happens in an expert system. But the role of abduction in multi-agent systems can go beyond the internal agent reasoning.

In general, sociable agents will exchange knowledge, ask questions, provide services to each other and, eventually, get to reasonable agreements when decisions are necessary. In this paper, we propose a Computational Logic-based framework for the integration of abductive reasoning and communication.

One of the first approaches to modelling agents based on Computational Logics was proposed by Kowalski and Sadri [2]. The authors propose an agent cycle where logic agents reason based on an abductive logic program, the hypotheses produced within the agent represent actions in the outer world, and the observations from the outer world are mapped into "abduced" that enlarge the agent's knowledge base. Communication primitives are considered as a particular case of actions. Agent communication can take place for various reasons, e.g., in reaction to stimuli, or as part of a plan to achieve a goal.

J. Dix and J. Leite (Eds.): CLIMA IV, LNAI 3259, pp. 34–52, 2004.

The sequence of communicative actions can follow a certain protocol, or else they can be less constrained like in the case of agent dialogues. In this setting, the communication plan is based on the abductive reasoning of the agents. The communication primitives are modelled as predicates at the object level. The integrity constraints and the knowledge base that constitute the agent's abductive logic program define the communication protocol by stating explicitly how to react to incoming communication actions. Building on [2], several other proposals have been published that map agent communication acts into abductive atoms [3, 4, 5].

In the present work, we take a different approach. By means of the well-understood declarative semantics of abduction, we give a formal understanding of information exchange. Similarly to the above cited work, we achieve information exchange by means of abducible predicates, but the purpose of this work is to give an abductive semantics to the reasoning activity of the overall group of agents involved in the derivation of goals. Our approach can be considered top-down, meant to define the semantics of a group reasoning activity, while many approaches are more bottom-up, in the sense that they give a declarative reading of the individual agents' knowledge bases, and derive a group behaviour which is hopefully sound to the semantics. With this we do not mean that we model through abduction all the possible flavours of emergent behaviour in a bunch of agents, but that the user can state a common goal of the agent group, and the group will try and find an abductive solution to the goal of the group. Moreover, this work is not about agent communication in the sense that we do not provide a semantics at a the high abstraction level, such as social semantics [6, 7, 8] or semantics based on speech acts [9, 10, 11]. We do not model roles and contexts. We put our work at a lower abstraction level, which nicely integrates the two essential concepts of reasoning and information exchange in a uniform semantic characterisation. We identify the information exchanged when agents come to a global agreement upon hypotheses.

Drawing inspiration from ALIAS [12], we group abductive agents interacting together and provide them with a shared repository of communicative actions, which we call Δ. Based on it, we establish abduction as a virtual machine given by communicating agents. All the agents will share the same Δ and a solution must satisfy all the (local) integrity constraints. In this way, communication primitives are transparent to the abductive reasoners and the communication protocol is implicitly defined in the program and in the integrity constraints of the agents. In a sense, we abstract away from protocols: the agents do not need to name explicitly the others in the group, they do not even need to know how many agents participate in the distributed computation, while trying and find a global agreement.

Consider, for example, a system that monitors some electronic equipment. We may have an abductive agent that monitors each of the alarms. A first agent, C_1, is responsible for checking the temperature of the whole system. It may have rules saying that the temperature can get high if the fan in one of the subsystems is broken, or in case of short circuit in one subsystem:

$$KB_1 \quad \begin{aligned} &high\_temp \leftarrow broken\_device(fan, System). \\ &high\_temp \leftarrow short\_circuit(System). \end{aligned}$$

A second abductive agent, C_2, checks the output of each subsystem, and knows that the wrong output of a system can be due to a failure in a device of such a system.

KB_2 $wrong\_output(System) \leftarrow broken\_device(Device, System).$

Finally, a third agent, C_3, checks the current absorption, and may have an integrity constraint saying that there cannot be, in a subsystem, low current and short-circuit:

IC_3 $\leftarrow low\_current(System), short\_circuit(System).$

Now, if we have high temperature, low current in all subsystems, and wrong output on subsystem *amplifier2*, none of the single agents can get to the right solution; however, together they can identify the failing device (namely, the *fan* in *amplifier2*). Notice that they will need to unify their possible guesses (C_1 could hypothesise $broken\_device(fan, S)$ and C_2 $broken\_device(D, amplifier2)$) to get to the complete solution. Moreover, they will need to check the integrity constraints of all the abductive agents to get a consistent solution. We see by this simple example how variable binding can be considered as both the subject and the vehicle of information exchange.

In this paper, we propose a framework of abductive reasoners that share a common hypothesis space. We do not explicitly address some typical issues of Multi-Agent Systems, like autonomy and pro-activity. Our focus is rather on the communication part and its relation with the agent's reasoning. Notice that it is not necessary that each agent exports its whole hypothesis space, but only the part related to communication, while its internal reasoning may remain private. We formally define the framework and theoretically show how the information is passed (Sect. 3).

In this work, we also discuss about the outcome of the collaborative reasoning process in terms of local vs. global consistency. To this end, we introduce the concepts of independence and compositionality of programs, and we prove that, in terms of consistency and under certain conditions, collaborative reasoning is equivalent to local abductive reasoning.

We show various examples of communication patterns that can be obtained in our framework (Sect. 4). We provide a prototypical implementation of our framework (Sect. 5), we discuss related work in Sect. 6 and, finally, we conclude.

2 Preliminaries on Abductive Logic Programming (ALP)

If F is a formula, with $\tilde{\exists}F$ (resp. $\tilde{\forall}F$) we denote the existential (resp. universal) closure of the formula. If t is a term, with $\tilde{\exists}_t F$ (resp. $\tilde{\forall}_t F$) we will indicate the existential (universal) closure of F restricted to the variables in t.

Definition 1. *An* abductive logic program *is a triple* $\langle KB, Ab, IC \rangle$ *where:*

- KB *is a (normal) logic program, that is, a set of clauses ("definitions") of the form* $A_0 \leftarrow A_1, \ldots, A_m$, *where each* A_i ($i = 1, \ldots, m$) *is a positive or negative literal;*
- Ab *a set of* abducible predicates, *p, such that p does not occur in the head of any clause of* KB;
- IC *is a set of* integrity constraints, *that is, a set of closed formulae.*

Following Eshghi and Kowalski [13], an abductive logic program $\langle KB, Ab, IC \rangle$ can be transformed into its *positive version*. The idea is to view default literals as new abducible positive atoms. In the rest of the paper, we will use the symbol not to indicate negation, and suppose that it is treated as by Eshghi and Kowalski [13].

Definition 2. *Given an abductive program $\langle KB, Ab, IC \rangle$ and a goal G, an abductive explanation for G is a set Δ (such that $\Delta \subseteq Ab$) with a substitution θ such that $KB \cup \Delta$ is consistent and*

- $KB \cup \Delta \models \tilde{\forall}(G/\theta)$
- $KB \cup \Delta \models IC$

We suppose that each integrity constraint has the syntax

$$(\bot) \leftarrow A_1, \ldots, A_n.$$

where $A_1, \ldots, A_n$ is a conjunction of atoms. Let I be the implication $A_0 \leftarrow A_1, \ldots, A_m$; we call $head(I)$ the atom A_0 and we denote with $body(I)$ the set $\{A_1, \ldots, A_m\}$.

Given this syntax, the previous definition $KB \cup \Delta \models IC$ is equivalent to saying that the atoms appearing in the body of an integrity constraint cannot be all true in order for the program (with the Δ) to be consistent: $\forall ic \in IC, \exists a \in body(ic)$ s.t. $KB \cup \Delta \not\models a$.

3   Formalisation

In this section, we give the formalisation of our framework for information sharing.

Let C_i denote an agent, provided with an abductive logic program $\langle KB_i, Ab, IC_i \rangle$.[1] In order to (abductively) prove a goal G_i, C_i will try to find a binding θ_i and a set of abductive hypotheses δ_i such that

$$KB_i \cup \delta_i \models G_i/\theta_i$$

that satisfies all the integrity constraints:

$$KB_i \cup \delta_i \models IC_i.$$

If the set δ_i can contain non ground literals, then the substitution θ_i will also apply to the set δ_i; all the remaining variables in δ_i/θ_i should be considered existentially quantified[2]

$$\tilde{\exists}_{\delta_i/\theta_i}(KB_i \cup \delta_i/\theta_i \models G_i/\theta_i).$$

---

[1] Since in this work we are tackling the problem of information sharing in the context of agents reasoning based on abductive logic programs, from now on we will use – with abuse of notation – the same symbol to denote both the agents and the ALP that they enclose. Indeed, in a more elaborated agent architecture, the abductive logic program will only represent a part of the whole agent. Also, in this simplified setting we consider – without loss of generality – the set Ab to be the same for all the agents in the system.

[2] Other variables which may appear in $G_\square$ are considered free, as in the IFF proof procedure [14].

Communication between agents will appear as a binding on the set of abduced hypotheses. Given n abductive agents C_i, $i = 1..n$, each providing an answer to a goal:

$$\tilde{\exists}_{\delta_i/\theta_i}[KB_i \cup \delta_i/\theta_i \models G_i/\theta_i]$$

communication will appear as (one) solution of the following equations:

$$\Delta = \overset{\square}{\underset{k}{}} \delta_k \tag{1}$$

$$\tilde{\exists}_{\Delta}\forall k(KB_k \cup \Delta \models IC_k). \tag{2}$$

that can be seen as a $CLP(\mathcal{SET})$ problem [15, 16].

Definition 3. *The property in Eq. 2 will be referred to as* Global Consistency.

Global consistency is equivalent to abduction performed by a single agent that has the union of the KBs and the union of the ICs. In order to prove this property, we introduce the concepts of *independency* and *compositionality* of programs, and show that independency implies compositionality.

Definition 4. *A set of atoms Δ is* independent *of a logic program KB, and we write $ind(\Delta, KB)$, iff $\forall a \in \Delta$ $\nexists d \in KB$ s.t. $a/head(d)$.*

Definition 5. *A logic program KB_1 is* independent *of a program KB_2, and we write $ind(KB_1, KB_2)$, iff $\forall d_i \in KB_1$ $ind(\{head(d_i)\} \cup body(d_i), KB_2)$.*

Note that this definition is not symmetric: $ind(KB_1, KB_2) \not\Rightarrow ind(KB_2, KB_1)$.

Theorem 1. **Compositionality.** *Suppose that KB_1 and KB_2 are mutually independent and that Δ is a set of ground facts independent of KB_1 and KB_2 (but, nevertheless, KB_1 and KB_2 may depend on Δ).*
Then, $\forall a$,

$$KB_1 \cup KB_2 \cup \Delta \models a \quad\Longleftrightarrow\quad (KB_1 \cup \Delta \models a) \vee (KB_2 \cup \Delta \models a)$$

Proof. Let us consider the immediate consequence operator, T; we will show that, $\forall n, T^n_{KB_1 \cup KB_2 \cup \Delta} = T^n_{KB_1 \cup \Delta} \cup T^n_{KB_2 \cup \Delta}$.

$T^1_{KB_1 \cup KB_2 \cup \Delta} = T^1_{KB_1 \cup \Delta} \cup T^1_{KB_2 \cup \Delta}$, as it only contains the ground facts in the Δ and in the two KBs.

By induction, let us suppose that $T^n_{KB_1 \cup KB_2 \cup \Delta} = T^n_{KB_1 \cup \Delta} \cup T^n_{KB_2 \cup \Delta}$. By definition of T, since Δ only contains facts,

$$T^{n+1}_{KB_1 \cup \Delta} = T^n_{KB_1 \cup \Delta} \cup \overset{\square}{} X : X \leftarrow B \in KB_1, B \subseteq T^n_{KB_1 \cup \Delta} \overset{\square}{}$$

and analogously for agent A_2.

$$T^{n+1}_{KB_1 \cup KB_2 \cup \Delta} = T^n_{KB_1 \cup KB_2 \cup \Delta} \cup$$
$$\cup \, X : X \leftarrow B \in KB_1, B \subseteq T^n_{KB_1 \cup KB_2 \cup \Delta} \cup$$
$$\cup \, X : X \leftarrow B \in KB_2, B \subseteq T^n_{KB_1 \cup KB_2 \cup \Delta} =$$
$$= T^n_{KB_1 \cup \Delta} \cup \, X : X \leftarrow B \in KB_1, B \subseteq T^n_{KB_1 \cup \Delta} \cup T^n_{KB_2 \cup \Delta} \cup$$
$$T^n_{KB_2 \cup \Delta} \cup \, X : X \leftarrow B \in KB_2, B \subseteq T^n_{KB_1 \cup \Delta} \cup T^n_{KB_2 \cup \Delta}$$

Now we only have to show that

$$
\begin{aligned}
&\overset{\square}{} \overset{\square}{X} : X \leftarrow B \in KB_1, B \subseteq T^n_{KB_1 \cup \Delta} \overset{\square}{=} \\
&= \overset{\square}{X} : X \leftarrow B \in KB_1, B \subseteq T^n_{KB_1 \cup \Delta} \cup T^n_{KB_2 \cup \Delta}
\end{aligned} \qquad (3)
$$

(and the same for KB_2).

Eq. 3 is true if for each clause $(X \leftarrow B) \in KB_1$ and each atom $S \in B$, $S \notin T^n_{KB_2 \cup \Delta} \setminus T^n_{KB_1 \cup \Delta}$. If S belonged to that set, then there would be a clause $(S' \leftarrow B') \in KB_2$ that unifies with S (by definition of $T_{KB_2 \cup \Delta}$), and this is impossible by hypothesis. $\square$

Achieving compositionality in a system of autonomous agents is not difficult: in fact, we can assume that the "private" atoms used by the various agents (those that are not intended for direct sharing) can either have different functor names or arity, or they can be labelled with the name of the agent. Instead, for what regards the abducible predicates used for communication, we can assume [17] that they have no definition.

We now extend Definition 5 for Abductive Logic Programs; intuitively, integrity constraints in one of the programs should not reference predicates defined in the other.

Definition 6. *An* Abductive Logic Program $\langle KB_1, Ab, IC_1 \rangle$ *is independent of a program* $\langle KB_2, Ab, IC_2 \rangle$ *iff*

- $ind(KB_1, KB_2)$, *and*
- $\forall ic_i \in IC_1, \forall a \in body(ic_i), ind(\{a\}, KB_2)$.

Theorem 2. *Let* $\langle KB_1, Ab, IC_1 \rangle$ *and* $\langle KB_2, Ab, IC_2 \rangle$ *be two mutually independent abductive logic programs. Then, global consistency is equivalent to (centralised) abduction, with* $KB = \cup_i KB_i$ *and* $IC = \cup_i IC_i$*; i.e., the two following conditions are equivalent*

- $\tilde{\exists}_\Delta \forall i (KB_i \cup \Delta \models IC_i)$
- $\cup_i KB_i \cup \tilde{\exists} \Delta \models \cup_i IC_i$

Proof. The set Δ is existentially quantified; let us take a ground version of it.

Suppose that the first condition holds. This means that for each abductive logic program i, for each integrity constraint $ic^i_j \in IC_i$ there is an atom a that is not entailed by KB_i:

$$\forall i \, \forall ic^i_j \in IC_i \, \exists a \in ic^i_j : KB_i \cup \Delta \not\models a.$$

If a is abducible, it can be true only if $a \in \Delta$, but this is not the case, since we know that $KB_i \cup \Delta \not\models a$. Since $a \in ic^i_j \in IC_i$, a cannot be defined in any KB_m with $m \neq i$. Thus, we have that a is not entailed by any of the KBs (union Δ):

$$\forall i \, \forall ic^i_j \in IC_i \, \exists a \in ic^i_j : \forall_m KB_m \cup \Delta \not\models a.$$

By Theorem 1, $\forall i \forall ic^i_j \in IC_i \, \exists a \in ic^i_j : \cup_m KB_m \cup \Delta \not\models a$, thus $\forall i \forall ic^i_j \cup_m KB_m \cup \Delta \models ic^i_j$. Since this holds for every integrity constraint, we have that $\cup_m KB_m \cup \Delta \models \cup_i \cup_j ic^i_j$ that is

$$\cup_m KB_m \cup \Delta \models \cup_i IC_i.$$

Viceversa, suppose that the second condition holds. This means that for each agent i, for each integrity constraint $ic_j^i \in IC_i$ there is an atom that is not entailed by the union of the KBs:

$$\forall i \,\forall ic_j^i \,\exists a \in ic_j^i : \cup_m KB_m \cup \Delta \not\models a.$$

By Theorem 1, this is equivalent to

$$\forall i \,\forall ic_j^i \,\exists a \in ic_j^i : \forall_m KB_m \cup \Delta \not\models a$$

In particular, if none of the KBs (union Δ) entails a, even more so neither the KB of the agent i (union Δ) to which ic_j^i belongs entails a:

$$\forall i \,\forall ic_j^i \,\exists a \in ic_j^i : KB_i \cup \Delta \not\models a$$

which means that

$$\forall i \,\forall ic_j^i : KB_i \cup \Delta \models ic_j^i$$

since every integrity constraint of the agent is entailed, also their union is entailed □

Note that Global Consistency requires that all the abductive reasoners will "agree" on one substitution of the variables in Δ. A weaker variant is *Local Consistency*:

Definition 7. *A set Δ of abduced hypotheses is* Locally Consistent *if the following condition holds:*

$$\forall i (KB_i \cup \tilde{\exists}\Delta \models IC_i). \tag{4}$$

If each of the agents checks the consistency of the set Δ locally, local consistency is ensured. However, local and global consistency are different properties:

Example 1. Consider the following situation, where $p/2$ is abducible.

$$
\begin{array}{lll}
\text{Agent 1} & IC_1 & \leftarrow p(X,Y), not\ q(X,Y). \\
& KB_1 & q(X,Y) \leftarrow X > Y.
\end{array}
$$

$$
\begin{array}{lll}
\text{Agent 2} & IC_2 & \leftarrow p(X,1), not\ f(X). \\
& KB_2 & f(X) \leftarrow X < 0.
\end{array}
$$

Should both agents try to assume $p(X,Y)$, we could obtain $\Delta = \{p(X,1)\}$, and Agent 1 will receive the binding $Y/1$. This is locally consistent, in fact for Agent 1 there exists a value of X that satisfies its integrity constraint (every value greater than one), and, similarly, for Agent 2 there exists at least one value (any value less than zero) that satisfies IC_2. Obviously, it is not consistent, because there is no value for X that satisfies all the integrity constraints, thus it is not globally consistent, and the hypothesis $(\exists X)p(X,1)$ should be rejected.

One may think, operationally, to enforce only local consistency, because it is less expensive. However, in this case, an eventual inconsistency might not be detected, and an expensive failure would be obtained in a later computation.

Various types of communication may appear in this framework, e.g., communication of a failure, communication triggered by integrity constraints, etc. In this paper, we focus on the communication given by a shared abduced hypothesis. Intuitively, when hypotheses made by different agents are unified, communication appears as a binding.

3.1   Communication Through a Shared Abduced Hypothesis

Once global consistency is enforced, we can identify the information exchanged among agents, if some of them share (at least) one predicate name in the abducible space. In fact, given two abductive agents, x_i, $i = 1..2$, each enclosing an abductive logic program $\langle KB_i, Ab, IC_i \rangle$, for all i we have:

$$\tilde{\exists}_{\delta_i/\theta_i} KB_i \cup \delta_i/\theta_i \models G_i/\theta_i.$$

If the set inequality $\delta_1/\theta_1 \cap \delta_2/\theta_2 \neq \emptyset$ has solutions, i.e., if there is a substitution θ' such that

$$\exists \theta' : (\delta_1/\theta_1)\theta' \cap (\delta_2/\theta_2)\theta' \neq \emptyset$$

then information exchange can occur by way of a variable binding.

The communication is, in general, bidirectional: both agents will receive the binding θ'. The information that agent 1 will receive is the substitution for its variables, $\theta'|_{\delta_1/\theta_1}$, and, in the same way, agent 2 will receive the information $\theta'|_{\delta_2/\theta_2}$.

Example 2. Let us consider the following instance, where $a/1$ is the only abducible.

	Agent 1		Agent 2
IC_1	$\leftarrow a(X), a(Y), X \neq Y.$		$q(X) \leftarrow a(X), f(X).$
KB_1	$p(X) \leftarrow a(X), b(X).$ $b(r(1, B)).$	KB_2	$f(r(A, 2)).$

The integrity constraint IC_1 tells that there can be only one atom $a/1$ in the Δ. If the first agent proves $p(Z)$ and the second one $q(Q)$, the individual results will be:

$$\theta_1 = \{Z/r(1, B)\} \qquad \delta_1 = \{a(r(1, B))\}$$
$$\theta_2 = \{Q/r(A, 2)\} \qquad \delta_2 = \{a(r(A, 2))\}$$

In this case there is only one most general unifier, namely $\theta' = \{B/2, A/1\}$. Both of the agents receive this substitution; the received information is the substitution restricted to their variables, i.e., Agent 1 receives $\theta'|_{\delta_1/\theta_1} = \{B/2\}$ and Agent 2 $\theta'|_{\delta_2/\theta_2} = \{A/1\}$.

4   Examples

Various information exchange patterns can be implemented on top of our the framework of abductive communication. In this section, we show some simple examples, that exploit non trivial communication patterns enclosed in the framework.

4.1   Dining Philosophers

The *dining philosophers* problem [18] is a classic problem in inter-process synchronisation. The problem consists of a group of philosophers sitting at a table; each philosopher has a chopstick on his right and one on his left. A chopstick cannot be used by two philosophers at the same time, and one philosopher needs both the chopstick on his right and the one on his left to eat.

We do not wish to propose with our framework a new solution to the dining philosophers, but instead, we will use the well-known example to show the inter-process communication involved and the abductive semantics that we give to it.

We propose a model based on abductive agents, each one representing a philosopher; agents share resources (the chopsticks), and communicate by means of abducible predicates that they derive within the knowledge base. Such predicates represent the state of the philosophers with respect to the chopsticks: $chop(C, F, T)$, where C indicates a chopstick, F represents a philosopher (abductive agent) and T is the time.

The set Δ, which grows during the individual computation activities of agents, contains all their abducible predicates, which must be agreed upon by all of them at all times. It represents a partial schedule of the allocation of chopsticks in time. Due to the conflicts on the use of resources (the chopsticks), the reasoning activity must be coordinated, and in particular it must comply with some constraints that must never be violated. For example, a chopstick cannot be taken by two different agents at the same time. In ALP terms, we would impose an integrity constraint such as:

$$\leftarrow \text{chop(C,F,T)}, \quad \text{chop(C,F1,T)}, \quad F \neq F1 \tag{5}$$

This constraint implies that for all ground instances of the first two predicates, the third one must fail (F must be equal to $F1$). That is, if an agent abduces $chop(1, 1, t)$, then $\forall X, chop(1, X, t) \notin \Delta \setminus \{chop(1, 1, t)\}$.

A resource at a given time is denoted as free by leaving its second parameter – the one representing the owner – as a variable. In this way, releasing a resource means abducing a fact with a variable as owner. Acquiring a resource means abducing a chop atom in which the second variable is not free. If a chopstick was released at a given time point, then Δ contains $chop(C, F, T)$, where F is a variable. A philosopher $F1$ can take it by abducing $chop(C, F1, T)$, and either F will be unified with $F1$ or (as a choice point) Δ will contain both the abducibles and the constraint $F \neq F1$.

This predicate shows the behaviour of a single philosopher:

```
phil(P) ←
   compute_needed_chops(P,Chop1,Chop2),
   % Get needed resources
   chop(Chop1,P,T), chop(Chop2,P,T),
   eat(T,T1),
   % Release the resources
   chop(Chop1,_,T1), chop(Chop2,_,T1).

compute_needed_chops(P,P,P1) ←
   number_philosophers(Pn), P<Pn, P1 is P+1.
compute_needed_chops(P,1,P) ← number_philosophers(P).
```

Let us see an example with three philosophers: p_1, p_2, and p_3 (all philosophers will have $number\_philosophers(3) \leftarrow$. in their knowledge base). At the beginning (time zero) all the resources are free. We model this by introducing in the Δ three atoms chops(i,_,0), where $i = 1..3$. Let us suppose the first philosopher, p_1, tries to get its needed resource first: it will abduce $chop(1, p_1, T1), chop(2, p_1, T1)$, i.e., it will try to get two chopsticks in a same time stamp. Since the set Δ currently leaves all the resources free at time zero, the philosopher gets the binding $T1/0$ and the Δ will contain information that two chopsticks are no more available. If philosopher p_2 tries to get its resources, it cannot get them at time zero, because the integrity constraint forbids to abduce both $chop(2, p_1, 0)$ and $chop(2, p_2, 0)$ $(p_1 \neq p_2)$; the only possibility is to abduce new facts $chop(2, p_2, T2)$, $chop(3, p_2, T2)$. The second philosopher still does not know in which time tick it will get the resources (T_2 is still a variable). If now p_1 releases its resources at time 3, abducing $chop(2, \_, 3)$, this atom unifies with one request of p_2, so p_2 gets the binding $T2/3$.

Step	Δ		
start	chop(1,_,0)	chop(2,_,0)	chop(3,_,0)
p_1 get chops	chop(1,p_1,0)	chop(2,p_1,0)	chop(3,_,0)
p_2 ask chops	chop(1,p_1,0)	chop(2,p_1,0)	chop(3,_,0)
		chop(2,p_2,T2)	chop(3,p_2,T2)
p_1 release chops	chop(1,p_1,0)	chop(2,p_1,0)	chop(3,_,0)
	chop(1,_,3)	chop(2,p_2,3)	chop(3,p_2,3)

We specified the program in a general way, i.e., independent of the philosopher. In fact, if we instantiate it to a specific philosopher (e.g., we define $phil(p_1)$ and $compute\_needed\_chops(p_1, P, P1)$ instead of the generic predicates $phil(P)$ and $compute\_needed\_chops(P, P, P1)$ that we defined above) we obtain three mutually independent programs, for which the results of Theorem 2 hold. In that case, global consistency is equivalent to centralised abduction. Similar considerations apply to the other examples that will follow this section.

This example must not be seen as a possible solution to the synchronisation problems of the dining philosophers, but rather as an example of information sharing. p_1, p_2, and p_3 will collaborate to generate a schedule of resource usage, and the semantics and properties of the framework ensure that their constraints are not violated. Indeed, different agents with different programs and constraints can participate in the solution of this problem, each one adopting suitable strategies (e.g., coordination mechanisms or ad-hoc ordering to prevent starvation).

4.2   Dialogues and Negotiation

In this section we would like to show how it is possible to model in our framework a two-agent dialogue. We will take as an example the negotiation dialogues produced by $\mathcal{N}^+$-systems [4]. Such dialogues – sequences of dialogue moves satisfying certain requirements – can be used to solve a *resource reallocation problem*. $\mathcal{N}^+$-agents produce dialogue moves produced by means of an abductive proof procedure, during the *think* phase of an observe-think-act life cycle [2]. In the context of resource reallocation considered in [4], agents have goals to achieve, resources to use in order to achieve them, and they produce dialogues among each other in order to obtain the resources that they miss to make a certain plan feasible. In the simplified setting that we are considering now, the purpose of producing a dialogue move is either to reply to a request, or to request a missing resource. $\mathcal{N}^+$-agents keep requesting resources to the other agents until they either obtain all the missing resources or they realise that there are not enough resources in the system to make their plan feasible. At the same time, agents must reply to asynchronously incoming requests. The policy used to produce requests and to reply to the other agents' requests is encoded into an abductive logic program.

We propose here an alternative implementation of $\mathcal{N}^+$-agents based on non-ground abducible predicates where an agent does not explicitly poll each other agent in the group, but posts a request in the common Δ with a variable as addressee. Other agents can hypothesise to be the addressee of the message and, consequently, reply.

We express dialogue moves by means of envelopes t/3 that have the following syntax: tell(Sender, Receiver, Subject), where Sender, Receiver, and Subject are terms that carry the obvious meaning.

The definition of the predicates is below. We divide the agent resources into two groups: those that are missing (and that the agent must somehow obtain in order to succeed in its goal, make_plan_feasible), and those that the agent may give away. For the sake of simplicity, we adopt here a static representation of the problem in which the set of missing resources is defined through a missing/1 predicate. A resource r is instead available if a predicate available(r) is true. We consider a setting in which three agents (a, b, and c) have the program below. It is given independently of the agent, but we assume that each agent has its own definition of missing/1, available/1, and self/1, this latter used to provide each agent with a unique identifier.

```
make_plan_feasible ← missing(M), get_all(M).
get_all([]).
get_all([R|R1]) ← get(R), get_all(R1).
get(R) ← self(S),
  tell(S,A,request(give(R))), S ≠ A,
  tell(A,S,accept(give(R))).
manage_request(S,X,R) ← available(R),
  tell(S,X,accept(give(R))).
manage_request(S,X,R) ← not(available(R)),
  tell(S,X,refuse(give(R))).
```

The integrity constraints are the following:

$$\leftarrow \texttt{tell(S,R,refuse(give(R)))},\ \texttt{tell(S,R,accept(give(R)))}. \tag{6}$$

$$\begin{aligned}\leftarrow \texttt{self(S)},\ \texttt{tell(Y,S,request(give(R)))},\\ \texttt{not manage\_request(S,Y,R)}.\end{aligned} \tag{7}$$

The first one states that an agent cannot reply both *accept* and *refuse* to the same request. The second one is used to react to a request of other agents by invoking manage_request if a request is addressed to the agent.

Let us see an example with three agents, called a, b and c. Suppose that the individual knowledge bases of the three agents are the following:

Agent a	Agent b	Agent c
self(a).	self(b).	self(c).
missing([nail]).	missing([pen]).	missing([knife]).
available(pen).	available(pen).	available(nail).
available(knife).		

Suppose that agent a starts first, and posts a request for its missing resource: tell(a, X, request(give(nail))). It will also try to abduce that the same agent that will reply, X, will accept to give the resource: t(X, a, request(give(nail))). This second hypothesis is motivated by the fact that without the resource, a cannot execute its plan, so a's computation would fail.

Agent b considers its integrity constraint (7) and has two possibilities: either variable X of the atom in the Δ is equal to b, or it is different from b. In other words, either it supposes to be the addressee of the request or not. In the first case it should reply refuse, as it does not have an available nail; however this reply would not be consistent with the hypothesis formulated by a that the reply would be accept. The Δ would contain both answers accept and refuse from b to a, and this is inconsistent with the integrity constraint (6). The only globally consistent possibility is that b is not the addressee of the request. Agent c will, in its turn, hypothesise to be the addressee: it will reply accept, which is consistent with both ICs.

4.3 A Meeting Room Reservation Problem

Speculative computation by Satoh et al. [19] is a technique used to carry on with a distributed computation where information exchange is involved, without waiting for such information to be available. To this purpose, it uses default assumptions on the missing information, and it provides an operational model for the consistency of the overall computation with the assumed defaults – once the information becomes available – or for activating alternative branches in case of inconsistency. The authors present a meeting room reservation problem as an example of computation with defaults, in an environment with unreliable communication. The problem is to organise a meeting among three agents: a, b, and c. If less than two agents attend the meeting, the meeting is cancelled. If exactly two agents attend the meeting, we book a small room. If three agents come, we book a big room.

The problem is modelled in [19] by adopting a master-slave system architecture, where $\{a, b, c\}$ are the *slave* agents, and a master agent m is introduced, whose goal is to reserve the meeting room. By default, m assumes that a and b are available, while c is not. In the reservation process m asks all agents about their availability, while it continues reasoning based on its default assumptions. If m does not receive any answer, a small room is reserved. If m receives an answer that contradicts its assumptions before a certain timeout, e.g., the end of the computation required to solve the top-goal, m backtracks and proceeds accordingly to the received replies.

Roughly speaking, the approach proposed in [19] to this problem is to activate several concurrent processes, each representing a positive or negative assumed answer to a certain question that has been made to the other agents. The processes waiting for an answer are suspended, while those that contain an assumption that is contradicted by an already received answer are killed (in a further refinement of the algorithm [20], such processes are not killed but only suspended, in order to allow further revision of a given answer).

We could model the communication underlying the meeting room reservation problem by means of abduction, and the shared Δ, with a common abducible predicate free/2. The master agent has the following program[3]:

```
plan(small_room,[X,Y]) ←
   free(X,true), free(Y,true), free(Z,false), X ≠ Y.
plan(big_room,[X,Y,Z]) ←
   free(X,true), free(Y,true), free(Z,true),
   alldifferent([X,Y,Z]).
plan(cancel_meeting,[]) ←
   free(Y,false), free(Z,false), Y ≠ Z.
← free(X,true), free(X,false).
```

For each case (i.e., reserve a small or big room or even cancel the meeting), the master abduces a reply, one for each agent involved in the meeting. For instance, if the (expected) default answer is two agents are available, and one busy, then the master agent plans to reserve a small room, on the basis of the abduced replies (e.g., free(X, true), free(Y, false) and free(Z, true)), and the computation proceeds.

In the program of the master agent, while exploiting abduction, we can constrain variables X, Y and Z to be all different and each assuming one value among a, b or c. Thus, abduced atoms are ground. However, in our framework, we can also abduce hypotheses with unbound variables, lifting the approach of speculative computation to non ground-terms.

As the computation proceeds, it can be the case that a reply comes from the agents (all, or some of them). In our framework, this reply is abduced by each agent itself, and stored in the common Δ. For each abducible free(X, true) a choice point is left open, e.g., $X/a \vee X \neq a$. If the reply provided by some of the agents, a, violates the integrity constraint, i.e., the master agent has assumed the availability of a, and this is not the case since a is busy, then the master agent has to backtrack, and consider a different set of abducibles. Nonetheless, if no answer comes from the agents, then the default is assumed, once and forever. This framework is able to provide the same answer also in case an atom free(a, true) is posted in the blackboard by agent a before the room reservation process is started by m: in this way, we give a declarative counterpart to a multiple-party speculative computation setting, more general than the one considered in [19], and a framework capable of dealing with non-ground terms. We see by this example how the communication can be obtained through bindings of variables in abduced literals, and how a default can be taken: agent m receives the names of the agents that will participate to the meeting and will retract its default assumption (that exactly two agents will participate) only if it is proven false, independently on *who* are the agents participating.

---

[3] We report only the part related to the replies, which is the most interesting, being the request and the reservation of the room quite straightforward. Also, we associate to the variables X, Y, Z the domain [a,b,c].

In future work, a full operational semantics should be given, and could be inherited from the works by Satoh et al., possibly extended in order to recover both synchronous or asynchronous communication: when abducing an atom with non-ground terms, the process can suspend thus miming the behaviour of read-only variable of concurrent logic languages (and obtain a synchronous communication), or proceed (asynchronous communication).

5 Abduction and Set Operations: Experiments with $CLP(\mathcal{SET})$

As we noticed in Sect. 3, communication is based on operations on *sets*. For this reason, we decided to perform our experiments on $CLP(\mathcal{SET})$ [15], a constraint language based on sets. $CLP(\mathcal{SET})$ is an instance of the general CLP framework [21] which provides finite sets, along with a few set-based operations, as primitive objects of the language.

Each of the agents could use one of the existing abductive proof procedures (e.g., [22, 14, 23, 24]) to perform abductive reasoning, and produce a set of abducibles. The hypotheses proposed by the various agents, δ_i, could be combined as explained in Sect. 3 with $CLP(\mathcal{SET})$, in order to obtain a globally consistent set of hypotheses Δ (Def. 3).

It is worth noticing that abduction itself can be thought of as based on set operations, thus one may implement also the abductive proof procedure in $CLP(\mathcal{SET})$. In fact, in the abductive computation of each agent, the expected result includes the set δ_i of abduced hypotheses, along with bindings of variables. Each hypothesis is inserted in the set δ_i by an abductive step, affirming that the hypothesis belongs to the set δ_i. The space of possible hypotheses is limited by ICs, that forbid some conjunctions of hypotheses in δ_i. Consider, for example, the IC:

$$\leftarrow L_1, L_2.$$

where both L_1 and L_2 are abducibles. This integrity constraint limits the possible hypotheses: if δ contains the atom L_1, then it cannot contain L_2 and viceversa.

All the operations on the set δ_i can be defined in terms of two basic operations: the abduction step (making an hypothesis, i.e., $L \in \delta_i$) and the check/propagation of the integrity constraints, that can reject some possible hypotheses (state that some hypotheses cannot belong to δ_i, i.e., $L \notin \delta_i$). Both these operations, the set membership operation and its denial, can be considered as *constraints*, meant to *define* the set δ_i, which is the result of the computation.

We made our experiments by defining a simplified abductive proof procedure in $CLP(\mathcal{SET})$. In our implementation, the abduction of an atom, L_1, is given by two steps. Firstly, we impose that the set δ_i contains the atom L_1, with the constraint $L_1 \in \delta_i$. This will result in the unification $\delta_i = \{L_1|\delta_i'\}$, which, in $CLP(\mathcal{SET})$ syntax, means that $\delta_i = \{L_1\} \cup \delta_i'$.

The second step is imposing integrity constraints. Whenever a new atom is abduced, constraints are imposed on the rest of the set δ_i. In our example, when abducing L_1, we impose that the rest of δ_i should not contain the abducible L_2: $L_2 \notin \delta_i'$. The structure of the predicate responsible for abduction can be the following:

```
abduce(Atom,Delta) ← Delta = Atom | D1,
    collect_ics(Atom,ICs), impose_ics(ICs,D1,Atom).
```

`collect_ics` collects all the variants of ICs that contain an atom unifying with the abduced atom, together with the corresponding substitution θ. Intuitively, when we abduce an atom L_1, we want to falsify at least one atom in each integrity constraint. `impose_ics` tries to find, in each IC/θ, an atom which is false for all the possible instantiations of its (remaining) universally quantified variables.

It is worth noticing that some of the transitions in the operational semantics of abductive proof procedures are automatically performed by constraint propagation in $CLP(\mathcal{SET})$. For example, proof procedures typically try to find a possibly minimal set of hypotheses, thus they try to unify couples of hypotheses in δ (with transitions called *solution reuse* [23] or *factoring* [14]). Given two hypotheses $p(X)$ and $p(Y)$, abductive proof procedures unify X and Y, but also consider $X \neq Y$ upon backtracking. In $CLP(\mathcal{SET})$, if δ contains a non-ground atom $p(X)$, i.e., $\delta = \{p(X)|\delta'\}$, when abducing a new atom $p(Y)$ (i.e., imposing the constraint $p(Y) \in \delta$) the nondeterministic propagation provides the two alternative solutions $\delta = \{p(X)|\delta'\}$ with $X = Y$ and $\delta = \{p(X), p(Y)|\delta''\}$ with $X \neq Y$.

Future work will focus on a fully distributed implementation of Global and Local Consistency algorithms.

6   Related Work and Discussion

Torroni [25] investigates how to coordinate the abductive reasoning of multiple agents, developing an architecture (ALIAS) where several coordination patterns can be chosen. A logic-based language (LAILA) is defined for expressing communication and coordination between logic agents, each one equipped with abductive reasoning capability [12]. LAILA can be used to model the social behaviour of logic-based agents, enabling them to express at a high level several ways to join and coordinate with one another. Our work approaches agent interaction from another perspective: no explicit coordination operators are needed, and the role of abduction is mainly in giving a semantics to interaction seen as information exchange, and not in the agent's internal reasoning. Differently from [12], in this work agents share predicates which are not necessarily ground, and a form of information exchange results from unification and variable binding. This allows for asynchronous interaction patterns, where in principle no agent needs "starting" the distributed proof of a goal, nor coordinating the reasoning activity of others. Following ALIAS, in [26] the authors propose an operational semantics based on a proof system for the consistent execution of tasks in a constrained multi-agent setting, and they prove the soundness and completeness of such operational semantics to be used to verify the correct execution of tasks. This work and [26] propose two logic based approaches to reasoning on the group activity of agents and enforcing properties such as consistency. However, their scope and purpose are different: here, the semantics of information exchange for abductive logic agents, in [26], the consistency of a joint work activity.

Hindriks et al. [27] propose a logic-based approach to agent communication and negotiation where deduction is used to derive information from a received message, and abduction is used to obtain proposals in reply to requests. In particular, deduction serves to derive information from a received message. Abduction serves to obtain proposals in reply to requests. A semantics based on deduction is proposed for the ask and tell primitives, similarly to other proposals in the literature, while a semantics based on abduction is proposed for the req and offer primitives. The semantics that they propose, based on the existence of free variables in the communicative acts, shows some similarities with ours; the main difference is that we do not distinguish among the different kinds of communication primitives, and the semantics of information exchange is uniformly based on abduction.

Sadri et al. [4] propose a framework for agent negotiation based on dialogue, which we sketched in section 4. The work of Sadri et al. [4] differs from ours in its purpose, which is not to give a semantics to agent interaction, but to give an execution model for the activity of the single agent and - based on it - to study formal properties of agents interacting with each other. In [3], the authors represent Kowalski-Sadri agents as abducible theories, and formalise communication acts by means of inter-theory reflection theorems, based on the predicate symbols $tell$ and $told$. Intuitively, each time a $tell(a_1, A)$ atom is derived from a theory represented by an agent a_2, the atom $told(a_2, A)$ is consequently derived in the theory represented by a_1, and therefore the proposition A becomes available to it. The framework is provided with a nice formalisation, and is based on two particular predicates ($tell/told$) that allow peer-to-peer communication. In our work, we aim to cater for different interaction patterns, possibly involving more than one peer, and to consider communication acts as bi-directional knowledge sharing activities, where several parties may contribute in shaping new information through the unification mechanism.

Bracciali and Torroni [28] propose a framework for knowledge revision of abductive agents through their interaction. They focus on several aspects of agent interaction at a higher level than the one we study in this work, by showing how negotiation about knowledge can be used to make the agents' knowledge evolve as they interact.

Satoh et al. [19] present a master-slave system in a setting where communication is assumed to be unreliable, which we briefly introduced in Section 4. The system is given a formal proof-procedure, that consists of two steps: a process reduction phase, and a fact arrival phase. Differently from our work (more focussed on the declarative semantics), speculative computation is an operational model.

Finally, a comment about the proof procedure for abduction. We chose to make our experiments with $CLP(\mathcal{SET})$, that has the advantage that it provides set unification as a first class operation. But there are several abductive proof procedures that could be used instead for our purpose. Of course, our framework requires abduction of non ground atoms, as variables in abducibles can represent request for information.

Denecker and De Schreye [22] introduce a proof procedure for normal abductive logic programs by extending the SLDNF resolution to the case of abduction. The resulting proof procedure (SLDNFA) is correct with respect to the completion semantics. A crucial property of this abductive procedure is the treatment of *non-ground* abductive goals. The authors do not consider general integrity constraints, but only constraints of the kind $\leftarrow A, not A$. To overcome this limitation, in a later work [29], they consider the treatment of general integrity constraints but in a quite inefficient way. In practice, they check all the integrity constraints at the end of the proof for a query, i.e., only when the overall set of abductive hypotheses supporting the query has been computed. More recent work is represented by the SLDNFA(C) system [30] which extends SLDNFA with constraints.

A recent abductive proof procedure dealing with constraints on finite domains is ACLP [23]. ACLP interleaves consistency checking of abducible assumptions and constraint satisfaction. Finally, $\mathcal{A}$-system [24], follow-up of ACLP and SLDNFA(C), differs from previous two for the explicit treatment of non-determinism that allows the use of heuristic search with different types of heuristics.

A different viewpoint of integration of constraints and abducibles has been studied by Kowalski et al. [31]. The authors group in a same framework the concepts of constraint logic programming, abduction and semantic query optimisation.

7   Conclusions and Future Work

In this work, we presented a framework that gives a uniform treating of abductive reasoning and communication. Groups of abductive agents communicate by abducing non-ground terms and obtain binding for their variables as the result of an (implicit) agreement with other agents. The result of the interaction is modelled as a set of abductive predicates (Δ), consistent with all the local integrity constraints of the agents. We showed some properties of the framework which make it possible to give a semantic characterisation to the information exchanged in the abductive process. We presented various examples of communication patterns that can be emulated, like the the dining philosophers and speculative computation. We gave them semantics in terms of abduction and set-based unification. Since the set Δ is constructed by the union of the local hypotheses, we sketched a prototypical implementation in $CLP(\mathcal{SET})$.

In future work, we plan to implement the framework in a fully distributed environment, possibly by exploiting proof procedures based on constraint satisfaction technology. We also plan to provide an operational semantics for our framework, with the semantics of suspension, possibly drawing inspiration from concurrent logic languages.

Acknowledgements

This work was partially funded by the Information Society Technologies programme of the European Commission, Future and Emerging Technologies under the IST-2001-32530 SOCS project, within the Global Computing proactive initiative, and by the MIUR COFIN 2003 projects *Sviluppo e verifica di sistemi multiagente basati sulla logica*, and *La Gestione e la negoziazione automatica dei diritti sulle opere dell'ingegno digitali: aspetti giuridici e informatici*.

References

1. Dix, J., Leite, J.A., Satoh, K., eds.: Computational Logic in Multi-Agent Systems: 3rd International Workshop, CLIMA'02, Copenhagen, Denmark, August 1, 2002, Proceedings. Volume 70 of Electronic Notes in Theoretical Computer Science. Elsevier Science Publishers (2002)

2. Kowalski, R.A., Sadri, F.: From logic programming towards multi-agent systems. Annals of Mathematics and Artificial Intelligence **25** (1999) 391–419

3. Dell'Acqua, P., Sadri, F., Toni, F.: Combining introspection and communication with rationality and reactivity in agents. In Dix, J., Fariñas del Cerro, L., Furbach, U., eds.: Logics in Artificial Intelligence, European Workshop, JELIA'98, Dagstuhl, Germany, October 12–15, 1998, Proceedings. Volume 1489 of Lecture Notes in Computer Science., Springer-Verlag (1998) 17–32

4. Sadri, F., Toni, F., Torroni, P.: An abductive logic programming architecture for negotiating agents. In Greco, S., Leone, N., eds.: Proceedings of the 8th European Conference on Logics in Artificial Intelligence (JELIA). Volume 2424 of Lecture Notes in Computer Science., Springer-Verlag (2002) 419–431

5. Dell'Acqua, P.: Weighted multi dimensional logic programs. In Dix, J., Leite, J., eds.: Computational Logic in Multi-Agent Systems. 4th International Workshop, CLIMA IV, Fort Lauderdale, Florida, USA, (2004) 162–178

6. Singh, M.: Agent communication language: rethinking the principles. IEEE Computer (1998) 40–47

7. Colombetti, M., Fornara, N., Verdicchio, M.: A social approach to communication in multiagent systems. In Leite, J., Omicini, A., Sterling, L., Torroni, P., eds.: Declarative Agent Languages and Technologies: Theory and Practice. Volume 2990 of Lecture Notes in Artificial Intelligence., Springer-Verlag (2004) 193–222

8. Alberti, M., Ciampolini, A., Gavanelli, M., Lamma, E., Mello, P., Torroni, P.: A social ACL semantics by deontic constraints. In Mařík, V., Müller, J., Pěchouček, M., eds.: Multi-Agent Systems and Applications III. Proceedings of the 3rd International Central and Eastern European Conference on Multi-Agent Systems, CEEMAS 2003. Volume 2691 of Lecture Notes in Artificial Intelligence., Prague, Czech Republic, Springer-Verlag (2003) 204–213

9. Cohen, P.R., Perrault, C.R.: Elements of a plan-based theory of speech acts. Cognitive Science **3** (1979)

10. FIPA: Communicative Act Library Specification (2001) Published on August 10th, 2001, available for download from the FIPA website.

11. Labrou, Y., Finin, T.W.: Semantics for an agent communication language. In: Intelligent Agents IV, Agent Theories, Architectures, and Languages, 4th International Workshop, ATAL '97, Providence, Rhode Island, Proceedings. Volume 1365 of Lecture Notes in Computer Science., Springer-Verlag (1998) 209–214

12. Ciampolini, A., Lamma, E., Mello, P., Toni, F., Torroni, P.: Co-operation and competition in *ALIAS*: a logic framework for agents that negotiate. Computational Logic in Multi-Agent Systems. Annals of Mathematics and Artificial Intelligence **37** (2003) 65–91

13. Eshghi, K., Kowalski, R.A.: Abduction compared with negation by failure. In Levi, G., Martelli, M., eds.: Proceedings of the 6th International Conference on Logic Programming, MIT Press (1989) 234–255

14. Fung, T.H., Kowalski, R.A.: The IFF proof procedure for abductive logic programming. Journal of Logic Programming **33** (1997) 151–165

15. Dovier, A., Piazza, C., Pontelli, E., Rossi, G.: Sets and constraint logic programming. ACM Transactions on Programming Languages and Systems **22** (2000) 861–931

16. Dovier, A., Pontelli, E., Rossi, G.: Constructive negation and constraint logic programming with sets. New Generation Computing **19** (2001)

17. Kakas, A.C., Kowalski, R.A., Toni, F.: The role of abduction in logic programming. In Gabbay, D.M., Hogger, C.J., Robinson, J.A., eds.: Handbook of Logic in Artificial Intelligence and Logic Programming. Volume 5., Oxford University Press (1998) 235–324

18. Dijkstra, E.: Hierarchical ordering of sequential processes. Acta Informatica **1** (1971) 115–138

19. Satoh, K., Inoue, K., Iwanuma, K., Sakama, C.: Speculative computation by abduction under incomplete communication environments. In: Proceedings of the 4th International Conference on Multi-Agent Systems, Boston, USA, IEEE Press (2000) 263–270
20. Satoh, K., Yamamoto, K.: Speculative computation with multi-agent belief revision. In Castelfranchi, C., Lewis Johnson, W., eds.: Proceedings of the First International Joint Conference on Autonomous Agents and Multiagent Systems (AAMAS-2002), Part II, Bologna, Italy, ACM Press (2002) 897–904
21. Jaffar, J., Maher, M., Marriott, K., Stuckey, P.: The semantics of constraint logic programs. Journal of Logic Programming **37(1-3)** (1998) 1–46
22. Denecker, M., Schreye, D.D.: SLDNFA: An abductive procedure for normal abductive programs. In Apt, K., ed.: Proceedings of the Joint International Conference and Symposium on Logic Programming, Cambridge, MIT Press (1992) 686–702
23. Kakas, A.C., Michael, A., Mourlas, C.: ACLP: Abductive Constraint Logic Programming. Journal of Logic Programming **44** (2000) 129–177
24. Kakas, A.C., van Nuffelen, B., Denecker, M.: A-System: Problem solving through abduction. In Nebel, B., ed.: Proceedings of the 17th International Joint Conference on Artificial Intelligence, Seattle, Washington, USA, Morgan Kaufmann Publishers (2001) 591–596
25. Torroni, P.: Reasoning and interaction in logic-based multi-agent systems. PhD thesis, Department of Electronics, Computer Science, and Systems, University of Bologna, Italy (2001)
26. Ciampolini, A., Lamma, E., Mello, P., Torroni, P.: A proof-system for the safe execution of tasks in multi-agent systems. In Greco, S., Leone, N., eds.: Proceedings of the 8th European Conference on Logics in Artificial Intelligence (JELIA). Volume 2424 of Lecture Notes in Computer Science., Springer-Verlag (2002) 14–26
27. Hindriks, K., de Boer, F., van der Hoek, W., Meyer, J.J.: Semantics of communicating agents based on deduction and abduction. In: Foundations And Applications Of Collective Agent Based Systems (CABS). (1999)
28. Bracciali, A., Torroni, P.: A new framework for knowledge revision of abductive agents through their interaction (preliminary report). In Dix, J., Leite, J., eds.: CLIMA-IV: Computational Logic in Multi-Agent Systems, Fourth International Workshop. Proceedings, Fort Lauderdale, FL, USA (2004) To Appear.
29. Denecker, M., Schreye, D.D.: Representing Incomplete Knowledge in Abductive Logic Programming. In: Logic Programming, Proceedings of the 1993 International Symposium, Vancouver, British Columbia, Canada, The MIT Press (1993) 147–163
30. van Nuffelen, B., Denecker, M.: Problem solving in ID-logic with aggregates. In: Proceedings of the 8th International Workshop on Non-Monotonic Reasoning, NMR'00, Breckenridge, CO. (2000) 1–9
31. Kowalski, R., Toni, F., Wetzel, G.: Executing suspended logic programs. Fundamenta Informaticae **34** (1998) 203–224

Fault Tolerant and Fixed Scalable Structure of Middle-Agents

Pavel Tichý

Rockwell Automation Research Center & Czech Technical University,
Prague, Czech Republic
ptichy@ra.rockwell.com

Abstract. Middle-agents are used by end-agents to locate service providers in multi-agent systems. One central middle-agent represents a single point of failure and communication bottleneck in the system. Thus a structure of middle-agents can be used to overcome these issues. We designed and implemented a structure of middle-agents called dynamic hierarchical teams that has user-defined level of fault-tolerance and is moreover fixed scalable. We prove that the structure that has teams of size λ has edge and vertex connectivity equal to λ and is maximally fault tolerant. We focus on social knowledge management describing several methods that can be used for social knowledge propagation and related methods to search for knowledge in this structure. We also test the fault-tolerance of this structure in practical experiments.

1 Introduction

Social knowledge in multi-agent systems can be understood as knowledge that is used to deal with other agents in the multi-agent system. Social knowledge consists of the information about the name of agents, their location (address), their capabilities (services), the language they use, their actual state, their conversations, behavioral patterns, and so on [13]. Knowledge that is located in agents can be formally split into two distinct types [2]:

- *domain knowledge* (or *problem-solving knowledge* [13]) - concerns a problem-solving domain and an environment of an agent. Domain knowledge represents the decision-making process of an agent.
- *social knowledge* - allows an agent to interact with other agents and possibly improves this process.

One of the main advantages in using multi-agent systems is fault tolerance. When an agent fails a multi-agent system could 'offer' another agent that can be used instead. Is this enough to ensure fault tolerant behavior? If a multi-agent system uses a middle-agent [4] to search for the capabilities of providers, i.e., to search for an alternative agent with the same capability, then this middle-agent can become a single point of failure, i.e., social knowledge is centralized in this case. It is not possible to search for capabilities of other agents and to form virtual organizations

J. Dix and J. Leite (Eds.): CLIMA IV, LNAI 3259, pp. 53–70, 2004.

any more if the system looses the middle-agent. Fault tolerance issue is tightly coupled with load sharing. When only one middle-agent is used then it becomes a communication bottleneck and can be easily overloaded.

Several approaches have been used already to deal with these issues. Mainly the teamwork-based technique [11] has been proposed that uses a group of N middle-agents where each middle-agent is connected to all other middle-agents forming a complete graph. This technique offers fault tolerance but since it uses a complete graph this structure is not fixed scalable as shown in section 2.4. Another example is distributed matchmaking [18] that focuses on increasing the throughput of matchmaking services by creation of hierarchy but does not deal with fault tolerance. Another approach to distribute social knowledge among agents is to use for instance acquaintance models [13], but this technique implicitly does not ensure fixed scalability since in the worst case each agent keeps knowledge about all other agents (see section 2.4).

2   Dynamic Hierarchical Teams Architecture

We propose the dynamic hierarchical teams (DHT) architecture [20] to take advantage of both hierarchical and distributed architectures. The pure hierarchical architectures offer the scalability, but they are not designed to be fault-tolerant. On the other hand, the pure distributed architectures offer the robustness, but they are not scalable since any middle-agent is connected to all other middle-agents.

2.1   DHT Architecture Description

Assume that a multi-agent system consists of middle-agents and end-agents. Middle-agents form a structure that can be described by the graph theory. Graph vertices represent middle-agents and graph edges represent a possibility for direct communication between two middle-agents, i.e., communication channels.

The first main difference from the pure hierarchical architecture is that the DHT architecture is not restricted to have a single root of the tree that serves as a global middle-agent. The single global middle-agent easily becomes a single point of failure and possibly also a communication bottleneck. In addition, any other middle-agent that is not in a leaf position in the tree has similar disadvantages.

Therefore, to provide a more robust architecture, each middle-agent that is not a leaf in the tree should be backed up by another middle-agent. Groups of these middle-agents we call *teams* (see Fig. 1). Whenever one of the middle-agents from the team fails, other middle-agents from the team can subrogate this agent.

During the normal operation of the DHT structure all middle-agents use only primary communication channels. The usage of secondary communication channels will be further described in section 2.5.

The DHT structure is not limited only to two levels, but it can support an N-level structure. For the cases where $N > 2$ teams compose a hierarchical structure in the form of a tree (see Fig. 2), i.e., the structure of teams does not contain cycles and

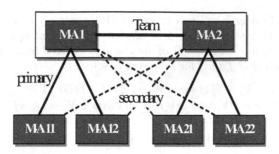

Fig. 1. Example of 2-level DHT architecture

the graph is connected. The tree structure holds only if we consider one edge of the resulting graph per a set of primary and secondary connections between two teams.

More complex is the structure of middle-agents (not teams), since this structure is not limited to be a tree. First of all, a team consists of at least one middle-agent. To increase fault tolerance, a team should consist of two or more middle-agents. All members of a team are interconnected via communication channels, forming a complete graph. The members of the top most team (Team1) are interconnected via primary communication channels while the members of other teams are interconnected via secondary ones.

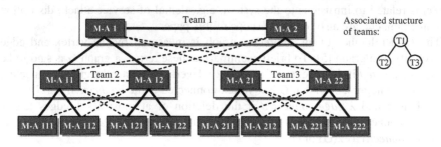

Fig. 2. Example of 3-level DHT architecture and associated structure of teams

If we restrict the DHT structure to contain only teams that consist of only one middle-agent then we end up with hierarchical structure (a tree). On the other hand, if we restrict it to one team plus possibly one middle-agent that is not a part of this team then full-connected network of middle-agents is created, i.e., a structure similar to the teamwork-based technique [11]. The DHT structure is therefore flexible in this respect.

Let G be a graph where each middle-agent i in the dynamic hierarchical teams (DHT) structure is represented by a graph vertex $v_i \in V$ and each primary or secondary connection among middle-agents i and j is represented by an edge $e = \{v_i, v_j\}$ between v_i and v_j.

Definition 1. (DHT) *A graph G will be called* DHT *graph if there exist non-empty sets $V_1, ..., V_n \subset V(G)$ such that they are pairwise disjoint and $V_1 \cup ... \cup V_n \neq V(G)$. In that case, the complete subgraph G_i of the graph G induced by the set of vertices V_i will be called a* team *of G if all of the following is satisfied:*

1) $\forall v(v \in V(G) \setminus V_1 \rightarrow \exists j \, \forall w(w \in V_j \rightarrow \{v, w\} \in E(G)))$[1]
2) $\forall v(v \in V(G) \wedge v \notin V_1 \cup ... \cup V_n) \rightarrow \exists! j \, \forall w(w \notin V_j \rightarrow \{v, w\} \notin E(G)))$[2]
3) $\forall j((j > 1) \wedge (j \leq n) \rightarrow \exists! k((k < j) \wedge \forall v \, \forall w(v \in V_j \wedge w \in V_k \rightarrow \{v, w\} \in E(G)) \wedge \forall u \, \forall m(u \in V_m \wedge (m < j) \wedge (m \neq k) \rightarrow \{v, u\} \notin E(G)))$[3]

Definition 2. (DHT-λ) *The graph G is called* DHT-λ *if G is DHT and $|V_i| = \lambda$ for every $i = 1,...,n$, where $\lambda \in N$.*

2.2   Fault Tolerance in DHT Architecture

The vertex and edge connectivity of a graph (see below) provide information about possibility to propagate knowledge through the network of middle-agents and communication channels despite failures on these multi-agent system components. Therefore, only the dynamic impact of these failures is studied in this paper. Static impact of these failures is out of scope of this paper. In that case we study various static parameters, e.g., a minimal/maximal percentage of end-agents about which social knowledge stored in middle-agents is lost when k middle-agents fail simultaneously, minimal/average redundancy of the social knowledge, etc. Also problems related to intrusions to the system, e.g., denial of service attack, disruption of connection, etc. are also out of the scope of this paper.

The fault tolerance of an undirected graph is measured by the vertex and edge connectivity of a graph [5]. To briefly summarize these terms, a graph G is said to be *λ vertex-connected* if the deletion of at most λ - 1 vertices leaves the graph connected. The greatest integer λ such that G is λ vertex-connected is the *connectivity* $\kappa(G)$ of G. A graph is called *λ edge-connected* if the deletion of at most λ - 1 edges leaves the graph connected. The greatest integer λ such that G is λ edge-connected is the *edge-connectivity* $\lambda(G)$ of G.

Claim 1. *If the graph G is DHT-λ then for each vertex $v \in V(G)$ there exists a vertex $w \in V_1$ such that there is a path in G starting from v and ending at w after **removing** λ - 1 vertices or λ - 1 edges from G.*

Proof. Assume the case where $v \notin V_1$ since otherwise the path is v itself. For each team of DHT-λ $|V_j| = \lambda$. Thus there are at least λ edges $\{v, w_1\}$ such that $\exists j \forall w_1$ $(w_1 \in V_j \rightarrow \{v, w_1\} \in E(G))$. Since $|V_j| = \lambda$ then after the elimination of λ - 1 vertices

---

[1] For all vertices v of G except V_1 (since there is no team with lower index than V_1) there has to be a team such that v is connected to all members of this team.

[2] For all vertices v that are not members of any team there are only connections to one team and there cannot be any other connection from v.

[3] All members of each team except G_1 are connected to all members of exactly one other team with lower index.

or λ - 1 edges there exists a path starting from v and ending at w_1 where $w_1 \in V_j$. If $j = 1$ then the resulting path is vw_1. Otherwise, since $|V_j| = \lambda$ the rule 3) from the definition of DHT can be repeatedly applied to construct a path in G despite the elimination of λ - 1 vertices or λ - 1 edges starting from w_1 and ending at w_k where $w_k \in V_1$. Therefore the resulting path in this case is $vw_1w_2...w_k$. □

Lemma 1. *If the graph G is DHT-λ then G is λ vertex-connected and λ edge-connected.*

Proof. 1) We prove that the graph G of type DHT-λ is λ edge-connected. Suppose (for contradiction) that there is a λ - 1 edge cut set in G. Assume that it separates G into pieces C_1 and C_2. Let $v_1 \in V(C_1)$ and $v_2 \in V(C_2)$. We already proved that after removing λ - 1 edges there exists a path starting from a vertex v_1 (or v_2 respectively) and ending at w_1 (or w_2 respectively) where $w_1 \in V_1$ and $w_2 \in V_1$. If $w_1 = w_2$ then a path from v_1 to v_2 already exists. Otherwise it remains to prove that any two vertices $w_1 \neq w_2$ such that $w_1 \in V_1$ and $w_2 \in V_1$ are connected after elimination of λ - 1 edges from G. At least λ - 1 edge cut set is required to split the complete graph G_1 into two pieces but since $G_1 \neq G$ thus $\exists w_3(w_3 \notin V_1 \wedge w_3 \in V(G))$ for which $\forall v_k(v_k \in V_1 \rightarrow \{w_3, v_k\} \in E(G)$ holds since either $w_3 \in V_2$ or the number of teams $n = 1$. Then a subgraph of G induced by $V(G_1) \cup \{w_3\}$ is a complete graph of order $\lambda + 1$ and therefore there is at least one path in G after elimination of λ - 1 edges from G that leads from w_1 to w_2. Thus there is no edge cut set of size λ - 1.

2) We prove that the graph G of type DHT-λ is λ vertex-connected. Suppose (for contradiction) that there is a λ - 1 vertex cut set in G. Assume that it separates the graph at least into pieces C_1 and C_2. Let $v_1 \in V(C_1)$ and $v_2 \in V(C_2)$. We already proved that after removing λ - 1 vertices there exists a path starting from a vertex v_1 (or v_2 respectively) and ending at w_1 (or w_2 respectively) where $w_1 \in V_1$ and $w_2 \in V_1$. If $w_1 = w_2$ then a path from v_1 to v_2 already exists. Otherwise since G_1 is a complete graph then any two vertices $w_1 \neq w_2$ where $w_1 \in V(G_1)$ and $w_2 \in V(G_1)$ are connected after elimination of λ - 1 vertices from G. Thus there is no vertex cut set of size λ - 1.   □

Claim 2. *If the graph G is DHT-λ then the minimum degree $\delta(G) = \lambda$.*

Proof. We already proved that G is λ edge-connected and therefore $\delta(G) \geq \lambda$. From the definition of DHT rule 1) and the fact that $V_1 \cup ... \cup V_n \neq V(G)$ there has to be at least one vertex $v' \in V(G)$ for which $v' \notin V_1 \cup ... \cup V_n$ holds and $\exists j \forall w(w \in V_j \rightarrow \{v', w\} \in E(G)$). Since $|V_j| = \lambda$ for DHT- λ thus there are at least λ edges $\{v', w\}$ and since from the definition of DHT rule 2) $\exists ! j \forall w(w \notin V_j \rightarrow \{v', w\} \notin E(G)$) holds there are no more than λ edges $\{v', w\}$ and therefore $d(v') = \lambda$. Since $\delta(G) \geq \lambda$ and $d(v') = \lambda$ thus $\delta(G) = \lambda$.   □

Theorem 1. *If the graph G is DHT-λ then the vertex connectivity $\kappa(G) = \lambda$ and the edge-connectivity $\lambda(G) = \lambda$.*

Proof. We already proved that the graph G of type DHT-λ is λ vertex-connected and λ edge-connected thus it remains to prove that $\kappa(G) \leq \lambda$ and $\lambda(G) \leq \lambda$. For every non-trivial graph G the equation $\kappa(G) \leq \lambda(G) \leq \delta(G)$ holds [5]. We already proved that $\delta(G) = \lambda$ therefore $\kappa(G) \leq \lambda$ and $\lambda(G) \leq \lambda$.   □

The DHT structure where teams consist of λ middle-agents is therefore fault tolerant to simultaneous failure of at least λ - 1 middle-agents and also to simultaneous failure of at least λ - 1 communication channels.

A graph G is called *maximally fault tolerant* if vertex connectivity of the graph G equals the minimum degree of a graph $\delta(G)$ [22].

Theorem 2. *The graph G of type DHT-λ is* maximally fault tolerant.

Proof. We already proved that the graph G of type DHT-λ has vertex connectivity $\kappa(G) = \lambda$ and we also proved that it has the minimum degree $\delta(G) = \lambda$.   □

The maximally fault tolerant graph means that there is no bottleneck in the structure of connections among nodes, i.e., middle-agents in the case of the DHT architecture.

The problem of directly computing the most survivable deployment of agents has been introduced recently in [10]. Although, disconnect probabilities of all nodes have to be known either by collecting statistical data or by experts (that can be hard to obtain and values are not only application specific but can also vary in time) then it is possible to compute the optimal survivable deployment. This probabilistic approach cannot be used in our study since these values are not available.

In addition, N-version programming [3] can be directly applied to the DHT architecture to increase robustness of the whole system. Assume that the teams are of size N and consist of N independently developed middle-agents (by N different developers, by N different programming languages, etc.). Then the whole structure of middle-agents is fault tolerant to the simultaneous failure of all middle-agents that were developed by N-1 development processes.

2.3   Social Knowledge Management in DHT Architecture

We identified several approaches to social knowledge management based on the amount of social knowledge that is stored in the low-level middle-agents. In this section we describe breadth knowledge propagation, depth knowledge propagation, and no knowledge propagation. The efficiency of these three methods can be further improved by knowledge propagation on demand or by knowledge caching. To formally describe these methods, we first define neighbors, parents, and team members of a middle-agent.

Definition 3. *Assume that a graph G is DHT with G_1, ..., G_n its teams. Then we define all of the following:*

1) $E^p(G) \subseteq E(G)$ *as a set of edges where each $e \in E^p(G)$ represents a primary communication channel.*
2) Neighbors$(v, G) = \{ w | \{v, w\} \in E^p(G) \}$.

3) Parents$(v, G) = \{ w | \{v, w\} \in E^v(G) \wedge \exists j \, \forall k(w \in V(G_j) \wedge v \in V(G_k) \rightarrow k > j)\}$.
4) If $v \in V(G_j)$ then TeamMemembers$(v, G) = V(G_j) \setminus \{v\}$.

If $v \notin V(G_j)$ for every $j = 1,..., n$ then TeamMemembers$(v, G) = \emptyset$.

Breadth Knowledge Propagation. We define *breadth knowledge propagation* in such a way that every middle-agent in the system ultimately knows social information about all end-agents in the system.

The following message routing algorithm is used for routing messages in the breadth knowledge propagation approach and holds for each middle-agent:

Definition 4. (full message routing) *Assume that a graph G is DHT. Let m be a message instance that the middle-agent represented by vertex $v \in V(G)$ received from a middle-agent represented by vertex $v^{orig} \in V(G)$ or from an end-agent for which $v^{orig} \notin V(G)$. Let AddOrig(m, V'(G)) be a subroutine that stores a set of vertices $V'(G) \subset V(G)$ in the message m and returns this result as a message m'. Let $V^{orig}(m) \subset V(G)$ be a set of vertices stored in the message m such that $v \in V^{orig}(AddOrig(m, \{v\}))$*[4]. *Let Send(H, m) be a subroutine that sends a message m to all middle-agents that are represented by vertices $v \in H$ where $H \subset V(G)$. Let KB(v) be an internal knowledge base of the middle-agent represented by a vertex v. Let Update(v, m) be a subroutine that updates KB(v) of the middle-agent v based on message m*[5]. *Let Store(v, w, c) be a subroutine that stores a reference to the middle-agent w under the message context c into KB(v) and let Retrieve(v, c) be a subroutine that returns $H \subseteq V(G)$ where a vertex $w \in H$ iff KB(v) contains w under the message context c. Let Context(m) be a subroutine that returns context of a message m, i.e., the same value for all messages that are successors of the original request message. Then the* full message routing *in G is defined by the following algorithm that is performed by a middle-agent v upon receiving a message m:*

```
IF Retrieve(v, Context(m)) = Ø THEN
{    Update(v, m)
     Let R(v) = {w | w ∈ Neighbors(v, G) ∧ w ≠ v^orig ∧
               w ∉ V^orig(m)} be a set of potential receivers.
     Let S(v) = {w | w ∈ R(v) ∧ w ∈ TeamMemembers(v, G)}
     FOR EACH w ∈ R(v)
     {        IF w ∉ TeamMemembers(v, G) THEN Send({w}, m)
              ELSE Send({w}, AddOrig(m, {v} ∪ (S(v)\{w})))
     }
     IF R(v) ≠ Ø THEN Store(v, v^orig, Context(m))
}
```

---

[4] AddOrig subroutine is typically used to store a set of vertices into the message m and then the resulting message m' is sent to other middle-agents. The receiver of this message m' can retrieve this set of vertices by $V^{orig}(m')$ and avoid to contact these middle-agents thus avoiding circuits in communication.

[5] Update subroutine is one of the main parts of a middle-agent where information from the message is processed and possibly stored to the internal knowledge base.

Based on this message routing in the breadth knowledge propagation we can distinguish how different types of messages are propagated.

1. Registration, unregistration or modification types of messages are routed to all middle-agents via the full message routing.
2. A search request is replied to the sender by using only the locally stored knowledge.

When an end-agent anywhere in the system contacts a local middle-agent and passes registration information to it, this middle-agent updates its internal database based on the incoming message and propagates this information to all neighbor middle-agents over primary communication channels except the sender and except any middle-agent that is already mentioned in the incoming message to avoid loops of size less than four. Since some of the communication channels can be faulty, the top most team that consists of more than three middle-agents can have a loop of size greater or equal to four. Therefore the context of the message is used to avoid these types of loops. The breadth knowledge propagation approach holds for requests for registration or unregistration of an end-agent and also for the modification of social knowledge. Search requests can be handled by middle-agents locally since knowledge about all end-agents in the system is ultimately present in every middle-agent.

Depth Knowledge Propagation. The second approach to social knowledge management is *depth knowledge propagation*, in which a middle-agent propagates social knowledge only to the higher level of the hierarchy of teams. In this approach only the topmost middle-agents contain social knowledge about all end-agents in the system. The following message routing algorithms are used for routing messages in the depth knowledge propagation approach and hold for each middle-agent:

Definition 5. (root message routing) *Apply the same set of assumptions as for the full message routing. Then the* root message routing *in G is defined by the following algorithm that is performed by a middle-agent v upon receiving a message m from* v^{orig}:

```
IF Retrieve(v, Context(m)) = Ø THEN
{   Update(v, m)
    Let R(v) = {w | (w ∈ Parents(v, G) ∪ TeamMemembers(v,
          G)) ∧ {v, w} ∈ E^p(G) ∧ w ≠ v^{orig} ∧ w ∉ V^{orig}(m)}
    Let S(v) = {w | w ∈ R(v) ∧ w ∈ TeamMemembers(v, G)}
    FOR EACH w ∈ R(v)
    {       IF w ∉ TeamMemembers(v, G) THEN Send({w}, m)
            ELSE Send({w}, AddOrig(m, {v} ∪ (S(v)\{w})))
    }
    IF R(v) ≠ Ø THEN Store(v, v^{orig}, Context(m)).
}
```

Definition 6. (parent retrieval message routing) *Apply the same set of assumptions as for the full message routing. Also let Process(v, m) be a subroutine that changes message m based on information of middle-agent represented by vertex v and returns*

true if all objectives of m have been satisfied and false otherwise. Then the parent
retrieval message routing *in G is defined by the following algorithm that is performed
by a middle-agent v upon receiving a message m from v^{orig}:*

```
IF Retrieve(v, Context(m)) = ∅ THEN
{   IF Process(v, m) THEN Send( Retrieve(v, Context(m)), m)
    ELSE
    {   FOR EACH w ∈ Parents(v, G)
            Send({w}, m)
        IF Parents(v, G) ≠ ∅ THEN Store(v, v^orig, Context(m))
        ELSE Send({v^orig}, m)
    }
}
ELSE Send( Retrieve(v, Context(m)), m)
```

Based on this message routing in the depth knowledge propagation we can
distinguish how different types of messages are propagated.

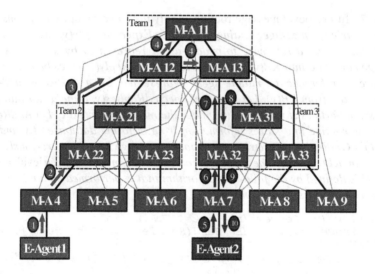

Fig. 3. Depth knowledge propagation example. Only interactions that are directly related to
the registration process and to the search process are described.
1. E-Agent1 sends a registration request to its local middle-agent (M-A 4).
2. M-A 4 forwards the registration information to M-A 22.
3. M-A 22 forwards the registration information to M-A 12.
4. M-A 12 forwards the registration information to M-A 11 and 13.
5. E-Agent2 sends a search request to its local middle-agent (M-A 7).
6. M-A 7 forwards the search request to M-A 32 since it cannot be satisfied locally.
7. M-A 32 forwards the search request to M-A 13.
8. M-A 13 is able to satisfy the search request and replies with the search result to M-A 32.
9. M-A 32 propagates the search result back to M-A 7.
10. M-A 7 finally replies with the search result to E-Agent2.

1. Registration, unregistration or modification types of messages are routed via the root message routing.
2. If a search request can be satisfied using local knowledge then reply with the result to the requester.
3. If a search request cannot be satisfied using local knowledge then it is routed via the parent retrieval message routing (if the set of receivers is non empty); otherwise, reply to the requester that the search was unsuccessful.
4. Forward the result of the search request back to the original requester (stored in v^{orig} under the same context as the result).

No Knowledge Propagation. The last approach to social knowledge propagation is *no knowledge propagation*. In this approach the end-agents register, unregister, and modify registration information only at the local middle-agents; this information is not further propagated. This type of technique is used for instance in multi-agent systems that are FIPA compliant [6] as JADE [8].

Definition 7. (full retrieval message routing) *Apply the same set of assumptions as for the parent retrieval message routing. Let StoreExpectedReply(v, w, c, m) be a subroutine that stores a reference to middle-agent represented by a vertex w under the message context c into KB(v) and RemoveExpectedReply(v, w, c) be a subroutine that removes a reference to middle-agent represented by a vertex w under the message context c from KB(v). Let RetrieveExpectedReplies(v, c) be a subroutine that returns a set of vertices stored in KB(v) under the message context c. Let AddReply(v, c, m) be a subroutine that stores information from m to the database of v under the context c and GetReply(v, c) retrieves composite message based on previously stored information in KB(v) under the message context c. Then the* full retrieval message routing *in G is defined by the following algorithm that is performed by a middle-agent v upon receiving a message m from v^{orig}:*

```
IF Retrieve(v, Context(m)) = Ø THEN
{   IF Process(v, m) THEN Send(Retrieve(v, Context(m)), m)
    ELSE
    {       Let R(v) = {w |w ∈ Neighbors(v, G) ∧ w ≠ v^orig ∧
                    w ∉ V^orig(m)}
            Let S(v) = {w |w ∈ R(v) ∧ w ∈ TeamMemembers(v, G)}
            FOR EACH w ∈ R(v)
            {       StoreExpectedReply(v, w, Context(m))
                    IF w ∉ TeamMemembers(v, G) THEN Send({w},m)
                    ELSE Send({w}, AddOrig(m, {v} ∪ (S(v)\{w})))
            }
            IF R(v) ≠ Ø THEN Store(v, v^orig, Context(m))
            ELSE Send({v^orig}, m)
    }
}
ELSE
    IF v^orig ∈ RetrieveExpectedReplies(v, Context(m)) THEN
    {       AddReply(v, Context(m), m)
            RemoveExpectedReply(v, v^orig, Context(m))
```

```
IF RetrieveExpectedReplies(v, c) = Ø THEN
    Send(Retrieve(v, Context(m)), GetReply(v,
        Context(m)))
}
```

The no knowledge propagation approach can be described by the following rules that hold for each middle-agent:

1. Registration, unregistration or modification types of messages are handled locally.
2. If a search request can be satisfied using the locally stored knowledge then reply to the requester with the result.
3. If a search request cannot be satisfied using the locally stored knowledge then it is routed via the full retrieval message routing (if the set of receivers is non empty); otherwise, reply to the requester with an unsuccessful result.
4. Store each result of a search request.
5. When all results of the search request are stored, assemble the results of the search request into a reply and send the reply back to the original requester (stored in v^{orig} under the same context as the result).

There is no communication among middle-agents during the registration phase, but there is much more communication during the search for information and the update of information. Since there is no clue where to search for any information, the searching process must be exhaustive. All middle-agents, both the ones upstream at the top of the hierarchy and the ones downstream in the lower levels of the hierarchy, must be searched.

The requester can, however, limit the search space. The information about the depth of search can be added to the request or the requester can limit the number of results (for instance specified by FIPA).

Knowledge Propagation on Demand. Both depth knowledge propagation and no knowledge propagation can be further improved with *knowledge propagation on demand*. Using this technique, information is discovered on demand and remembered for further use. Knowledge propagation on demand can be described by the following additional rule that holds for each middle-agent in the hierarchy:

1. During the forwarding of the result of the search request remember the information that is contained in the result of the search.

Suppose a middle-agent needs to contact the parent middle-agent to search for information. When a response propagates back with possibly a positive result, middle-agents remember this information along the propagation path.

Propagation on demand brings one complication to social knowledge update. To assure that information gathered on demand is up-to-date, we must introduce one of the refresh mechanisms.

- *Subscribe and advertise mechanism.* When a middle-agent remembers some social knowledge, it subscribes for the update of this knowledge with the middle-agent that supplied the knowledge. When this knowledge gets updated then all middle-agents on the path of this update also send updates to all of their subscribers of this knowledge. This mechanism is used for instance in KQML specification [9].

- *Time stamping mechanism.* When a middle-agent stores social knowledge gathered on demand, this knowledge is time-stamped. The middle-agent can then examine the time-stamp to determine whether this knowledge is still valid or too old to be used. The examination process happens either periodically or at the time when this knowledge is accessed. The time stamping is well known mechanism used for instance for revocation of certificates [15].

Knowledge Caching. Both depth knowledge propagation and no knowledge propagation can be further improved by using the *knowledge caching* mechanism. The knowledge caching mechanism can be described by the following additional rule that holds for each middle-agent in the hierarchy:

1. During the forwarding of the search result only remember the knowledge that is contained in the result if the receiver is the original requester of the search, i.e., the receiver is not a middle-agent.

Knowledge caching is an alternative approach to knowledge propagation on demand in which knowledge is not remembered all the way back to the requester, but only at the last middle-agent on the path to the requester. In this way the knowledge redundancy is very low despite the fact that knowledge is located at the proper places.

Note that we omitted describing all the cases in which the search was unsuccessful. The subscribe-and-advertise or time stamping mechanism has to be used again to ensure that the registration information is up-to-date.

All of these techniques are intended to work behind the scenes as part of the agent platform functionality. The hierarchy of middle-agents should be transparent to end-agents in the system. The end-agents register and modify information using their local middle-agent and ask for information again from their local middle-agent.

2.4   Scalability of DHT Architecture

Although the term scalability is frequently used it is not precisely defined so far. Researchers in the parallel processing community have been using for instance Amdahl's Law and Gustafson's Law [7] and therefore tie notions of scalability to notions of speedup. Nevertheless, speedup is not the main concern in the area of social knowledge since there is not one task that is split and solved in parallel. Thus these definitions are not sufficient and we present several other definitions.

"A system is said to be scalable if it can handle the addition of users and resources without suffering a noticeable loss of performance or increase in administrative complexity" [16].

"A scalable parallel processing platform is a computer architecture that is composed of computing elements. New computing element can be added to the scalable parallel processing platform at a fixed incremental cost" [12].

A formal definition of scalability in distributed applications is given in [19]. An important aspect of this definition is the distinction between performance and extensibility since the previous definitions are based on just one of these attributes. Very roughly, an application A is scalable in an attribute a if A can accommodate a growth of a up to defined maximum, if it is possible to compensate a performance degradation caused by increase of a, and if the costs that compensate performance degradation are limited.

To determine scalability without measuring resulting performance we can use definitions that are based on the extensibility and evaluate whether the cost to add new computing element is fixed. Thus we reformulate the scalability definition that is based on extensibility [12] to be used in the area of social knowledge architectures.

Definition 8. *Let $G = (V(G), E(G))$ be a graph that represents the structure of middle-agents and assume that G is of type[6] T. Then let H be a graph of type T such that $V(H) = V(G) \cup V^\delta(H)$ and $E(H) = E(G) \cup E^\delta(H)$ where $V^\delta(H)$ is a set of vertices that were added to $V(G)$ and $E^\delta(H)$ is a set of edges where each edge is adjacent to at least one vertex from $V^\delta(H)$. If for each such G there exists $\varepsilon > 0$ such that for each $V^\delta(H)$ there is $E^\delta(H)$ with $|E^\delta(H)| \leq \varepsilon \cdot |V^\delta(H)|$ then G is called* fixed scalable.

Theorem 3. *If the graph G is DHT then G is* fixed scalable.

Proof. Assume that $G' \subset G$ is such team of G where its order λ is the biggest one. Assume that $H \supset G$ such that $V(H) = V(G) \cup \{v\}$. Then a set of edges $E^\delta(H)$ has to satisfy for instance that $\forall w(w \in V(G') \leftrightarrow \{v, w\} \in E^\delta(H))$ to ensure that H is also DHT[7]. Therefore $|E^\delta(H)| = \lambda$. We can repeat this process for all $v \in V^\delta(H')$ where $H' \supset G$, H' is again DHT, and where $V(H') = V(G) \cup V^\delta(H')$ and $E(H') = E(G) \cup E^\delta(H')$ hold. Therefore for each $V^\delta(H')$ exists $E^\delta(H')$ such that $|E^\delta(H')| = \lambda \cdot |V^\delta(H')|$.   □

Table 1. Fixed scalability of various types of social knowledge distributions

Social knowledge distribution		Fixed scalable?
Centralized		No
Distributed	Acquaintance models	No[8]
	Teamwork-based technique	No
Hybrid	Distributed matchmaking	Yes
	Dynamic hierarchical teams	Yes

---

[6] The type T is for instance DHT, structure defined by distributed matchmaking, teamwork-based, etc.

[7] Note that to ensure fixed scalability as defined above there is not requirement on the final structure of edges. Any structure that satisfies DHT type of graph is sufficient.

[8] Note that end-agents are used in this case instead of middle-agents. Also note that if we ensure that each end-agent has a limited number of connections to other end-agents than these structures become fixed scalable.

Note that, for instance, the centralized architecture is obviously not fixed scalable since it cannot accommodate more than one middle-agent. Also, for instance, the teamwork-based technique [11] is not fixed scalable since the structure of middle-agents has to form a complete graph. Thus we present Table 1 of fixed scalability for various structures of social knowledge distribution.

2.5   Reconfiguration in DHT Architecture

In Fig. 1 we present the concept of primary and secondary communication channels. During normal operation of the DHT architecture all middle-agents use only primary communication channels. Secondary communication channels are used in the case in which at least one of the following occurs:

- primary communication channels failed to transmit messages; or
- a receiving middle-agent failed.

These failures can be detected by various failure detection mechanisms, e.g., heartbeat mechanism [1], meta-agent observation [17], etc.

The secondary communication channel does not mean 'second'; there can be more than one secondary communication channel per primary one. When a middle-agent is unable to use the primary communication channel then one of the secondary ones is used instead. The structure of interconnections of the primary communication channels is dynamically reshaped by this change. Nevertheless, it is beyond the scope of this paper to describe the details of this reshaping process.

The same process of dynamic reconfiguration is used when a communication channel fails to transmit a message. In this case also the sender middle-agent will use the secondary one. Note that the secondary communication channels replace only the primary ones that failed.

Another type of dynamic reconfiguration occurs when a new (or possibly cloned) middle-agent tries to register into the system or a previously failed middle-agent tries to reregister into the system.

3   Experiments with DHT Architecture

To test the robustness of the DHT architecture and to test various knowledge propagation methods in practical experiments, we created the test case setting as follows. There are twelve possible types of end-agents. An end-agent that is registered into the system has one or two from the six possible capabilities. An end-agent location is randomly[9] chosen, i.e., an end-agent registers with one of the local middle-agents (M-As). The DHT structure of middle-agents has been practically tested in the Chilled Water System based on the Reduced Scale Advanced Development (RSAD) model that is a reconfigurable fluid system test platform, i.e., a chilled water part of a shipboard automation for US-Navy vessels. Nevertheless, the following experimental results have been obtained on the same system where all M-As and end-agents run on

---

[9] A uniform distribution of probability is used whenever we use the term randomly chosen.

a single computer Pentium III/800Mhz as separate threads under Agent-OS ([14] and [21]). The test case consists of an initial phase and a test phase described as follows:

1. During the *initial phase* 20 randomly chosen end-agents are created and registered into the system.
2. The *test phase* consists of 1000 actions. Three types of actions can occur.
   a) *Create* a new end-agent. A new end-agent of a randomly chosen type is created and registered to one randomly chosen M-A.
   b) *Delete* one of the existing end-agents. One randomly chosen end-agent is unregistered from its local M-A and then the end-agent is deleted.
   c) *Search* for a capability. One randomly chosen end-agent sends a search request to its local M-A for a randomly chosen capability.

The distribution of probability to choose an action is as follows. The probability that the search action is chosen, denoted as P_S, is used as a *parameter* for each test case. The create and delete actions each has in every test case the same probability to be chosen, i.e., $(1-P_S)/2$.

3.1   Comparison by the Number of Messages

The purpose of this test case is to determine which knowledge propagation method is the best one to be used when considering the number of messages, i.e., which method

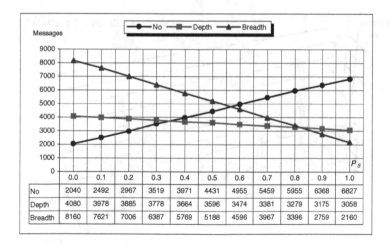

	0.0	0.1	0.2	0.3	0.4	0.5	0.6	0.7	0.8	0.9	1.0
No	2040	2492	2967	3519	3971	4431	4955	5459	5955	6368	6827
Depth	4080	3978	3885	3778	3664	3596	3474	3381	3279	3175	3058
Breadth	8160	7621	7006	6387	5769	5188	4596	3967	3396	2759	2160

Fig. 4. Test case of knowledge propagation methods for the number of messages. The X-axis represents the probability that the search action is chosen, denoted as P_S. The Y-axis represents the total number of messages in the test run, where only messages that are related to the registration, unregistration, and to the search process are considered. Each value of each graph is the average (arithmetic mean) of 50 measurements

needs fewer messages for a completion of the test case. The testing architecture consists of one global middle-agent (GM-A), i.e., a middle-agent in the top-most team, and five local middle-agents that have GM-A as their parent. The goal of these tests is not to test robustness since there is only one GM-A used, but to compare presented knowledge propagation methods.

From the measurements presented in Fig. 4 we can conclude that the no knowledge propagation method gives the best results in the case in which the probability that an agent uses the search action is less than 35%. The depth knowledge propagation method gives the best results in the case in which P_s is greater than 35% and less than 82% and the breadth knowledge propagation method gives the best results otherwise. These results have been proved also theoretically [20]. The depth knowledge propagation method is nearly independent of the search probability parameter since the average deviation is 276, whereas values measured for the other two methods have the average deviation greater than 1642.

3.2   Experiments with Robustness in DHT Architecture

To test the robustness of the DHT architecture in practical experiments, we created an experiment where the structure of middle-agents consists of three GM-As that form a team plus six M-As that are evenly distributed using their primary connections among the three GM-As. The test case should prove that the DHT architecture with teams that consist of N middle-agents (3 in this test case) is able to withstand at least $N - 1$ failures of the middle-agents

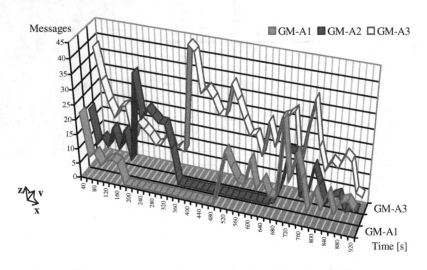

Fig. 5. Two failures of the global middle-agents in the DHT architecture with three members of the team. The architecture uses the depth knowledge propagation method. The graph depicts the communication frequency where the test run is split into time slots of 20 seconds (X-axis) with the number of messages in each time slot on the Z-axis connected by a line. The first graph on the Y-axis labeled GM-A1 is filtered in such a way that only outgoing messages from the first global middle-agent are considered, and so on

After 150 seconds the first GM-A simulates a failure and the system is not able to use it to propagate requests. The requests that are sent to this GM-A stay pending until the system discovers that it failed. The local M-As that are initially connected to the first GM-A dynamically switch to another GM-A, in this case the second one.

After 300 seconds from the beginning of the test case also the second GM-A simulates a failure. In this case also the local M-As that are initially connected to the first and to the second GM-A dynamically switch to the third GM-A and the system is still able to respond to the incoming requests.

After 450 seconds from the beginning of the test case the first GM-A is repaired, followed by the second GM-A 150 seconds later. The local M-As dynamically switch back to their preferred GM-As again.

4   Conclusion

We have proposed and implemented the DHT structure of middle-agents that can be used to increase the fault-tolerance of a multi-agent system. We have proved that the structure which consists of teams of size N is fault tolerant to failure of N-1 middle-agents or N-1 communication channels. Moreover, we have proved that the structure is maximally fault tolerant. We have proved that the DHT structure is fixed scalable, i.e., can be scaled-up at a fixed incremental cost. We defined several methods for social knowledge propagation, such as breadth, depth, and no knowledge propagation and corresponding search techniques.

We have experimentally tested proposed knowledge propagation methods in DHT structure to determine their advantages and disadvantages on a real multi-agent system. The experiments revealed that all proposed knowledge propagation methods can be efficiently used in presented testing environment based on the probability P_s that end-agents request the search action when measuring number of messages. We have experimentally tested robustness and reconfiguration of proposed architecture on a real multi-agent system with successful results. Despite the DHT structure has many advantages, it has also disadvantages. Namely, the development and debugging process is more complicated than previous designs. Also, since the social knowledge is distributed there are more possibilities for inconsistencies in social knowledge than, for example, in the centralized type of system.

References

1. Aguilera M. K., Chen W., and Toueg S.: Heartbeat: A Timeout-free Failure Detector for Quiescent Reliable Communication. In Proceedings of the 11th International Workshop on Distributed Algorithms, Springer-Verlag, Berlin (1997) 126-140
2. Byrne C. and Edwards P.: Refinement in Agent Groups. In G. Weiss, S. Sen, eds., Adaption and Learning in Multi-Agent Systems. Lecture Notes in Artificial Intelligence 1042, Springer-Verlag, Heidelberg (1996) 22-39
3. Chen L. and Avizienis A.: N-version Programming: A Fault-Tolerance Approach to Reliability of Software Operation. In Digest of Papers of the 8th Annual International Conference on Fault-Tolerant Computing, Toulouse, France (1978)

4. Decker, K., Sycara, K., Williamson, M.: Middle-Agents for the Internet. In Proceedings of the 15th IJCAI, Morgan Kaufmann, Nagoya, Japan (1997) 578-583
5. Diestel, R.: Graph Theory. Graduate Texts in Mathematics. Vol. 173, Springer-Verlag, New York (2000)
6. FIPA: The Foundation for Intelligent Physical Agents, http://www.fipa.org, Geneva, Switzerland (1997)
7. Gustafson, J.L.: Reevaluating Amdahl's Law. CACM, Vol. 31, No. 5 (1988) 532-533
8. JADE: Java Agent DEvelopment Framework, Telecom Italia Lab, Torino, Italy, http://sharon.cselt.it/projects/jade/.
9. Finin, T., McKay, D., Fritzson, R.: An Overview of KQML: A Knowledge Query and Manipulation Language, Technical Report, UMBC, Baltimore (1992)
10. Kraus S., Subrahmanian V.S., and Tas N.C.: Probabilistically Survivable MASs. In proceedings of IJCAI-03, Acapulco, Mexico (2003) 676-679
11. Kumar, S., Cohen, P.R.: Towards a Fault-Tolerant Multi-Agent System Architecture. In Proceedings of the 4th International Conference on Autonomous Agents, Barcelona, Spain (2000) 459-466
12. Luke, E.A.: Defining and Measuring Scalability. In Scalable Parallel Libraries Conference, Mississippi, USA (1994)
13. Mařík, V., Pěchouček, M., Štěpánková, O.: Social Knowledge in Multi-Agent Systems. In Multi-Agent Systems and Applications, LNAI 2086, Springer, Berlin (2001) 211-245
14. Maturana, F., Staron, R., Tichý, P., Šlechta, P.: Autonomous Agent Architecture for Industrial Distributed Control. 56th Meeting of the Society for Machinery Failure Prevention Technology, Sec. 1A, Virginia Beach (2002) 147-156
15. Naor, M., Nissim, K.: Certificate Revocation and Certificate Update. In Proceedings of the 7th USENIX Security Symposium, San Antonio, Texas, USA (1998) 217-228
16. Neuman, B.C.: Scale in Distributed Systems. In Readings in Distributed Computing Systems. IEEE Computer Society Press, Los Alamitos, CA (1994) 463-489
17. Pěchouček M., Macůrek F., Tichý P., Štěpánková O., and Mařík V.: Meta-agent: A Workflow Mediator in Multi-Agent Systems. In Watson, I., Gordon, J., McIntosh, A., eds. Intelligent Workflow and Process Management: The New Frontier for AI in Business IJCAI-99, Morgan Kaufmann Publishers, San Francisco (1999) 110-116
18. Pothipruk, P., Lalitrojwong, P.: An Ontology-based Multi-agent System for Matchmaking. ICITA 2002, section 201-2, Bathurst, Australia (2002)
19. van Steen, M., van der Zijden, S., Sips, H.J.: Software Engineering for Scalable Distributed Applications. The 22nd COMPSAC '98, IEEE Computer Society 0-8186-8585-9 (1998) 285-293.
20. Tichý, P.: Social Knowledge in Multi-agent Systems. Dissertation thesis, Czech Technical University, Prague, 2004.
21. Tichý, P., Šlechta, P., Maturana, F., and Balasubramanian, S.: Industrial MAS for Planning and Control. In (Mařík, V., Štěpánková, O., Krautwurmová, H., Luck, M., eds.) Proceedings of Multi-Agent Systems and Applications II: 9th ECCAI-ACAI/EASSS 2001, AEMAS 2001, HoloMAS 2001, LNAI 2322, Springer-Verlag, Berlin (2002) 280-295
22. Vadapalli, P., Srimani, P.K.: A New Family of Cayley Graph Interconnection Networks of Constant Degree Four. In IEEE Transactions on Parallel and Distributed Systems, Vol. 7, No. 1 (1996) 26-32

Symbolic Negotiation with Linear Logic

Peep Küngas[1] and Mihhail Matskin[2]

[1] Norwegian University of Science and Technology,
Department of Computer and Information Science,
Trondheim, Norway
peep@idi.ntnu.no
[2] Royal Institute of Technology,
Department of Microelectronics and Information Technology,
Kista, Sweden
misha@imit.kth.se

Abstract. Negotiation over resources and multi-agent planning are important issues in multi-agent systems research. Previously it has been demonstrated [18] how symbolic negotiation and distributed planning together could be formalised as distributed Linear Logic (LL) theorem proving. LL has been chosen mainly because of its expressive power for representation of resources and its computation-oriented nature. This paper extends the previous work by taking advantage of a richer fragment of LL and introducing two sorts of nondeterministic choices into negotiation. This allows agents to reason and negotiate under certain degree of uncertainty. Additionally, a way of granting unbounded access to resources during negotiation is considered. Finally we extend our framework with first-order LL for expressing more complex offers during negotiation.

1 Introduction

Although the idea of distributed theorem proving as a formalism for agent negotiation is not new, there are still many open issues which require special attention. In particular, not much is known about limits of logics when it comes to capturing encodings of certain offers and reasoning about specific dialogues. Another important issue is computation—in order to ensure finiteness and efficiency of negotiations we may have to develop a special technique for more efficient proof search. This paper contributes to both issues—we extend expressiveness of previous work based on linear logic [9] (LL) and introduce new LL inference figures, which allow us to simplify proof search in our fragment of LL.

It was argued in [18] that distributed LL theorem proving could be applied for symbolic agent negotiation. Also a formal mechanism for generating new offers was proposed there. The corresponding framework allows agents to negotiate over resources and to exploit capabilities of their partners. Since all participating agents have to achieve their personal goals, each agent has to make sure which resources could be given away and which capabilities could be accessed by other agents.

J. Dix and J. Leite (Eds.): CLIMA IV, LNAI 3259, pp. 71–88, 2004.

Agent reasoning in [18] is an interactive process involving Partial Deduction (PD) and LL theorem proving. PD is applied there as a method of deducing subproblems, which from negotiation point of view are interpreted as offers. However, it was assumed that all offers, that an agent distributes, are independent from each-other.

In this paper we augment the previous approach with a mechanism for producing multiple interdependent offers at once. This provides competing agents with some hints about other distributed offers and available resources. Although the LL fragment in [18] permits usage of nondeterministic offers, it was not described how these offers are generated. We cover this aspect in our paper.

While in [18] the propositional intuitionistic multiplicative additive fragment of LL was considered, here we take advantage of full intuitionistic LL. This allows us to describe unbounded access to certain resources. Additionally we take advantage of first-order intuitionistic LL as a negotiation language.

Although several articles discuss language and representation issues of symbolic negotiation, we are more concerned with the computational side of the negotiation process. This paper presents a formalism for generating new offers using PD during negotiation. We define PD steps as inference figures in LL. While using those inference figures instead of basic LL rules, we can achieve higher efficiency during proof search. These inference figures represent specialisation of LL to symbolic negotiation.

The paper is organised as follows. In Section 2 we present a general model of distributed problem solving and give an introduction to LL and PD. Additionally the LL formalisation to negotiation is given there. Section 3 describes a motivating example and illustrates how negotiation between agents works within our formalism. Section 4 presents new PD steps for agent negotiation. Section 5 reviews related work. The last section concludes the paper and discusses future work.

2 Formalisation of Negotiation

2.1 Agent Communication Architecture

In this paper we consider self-interested cooperative agents. This means that agents cooperate with each other as long as it does not prevent them to achieve their own goals.

We define offers as instances of the following structure:

$$(id_{req}, S, R, O),$$

where id_{req}, S, R and O denote respectively a message identifier, its sender, its receiver and an offer itself in a declarative language. The message identifier is needed to keep track of different negotiations. The sender and the receiver are identifiers of participating agents and the offer content is represented with a LL formula.

While naming message identifiers, we apply the following conventions:

- if agent $\mathcal{A}$ sends out an initial offer, then a is its message identifiers name
- if a represents an offer, then a' represents its counter-offer
- if an agent $\mathcal{A}$ sends out more than one offer, then their messages are indexed as $a_1, a_2, \ldots$

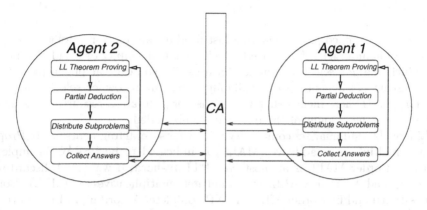

Fig. 1. General CPS model

Our general problem solving model is presented in Figure 1. In this model each agent initially tries to solve its problem alone. If the agent cannot find a solution then subproblems are generated. The subproblems are distributed among the partners and they are treated as offers to other agents. In other words, they present what an agent can provide and what it expects to get in return. If it should happen that an agent dies during symbolic negotiation, then possibly some negotiation steps should be cancelled or revised. CA in Figure 1 denotes to Communication Adapter, which translates offers from one agent such that a receiver could understand it. Formalisation of CA is given in Section 2.6.

2.2 Linear Logic

LL is a refinement of classical logic introduced by J.-Y. Girard to provide means for keeping track of "resources". In LL two copies of a propositional constant A are distinguished from a single copy of A. This does not apply in classical logic, since there the truth value of a fact does not depend on the number of copies of the fact. Indeed, LL is not about truth, it is about computation.

In the following we are considering intuitionistic fragment of LL (ILL) consisting of multiplicative conjunction ($\otimes$), additive disjunction ($\oplus$), additive conjunction (&), linear implication ($\multimap$) and "of course" operator (!). In terms of resource acquisition the logical expression $A \otimes B \vdash C \otimes D$ means that resources C and D are obtainable only if both A and B are obtainable. After the sequent has been applied, A and B are consumed and C and D are produced.

The expression $A \vdash B \oplus C$ in contrast means that, if we have resource A, we can obtain either B or C, but we do not know which one of those. The expression $A\&B \vdash C$ on the other hand means that while having resources A and B we can choose, which one of them to trade for C. Therefore it is said that $\oplus$ and $\&$ represent respectively *external* and *internal* choice. To increase the expressiveness of formulae, we use the following abbreviation $a^n = \underbrace{a \otimes \ldots \otimes a}_{n}$, for $n > 0$.

In order to illustrate the above-mentioned features we can consider the following LL sequent from [20]—$(D \otimes D \otimes D \otimes D \otimes D) \vdash (H \otimes C \otimes (O\&S) \otimes !F \otimes (P \oplus I))$, which encodes a fixed price menu in a fast-food restaurant: for 5 dollars (D) you can get an hamburger (H), a coke (C), either onion soup O or salad S depending, which one *you* select, all the french fries (F) you can eat plus a pie (P) or an ice cream (I) depending on availability (restaurant owner selects for you). The formula $!F$ here means that we can use or generate a resource F as much as we want—the amount of the resource is unbounded.

Lincoln [21] summarises complexity results for several fragments of LL. Propositional multiplicative additive (MALL) is indicated to be PSPACE-complete, whilst first-order MALL is at most NEXPTIME-hard. If we would discard additives $\oplus$ and $\&$ from MALL, we would get multiplicative LL (MLL). Both, propositional and first-order MLL, are NP-complete. According to Lincoln these complexity results do not change, if respective intuitionistic fragments of LL are considered. These results hint that for practical computations either MLL or propositional MALL (or their intuitionistic variants MILL and MAILL (IMALL), respectively) might be applied.

2.3   Agents in LL

An agent is presented with the following LL sequent:

$$\Gamma; S \vdash G,$$

where Γ is a set of extralogical LL axioms representing agent's capabilities, S is the initial state and G is the goal state of the agent. Both S and G are multiplicative conjunctions of literals. Every element of Γ has the form

$$\vdash I \multimap O,$$

where I and O are formulae in conjunctive normal form which are, respectively, consumed and generated when a particular capability is applied. It has to be mentioned that a capability can be applied only, if conjuncts in I form a subset of conjuncts in S. It should be also underlined that in order to achieve their goals, agents have to construct (and then execute) the following program/plan from the elements of Γ:

$$\vdash S \multimap G.$$

2.4   Partial Deduction and LL

Partial deduction (PD) (or partial evaluation of logic programs first introduced in [16]) is known as one optimisation technique in logic programming. Given a logic program, partial deduction derives a more specific program while preserving the meaning of the original program. Since the program is more specialised, it is usually more efficient than the original program, if executed. For instance, let A, B, C and D be propositional variables and $A \multimap B$, $B \multimap C$ and $C \multimap D$ computability statements in LL. Then possible partial deductions are $A \multimap C$, $B \multimap D$ and $A \multimap D$. It is easy to notice that the first corresponds to forward chaining (from initial states to goals), the second to backward chaining (from goals to initial states) and the third could be either forward or backward chaining.

Although the original motivation behind PD was to deduce specialised logic programs with respect to a given goal, our motivation for PD is a bit different. We are applying PD for determining subtasks, which cannot be performed by a single agent, but still are possibly closer to a solution than an initial task. This means that given a state S and a goal G of an agent we compute a new state S' and a new goal G'. This information is forwarded to another agent for further inference. From PD point of view this means that the program $\Gamma \vdash S' \multimap G'$ would be derived from $\Gamma \vdash S \multimap G$. Then the derived program is sent to other entities, who modify it further.

The main problem with PD in LL is that although new derived states and goals are sound with respect to an initial specification, they may not preserve completeness anymore. This is due to resource-consciousness of LL—if a wrong proof branch is followed, literals in the initial state may be consumed and thus further search becomes more limited. Therefore agents have to search, in the worst case, all possible PDs of an initial specification to preserve completeness of the distributed search mechanism. In [22] completeness and soundness issues of PD are considered for classical logic programs. Issues of completeness and soundness of PD in LL will be considered within another paper.

The following LL inference figures, $\mathcal{R}_b(L_i)$ and $\mathcal{R}_f(L_i)$, were defined in [18] for PD back- and forward chaining steps respectively:

$$\frac{S \vdash B \otimes C}{S \vdash A \otimes C} \; \mathcal{R}_b(L_i) \qquad \frac{A \otimes C \vdash G}{B \otimes C \vdash G} \; \mathcal{R}_f(L_i)$$

L_i in the inference figures is a labelling of a particular LL axiom representing an agent's capability (computability clause in PD) in the form $\vdash B \multimap_{L_i} A$. $\mathcal{R}_f(L_i)$ and $\mathcal{R}_b(L_i)$ apply clause L_i to move the initial state towards the goal state or the other way around. A, B and C are formulae in ILL.

In $\mathcal{R}_b(L_i)$ inference figure formulae $A \otimes C$ and $B \otimes C$ denote respectively goals G and G'. The inference figure encodes that, if there is an extralogical axiom $\vdash B \multimap A$, then we can change goal $A \otimes C$ to $B \otimes C$. Analogously, in the inference figure $\mathcal{R}_f(L_i)$ formulae $B \otimes C$ and $A \otimes C$ denote states S and S' respectively. The inference figure encodes that, if there is an extralogical axiom $\vdash B \multimap A$, then we can change initial state $B \otimes C$ to $A \otimes C$.

Although the defined PD steps consider only application of agent capabilities, they can be used for modelling resource exchange as well. We model exchange of resources with execution of capabilities, which generate those resources.

In addition to $\mathcal{R}_b(L_i)$ and $\mathcal{R}_f(L_i)$ we define other PD steps for constructing nondeterministic offers, to handle first-order representation and nondeterminism arising from usage of unbounded resources. Finally we introduce macros for more efficient PD.

2.5   Encoding Offers in LL

Harland and Winikoff [11] presented the first ideas about applying LL theorem proving for agent negotiation. The main advantages of LL over classical logic are its resource-consciousness and existence of two kinds of nondeterminism. Both internal and external nondeterminism in negotiation rules can be represented. In the case of internal nondeterminism a choice is made by resource provider, whereas in the case of external nondeterminism a choice is made by resource consumer. For instance, formula $Dollar^5 \multimap Beer \oplus Soda$ (at the offer receiver side) means that an agent can provide either some $Beer$ or $Soda$ in return for 5 dollars, but the choice is made by the provider agent. The consumer agent has to be ready to obtain either a beer or a soda. The formula $Dollar \multimap Tobacco \& Lighter$ (again at the offer receiver side) in contrary means that the consumer may select which resource, either $Tobacco$ or $Lighter$, s/he gets for a $Dollar$.

In the context of negotiation, operators $\&$ and $\oplus$ have symmetrical meanings—what is $A \oplus B$ for one agent, is $A \& B$ to its partner. This means that if one agent gives an opportunity to another agent to choose between A and B, then the former agent has to be ready to provide both choices, A and B. When initial resources owned by agents and expected negotiation results have been specified, LL theorem proving is used for determining the negotiation process.

In [18] the ideas of Harland and Winikoff were augmented by allowing trading also services (agent capabilities). This is a step further toward the world where agents not only exchange resources, but also work for other agents in order to achieve their own goals. We write $A \vdash B \multimap C$ to indicate that an agent can trade resource A for a service $B \multimap C$. $B \multimap C$ denotes to a service, which consumes B and generates C.

There is another kind of nondeterministic construction in LL, namely the ! operator. Since $!A$ means that an agent can generate as many copies of A as required, the number of literals A is unbounded and represents additional kind of nondeterminism. From negotiation point of view, $!A$ represents unbounded access to resource A.

2.6   Communication Adapter

In [24] bridge rules are used for translating formulae from one logic to another, when agents exchange offers. We adopt this idea of Communication Adapter (CA) for two reasons. First, it would allow us to encapsulate agents' internal states and, second, while offers are delivered by one agent to another, viewpoint to the offer is changing and internal and external choices are inversed. By viewpoint we mean an agent's role, which can be either receiver or sender of an offer. Additionally, we could consider CA as a component in a distributed problem solving system, where agent communication protocols are implemented and target agents are determined, if an agent proposes an offer.

The *CA* rule is described as follows. As long as formulae on the left and the right hand side of sequents consist of only $\otimes$ and $\multimap$ operators, the left and the right hand sides of sequents are inversed. However, if formulae contain disjunctions, their types have to be inversed as well. This has to be done because there are 2 disjunctions in LL—one with internal and another with external choice. Since internal and external choices are context-dependent, they have to be inversed, when changing viewpoints. For instance, sequent $A \otimes (A \multimap B) \vdash C \oplus D$ is translated to $C \& D \vdash A \otimes (A \multimap B)$ by the *CA* rule:

$$\frac{\underset{j}{\&} B_j \vdash \underset{i}{\bigoplus} A_i}{\underset{i}{\&} A_i \vdash \underset{j}{\bigoplus} B_j} \; CA$$

Although reversion of offers is not needed for PD itself, it is essential when an agent checks whether the offer matches its own initial state and goal. For instance, if agent's initial state and goal are described with sequent $X \vdash Y$, then the agent would definitely accept offer $X \vdash Y$, since the latter satisfies completely agent's requirements. However, the offer is sent by another agent in form $Y \vdash X$. Therefore it has to be reversed when it arrives to its target.

In the *CA* rule A and B consist of multiplicative conjunctions and linear implications. We allow $\&$ only in the left hand side and $\oplus$ only in the right hand side of a sequent. Due to LL rules $R\&$ and $L\oplus$ the following conversions are allowed:

$$D \vdash \underset{j}{\&} D_j \implies \bigcup_j (D \vdash D_j),$$

$$\underset{j}{\bigoplus} D_j \vdash D \implies \bigcup_j (D_j \vdash D).$$

Therefore we do not lose in expressive power of LL, when limiting the syntax of offers in that way. Although this bridge rule is intended for agents reasoning in LL only, additional bridge rules may be constructed for communication with other non-LL agents.

3   A Motivating Example

To illustrate the symbolic negotiation process with our formalism, we consider the following example. Let us have 3 agents representing a musician $\mathcal{M}$, a writer $\mathcal{W}$ and an artist $\mathcal{A}$. They all have personal goals they would like to achieve. We would like to emphasise that this example is supposed to demonstrate syntactical and computational aspects only and no pragmatic issues are considered here. We have considered more practical examples in the field of automated Web service synthesis [25]. The examples involve more extralogical axioms and longer proofs. They are, however, not so sophisticated from formal point of view.

The musician would like to go out with her husband and therefore needs 2 concert tickets. Unfortunately the concert, she is interested in, has been sold out and therefore the only way to acquire the tickets is to ask them from other agents. In return she can grant a certain book and unlimited access to digital version of her albums. Thus

$$G_{\mathcal{M}} = \{ Ticket^2 \},$$

$$S_{\mathcal{M}} = \{ !MP3 \otimes Book \}$$

and

$$\Gamma_{\mathcal{M}} = \emptyset.$$

The artist has promised to perform at a conference and thus needs 2 hours of background music and an MP3 player. Since the performance takes place at the same time as the concert he can give away the concert ticket. Formally,

$$G_{\mathcal{A}} = \{ Perf \},$$

$$S_{\mathcal{A}} = \{ Ticket \}$$

and

$$\Gamma_{\mathcal{A}} = \{ \vdash MP3^2 \otimes MP3Player \multimap Perf \}.$$

The writer wants to relax and this can be achieved by reading a book and listening to music. He has both—a CD player and an MP3 player. Additionally he can write CDs from MP3 files. He also has a ticket to the same concert with the artist. However, he prefers staying at home this time. Thus formally this is described as follows:

$$G_{\mathcal{W}} = \{ Relaxed \},$$

$$S_{\mathcal{W}} = \{ Ticket \otimes CDPlayer \otimes MP3Player \},$$

$$\Gamma_{\mathcal{W}} = \begin{array}{l} \vdash (CD \otimes CDPlayer) \oplus (MP3 \otimes MP3Player) \multimap Music, \\ \vdash Music \otimes Book \multimap Relaxed, \\ \vdash MP3 \multimap CD. \end{array}$$

Our representation language so far differs from [18] by additional usage of $\oplus$ and !. While ! allows representing unbounded usage or access to a resource, $\oplus$ represents nondeterministic choice, which will be discussed below in more details.

Let us describe now the symbolic negotiation process between these 3 agents. The negotiation is initiated by agents $\mathcal{M}$ and $\mathcal{W}$. Agent $\mathcal{M}$ is unsure whether anyone has two tickets left to the concert. Therefore she decides to propose 2 separate offers instead of a single one and delivers them to $\mathcal{A}$ and $\mathcal{W}$:

$$(m_1, \mathcal{M}, \mathcal{A}, !MP3 \oplus Book \vdash Ticket)$$

and

$$(m_2, \mathcal{M}, \mathcal{W}, !MP3 \& Book \vdash Ticket).$$

The first offer means that $\mathcal{M}$ gives $\mathcal{A}$ an opportunity to choose between $!MP3$ and $Book$. The proposal to $\mathcal{W}$, however, means that $\mathcal{W}$ could get either $!MP3$ or $Book$, but the choice is made by $\mathcal{M}$. This is intuitive since $\mathcal{M}$ has no idea whether $\mathcal{A}$ would choose either $!MP3$ or $Book$.

The proposals describe internal and external choices in LL and are represented with operators $\&$ and $\oplus$ respectively. While $\oplus$ from the sender's point of view gives choice to the receiver, $\&$ is the opposite—the sender makes the decision of which resource to deliver. It should be mentioned that messages, when received by agents, are translated using the CA rule.

Agent $\mathcal{W}$ sends out the following offer:

$$(w_1, \mathcal{W}, \mathcal{A}, MP3Player \vdash MP3 \otimes Book)$$

which means that he can trade an MP3 player and a book for 1 hour of MP3 music. The offer was achieved in the following way:

$$
\cfrac{
\cfrac{
\cfrac{
\cfrac{
\cfrac{Ticket \otimes MP3Player \vdash MP3 \otimes Book \qquad CDPlayer \vdash CDPlayer}{Ticket \otimes CDPlayer \otimes MP3Player \vdash MP3 \otimes CDPlayer \otimes Book} \; Id}{Ticket \otimes CDPlayer \otimes MP3Player \vdash CD \otimes CDPlayer \otimes Book} \; L\otimes, R\otimes}{Ticket \otimes CDPlayer \otimes MP3Player \vdash Music \otimes Book} \; \mathcal{R}_b(burnCD)}{Ticket \otimes CDPlayer \otimes MP3Player \vdash Relaxed} \; \mathcal{R}_b(playCD)}{} \; \mathcal{R}_b(relax)
$$

It has to be mentioned, that the agent omitted literal $Ticket$ from its offer since a particular PD strategy determined that only a part of the resulting state could be made public through an offer. Although the strategy may slow down the negotiation process, it allows agents to hide partially their internal states and optimise resource usage according to certain policies.

The following responses are received:

$$(m_1', \mathcal{A}, \mathcal{M}, Ticket \vdash !MP3)$$

and

$$(w_1', \mathcal{A}, \mathcal{W}, MP3 \vdash MP3Player).$$

Based on the message from $\mathcal{A}$ to $\mathcal{W}$, the latter generates a new offer:

$$(m_2', \mathcal{W}, \mathcal{M}, Ticket \vdash Book).$$

The message from $\mathcal{W}$ to $\mathcal{M}$ means that $\mathcal{W}$ is not satisfied with the proposal and wants to be more precise. Namely, he is ready to trade his ticket for the book. Fortunately, $\mathcal{A}$ has chosen $!MP3$ and the proposal from $\mathcal{W}$ to $\mathcal{M}$ can be satisfied now. Additionally $\mathcal{W}$ accepts the proposal from $\mathcal{A}$ and everybody is now satisfied.

The result of symbolic negotiation is depicted in Figure 2. Circles denote there resource exchange events between agents, while rounded rectangles represent execution of agents' capabilities. The vertical arrows between circles and

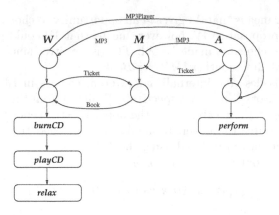

Fig. 2. The result of symbolic negotiation

rectangles represent ordering of activities, which was achieved through symbolic negotiation. The horizontal arrows represent which resources are exchanged at particular time points.

The scenario presented in this section describes only which proposals were exchanged. The methodology for constructing these offers deserves special attention and is clarified in the following sections. However, we only define new PD steps. Which steps and in which order are chosen during PD, depends on a particular PD strategy and is not covered here. This would be covered in another paper together with other formal results.

4   Additional PD Steps for Agent Negotiation

In this section we describe additional PD steps, which are needed for generating offers in ILL. These PD steps allow construction of nondeterministic offers and to handle unbounded access to resources. Additionally special PD steps for first-order ILL are introduced.

4.1   Generating Nondeterministic Offers

Nondeterministic offers can be generated basically in two ways. First, there may exist a particular capability having nondeterministic effects. Second, an agent uses some internal mechanism for composing such offers from scratch. Since in the first case nondeterministic offers are achieved via basic PD forward and backward steps, we consider here only the second case.

In order to describe how offers $!MP3 \oplus Book \vdash Ticket$ and $!MP3 \& Book \vdash Ticket$ were achieved from $!MP3 \otimes Book \vdash Ticket$[2] in Section 3 we present the following LL proof (M, T and B stand for $MP3$, $Ticket$ and $Book$, respectively):

$$\cfrac{\cfrac{\cfrac{\overline{B \vdash B}^{\,Id}}{\cfrac{\overline{!M \vdash !M}^{\,Id} \quad \cfrac{\overline{B \vdash B}^{\,Id}}{B \vdash !M \oplus B}^{R \oplus (b)}}{!M, B \vdash !M \otimes (!M \oplus B)}^{R \otimes}}{!M \otimes B \vdash !M \otimes (!M \oplus B)}^{L \otimes} \quad \cfrac{\cfrac{\overline{B \vdash B}^{\,Id} \quad \cfrac{\overline{!M \vdash !M}^{\,Id}}{!M \vdash !M \oplus B}^{R \oplus (a)}}{!M, B \vdash B \otimes (!M \oplus B)}^{R \otimes}}{!M \otimes B \vdash B \otimes (!M \oplus B)}^{L \otimes}}{\cfrac{!M \otimes B \vdash (!M \otimes (!M \oplus B)) \& (B \otimes (!M \oplus B))}{!M \otimes B \vdash (!M \& B) \otimes (!M \oplus B)}^{Rewrite}}^{R \&} \quad \cfrac{\cfrac{!M \& B \vdash T \quad !M \oplus B \vdash T}{(!M \& B), (!M \oplus B) \vdash T \otimes T}^{R \otimes}}{(!M \& B) \otimes (!M \oplus B) \vdash T \otimes T}^{L \otimes}}{!M \otimes B \vdash T \otimes T}^{Cut}$$

The proof can be generalised to a Partial Deduction (PD) step. This step generates multiple nondeterministic offers at once. This forward chaining PD step, called *Branch* in other sections of the paper, is defined as follows:

$$\cfrac{\cfrac{\vdots}{\overset{n}{\underset{i=1}{\otimes}} A_i \vdash (\overset{k}{\underset{i=1}{\&}} A_i) \otimes \cdots \otimes (\overset{n}{\underset{i=l}{\oplus}} A_i)}^{Rewrite} \quad \cfrac{\cfrac{\overset{n}{\underset{i=l}{\oplus}} A_i \vdash B_m}{\vdots} \quad \cfrac{\overset{k}{\underset{i=1}{\&}} A_i \vdash B_1 \quad \cdots \otimes (\overset{n}{\underset{i=l}{\oplus}} A_i) \vdash \overset{m}{\underset{i=2}{\otimes}} B_i}{\cfrac{(\overset{k}{\underset{i=1}{\&}} A_i), \dots \otimes (\overset{n}{\underset{i=l}{\oplus}} A_i) \vdash \overset{m}{\underset{i=1}{\otimes}} B_i}{(\overset{k}{\underset{i=1}{\&}} A_i) \otimes \cdots \otimes (\overset{n}{\underset{i=l}{\oplus}} A_i) \vdash \overset{m}{\underset{i=1}{\otimes}} B_i}^{L \otimes}}^{R \otimes}}{\overset{n}{\underset{i=1}{\otimes}} A_i \vdash \overset{m}{\underset{i=1}{\otimes}} B_i}^{Cut}$$

where $1 \leq l, k \leq n, n > 1$. While the right branch of that inference figure generates multiple nondeterministic offers at once, the left branch ensures consistency of the offers. *Rewrite* indicates that the right hand side of a sequent is transformed to disjunctive normal form with respect to the & operator. From a negotiation point of view this represents a higher priority of offers, which include &, at the offer receiver side.

The number of nondeterministic branches cannot be larger than n, since we have only n resources. Additionally, the number of $\oplus$-offers (at sender side) is not greater than $n/2$. The latter derives from 2 assumptions: (1) for a choice at least 2 literals are needed and (2) $\oplus$-offers (from proposer point of view) must not overlap (otherwise it may happen that 2 agents choose the same resource and conflicts may occur). Generally, we assume that we can insert as many constants 1 as needed to enlarge m, since m has to be greater than or equal to the number of branches, which is limited by n.

Therefore, offers $!MP3 \oplus Book \vdash Ticket$ and $!MP3 \& Book \vdash Ticket$ were achieved from $!MP3 \otimes Book \vdash Ticket^2$ by applying inference figure *Branch* in the following manner:

$$\cfrac{!MP3 \oplus Book \vdash Ticket \quad !MP3 \& Book \vdash Ticket}{!MP3 \otimes Book \vdash Ticket^2}\ Branch$$

4.2   First-Order Offers

So far we have employed only the propositional part of ILL. Let us consider now the same example from Section 3 but we modify it by replacing $G_\mathcal{M}$, $\Gamma_\mathcal{M}$, $S_\mathcal{W}$ and $S_\mathcal{A}$ with the following formulae:

$$G_{\mathcal{M}} = \{\,Concert(c)\}$$

$$\Gamma_{\mathcal{M}} = \{\vdash \forall x \forall y.(\,Ticket(x,y) \otimes Ticket(x,y+1) \multimap Concert(x))\}$$

$$S_{\mathcal{A}} = \{\,Ticket(c,4)\}$$

$$S_{\mathcal{W}} = \{\,Ticket(c,5) \otimes CDPlayer \otimes MP3Player\}$$

Here $Ticket(x,y)$ denotes a ticket to concert x and seat y (for simplicity we assume that all places have unique sequential number—this can be easily modified to a row and places system). It means that the musician goes to a concert only, if she has 2 tickets to the concert c and, moreover, only tickets for seats next to each-other are accepted.

In our formulae we allow only usage of the universal quantifier $\forall$. Its intended meaning is rather *for any* than *for every*. Although agents may send out first order offers, which have not been instantiated yet, their current state must be ground. To illustrate the construction of first-order offers, let us consider how agent $\mathcal{M}$ should proceed (again we indicate predefined literal symbols with their first letters):

$$
\cfrac{
\cfrac{
\cfrac{
\cfrac{\forall y.(T(c,y) \otimes T(c,y+1)) \vdash \forall y.(T(c,y) \otimes T(c,y+1)) \quad \overline{C(c) \vdash C(c)}^{\;Id}}{\forall y.(T(c,y) \otimes T(c,y+1) \otimes (T(c,y) \otimes T(c,y+1) \multimap C(c))) \vdash C(c)}^{\;Id}
}{\forall x \forall y.(T(c,y) \otimes T(c,y+1) \otimes (T(x,y) \otimes T(x,y+1) \multimap C(x))) \vdash C(c)}^{\;L\multimap}
}{\vdots}^{\;L\forall}
}{ }
$$

$$
\cfrac{!M \otimes B \vdash \forall y.(T(c,y) \otimes T(c,y+1)) \qquad \cfrac{\vdash \forall x \forall y.(T(x,y) \otimes T(x,y+1) \multimap C(x))}{\begin{array}{c}\vdots \\ {}\end{array}}^{\;Axiom}_{\;R\otimes} \quad \begin{array}{c}\vdots \\ {}\end{array}^{\;L\forall}}{\cfrac{!M \otimes B \vdash \forall x \forall y.(T(c,y) \otimes T(c,y+1) \otimes (T(x,y) \otimes T(x,y+1) \multimap C(x)))}{!M \otimes B \vdash C(c)}}^{\;Cut}
$$

Thus a new offer was generated:

$$!M \otimes B \vdash \forall y.(T(c,y) \otimes T(c,y+1)).$$

However, if the current state/goal pair of agent $\mathcal{M}$ is described with

$$Ticket(c,4) \otimes Ticket(c,5) \vdash A,$$

where A is an arbitrary goal, then the following inference could be applied and a new offer $C(c) \vdash A$ is generated:

$$
\cfrac{
\cfrac{
\cfrac{\overline{T(c,4) \otimes T(c,5) \vdash T(c,4) \otimes T(c,5)}^{\;Id} \quad \overline{C(c) \vdash A}}{T(c,4) \otimes T(c,5) \otimes (T(c,4) \otimes T(c,5) \multimap C(c)) \vdash A}^{\;L\multimap}
}{T(c,4) \otimes T(c,5) \otimes (\forall x \forall y.(T(x,y) \otimes T(x,y+1) \multimap C(x))) \vdash A}^{\;L\forall}
}{\vdots}
$$

$$
\cfrac{\cfrac{\overline{T(c,4) \otimes T(c,5) \vdash T(c,4) \otimes T(c,5)}^{\;Id} \quad \cfrac{\vdash \forall x \forall y.(T(x,y) \otimes T(x,y+1) \multimap C(x))}{}^{\;Axiom}\; \begin{array}{c}\vdots\end{array}^{\;L\forall}}{T(c,4) \otimes T(c,5) \vdash T(c,4) \otimes T(c,5) \otimes (\forall x \forall y.(T(x,y) \otimes T(x,y+1) \multimap C(x)))}^{\;R\otimes}}{T(c,4) \otimes T(c,5) \vdash A}^{\;Cut}
$$

We can generalise these inferences to PD steps:

$$\cfrac{S \vdash A \otimes C}{S \vdash B \otimes C}\;\mathcal{R}_b(L_i(\underline{x})) \qquad \cfrac{A \otimes C \vdash G}{B \otimes C \vdash G}\;\mathcal{R}_f(L_i(\underline{x}))$$

where $L_i(\underline{x})$ is defined as $\vdash \forall \underline{x}.(A' \multimap_{L_i(\underline{x})} B')$ for $\mathcal{R}_b(L_i(\underline{x}))$ and as $\vdash \forall \underline{x}.(B' \multimap_{L_i(\underline{x})} A')$ for $\mathcal{R}_f(L_i(\underline{x}))$. A, B, C are LL formulae. Additionally we assume that $\underline{a} \stackrel{def}{=} a_1, a_2, \ldots$ is an ordered set of constants, $\underline{x} \stackrel{def}{=} x_1, x_2, \ldots$ is an ordered set of variables, $[\underline{a}/\underline{x}]$ denotes substitution, and $X = X'[\underline{a}/\underline{x}]$. When substitution is applied, elements in $\underline{a}$ and $\underline{x}$ are mapped to each other in the order they appear in the ordered sets. These sets must have the same number of elements.

LL inference figures for $\mathcal{R}_b(L_i(\underline{x}))$ and $\mathcal{R}_f(L_i(\underline{x}))$ look as follows. Backward chaining step $\mathcal{R}_b(L_i(\underline{x}))$:

$$
\cfrac{
\cfrac{S \vdash A \otimes C \qquad \cfrac{}{\vdash \forall \underline{x}.(A' \multimap_{L_i(\underline{x})} B')} \; Axiom}{S \vdash A \otimes C \otimes (\forall \underline{x}.(A' \multimap_{L_i(\underline{x})} B'))} \; R\otimes
\qquad
\cfrac{
\cfrac{
\cfrac{
C \vdash C \quad
\cfrac{
\cfrac{
\cfrac{A \vdash A \;\; Id \quad B \vdash B \;\; Id}{A, (A \multimap_{L_i(\underline{a})} B) \vdash B} \; L\multimap
}{A \otimes (A \multimap_{L_i(\underline{a})} B) \vdash B} \; L\otimes
}{C, A \otimes (A \multimap_{L_i(\underline{a})} B) \vdash B \otimes C} \; R\otimes
}{A \otimes C \otimes (A \multimap_{L_i(\underline{a})} B) \vdash B \otimes C} \; L\otimes
}{A \otimes C \otimes (\forall \underline{x}.(A' \multimap_{L_i(\underline{x})} B')) \vdash B \otimes C} \; L\forall
}{S \vdash B \otimes C} \; Cut
$$

Forward chaining step $\mathcal{R}_f(L_i(\underline{x}))$:

$$
\cfrac{
\cfrac{B \otimes C \vdash B \otimes C \;\; Id \qquad \cfrac{}{\vdash \forall \underline{x}.(B' \multimap_{L_i(\underline{x})} A')} \; Axiom}{B \otimes C \vdash B \otimes C \otimes (\forall \underline{x}.(B' \multimap_{L_i(\underline{x})} A'))} \; R\otimes
\qquad
\cfrac{
\cfrac{
\cfrac{
C \vdash C \quad
\cfrac{
\cfrac{
\cfrac{B \vdash B \;\; Id \quad A \vdash A \;\; Id}{B, (B \multimap_{L_i(\underline{a})} A) \vdash A} \; L\multimap
}{B \otimes (B \multimap_{L_i(\underline{a})} A) \vdash A} \; L\otimes
}{C, B \otimes (B \multimap_{L_i(\underline{a})} A) \vdash A \otimes C} \; R\otimes
}{B \otimes C \otimes (B \multimap_{L_i(\underline{a})} A) \vdash A \otimes C} \; L\otimes
}{B \otimes C \otimes (\forall \underline{x}.(B' \multimap_{L_i(\underline{x})} A')) \vdash A \otimes C} \; L\forall
\qquad A \otimes C \vdash G
}{B \otimes C \otimes (\forall \underline{x}.(B' \multimap_{L_i(\underline{x})} A')) \vdash G} \; Cut
}{B \otimes C \vdash G} \; Cut
$$

4.3   Unbounded Access to Resources

In order to manage access to unbounded resources, we need PD steps $\mathcal{R}_{C_l}$, $\mathcal{R}_{L_l}$, $\mathcal{R}_{W_l}$. They are formalised as the following LL inference figures:

$$
\cfrac{!A \otimes !A \otimes B \vdash C}{!A \otimes B \vdash C} \; \mathcal{R}_{C_l}
\qquad
\cfrac{A \otimes B \vdash C}{!A \otimes B \vdash C} \; \mathcal{R}_{L_l}
\qquad
\cfrac{B \vdash C}{!A \otimes B \vdash C} \; \mathcal{R}_{W_l}
$$

The inference figures reflect directly LL rules $!C$, $!L$ and $!W$.
PD step $\mathcal{R}_{C_l}$:

$$
\cfrac{
\cfrac{
\cfrac{
\cfrac{
\cfrac{!A \vdash !A \;\; Id \quad !A \vdash !A \;\; Id}{!A, !A \vdash !A \otimes !A} \; R\otimes
}{!A \vdash !A \otimes !A} \; C!
\qquad B \vdash B \;\; Id
}{!A, B \vdash !A \otimes !A \otimes B} \; R\otimes
}{!A \otimes B \vdash !A \otimes !A \otimes B} \; L\otimes
\qquad !A \otimes !A \otimes B \vdash C
}{!A \otimes B \vdash C} \; Cut
$$

PD step $\mathcal{R}_{L_l}$:

$$\cfrac{\cfrac{\cfrac{\overline{A \vdash A}\ Id}{!A \vdash A}\ L!\quad \overline{B \vdash B}\ Id}{\cfrac{!A, B \vdash A \otimes B}{!A \otimes B \vdash A \otimes B}\ L\otimes}\ R\otimes \quad \overline{A \otimes B \vdash C}}{!A \otimes B \vdash C}\ Cut$$

PD step $\mathcal{R}_{W_l}$:

$$\cfrac{\cfrac{\cfrac{\overline{B \vdash B}\ Id}{!A, B \vdash B}\ W!}{!A \otimes B \vdash B}\ L\otimes \quad \overline{B \vdash C}}{!A \otimes B \vdash C}\ Cut$$

Additionally we define a macro, $\mathcal{R}_{!_l}(n)$ using the previously specified inference figures:

$$\cfrac{\cfrac{\cfrac{\begin{array}{c}!A \otimes A^n \otimes B \vdash C\\ \vdots\\ !A \otimes A \otimes B \vdash C\end{array}}{!A \otimes !A \otimes B \vdash C}\ \mathcal{R}_{L_l}}{!A \otimes B \vdash C}\ \mathcal{R}_{C_l}}{}$$

5   Related Work

As it has been indicated in [14] negotiation is the most fundamental and powerful mechanism for managing inter-agent dependencies at run-time. Negotiation may be required both for self-interested and cooperative agents. It allows to reach a mutually acceptable agreement on some matter by a group of agents.

Kraus et al [17] give a logical description for negotiation via argumentation for BDI agents. They classify arguments as threats and promises, which are identified as most common arguments in human negotiations. In our case only promises are considered, since in order to figure out possible threats to goals of particular agents, agents' beliefs, goals and capabilities should be known in advance to the persuader. We assume, that our agents do not explicitly communicate about their internal state. Thus, our agents can provide higher degree of privacy in agent applications compared to particular BDI agents.

Fisher [6] introduced the idea of distributed theorem proving in classical logic as agent negotiation. In his approach all agents share the common view to the world and if a new clause is inferred, all agents would sense it. Inferred clauses are distributed among agents via broadcasting. Then, considering the received information, agents infer new clauses and broadcast them further again. Although agents have a common knowledge about inferred clauses, they may hold different sets of inference rules. Distribution of a collection of rules between agents means that different agents may have different capabilities and make different inferences. The latter implies that different agents contribute to different phases of proof search. Our approach differs from that work mainly in 2 aspects (in addition to usage of another logic): (1) our agents do not share a common view of a world and (2) inference results are not broadcasted.

Parsons et al [24] defined negotiation as interleaved formal reasoning and arguing in classical logic. Arguments and contra arguments are derived using theorem proving whilst taking into consideration agents' own goals. Sadri et al [26] propose an abductive logic programming approach to automated negotiation, which is built on Amgoud et al [1] work on argumentation. The work of Sadri et al is more specialised and detailed than the work by Amgoud et al. That allows deeper analysis of the reasoning mechanism and the knowledge required to build negotiation dialogues.

There are some similarities between abduction and PD. However, while abduction is about finding a hypothesis to explain given results, then PD achieves the hypothesis as a side-effect. The latter could be explained by stating that in our case the given results are a part of a program and PD is about program transformation, not about finding an hypothesis. By taking into account the preceding, abduction could be implemented through PD.

Our approach could be viewed as distributed planning similarly to the work in [5]. Case-based planning has been used for coordinating agent teams in [8]. The planner generates a so called shared mental model of the team plan. Then all agents adapt their plans to the team plan. This work is influenced by the joint intentions [19, 4] and shared plans [10] theory.

In [3] LL has been used for prototyping multi-agent systems at conceptual level. Because of the fixed semantics of LL, it is possible to verify whether a system functions as intended at conceptual level. Although the prototype LL program is executable, it is still too high level to produce a final agent-based software. Thus another logic programming language is embedded to compose the final software.

Harland and Winikoff [12] address the question of how to integrate both proactive and reactive properties of agents into LL programming framework. They use forward chaining to model the reactive behaviour of an agent and backward chaining to model the proactive behaviour. This type of computation is called as mixed mode computation, since both forward and backward chaining are allowed.

According to [2] our theorem proving methodology is characterised with *parallelism at the search level*. The approach relates by theorem proving methodology mostly to the successors of Team-Work [7]. Fuchs [7] describes an approach, where distribution of facts and sub-problems is organised on request—that is the basic mechanism behind our methodology as well. However, Fuchs considers first-order logic with equality, which is somehow different from LL.

6   Conclusions and Future Work

In this paper we augmented a symbolic negotiation framework, which was initially introduced in [18]. More specifically, we introduced PD steps for generating nondeterministic offers and handling unbounded access to resources. We also extended the framework with first-order PD steps and thus increased expressiveness of offers. We defined PD steps as special LL inference figures. While applying these inference figures during proof search instead of basic LL rules we can gain higher efficiency.

We have implemented a planner on top of a first-order MILL theorem prover. Instead of applying individual LL inference rules, the theorem prover behind the planner applies the inference figures presented in [18]. Although that approach makes the prover application specific, it allows higher computational efficiency. In future we would like to extend the prover to cover ILL as well. The planner is available at `http://www.idi.ntnu.no/~peep/RAPS`. Additionally we have implemented an agent system, where the planner is applied during symbolic negotiation for constructing new offers. The agent system is based on JADE and can be download from `http://www.idi.ntnu.no/~peep/symbolic`. Although in the current version of the agent software the derived offers are broadcasted, we are working on a P2P implementation of the symbolic negotiation system. The P2P implementation would release agents/mediators in the system from the burden of keeping track of all participating agents in the system. Relevant agents are discovered dynamically during problem solving.

One significant disadvantage of symbolic negotiation is that agents lack an opportunity to negotiate over the amount of information (in terms of the number of literals) which should be exchanged. Anyway, by applying PD, certain PD strategies could be developed for optimal resource usage according to different criteria. Then the strategy would guide agents to achieve their goals by providing the least amount of information/resources.

There are many open issues related to agent systems, negotiation and LL. Since LL has been extended with temporal properties [13, 15], we would like to introduce the notion of time to our framework as well. Additionally it has been indicated in [23] that modal logic S4 has a direct translation to LL. This result is motivating for considering whether current BDI-theories could be embedded into our framework. We also have plans to apply our approach to some more practical cases of negotiation, in particular, to distributed Web service composition.

Acknowledgements

This work is partially supported by the Norwegian Research Foundation in the framework of the Information and Communication Technology (IKT-2010) program—the ADIS project. We would like to thank the anonymous referees for their comments.

References

1. L. Amgoud, S. Parsons, N. Maudet. Arguments, Dialogue and Negotiation. In Proceedings of 14th European Conference on Artificial Intelligence, Berlin, Germany, August 20–25, 2000, pp. 338–342, IOS Press, 2000.

2. M. P. Bonacina. A Taxonomy of Parallel Strategies for Deduction. Annals of Mathematics and Artificial Intelligence, Vol. 29, No. 1–4, pp. 223–257, 2000.

3. M. Bozzano, G. Delzanno, M. Martelli, V. Mascardi, F. Zini. Logic Programming & Multi-Agent Systems: a Synergic Combination for Applications and Semantics. In The Logic Programming Paradigm: a 25-Year Perspective, pp. 5–32, Springer-Verlag, 1999.

4. P. R. Cohen, H. J. Levesque. Teamwork. Nous, Vol. 25, No. 4, pp. 487–512, 1991.

5. M. Fisher, M. Wooldridge. Distributed Problem-Solving as Concurrent Theorem Proving. In Proceedings of 8th European Workshop on Modelling Autonomous Agents in a Multi-Agent World, Ronneby, Sweden, May 13-16, 1997. Lecture Notes in Computer Science, Vol. 1237, pp. 128–140, Springer-Verlag, 1997.

6. M. Fisher. Characterising Simple Negotiation as Distributed Agent-Based Theorem-Proving—A Preliminary Report. In Proceedings of the Fourth International Conference on Multi-Agent Systems, Boston, July 2000, IEEE Press.

7. D. Fuchs. Requirement-Based Cooperative Theorem Proving. In Proceedings of JELIA-1998, Dagstuhl, Germany, October 12–15, 1998, Lecture Notes in Artificial Intelligence, Vol. 1489, pp. 139–153, Springer, 1998.

8. J. A. Giampapa, K. Sycara. Conversational Case-Based Planning for Agent Team Coordination. In D. W. Aha, I. Watson (eds). Case-Based Reasoning Research and Development: Proceedings of the Fourth International Conference on Case-Based Reasoning, ICCBR 2001, July 2001, Lecture Notes in Artificial Intelligence, Vol. 2080, pp. 189–203, Springer-Verlag, 2001.

9. J.-Y. Girard. Linear Logic. Theoretical Computer Science, Vol. 50, pp. 1–102, 1987.

10. B. Grosz, S. Kraus. Collaborative Plans for Complex Group Actions. Artificial Intelligence, Vol. 86, pp. 269–357, 1996.

11. J. Harland, M. Winikoff. Agent Negotiation as Proof Search in Linear Logic. In Proceedings of the First International Joint Conference on Autonomous Agents and Multi-Agent Systems (AAMAS 2002), July 15–19, 2002, Bologna, Italy.

12. J. Harland, M. Winikoff. Language Design Issues for Agents based on Linear Logic. In Proceedings of the Workshop on Computational Logic in Multi-Agent Systems (CLIMA'02), August 2002.

13. T. Hirai. Propositional Temporal Linear Logic and its Application to Concurrent Systems. IEICE Transactions on Fundamentals of Electronics, Communications and Computer Sciences (Special Section on Concurrent Systems Technology), Vol. E83-A, No. 11, pp. 2219–2227, November 2000.

14. N. R. Jennings, P. Faratin, A. R. Lomuscio, S. Parsons, C. Sierra, M. Wooldridge. Automated Negotiation: Prospects, Methods and Challenges, International Journal of Group Decision and Negotiation, Vol. 10, No. 2, pp. 199–215, 2001.

15. M. Kanovich, T. Ito. Temporal Linear Logic Specifications for Concurrent Processes (Extended Abstract). In Proceedings of the Twelfth Annual IEEE Symposium on Logic in Computer Science, Warsaw, Poland, June 29–July 2, 1997, pp. 48–57, IEEE Computer Society Press, 1997.

16. J. Komorowski. A Specification of An Abstract Prolog Machine and Its Application to Partial Evaluation. PhD thesis, Technical Report LSST 69, Department of Computer and Information Science, Linkoping University, Linkoping, Sweden, 1981.

17. S. Kraus, K. Sycara, A. Evenchik. Reaching Agreements through Argumentation: A Logical Model and Implementation. Artificial Intelligence, Vol. 104, No. 1–2, pp. 1–69, 1998.

18. P. Küngas, M. Matskin. Linear Logic, Partial Deduction and Cooperative Problem Solving. Proceedings of the First International Workshop on Declarative Agent Languages and Technologies (DALT 2003), Melbourne, Australia, July 15, 2003, Lecture Notes in Artificial Intelligence Series, Vol. 2990, Springer-Verlag, 2004.

19. H. J. Levesque, P. R. Cohen, J. H. T. Nunes. On Acting Together. In Proceedings of the Eighth National Conference on Artificial Intelligence, AAAI-90, pp. 94–99, 1990.

20. P. Lincoln. Linear Logic. ACM SIGACT Notices, Vol. 23, No. 2, pp. 29–37, Spring 1992.

21. P. Lincoln. Deciding Provability of Linear Logic Formulas. In J.-Y. Girard, Y. Lafont, L. Regnier (eds). Advances in Linear Logic, London Mathematical Society Lecture Note Series, Vol. 222, pp. 109–122, 1995.

22. J. W. Lloyd, J. C. Shepherdson. Partial Evaluation in Logic Programming. Journal of Logic Programming, Vol. 11, pp. 217–242, 1991.

23. S. Martini, A. Masini. A Modal View of Linear Logic. Journal of Symbolic Logic, Vol. 59, No. 3, pp. 888–899, September 1994.

24. S. Parsons, C. Sierra, N. Jennings. Agents that Reason and Negotiate by Arguing. Journal of Logic and Computation, Vol. 8, No. 3, pp. 261–292, 1998.

25. J. Rao, P. Küngas, M. Matskin. Application of Linear Logic to Web Service Composition. In Proceedings of the First International Conference on Web Services (ICWS 2003), Las Vegas, USA, June 23–26, 2003, pp. 3–9, CSREA Press, 2003.

26. F. Sadri, F. Toni, P. Torroni. Logic Agents, Dialogues and Negotiation: An Abductive Approach. In Proceedings of the Symposium on Information Agents for E-Commerce, Artificial Intelligence and the Simulation of Behaviour Convention (AISB-2001), York, UK, March 21–24, 2001.

Planning Experiments
in the DALI Logic Programming Language*

Stefania Costantini and Arianna Tocchio

Università degli Studi di L'Aquila,
Dipartimento di Informatica,
Via Vetoio, Loc. Coppito, I-67010 L'Aquila - Italy
{stefcost, tocchio}@di.univaq.it

Abstract. We discuss some features of the new logic programming language DALI for agents and multi-agent systems, also in connection to the issues raised in [12]. We focus in particular on the treatment of proactivity, which is based on the novel mechanism of the *internal events* and *goals*. As a case-study, we discuss the design and implementation of an agent capable to perform simple forms of planning. We demonstrate how it is possible in DALI to perform STRIPS-like planning without implementing a meta-interpreter. In fact a DALI agent, which is capable of complex proactive behavior, can build step-by-step her plan by proactively checking for goals and possible actions.

1 Introduction

The new logic programming language DALI [2], [4], [3] has been designed for modeling Agents and Multi-Agent systems in computational logic. Syntactically, DALI is close to the Horn clause language and to Prolog. In fact, DALI can be seen as a "Prolog for agents" in the sense that it is a general-purpose language, without prior commitment to a specific agent architecture. Rather, DALI provides a number of mechanisms that enhance the basic Horn-clause language to support the "agent-oriented" paradigm.

The definition of DALI has been meant to be a contribution to the understanding of what the agent-oriented paradigm may mean in computational logic. In fact, in the context of a purely logic semantics and of a resolution-based interpreter, some new features have been introduced: namely, events can be considered under different perspectives, and there is a careful treatment of proactivity and memory. In his new book [12], R. A. Kowalski discusses at length, based on significant examples, the principles and techniques an intelligent logical agent should be based upon. In this paper we will argue that DALI, although developed independently, is able to cope with many of the issues raised in [12].

DALI programs may contain a special kind of rules, reactive rules, aimed at interacting with an external environment. The environment is perceived in the form of external

---

* We acknowledge the support by MIUR 40% project *Aggregate- and number-reasoning for computing: from decision algorithms to constraint programming with multisets, sets, and maps* and by the *Information Society Technologies programme of the European Commission, Future and Emerging Technologies* under the IST-2001-37004 WASP project.

J. Dix and J. Leite (Eds.): CLIMA IV, LNAI 3259, pp. 89–107, 2004.

events, that can be exogenous events, observations, or messages from other agents. In response, a DALI agent can either perform actions or send messages. This is pretty usual in agent formalisms aimed at modeling reactive agents (see among the main approaches [10], [6], [7] [21], [20], [24]).

There are however in DALI some aspects that can hardly be found in the above-mentioned approaches. First, the same external event can be considered under different points of view: the event is first perceived, and the agent may reason about this perception; then a reaction can take place; finally, the event and the (possible) actions that have been performed are recorded as past events and past actions. The language has advanced proactive features, on which we particularly focus in this paper.

The new approach proposed by DALI is compared to other existing logic programming languages and agent architectures such as ConGolog, 3APL, IMPACT, METATEM, AgentSpeak in [4]. It is useful to remark that DALI is meant to be a general-purpose language, and thus does not commit to any specific agent architecture. Differently from other significant approaches, e.g., DESIRE [9], DALI agents do not have pre-defined submodules. Thus, different possible functionalities (problem-solving, cooperation, negotiation, etc.) and their interactions must be implemented specifically for the particular application. DALI is not directly related to the BDI approach, although its proactive mechanisms allow BDI agents to be implemented.

The declarative semantics of DALI, briefly summarized in Section 4, is an *evolutionary semantics,* where the meaning of a given DALI program P is defined in terms of a modified program P_s, where reactive and proactive rules are reinterpreted in terms of standard Horn Clauses. The agent receiving an event/making an action is formalized as a program transformation step. The evolutionary semantics consists of a sequence of logic programs, resulting from these subsequent transformations, together with the sequence of the models of these programs. Therefore, this makes it possible to reason about the "state "of an agent, without introducing explicitly such a notion, and to reason about the conclusions reached and the actions performed at a certain stage. Procedurally, the interpreter simulates the program transformation steps, and applies an extended resolution which is correct with respect to the model of the program at each stage.

The proactive capabilities of DALI agents, on which we concentrate in this paper, are based on considering (some distinguished) internal conclusions as events, called "internal events": this means, a DALI agent can "think" about some topic, the conclusions she takes can determine a behavior, and, finally, she is able to remember the conclusion, and what she did in reaction. Whatever the agent remembers is kept or "forgotten" according to suitable conditions (that can be set by directives). Then, a DALI agent is not a purely reactive agent based on condition-action rules: rather, it is a reactive, proactive and rational agent that performs inference within an evolving context.

An agent must be able to act in a goal-oriented way, to solve simple planning problems (regardless to optimality) and to perform tasks. To this aim, we have introduced a subclass of internal events, namely the class of "goals", that once invoked are attempted until they succeed, and then expire. For complex planning tasks however, from DALI rules it is possible to invoke an Answer Set Solver [23]. In fact, Answer Set Programming [17] [16] (based on the Answer Set Semantics of [13] [14]) is a new logic programming paradigm particularly well-suited for planning. In particular, given (in a file) a knowledge base describing actions, constraints and the goal to be reached, the solver returns possible plans in the form of *Answer Sets*, each of them containing the composing steps of a single plan. The DALI agent can then choose among the Answer Sets according to her criteria.

To demonstrate the usefulness of the "internal event" and "goal" mechanisms, we consider as a case-study the implementation of STRIPS-like planning. We will show that it is possible to design and implement this kind of planning without defining a meta-interpreter like is done in [18] (Ch. 8, section on Planning as Resolution). Rather, each feasible action is managed by the agent's proactive behavior: the agent checks whether there is a goal requiring that action, sets up the possible subgoals, waits for the preconditions to be verified, performs the actions (or records the actions to be done if the plan is to be executed later), and finally arranges the postconditions.

The paper is organized as follows. In Section 2 we summarize how we have understood the discussion in [12]; in Section 3 the language syntax, main constructs and their use are illustrated; in Section 4 the evolutionary semantics is briefly recalled; in Section 5 we present the case-study, and finally in Section 6 we conclude.

2   How to be Artificially Intelligent, the Logical Way

This is the topic treated at length by R. A. Kowalski in his new book [12], which is aimed at understanding which principles an intelligent logical agent should be based upon. According to our understanding of the interesting and deep discussion reported there, there are some important features and functionalities that any approach to agents in computational logic should include, mainly the following:

- Being able of forward reasoning, for interacting with the external world: on the one hand, for going from perceptions to goals; on the other hand, for going from goals or candidate actions to actions.
- Making a distinction between high-level *maintenance goals* and *achievement goals* Maintenance goals constitute the "consciousness " of what the agent has to fulfill in order to stay alive, keep herself in an acceptable state, be able to perform her main tasks. Achievement goals are needed in order to reach maintenance goals, and can in turn leave to low-level subgoals. The step between a maintenance goal and the achievement goals that are needed in order to make it done is in principle a step of forward reasoning. Instead, achievement goals can be coped with by means of backward reasoning, unless they are low-level, and thus require a forward reasoning step for making actions that affect the world.
- Combining different *levels of consciousness*. An agent is computationally conscious when she is aware of what she is doing and why she is doing it, which means that her behaviour is described by means of an high-level program, which manipulates symbols that have meaningful interpretations in the environment. Equivalently, an agent is logically conscious when her behaviour is generated by reasoning with goals and beliefs. Consciousness must be suitably combined with lower-level input-output associations or condition-action rules, which can also be represented as goals in logical form. Wishfully, it should be possible to compile and de-compile between high-level and low-level representations.

– Keeping track of time, both to timestamp externally observed events and to compare the current time with the deadlines of any internally derived future actions.
– Keeping memory of past observations, so as to be able to generate hypothetical beliefs, to explain the past and predict the future.
– Coping with a changing world, possibly by an approach focused on the occurrence of events and on the effect of events on local states of affairs, such as the Event Calculus [11].

In the rest of this paper we will argue that DALI, although developed independently, is able to cope with many of the issues raised in [12].

3   DALI

DALI is a logic programming agent-oriented language, aimed at a declarative specification of agents and multi-agent systems. While describing the main features of DALI, we will try to focus where these features find a convergence with the points raised in [12] that we have reported above.

A DALI program is syntactically very close to a traditional Horn-clause program. In fact, a Horn-clause program is a special case of a DALI program. Specific syntactic features have been introduced to deal with the agent-oriented capabilities of the language, and in particular to deal with events, actions and goals.

Having been designed for defining agents and multi-agent systems, DALI has been equipped with a communication architecture [5]. For the sake of interoperability, the DALI communication protocol is FIPA compliant, where FIPA (Foundation for Intelligent Physical Agents) is the most widely acknowledged standard for Agent Communication Languages. We have implemented the relevant FIPA primitives, plus others which we believe to be suitable in a logic setting. We have designed a meta-level where: on the one hand the user can specify, via two distinguished primitives tell/told, constraints on communication and/or a communication protocol; on the other hand, meta-rules can be defined for filtering and/or understanding messages via applying ontologies and forms of commonsense and case-based reasoning. These forms of meta-reasoning are automatically applied when needed by form of *reflection* [1].

3.1   Events

Let us consider an event arriving to the agent from its "external world", like for instance $bell\_ringsE$ (postfix E standing for "external"). From the agent's perspective, this event can be seen in different ways.

Initially, the agent has perceived the event, but she still has not reacted to it. The event is now seen as a present event $bell\_ringsN$ (postfix N standing for "now"). She can at this point reason about the event: for instance, she concludes that a visitor has arrived, and from this she realizes to be happy.

$visitor\_arrived$:- $bell\_ringsN$.
   $happy$:- $visitor\_arrived$.

Then, the reaction to the external event *bell_ringsE* consists in going to open the door. This is specified by the following *reactive rule*. The new token :> used instead of :- emphasizes that this rule performs forward reasoning, and is activated by the occurrence of the event which is in the head.

> *bell_ringsE* :> *go_to_open.*

About opening the door, there are two possibilities: one is that the agent is dressed already, and thus can perform the action directly (*open_the_doorA*, postfix *A* standing for "action"). The other one is that the agent is *not* dressed, and thus she has to get dressed before going. The action *get_dressedA* has a defining rule. This is just a plain horn rule, but in order to emphasize that it has the role of specifying the preconditions of an action, the new token :< is used instead of :- .

> *go_to_open* :- *dressed, open_the_doorA.*
>
> *go_to_open* :- *not dressed,*
>
> > *get_dressedA, open_the_doorA.*
>
> *get_dressed* :< *grab_clothes.*

DALI makes a distinction between low level *reaction* to the external events, and high-level *thinking* about these events. Since thinking and reacting are in principle different activities, we have introduced the two different *points of view* of the same event: as an external event to be reacted to, and as a present event to be conscious of. Then, when coping with external events DALI is able to combine, as advocated in [12], different "levels of consciousness": high-level reasoning performed on present events, that may lead the agent to revise or augment her beliefs; low-level forward reasoning for reaction.

DALI keeps track of time, since all events are timestamped. As we will see later, DALI also keeps track of events and actions that occurred in the past. The timestamp can be explicitly indicated when needed, and omitted when not needed. I.e., for any timestamped expression $Expr$, one can either write simply $Expr$, or $Expr : T$. External events and actions are used also for sending and receiving messages [5].

3.2   Proactivity in DALI

The basic mechanism for providing proactivity in DALI is that of the *internal events*. Namely, the mechanism is the following: an atom A is indicated to the interpreter as an internal event by means of a suitable directive. If A succeeds, it is interpreted as an event, thus determining the corresponding reaction. By means of another directive, it is possible to tell the interpreter that A should be attempted from time to time: the directive also specifies the frequency for attempting A, and the terminating condition (when this condition becomes true, A will be not attempted any more).

Thus, internal events are events that do not come from the environment. Rather, they are predicates defined in the program, that allow the agent to introspect about the state of her own knowledge, and to undertake a behavior in consequence. This mechanism has many uses, and also provides a mean for gracefully integrating object-level and meta-level reasoning. It is also possible to define priorities among different internal events, and/or constraints stating for instance that a certain internal event is incompatible with another one. Internal events start to be attempted when the agent is activated, or upon a certain condition, and keep being attempted (at the specified frequency) until the terminating condition occurs. The syntax of a directive concerning an internal event p is the following:

try p [since *SCond*] [frequency f] [until *TCond*].

It states that: p should be attempted at a frequency f; the attempts should start whenever the initiating condition *SCond* becomes true; the attempts should stop as soon as the terminating condition *TCond* becomes true. All fields are optional. If all of them are omitted, then p is attempted at a default frequency, as long as the agent stays alive.

Whenever p succeeds, it is interpreted as an event to which the agent may react, by means of a *reactive rule*:

$pI :> R_1, \ldots, R_n$.

The postfix I added to p in the head of the reactive rule stands for "internal", and the new connective $:>$ stands for *determines*. The rule reads: "if the internal event pI has happened, pI will determine a reaction that will consist in attempting $R_1, \ldots, R_n$". The reaction may involve making actions, or simply reasoning on the event.

Internal events are the DALI way of implementing *maintenance goals*. The relevant aspects of the agent's state are continuously kept under control. In fact, repeatedly attempting an internal event A means checking whether a condition that must be taken care of has become true. Success of A triggers a reaction: by means of a step of forward reasoning, the DALI agent goes from the internal event to whatever needs to be done in order to cope with it.

Frequency and priorities are related to the fact that there are conditions that are more critical then others, and or that evolve differently with time.

The reasons why A may fail in the first place and succeed later may be several. As a possible reason, the agent's internal state may change with time:

time_to_go_home :- *time(T), T >= 17:00pm*.

time_to_go_homeI :> *stop_work, go_to_bus_stopA, take_busA*.

Or, the agent's internal state may change with time, given her internal rules of functioning (below, she gets hungry after some time from last meal), which may imply setting achievement goals (*get_food*) and making actions (*eat_food*):

hungry :- *time(T), time_last_meal(T1), finished_energy(T,T1)*.

hungryI :> *get_food, eat_foodA*.

Notice that the reaction to an internal event corresponding to a maintenance goal resembles what in the BDI approach is called an "intention", i.e., the act of taking measures in order to reach a desirable state.

Another reason why an internal event may initially fail and then succeed is that the state of the external world changes with time. In the example below, a meal is ready as soon as the cooking time has elapsed. The definition uses timestamps: the agent knows when the soup was previously (postfix P) put on fire from the enclosed timestamp, and can thus estimate whether the cooking time has elapsed:

soup_ready :- *soup_on_fireP:T*,

                cooking_time(soup,K), *time_elapsed(T,K)*.

soup_readyI :> *take_off_pan_from_stoveA*, *turn_off_the_fireA*.

Or also, there may be new observations that make the internal event true:

     ready(cake) :- *in_the_oven(cake)*, *color(cake,golden)*, *smell(cake,good)*.

     readyI(cake) :> *take_from_oven(cake)*, *switch_off_the_oven*, *eat(cake)*.

Or, the reasoning about a present event may lead to a conclusion or to a new belief, that may trigger further activity. In a previous example, we have the conclusion *happy*, drawn from the present event *bell_rings* (but in general, this conclusion will be possibly drawn from several other conditions). It may be reasonable to consider "happiness" as a relevant aspect of the agent's state, and thus interpret predicate *happy* as an internal event, that causes a reaction (e.g., a smile) whenever true.

       visitor_arrived :- *bell_ringsN*.

          happy :- *visitor_arrived*.

         happyI :> *smileA*.

This shows that internal events not only can model maintenance goals, but can also model a kind of "consciusness" or "introspection" of the agent about her private state of affairs. When internal events are used in this way, the definition of the reaction specifies a sort of "individuality" of the agent, i.e., a kind of peculiar behaviour not strictly related to a need.

3.3   Past Events

The agent remembers events and actions, thus enriching her reasoning context. An event (either external or internal) that has happened in the past will be called *past event,* and written *bell_ringsP*, *happyP*, etc., postfix *P* standing for "past". Similarly for an action that has been performed. It is also possible to indicate to the interpreter plain conclusions that should be recorded as *past conclusions* (which, from a declarative point of view, are just lemmas). Past events are time-stamped, i.e., they are actually stored in the form: *predP* : *timestamp*.

Then, past events can remind the agent of:

- An external event that has happened; in this case, the time-stamp refers to the moment in time when the agent has reacted to the event.
- An internal event that has taken place; also in this case, the time-stamp refers to reaction.
- An action that has been performed; the time-stamp refers to when the action has been done.
- A conclusion that has been reached; the time-stamp records when.

It is important to notice that an agent cannot keep track of *every* event and action for an unlimited period of time, and that, sometimes, subsequent events/actions can make former ones no more valid. Then, we must equip an agent with the possibility to remember, but also to forget things.

According to the specific item of knowledge, the agent may want:

- To remember it forever.
- To forget it after a certain time.
- To forget it as as soon as subsequent knowledge makes it no more valid.

Moreover, if the recorded item concerns an event that may happen several time (i.e., $rain$) the agent may want:

- To remember all the occurrences.
- To remember only some of them, according to some conditions (the simplest one is a time-interval).
- To remember only the last occurrence.

In essence, there is a need to express forms of meta-information about the way in which the agent manages her knowledge base. Modifying this meta-information makes the behavior of the agent different. However, these aspects cannot be expressed in the agent logic program, which is a first-order Horn theory. Nor we want to hardwire them in the implementation.

Then, we have introduced the possibility of defining *directives*, that are by all means part of the specification of an agent, but are not part of the logic program. They are an input to the interpreter, and can be modified without altering (and even without looking at) the logic program, in order to "tune" the agent behavior.

Then, all the above-mentioned conditions can be specified via directives. Examples of directives are the following:

$keep \ predP \ until \ Time.$

where $PredP$ is removed at the time $Time$,

$keep \ predP \ until \ Condition.$

where $PredP$ is removed when $Condition$ becomed true,

$keep \ predP \ forever.$

where $PredP$ is never removed (think as an example to the birth-date of people, as a kind of information that never expires).

As a default, just the last occurrence of $PredP$ is kept, with its time-stamp, thus overriding previous ones. A directive can however alter this behavior, and the agent can look for various versions (for the sake of simplicity, we do not detail this point here). In the agent program, when referring to $PredP$ the agent implicitly refers to the last version.

If the directives for keeping/removing past events/actions/conclusions are specified carefully, we can say that the set of the last versions of past events/actions/conclusions constitutes an implicit representation of the *frame axiom*. This because this set represents what has happened/has been concluded, and has not been affected yet by what has happened later in the agent evolution.

Past events, past conclusions and past actions, which constitute the "memory" of the agent, are an important part of the (evolving) context of an agent. Memories make the agent aware of what has happened, and allow her to make predictions about the future.

It is interesting to notice that DALI management of past events allows the programmer to easily define *Event Calculus* expressions. The Event Calculus (EC) has been proposed by Kowalski and Sergot [11] as a system for reasoning about time and actions in the framework of Logic Programming. The essential idea is to have terms, called *fluents*, which are names of time-dependent relations. Kowalski and Sergot write $holds(r(x,y),t)$ which is understood as "fluent $r(x,y)$ is true at time t".

Take for instance the default inertia law formulated in the event calculus as follows:

> *holds(f,t)* ← *happens(e)*,
>
> *initiates(e,f)*,
>
> *date(e,t_s)*,
>
> *t_s < t*,
>
> *not clipped(t_s,f,t)*

where $clipped(t_s, f, t)$ is true when there is record of an event happening between t_s and t that terminates the validity of f. In other words, $holds(f,t)$ is derivable whenever in the interval between the initiation of the fluent and the time the query is about, no terminating events has happened.

In DALI, assuming that the program contains suitable assertion for *initiates* as well as the definition of *clipped*, this law could be immediately reformulated as follows. We just reinterpret $Happens(e), date(e, t_s)$ as a lookup in the knowledge base of past events, where *evp* finds an event E with its timestamp T_s (where, in this case, T_s initiates fluent f):

> *holds(f,T)* :- *evp(E,T_s)*,
>
> *initiates(E,T)*,
>
> *T_s < t*,
>
> *not Clipped(T_s,f,T)*

The representation can be enhanced by defining *holds* as an internal event. This means, the interpreter repeatedly attempts to prove $holds(f,T)$. Upon success, a reactive rule can state what to do in consequence of this conclusion. Then, $holds(f,T)$ will be recorded as a past event $holdsP(f,T)$, thus creating a temporal database where *holds* atoms are kept, and possibly removed according to the associated directives.

3.4 Goals

A special kind of internal event is a *goal*. Differently from the other internal events, goals start being attempted either when encountered during the inference process, or when invoked by an external event. Each goal G will be automatically attempted until it succeeds, and then expires. Moreover, if multiple definitions of G are available, they are (as usual) applied one by one by backtracking, but success of one alternative prevents any further attempt. attempt. DALI goals are a way of implementing [12] *achievement goals*, that must be attempted whenever needed, and possibly decomposed into subgoals.

We have implemented goals (postfix G) on top of internal events, by exploiting a practically useful role of past conclusions: i.e., that of allowing one to eliminate subsequent alternatives of a predicate definition upon success of one of them. Assume that the user has designated predicate q as a conclusion to be recorded (it will be recorded with syntax qP). Then, she can state that only one successful alternative for q must be considered (if any), by means of the following definition:

q :- $not\ qP, \langle def_1 \rangle$.

$\dots$

q :- $not\ qP, \langle def_n \rangle$.

Coming back to goals, whenever $goalG$ becomes true, a reaction may be triggered, by means of an (optional) reactive rule:

$goalGI :> R_1, \dots, R_k$

A slightly different postfix, namely GI, is used to distinguish the head of the reactive rule, so as to visually remark that this internal event is in particular a goal. After reaction, the goal is recorded as a past event $goalP$, so as the agent is aware that it has been achieved. If there is no reactive rule, the past event is recorded as soon as $goalG$ becomes true. This past event may in turn allow other internal events or goals to succeed, and so on. Then, a DALI agent is in constant evolution.

Goals can be used in a planning or problem-solving mechanism, for instance by employing the following schema.

> *RULE 1: goal prerequisites*
> $$goalG \ :- \ condition_1, \dots, condition_k(1)$$
> $$subgoalG_1, \dots, subgoalG_n(2)$$
> $$subgoalP_1, \dots, subgoalP_n(3)$$
> *RULE 2: goal achievement*
> $$goalGI \ :> \ actionA_1, \dots, actionA_m$$

where:

part (1) of Rule 1 verifies the preconditions of the goal;
part (2) of Rule 1 represents the invocation of the subgoals;
part (3) of Rule 1 verifies that previously invoked subgoals have been achieved (they have become past conclusions);
Rule 2 (optional) performs the actions which are needed to achieve the present goal, and to set its postconditions.

The reason why $goalG$ must be attempted repeatedly by Rule 1 is that, presumably, in the first place either some of the preconditions will not hold, or some of the subgoals will not succeed. The reason why part 3 of Rule 1 is needed is that each of the subgoals has the same structure as the overall goal. I.e., first its prerequisites have to succeed by Rule 1, and then it is actually achieved by the reaction in Rule 2 (if present), and finally becomes a past event. Then, by looking for past events part 3 checks that the subgoals have been properly achieved.

If the given goal is part of a problem-solving activity, or if it is part of a task, then the reaction may consist in directly making actions. In planning, the reaction may consist in updating the plan (by adding to it the actions that will have to be performed whenever the plan will be executed).

For convenience, a conjunction *goalG,goalP* that attempts a goal and waits for it to be achieved is denoted by the shorthand *goalD*, *D* standing for "done". Then, the above rules can be rewritten more shortly as:

RULE 1: goal prerequisites

$$goalG \; :- \; condition_1, \ldots, condition_k$$
$$subgoalD_1, \ldots, subgoalD_n.$$

RULE 2: goal achievement

$$goalGI \; :> \; actionA_1, \ldots, actionA_m$$

Also, it is possible to associate a timeout to the goal: by writing *goalD:T* we say that if the goal has not been achieved within the given time period T, then it fails.

Notice that the mechanism of DALI goals fulfills the structure advocated in [12] for achievement goals: there is a backward reasoning part in Rule 1, that possibly splits the goal into subgoals; there is (if needed) a forward reasoning part in Rule 2, for performing actions.

An easy improvement, demonstrated below, copes with situation where there are goals, and the agent may want to achieve as many of them as possible, regardless to the others.

$$many\_goals \; :- \; condition_1, \ldots, condition_k, goalsG.$$
$$goalsG \; :- \; goalD_1:T_1 \; :: \; \ldots \; :: \; goalD_n:T_n.$$

On the invocation of *goalsG*, the interpreter invokes all goals in the body of the rule. The body succeeds if at least one of them succeeds. This mechanism is composable, in the sense that any of the $goalG_i$'s can in turn be defined in this way.

Conceptually, there is a declarative rewriting of the above rule, taking profit of the fact that if there are alternative definitions for *goalG*, then the first successful alternative is taken. One should then specify as many rules as the possible combinations.

The examples that we propose in the ongoing for STRIPS-like planning are aimed at showing the power, generality and usability of DALI internal events and goals.

3.5   Coordinating Actions Based on Context

A DALI agent builds her own context, as suggested in [12], by keeping track of the events that have happened in the past, and of the actions that she has performed. As discussed above, whenever an event (either internal or external) is reacted to, whenever an action subgoal succeeds (and then the action is performed), and whenever a distinguished conclusion is reached, this is recorded in the agent knowledge base.

Past events and past conclusions are indicated by the postfix P, and past actions by the postfix PA. The following rule for instance says that Susan is arriving, since we know her to have left home.

$$is\_arriving(susan) \; :- \; left\_homeP(susan).$$

The following example illustrates how to exploit past actions. We consider an agent who opens and closes a switch upon a condition. For the sake of simplicity we assume that no exogenous events influence the switch. The action of opening (resp. closing) the switch can be performed only if the switch is closed (resp. open). The agent knows that the switch is closed if she remembers to have closed it previously. The agent knows that the switch is open if she remembers to have opened it. Predicates *open* and *close* are internal events, that periodically check the opening/closing condition, and, whenever true, perform the action (if feasible). previously.

$$open \ :- \ opening\_cond.$$
$$openI \ :> \ open\_switchA.$$
$$open\_switchA \ :< \ switch\_closed.$$
$$switch\_closed \ :- \ close\_switchPA.$$
$$close \ :- \ closing\_cond.$$
$$closeI \ :> \ close\_switchA.$$
$$close\_switchA \ :< \ switch\_open.$$
$$switch\_open \ :- \ open\_switchPA.$$

In the example, the agent will remember to have opened the switch. However, as soon as she closes the switch this record becomes no longer valid and should be removed: the agent in this case is interested to remember only the last action of a sequence. As soon as the *until* condition is fulfilled, i.e., the corresponding subgoal has been proved, the past action is removed. Then, the suitable directives for past actions will be in this case the following:

$$keep \ open\_switchPA \ until \ close\_switchA.$$

$$keep \ close\_switchPA \ until \ open\_switchA.$$

The following example illustrates the use of actions with preconditions. The agent emits an order for a product *Prod* of which she needs a supply. The order can be done either by phone or by fax, in the latter case if a fax machine is available. We want to express that the order can be done either by phone or by fax, but not both, and we do that by exploiting past actions, and say that an action cannot take place if the other one has already been performed. Here, *not* is understood as default negation.

$$need\_supplyE(Prod) \ :> \ emit\_order(Prod).$$
$$emit\_order(Prod) \ :- \ phone\_orderA(Prod),$$
$$not \, fax\_orderPA(Prod).$$
$$emit\_order(P) \ :- \ fax\_orderA(Prod),$$
$$not \, phone\_orderPA(Prod).$$

This can be reformulated in a more elaboration-tolerant way by the constraints:

$$:- fax\_orderA(Prod), phone\_orderPA(Prod)$$
$$:- fax\_orderPA(Prod), phone\_orderA(Prod)$$

thus eliminating negations from the body of the action rules.

4   Semantics

The DALI interpreter can answer user queries like the standard Prolog interpreter, but in general it manages a disjunction of goals. In fact, from time to time external and internal event will be added (as new disjuncts) to the current goal. The interpreter extracts the events from queues where they occur in the order in which they have been generated.

All the features of DALI that we have previously discussed are modeled in a declarative way. For a full definition of the semantics the reader may refer to [4]. We summarize the approach here, in order to make the reader understand how the examples actually work.

Some language features do not affect at all the logical nature of the language. In fact, attempting the goal corresponding to an internal event just means trying to prove something. Also, storing a past event just means storing a lemma.

Reaction and actions are modeled by suitably modifying the program. This means, inference is performed not in the given program, but in a modified version where language features are reformulated in terms of plain Horn clauses.

Reception of an event is modeled as a program transformation step. I.e., each event that arrives determines a new version of the program to be generated, and then we have a sequence of programs, starting from the initial one. In this way, we do not introduce a concept of state which is incompatible with a purely logic programming language. Rather, we prefer the concept of program (and model) evolution.

More precisely, we define the declarative semantics of a given DALI program P in terms of the declarative semantics of a modified program P_s, obtained from P by means of syntactic transformations that specify how the different classes of events/conclusions/actions are coped with. For the declarative semantics of P_s we take the Well-founded Model, that coincides with the the Least Herbrand Model if there is no negation in the program (see [19] for a discussion). In the following, for short we will just say "Model". It is important to notice that P_s is aimed at modeling the declarative semantics, which is computed by a bottom-up immediate-consequence operator. The declarative semantics will then correspond to the top-down procedural behavior of the interpreter.

We assume that events which have happened are recorded as facts. We have to formalize the fact that a reactive rule is allowed to be applied only if the corresponding event has happened. We reach our aim by adding, for each event atom $p(Args)E$, the event atom itself in the body of its own reactive rule. The meaning is that this rule can be applied by the immediate-consequence operator only if $p(Args)E$ is available as a fact. Precisely, we transform each reactive rule for external events:

$$p(Args)E \ :> \ R_1, \ldots, R_q.$$

into the standard rule:

$$p(Args)E \ :- \ p(Args)E, R_1, \ldots, R_q.$$

In a similar way we specify that the reactive rule corresponding to an internal event $q(Args)I$ is allowed to be applied only if the subgoal $q(Args)$ has been proved.

Then, we have to declaratively model actions, without or with an action rule. An action is performed as soon as its preconditions are true *and* it is invoked in the body of a rule, such as:

$$B \; :< \; D_1, \ldots, D_h, aA_1, \ldots, aA_k. \quad h \geq 1, k \geq 1$$

where the aA_i's are actions and the D_j's are not actions. Then, for every action atom aA, with action rule

$$aA \; :- \; C_1, \ldots, C_s. \quad s \geq 1$$

we modify this rule into:

$$aA \; :- \; D_1, \ldots, D_h, C_1, \ldots, C_s.$$

If aA has no defining clause, we instead add clause:

$$aA \; :- \; D_1, \ldots, D_h.$$

We repeat this for every rule in which aA is invoked.

In order to obtain the *evolutionary* declarative semantics of P, we explicitly associate to P_s the list of the external events that we assume to have arrived up to a certain point, in the order in which they are supposed to have been received. We let $P_0 = \langle P_s, [] \rangle$ to indicate that initially no event has happened.

Later on, we have $P_n = \langle Prog_n, Event\_list_n \rangle$, where $Event\_list_n$ is the list of the n events that have happened, and $Prog_n$ is the current program, that has been obtained from P_s step by step by means of a *transition function* Σ. In particular, Σ specifies that, at the n-th step, the current external event E_n (the first one in the event list) is added to the program as a fact. E_n is also added as a present event. Instead, the previous event E_{n-1} is removed as an external and present event, and is added as a past event.

Formally we have:

$$\Sigma(P_{n-1}, E_n) = \langle \Sigma_P(P_{n-1}, E_n), [E_n | Event\_list_{n-1}] \rangle$$

where

$$\Sigma_P(P_0, E_1) = \Sigma_P(\langle P_s, [] \rangle, E_1) = P_s \cup E_1 \cup E_{1N}$$
$$\Sigma_P(\langle Prog_{n-1}, [E_{n-1}|T] \rangle, E_n) =$$
$$\{\{Prog_{n-1} \cup E_n \cup E_{nN} \cup E_{n-1P}\} \setminus E_{n-1N}\} \setminus E_{n-1}$$

It is possible to extend Σ_P so as to deal with internal events, add as facts past actions and conclusions, and remove the past events that have expired.

Definition 1. *Let P_s be a DALI program, and $L = [E_n, \ldots, E_1]$ be a list of events. Let $P_0 = \langle P_s, [] \rangle$ and $P_i = \Sigma(P_{i-1}, E_i)$ (we say that event E_i determines the transition from P_{i-1} to P_i). The list $\mathcal{P}(P_s, L) = [P_0, \ldots, P_n]$ is the program evolution of P_s with respect to L.*

Notice that $P_i = \langle Prog_i, [E_i, \ldots, E_1] \rangle$, where $Prog_i$ is the program as it has been transformed after the ith application of Σ.

Definition 2. *Let P_s be a DALI program, L be a list of events, and PL be the* program evolution *of P_s with respect to L. Let M_i be the Model of $Prog_i$. Then, the sequence* $\mathcal{M}(P_s, L) = [M_0, \ldots, M_n]$ *is the* model evolution *of P_s with respect to L, and M_i the* instant model at step i .

The evolutionary semantics of an agent represents the history of the events received by the agents, and of the effect they have produced on it, without introducing a concept of a "state". It is easy to see that, given event list $[E_n, \ldots, E_1]$, DALI resolution simulates standard SLD-Resolution on $Prog_n$.

Definition 3. *Let P_s be a DALI program, L be a list of events. The* evolutionary semantics $\mathcal{E}_{P_s}$ *of P_s with respect to L is the couple* $\langle \mathcal{P}(P_s, L), \mathcal{M}(P_s, L) \rangle$.

The behaviour of DALI interpreter has been modeled and checked with respect to the evoltionary semantics by using the Murϕ model checker [8].

5   A Sample Application: STRIPS-Like Planning

In this section we show that the DALI language allows one to define an agent that is able to perform planning (or problem-solving) in a STRIPS-like fashion, without implementing a metainterpreter.

For the sake of simplicity, the planning capabilities that we consider are really basic, e.g., we do not consider here the famous STRIPS anomaly, and we do not have any pretense of optimality.

We consider the sample task of putting on socks and shoes. Of course, the agent should put her shoes on her socks, and she should put both socks and both shoes on.

We suppose that some other agent sends a message to ask our agent to wear the shoes. This message is an external event, which is the head of a reactive rule: the body of the rule specifies the reaction, which in this case consists in invoking the goal *put_your_shoesG*.

   goE :> *put_your_shoesG*.

This goal will be attempted repeatedly, until it will be achieved.

It is important to recall the mechanism of DALI goals:

- For a goal g to be achieved, first of all the predicate gG must become true, by means of a rule gG :- $Conds$, where $Conds$ specify preconditions and subgoals.
- For a goal g to be achieved, as soon as gG becomes true the (optional) reactive rule gGI :> $PostAndActions$ is activated, that performs the actions and/or sets the postconditions related to the goal.
- as soon as a goal gG is achieved (or, in short, we say that gG *succeeds*, even though this involves the above two steps), it is recorded as a past event, in the form gP.
- the conjunction gG, gP that invokes a goal and waits for it to be achieved is denoted by gD.

This explains the structure of the rule below:

   put_your_shoesG :- *put_right_shoeD, put_left_shoeD*.

In particular, it is required that the agent puts both the right and left shoe on. This means, *put_your_shoesG* will become true as soon as both of its subgoals will have been achieved. In practice, after the invocation of the subgoals, the overall goal is suspended until the subgoals become past events.

In the meantime, the subgoals *put_right_shoeG* and *put_left_shoeG* will be attempted.

> *put_right_shoeG* :- *have_right_shoe*, *put_right_sockD*.

This rule verifies a precondition, i.e., that of having the shoe to put on. Then it attempts the subgoal *put_right_sockG* and waits for its success, i.e., waits for the subgoal to become a past event. The rule for the subgoal is:

> *put_right_sockG* :- *have_right_sock*.

This rule doesn't invoke subgoals, but it just checks the precondition, i.e., to have the right sock. Upon success, the corresponding reactive rule is triggered:

> *put_right_sockGI* :> *right_sock_on*.

Now we have two possibilities: in a problem-solving activity, we will have the rule:

> *right_sock_on* :- *wear_right_sockA*.

that actually executes the action of wearing the sock.

In a planning activity, we will have instead the rule:

> *right_sock_on* :- *update_plan(wear_right_sock)*.

that adds to the plan that is being built the step of wearing the sock. In any case, the goal *put_right_sockG* has been achieved, and will be now recorded as past event, and thus *put_right_sockD* becomes true. Consequently, also *put_right_shoeG* becomes true, thus triggering the reactive rule:

> *put_right_shoeGI* :> *right_shoe_on*.

After having made (or recorded) the action of wearing the shoe, *put_right_shoeP* will become true, thus obtaining *put_right_shoeD*.

Analogously, the agent will eventually record the past event *put_left_shoeP*, thus obtaining *put_left_shoeD*. Since the subgoals of wearing the right and the left shoe are unrelated, no order is enforced on their execution. Only, the overall goal becomes true whenever both of them have been achieved.

At this point, the reactive rule related to the overall goal will be activated:

> *put_your_shoesGI* :> *message(tell_shoes_onA)*.

which means that the goal has succeeded, and in particular the agent declares to have the shoes on.

The planning mechanism that we have outlined consists of a descendant process that invokes the subgoals, and of an ascending process that executes (or records) the corresponding actions.

This methodology allows an agent to construct plans dynamically. In fact, a change of the context, i.e., new information received from the outside, can determine success of subgoals that could not succeed before.

A future direction of this experimental activity is that of writing a meta-planner with general meta-definitions for root, intermediate and leaf goals. This meta-planner would accept a list of goals, with the specification of their kind, and for each of them the list of preconditions, subgoals and actions.

Below we show an example of use of conditional goal rules, where

$$gG :\text{-} Conds, gD_1 :: , \ldots , , :: gD_n$$

means, as previously discussed, that if $Conds$ are true, then the body of the rule succeeds provided that at least one of the gD_i's succeeds (though the interpreter invokes them all, and tries to achieve as many as possible). The point is that the failure of non-critical partial objectives does not determine the failure of the overall goal. The example consists in an agent that has to go to the supermarket in order to buy milk and bananas, and to the hardware shop in order to buy a drill. He tries to go both to the supermarket and to the hardware shop. However, if one of them is closed he just goes to the other one. In each shop, he tries to buy what he needs, without making a tragedy if something is missing. There is a failure (and then the agent is disappointed) only if either both shops are closed, or all items are missing.

$$
\begin{aligned}
buy \;\; &:\text{-} \;\; buy\_allD. \\
disappointed \;\; &:\text{-} \;\; not\; buy. \\
buyI \;\; &:> \;\; go\_homeA. \\
disappointedI \;\; &:> \;\; some\_reaction. \\
buy\_allG \;\; &:\text{-} \;\; buy\_at\_supermarketD :: buy\_at\_hardware\_shopD. \\
buy\_at\_supermarketG \;\; &:\text{-} \;\; supermarket\_open, \\
&\quad\; buy\_bananasD :: buy\_milkD. \\
buy\_at\_hardware\_shopG \;\; &:\text{-} \;\; hardware\_shop\_open, \\
&\quad\; buy\_drillG.
\end{aligned}
$$

6   Conclusions

We have presented how to implement a naive version of STRIPS-like planning in DALI, mainly by using the mechanism of internal events and goals. However, the ability of DALI agents to behave in a "sensible" way comes from the fact that DALI agents have several classes of events, that are coped with and recorded in suitable ways, so as to form a context in which the agent performs her reasoning. In fact, we have argued that DALI fulfills many of the points raised in [12] about which features any logical formalism aimed at defining intelligent agents should possess.

A simple form of knowledge update and "belief revision" is provided by the conditional storing of past events, past conclusions and past actions. They constitute the "memory" of the agent, and are an important part of her evolving context: memories make the agent aware of what has happened, and allow her to make predictions about the future. The ability of specifying how long and under which conditions memories should be kept allows the agent behavior to be specified in a more sophisticated and flexible way. For the sake of flexibility and of conceptual clarity, the directives that cope with the knowledge base of the agent memories are distinct from the agent logic program. In the future however, more sophisticated belief revision strategies will be integrated into the formalism.

DALI is fully implemented in Sicstus Prolog [22]. The implementation, together with a set of examples, is available at the URL http://gentile.dm.univaq.it/dali/dali.htm.

Acknowledgments

Many thanks to Stefano Gentile, who joined the DALI project, cooperates to the implementation of DALI, has designed the language web site, and has supported the authors in many ways. We also gratefully acknowledge Prof. Eugenio Omodeo for useful discussions and for his support to this research.

References

1. J. Barklund, S. Costantini, P. Dell'Acqua e G. A. Lanzarone, *Reflection Principles in Computational Logic*, Journal of Logic and Computation, Vol. 10, N. 6, December 2000, Oxford University Press, UK.
2. S. Costantini, *Towards active logic programming*, In A. Brogi and P. Hill, (eds.), *Proc. of 2nd International Works. on Component-based Software Development in Computational Logic (COCL'99)*, PLI'99, Paris, France, September 1999, http://www.di.unipi.it/~brogi/ResearchActivity/COCL99/ proceedings/index.html.
3. S. Costantini, S. Gentile and A. Tocchio, *DALI home page:* http://gentile.dm.univaq.it/dali/dali.htm.
4. S. Costantini and A. Tocchio, *A Logic Programming Language for Multi-agent Systems*, In S. Flesca, S. Greco, N. Leone, G. Ianni (eds.), *Logics in Artificial Intelligence, Proc. of the 8th Europ. Conf., JELIA 2002*, Cosenza, Italy, September 2002, LNAI 2424: Springer-Verlag, Berlin, 2002.
5. S. Costantini, A. Tocchio (**submitted**). *Communication in the DALI Agent-Oriented Logic Programming Language.* submitted to ICLP'04, International Conference on Logic Programming.
6. P. Dell'Acqua, F. Sadri, and F. Toni, *Communicating agents*, In *Proc. International Works. on Multi-Agent Systems in Logic Progr., in conjunction with ICLP'99*, Las Cruces, New Mexico, 1999.
7. M. Fisher, *A survey of concurrent METATEM – the language and its applications*, In *Proc. of First International Conf. on Temporal Logic (ICTL)*, LNCS 827, Springer Verlag, Berlin, 1994.
8. B. Intrigila, I. Melatti, A. Tocchio, *Model-checking DALI with Murφ*, Tech. Rep., Univ. of L'Aquila, 2004.
9. C. M. Jonker, R. A. Lam and J. Treur, *A Reusable Multi-Agent Architecture for Active Intelligent Websites. Journal of Applied Intelligence*, vol. 15, 2001, pp. 7-24.

10. R. A. Kowalski and F. Sadri, *Towards a unified agent architecture that combines rationality with reactivity*, In *Proc. International Works. on Logic in Databases*, LNCS 1154,Springer-Verlag, Berlin, 1996.
11. R. A. Kowalski and M. A. Sergot, *A logic-based calculus of events*, New Generation Computing 4, 1986.
12. R. A. Kowalski, *How to be Artificially Intelligent - the Logical Way*, Draft, revised February 2004, Available on line, URL http://www-lp.doc.ic.ac.uk/UserPages/staff/rak/rak.html.
13. M. Gelfond and V. Lifschitz, *The Stable Model Semantics for Logic Programming,* In: R. Kowalski and K. Bowen (eds.), Logic Programming: Proc. of 5th International Conference and Symposium, The MIT Press, 1988.
14. M. Gelfond and V. Lifschitz, *Classical Negation in Logic Programming and Disjunctive Databases,* New Generation Computing 9, 1991: 365–385.
15. *How to be Artificially Intelligent – the Logical Way,* book drafta (revised February 2004), Available on-line at the URL: http://www-lp.doc.ic.ac.uk/UserPages/staff/rak/rak.html
16. V. Lifschitz, *Answer Set Planning,* in: D. De Schreye (ed.) Proc. of the 1999 International Conference on Logic Programming (invited talk), The MIT Press, 1999: 23–37.
17. W. Marek and M. Truszczyński, *Stable Models and an Alternative Logic Programming Paradigm,* In: The Logic Programming Paradigm: a 25-Year Perspective, Springer-Verlag, Berlin, 1999: 375–398.
18. D. Poole, A. Mackworth, R. Goebel, *Computational Intelligence*: ISBN 0-19-510270-3, Oxford University Press, New York, 1998.
19. H. Przymusinska and T. C. Przymusinski, *Semantic Issues in Deductive Databases and Logic Programs*, R.B. Banerji (ed.) Formal Techniques in Artificial Intelligence, a Sourcebook: Elsevier Sc. Publ. B.V. (North Holland), 1990.
20. A. S. Rao, *AgentSpeak(L): BDI Agents speak out in a logical computable language*, In W. Van De Velde and J. W. Perram, editors, *Agents Breaking Away: Proc. of the Seventh European Works. on Modelling Autonomous Agents in a Multi-Agent World*, LNAI: Springer Verlag, Berlin, 1996.
21. A. S. Rao and M. P. Georgeff, *Modeling rational agents within a BDI-architecture*, In R. Fikes and E. Sandewall (eds.), Proc. of Knowledge Representation and Reasoning (KR&R-91): Morgan Kaufmann Publishers: San Mateo, CA, April 1991.
22. SICStus home page: http://www.sics.se/sicstus/.
23. Web location of the most known ASP solvers:
    aspps: http://www.cs.uky.edu/ai/aspps/
    CCalc: http://www.cs.utexas.edu/users/tag/cc/
    Cmodels: http://www.cs.utexas.edu/users/tag/cmodels.html
    DLV: http://www.dbai.tuwien.ac.at/proj/dlv/
    NoMoRe: http://www.cs.uni-potsdam.de/~linke/nomore/
    SMODELS: http://www.tcs.hut.fi/Software/smodels/
24. V. S. Subrahmanian, P. Bonatti, J. Dix, T. Eiter, S. Kraus, F. Özcan, and R. Ross, *Heterogenous Active Agents*: The MIT Press, 2000.

A New HTN Planning Framework for Agents in Dynamic Environments

Hisashi Hayashi, Kenta Cho, and Akihiko Ohsuga

Knowledge Media Laboratory,
Corporate Research and Development Center,
Toshiba Corporation,
1 Komukai-Toshiba-cho, Saiwai-ku, Kawasaki-shi, 212-8582, Japan
{hisashi3.hayashi, kenta.cho, akihiko.ohsuga}@toshiba.co.jp

Abstract. In a dynamic environment, even if an agent makes a plan to obtain a goal, the environment might change while the agent is executing the plan. In that case, the plan, which was initially valid when it was made, might later become invalid. Furthermore, in the process of replanning, it is necessary to take into account the side effects of actions already executed . To solve this problem, we have previously presented an agent life cycle that interleaves HTN planning, action execution, knowledge updates, and plan modification. In that agent life cycle, the plans are always kept valid according to the most recent knowledge and situation. However, it deals with only total-order plans. This paper extends the agent life cycle so that the agent can handle partial-order plans.

1 Introduction

As agents are working on the Internet, adaptation to dynamic environments is becoming an important subject. Because environments change, even if the agent obtained a goal in the past, it does not mean that the agent can obtain the same goal in the same way. Making inferences is an effective approach to adapt to such a dynamic environment. In fact, mobile agents of *Jini* [19] and *MiLog* [6] make inferences using Prolog. Mobile agents of *Plangent* [16] make a plan before acting.

If an agent makes a complete plan just before acting, the agent can adapt to the dynamic world to some extent. However, this is not enough: the agent might not be able to execute some actions as expected; the agent might get new information which affects the plan. In the former case, the agent needs to suspend the plan currently being executed and switch to an alternative plan. In the latter case, the agent needs to check the validity of the plan and modify it if necessary. Therefore, in order to adapt to the changing environment, it is necessary to check and modify plans continually and incrementally.

As pointed out in [4], much of the research into continual, distributed planning is built around the notion of abstract plan decomposition such as *hierarchical task network (HTN) planning*. HTN planners, such as *SHOP* [14], decompose

J. Dix and J. Leite (Eds.): CLIMA IV, LNAI 3259, pp. 108–133, 2004.
© Springer-Verlag Berlin Heidelberg 2004

a task to more primitive tasks. If an agent keeps an abstract plan, the agent can successively decompose the abstract tasks in the plan as it gets new information from another agent, the user, or the environment. HTN planning is also useful for joint planning where one agent makes abstract plans and other agents decompose abstract tasks in the plans.

Unlike standard partial-order planners, when planning, HTN planners do not always connect preconditions and postconditions (effects) of actions. Instead, such HTN planners decompose an abstract task into a more detailed plan. In this approach, plan decomposition is done by replacing the abstract task into the ready-made plan that is chosen from the plan library. Obviously, in this case, the agent can save the time to construct the ready-made plan. Note that this task decomposition is similar to the literal decomposition of Prolog. Prolog decomposes a literal using a clause that is selected from the Prolog program. The clause shows a plan (the body of the clause) for the abstract task (the head of the clause), and the Prolog program corresponds to the plan library.

Although the task (or literal) decomposition of HTN planners or Prolog is useful for agents in dynamic environments, we need to extend them so that they can incrementally and dynamically modify the plans. This is an important subject, which is recognized also in [5]. To deal with this problem, we previously designed an HTN planner [9] for speculative computation in multi-agent systems that interleaves planning, action execution, knowledge updates, and plan modifications. We also implemented the dynamic planning mobile agent system [10] on top of our *picoPlangent* mobile agent system. Based on Prolog's proof procedure, this planner makes (possibly more than one) plans, and incrementally modifies the plans. When one plan does not work or other plans become more attractive, the agent switches to another plan. The agent checks and modifies plans when executing an action or updating the program (Prolog's clauses). Plans are checked and modified after executing an action in a plan because this action might prevent the execution of the other alternative plans. Plans are also checked and modified after updating the program because some plans, which were initially valid when they were made, might become invalid and also it might be possible to make new valid plans after the program update.

Our previous HTN planner made it possible to guarantee the validity of plans with regard to the newest knowledge of the agent and its history of action execution. However, it can handle only *total-order* plans, which causes another problem: when switching from one plan to another, the agent sometimes cancels an action and re-executes the same action. For example, consider the following two total-order plans:

- [buy(a), buy(b), assemble(pc)]
- [buy(c), buy(a), assemble(pc)]

Informally, according to the first plan, the agent is expected to buy the part a, buy the part b, and then assemble pc. (See Figure 1.) The second plan is interpreted in the same way. Suppose that the agent has executed the action buy(a). Our previous planner modifies the plans as follows:

Fig. 1. A Total-Order Plan

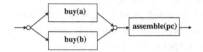

Fig. 2. A Partial-Order Plan

- $[\texttt{buy(b)}, \texttt{assemble(pc)}]$
- $[\texttt{return(a)}, \texttt{buy(c)}, \texttt{buy(a)}, \texttt{assemble(pc)}]$

From the first plan, the executed action (buy(a)) has been removed. There is no problem with regard to the first plan. However, according to the second plan, the agent is expected to return(a) and later buy(a). Although the second plan is correct, it is wasteful to redo what is undone. This problem is caused because the second total-order plan specifies the order of buying the parts a and c although the order is not a matter of concern. If we can use *partial-order* plans, we do not have to specify the order of buy(a) and buy(c). In order to avoid this kind of unnecessary execution of canceling actions, we have extended our previous planner so that it can handle (restricted) partial-order plans. If we can use partial-order plans, we can express plans such as:

- $[\{\texttt{buy(a)}, \texttt{buy(b)}\}, \texttt{assemble(pc)}]$
- $[\{\texttt{buy(c)}, \texttt{buy(a)}\}, \texttt{assemble(pc)}]$

In the first plan, the execution order of buy(a) and buy(b), which is written between "{" and "}", is not specified. (See Figure 2.) Similarly, the second plan does not specify the execution order of buy(c) and buy(a). Therefore, after executing buy(a), these plans can be modified as follows:

- $[\texttt{buy(b)}, \texttt{assemble(pc)}]$
- $[\texttt{buy(c)}, \texttt{assemble(pc)}]$

In summary, this paper presents a new agent life cycle that deals with (restricted) partial-order plans and that integrates the following:

- Decomposition of abstract tasks (literals);
- Action execution and plan modifications;
- Program updates and plan modifications.

This paper is organized as follows. In the next section, we define basic terminologies. Section 3 defines the procedure for task (literal) decomposition. This planning (task decomposition) procedure records extra information to prepare for future plan modifications. Section 4 shows how to modify the plans after

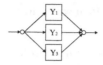

Fig. 3. Execution Order of a Plan (Type 1)

Fig. 4. Execution Order of a Plan (Type 2)

action execution. Plans are modified considering the side effects of actions. Section 5 shows how to modify the plans after a program update: invalid plans are removed; new valid plans are added. Section 6 introduces the agent life cycle that integrates task decomposition, action execution, program updates, and plan modifications. Section 7 evaluates the efficiency of the plan modification method in Section 5 by means of experiments. Section 8 defines an independent semantics and shows the soundness of the agent life cycle. Section 9 explains why our incremental plan modification approach is important in implementing multi-agent systems. Section 10 discusses related work.

2 Terminology

This section defines basic terminologies including plans, clauses, dynamic planning framework, action data, and history of action execution. Like Prolog, (positive) literals will be defined using *constants, variables, functions,* and *predicates.*

Definition 1. *A* **complex term** *is of the form:* $F(T_1, ..., T_n)$ *where* $n \geq 0$, F *is an n-ary function, and each* T_i *($1 \leq i \leq n$) is a term. A* **term** *is one of the following: a constant; a variable; a complex term. A* **literal** *is of the form:* $P(T_1, .., T_n)$ *where* $n \geq 0$, P *is an n-ary predicate, and each* T_i *($1 \leq i \leq n$) is a term. When* P *is a 0-ary predicate, the literal* $P()$ *can be abbreviated to* P.

Plans are defined using literals as follows.

Definition 2. *A* **plan** *is either* **Type 1** *of the form:* $[X_1, ..., X_n]$ *or* **Type 2** *of the form:* $\{Y_1, ..., Y_n\}$ *where* $n \geq 0$, *each* X_i *and each* Y_i *($1 \leq i \leq n$) is a literal or a plan, which is called a* **subplan**. *The plan* $[]$ *and the plan* $\{\}$ *are called* **empty plans**.

Intuitively, Figure 3 expresses the execution order of a plan (Type 1): $[X_1, X_2, X_3]$, and Figure 4 expresses the execution order of a plan (Type 2): $\{Y_1, Y_2, Y_3\}$. These execution orders will be reflected in the definition of *action consumability* of plans.

Example 1. Figure 5 expresses the execution order of a plan (Type 2): $\{$ [a1, a2] , a3, [a4,a5] $\}$ in which two subplans of Type 1 ([a1,a2] and [a4,a5]) occur.

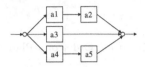

Fig. 5. Plan which has subplans

We define clauses using plans. Unlike Prolog's clauses, the execution order of literals in a clause is partially specified.

Definition 3. *A* **clause** *defining the literal* LIT *by the plan* PLAN *is of the form:* LIT ⇐ PLAN. *When* PLAN *is an empty plan, this clause is called a* **fact** *and can be abbreviated to* LIT.

Intuitively, in the above definition, LIT ⇐ PLAN means that LIT is satisfied when the execution of PLAN is completed.

Next, we define the *dynamic planning framework*, which will be used for our planning procedure.

Definition 4. *A* **dynamic planning framework** *is of the form:* ⟨A, D, P⟩ *where* A *is a set of literals (called* **actions***),* D *is a set of literals (called* **dynamic literals***) that are not actions,* P *is a set (called* **program***) of clauses that do not define any action. An instance of an action is also an action. An instance of a dynamic literal is also a dynamic literal.*

In the above definition, actions are executed by an agent. The program will be used for planning. The definition clauses of dynamic literals in the program might be updated in the future by adding (or deleting) a clause to (respectively, from) the program.

Following the intuitive execution order of plans, we define action consumability of plans as follows. Informally, a plan can consume an action if the action is one of the next actions to be executed according to the plan.

Definition 5. *In the dynamic planning framework, the action* A *is* **consumable** *for the plans of the form:*

1. $[X_1, ..., X_n]$ *where*
   - $n \geq 1$, *and* X_1 *is either an action that is unifiable with* A *or a subplan such that* A *is consumable.*
2. $\{Y_1, ..., Y_n\}$ *where*
   - $n \geq 1$, *and there exists* Y_i *($1 \leq i \leq n$) such that* Y_i *is either an action that is unifiable with* A *or a subplan such that* A *is consumable.*

Definition 6. *In the dynamic planning framework, the action* A *is* **inconsumable** *for the plans of the form:*

1. $[X_1, ..., X_n]$ *where*
   - *$n = 0$ or;*
   - *$n \geq 1$ and X_1 is either an action that is not unifiable with A or a subplan such that A is inconsumable.*
2. $\{Y_1, ..., Y_n\}$ *where*
   - *$n \geq 0$ and each Y_i ($1 \leq i \leq n$) is either an action that is not unifiable with A or a subplan such that A is inconsumable.*

Example 2. In a dynamic planning framework, suppose that a1, a2, a3, a4, and a5 are actions. The plan $\{$[a1,a2],a3,[a4,a5]$\}$ can consume a1, a3, and a4 but cannot consume a2 and a5. (See Figure 5.)

An action execution in a plan might affect the execution of other plans. The *action data* of an action, defined as follows, will be used to record the data regarding the side effects of the action.

Definition 7. *In the dynamic planning framework, the action data of the action* A *is one of the following forms:*

- $dataA(A, noSideEffect)$
- $dataA(A, undo(seq, A^-))$
- $dataA(A, undo(con, A^-))$
- $dataA(A, cannotUndo)$

Informally, in the above definition, each action data has the following meaning:

- A does not have side effects.
- A has side effects. A^- is the action that will undo the execution of A unless other actions with side effects are executed between the execution of A and A^-.
- A has side effects. A^- is the action that will undo the execution of A. We do not care when A^- undoes A.
- A has side effects that cannot be undone.

Finally, we define the *history of action execution*, which records the order of actions that have been executed recently. It also records the side effects of actions already executed. This information will be used for plan modification.

Definition 8. *A* **history of action execution** *is of the form:* $[H_1, ..., H_n]$ *where* $n \geq 0$, *and each* H_i *($1 \leq i \leq n$) is an action data.*

3   Decomposition of Abstract Tasks (Literals)

This section introduces a new procedure for planning via literal decomposition. In the dynamic planning framework, the program might be updated even after making plans. The planning procedure adds extra information to plans so that the plans can be modified when necessary. A *plan plus*, defined below, records such extra information (clauses and history of action execution) in association with a plan.

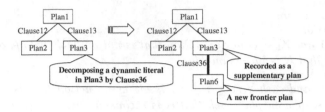

Fig. 6. Search Tree

Definition 9. *In the dynamic planning framework, a* **plan plus** *is of the form:* (PLAN, CSET, HISTORY) *where* PLAN *is a plan,* CSET *is a set of clauses (called* **prerequisite clauses** *of* PLAN*) in the program, and* HISTORY *is history of action execution.*

Prerequisite clauses of a plan were used to derive the plan. Therefore, if a prerequisite clause of a plan becomes invalid, the plan becomes invalid. The history of action execution (See Definition 7) that is recorded in association with a plan records actions already executed, which have not been reflected in the plan yet.

Two kinds of plan pluses will be used by our planning procedure. The following *plan goal* records these two kinds of plan pluses.

Definition 10. *In the dynamic planning framework, a* **plan goal** *is of the form:* (PLANS$^+$, SPP$^+$) *where* PLANS$^+$ *and* SPP$^+$ *are sets of plan pluses. Each plan plus in* PLANS$^+$ *is called a* **frontier plan plus**. *Each plan plus in* SPP$^+$ *is called a* **supplementary plan plus**. *The plan mentioned in a frontier plan plus is called a* **frontier plan**. *The plan mentioned in a supplementary plan plus is called a* **supplementary plan**. *For each supplementary plan, exactly one dynamic literal that occurs in the supplementary plan is* **marked**.

Frontier plans correspond to leaves in the search tree. In Figure 6, the left search tree means that Plan2 is derived from Plan1 using Clause12. Similarly, Plan3 is derived from Plan1 using Clause13. In this search tree, the frontier plans are Plan2 and Plan3. Our planning procedure will make plans by decomposing the selected literal in a frontier plan. If the selected literal is a dynamic literal, we record the frontier plan as a supplementary plan. For example, in Figure 6, when decomposing a dynamic literal in Plan3, Plan3 is recorded as a supplementary plan. Therefore, each supplementary plan has the selected dynamic literal, which is marked. Supplementary plans correspond to intermediate nodes (not leaves) from which another branch might be added. Note that a clause defining a dynamic literal might be added to the program later by a program update.

Like Prolog, a plan is resolved by a clause as follows.

Definition 11. *Let* PLANv *be a new variant[1] of* PLAN. *Suppose that the occurrence of the literal* LITv *in* PLANv *corresponds to the occurrence of the literal*

---

[1] A new variant of X is made by replacing all the variables in X with new variables.

LIT *in* PLAN. *Suppose that* HEAD $\Leftarrow$ BODY *is a new variant of the clause* CL, *and that* LIT, LITv, *and* HEAD *are unifiable.*

When LIT *in* PLAN *is selected, the resolvent of* PLAN *by* CL *is made from* PLANv *by first unifying* LITv *and* HEAD *with the most general unifier* θ, *and then replacing the occurrence of* θ(LITv) *in* θ(PLANv) *with* θ(BODY).

Example 3. When the literal x2(b) in the plan [x1(a),x2(b)] is selected, the resolvent of the plan [x1(a),x2(b)] by the clause x2(V) $\Leftarrow$ {y1(V),y2(V)} is [x1(a),{y1(b),y2(b)}].

Now, we define a *derivation* of plan goals. This derivation is our planning procedure. Not only does the derivation resolve plans, but it also records extra information which will be used for plan modification, when necessary.

Definition 12. *In the dynamic planning framework, a* **derivation** *from the plan goal* $GOAL_1$ *to the plan goal* $GOAL_n$ *(n $\geq$ 2) is a sequence of plan goals:* $GOAL_1$, ..., $GOAL_n$ *such that each* $GOAL_{k+1}$ *(1 $\leq$ k $\leq$ n - 1) is derived from* $GOAL_k$ *(= (PLANS$^+$, SPP$^+$)) by one of the following* **derivation rules**.

p1 *Select a plan plus* (PLAN, CSET, HISTORY) *which belongs to* PLANS$^+$. *Select a literal* L *that occurs in* PLAN *and that is not a dynamic literal. Suppose that* C_1, ..., C_s *(s $\geq$ 0) are all the clauses in the program such that each* C_u *(0 $\leq$ u $\leq$ s) defines a literal which is unifiable with the selected literal* L. *Suppose that* $RPLAN_i$ *(1 $\leq$ i $\leq$ s) is the resolvent of* PLAN *by* C_i. $GOAL_{k+1}$ *is made from* $GOAL_k$ *by replacing the occurrence of the selected plan plus:*
    (PLAN, CSET, HISTORY)
with the following plan pluses:
    ($RPLAN_1$, CSET, HISTORY), ..., ($RPLAN_s$, CSET, HISTORY).
p2 *Select a plan plus* (PLAN, CSET, HISTORY) *which belongs to* PLANS$^+$. *Select a literal* L *that occurs in* PLAN *and that is a dynamic literal. Suppose that* C_1, ..., C_s *(s $\geq$ 0) are all the clauses in the program such that each* C_u *(0 $\leq$ u $\leq$ s) defines a literal which is unifiable with the selected literal* L. *Suppose that* $RPLAN_i$ *(1 $\leq$ i $\leq$ s) is the resolvent of* PLAN *by* C_i. $GOAL_{k+1}$ *is made from* $GOAL_k$ *by replacing the occurrence of the selected plan plus:*
    (PLAN, CSET, HISTORY)
with the following plan pluses:
    ($RPLAN_1$, {C_1}∪CSET, HISTORY), ..., ($RPLAN_s$, {C_s}∪CSET, HISTORY),
and adding the selected plan plus: (PLAN, CSET, HISTORY) *to* SSP$^+$ *as a supplementary plan plus with the selected literal marked.*

Rule p1 decomposes a literal whose definition clause will not be updated. On the other hand, Rule p2 decomposes a dynamic literal whose definition clauses might be updated. When resolving a plan by a clause, Rule p2 records the clause in association with the resolved plan because if the clause becomes invalid, the resolved plan also becomes invalid. (See Figure 9.) Rule p2 also records the resolved plan as a supplementary plan because if another new clause which defines the selected literal becomes valid, it is possible to resolve the plan by the new valid clause.

Example 4. In the dynamic planning framework, suppose that x2(V) is a dynamic literal. When resolving the plan [x1(a), x2(b)], as shown in Example 3, using the clause x2(V) ⇐ {y1(V), y2(V)}, Rule p2 records this clause in association with the plan [x1(a), {y1(b), y2(b)}]. Also Rule p2 records [x1(a), x2(b)] as a supplementary plan with the selected literal x2(b) marked.

4   Action Execution and Plan Modification

When one plan does not work, we might want to suspend the plan execution and switch to another plan. However, some actions that have been executed following a plan might prevent another plan from functioning. This section defines how to modify plans after an action execution.

Definition 13. *In the dynamic planning framework, the* **plan modification rules after the execution of the action** A *are as follows where* PLAN *is the plan to be modified by a plan modification rule, and only one plan modification rule is applied to* PLAN *if more than one plan modification rule can be applied to* PLAN.

- *When* A *is consumable for* PLAN:

  a1 *If* PLAN *is of the form:* $[A', X_1, ..., X_n]$, $n \geq 0$, *and* A *and* A' *are unifiable, then unify* A *and* A' *with the most general unifier* θ *and modify* PLAN *to* $\theta([X_1, ..., X_n])$.

  a2 *If* PLAN *is of the form:* $[SUBPLAN, X_1, ..., X_n]$, $n \geq 0$, *and* SUBPLAN *is a subplan, then modify* SUBPLAN *following the plan modification rules after the execution of* A.

  a3 *If* PLAN *is of the form:* $\{X_1, ..., X_n\}$, $n \geq 1$, *and* X_i *(*$1 \leq i \leq n$*) is unifiable with* A, *then unify* X_i *and* A *with the most general unifier* θ, *and remove* $\theta(X_i)$ *from* $\theta(PLAN)$.

  a4 *If* PLAN *is of the form:* $\{X_1, ..., X_n\}$, $n \geq 1$, *and* X_i *(*$1 \leq i \leq n$*) is a subplan which can consume* A, *then modify* X_i *following the plan modification rules after the execution of* A.

- *When* A *is inconsumable for* PLAN *and* DATA *is the action data of* A:

  b1 *If* DATA *is of the form:* $dataA(A, noSideEffect)$, *then* PLAN *is not modified.*

  b2 *If* DATA *is of the form:* $dataA(A, undo(seq, A^-))$, *then modify* PLAN *to* $[A^-, PLAN]$.

  b3 *If* DATA *is of the form:* $dataA(A, undo(con, A^-))$, *then modify* PLAN *to* $\{A^-, PLAN\}$.

  b4 *If* DATA *is of the form:* $dataA(A, cannotUndo)$, *then delete* PLAN.

When PLAN can consume A, Rules a1-a4 removes A from the plan because A has been executed. When PLAN cannot consume A, one of the rules b1-b4 is applied to the plan. If A does not have side effects (b1), we do not have to care. If A has side effects (b2, b3, b4), it is necessary to undo A. As shown in

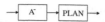

Fig. 7. Sequentially Undoing Action

Fig. 8. Concurrently Undoing Action

Figure 7, some A have to be undone before PLAN is executed (b2). As shown in Figure 8, some A can be undone anytime (b3). If A cannot be undone (b4), it is impossible to use PLAN. More intuitive meaning of undoing actions is explained in the following example:

Example 5. Four examples are shown to further understand the intuitive meaning of sequentially undoing actions, concurrently undoing actions, actions whose side effects cannot be undone, and actions that does not have side effects:

- Suppose that the agent has executed the action (scrap(pLine)) that scraps the production line of pc before executing the plan ([assemble(pc)]) for assembling pc. In order to reuse the plan, we need to rebuild the production line before assembling pc. In this case, we should modify the plan to:
    [build(pLine),[assemble(pc)]][2]
  where build(pLine) is the action that builds the production line of pc.
  We can express the action data of scrap(pLine) as follows:
    dataA(scrap(pLine),undo(seq,build(pLine)))
- Suppose that the agent has executed the action (buy(x)) that buys the part x which is not necessary for assembling pc. In order to use the plan ([assemble(pc)]) for assembling pc, we need to return the part x. However, it is not very important when the agent returns the part x. In this case, we should modify the plan to:
    {return(x),[assemble(pc)]}[3]
  where return(x) is the action that returns the part x. We can express the action data of buy(x) as follows:
    dataA(buy(x),undo(con,return(x)))
- In the previous example of buying x, if the part x cannot be returned, the plan [assemble(pc)] is discarded because the agent cannot use the plan. In this case, We can express the action data of buy(x) as follows:
    dataA(buy(x),cannotUndo)

---

[2] This plan will be simplified to [build(pLine),assemble(pc)] in the plan simplification step of the agent life cycle, which will be introduced in Section 6.
[3] This plan will be simplified to {return(x),assemble(pc)} in the plan simplification step of the agent life cycle, which will be introduced in Section 6.

– Suppose that the agent has executed the action (checkPrice(x)) that checks the price of the part x. This action execution is not related to the plan ([assemble(pc)]) for assembling pc, but this action does not have side effects. In this case, the agent does not modify the plan [assemble(pc)] because this plan is not affected by the execution of checkPrice(x). We can express the action data of checkPrice(x) as follows:

dataA(checkPrice(x),noSideEffect)

The plan modification rules after the execution of the action A can be applied to a plan only if it is possible to judge whether the plan can consume A or not. For example, if the literal lit1 is not an action, it is impossible to apply the plan modification rules to the plan [lit1,lit2]. However, when the plan is resolved further and the literal lit1 is decomposed into an action, we can apply the plan modification rules to the resolved plan. In order to apply plan modification rules later to this kind of plan, we record the history of action execution in association with the plan.

Definition 14. *In the dynamic planning framework, the* **plan plus modification rules after the execution of the action** A *are as follows where* $(PLAN, CSET, [H_1, ..., H_n])$ *(*$n \geq 0$*) is the plan plus to be modified by a plan plus modification rule.*

c1 *If* $n = 0$ *and* A *is either consumable or inconsumable for* PLAN, *then modify* PLAN *by applying a plan modification rule (defined in Definition 13) to* PLAN.

c2 *If* $n \geq 1$ *or* A *is neither consumable nor inconsumable for* PLAN, *update the history of action execution from* $[H_1, ..., H_n]$ *to* $[H_1, ..., H_n, H_{n+1}]$ *where* H_{n+1} *is the action data of* A.

Finally, we define how to modify a plan goal after an action execution.

Definition 15. *In the dynamic planning framework, the* **plan goal modification rule after the execution of the action** A *is as follows where* PGOAL *is the plan goal to be modified by the plan goal modification rule:*

d1 *Modify each plan plus that occurs in* PGOAL *by the plan plus modification rule (defined in Definition 14) after the execution of* A.

Even if an action is neither consumable nor inconsumable for a plan, after further resolving the plan, the action might become consumable or inconsumable for the resolved plan. In that case, we modify the resolved plan using the information that is recorded in the history of action execution.

Definition 16. *In the dynamic planning framework, the* **plan plus modification rule after resolution** *is as follows where* $(PLAN, CSET, [H_1, ..., H_n])$ *(*$n \geq 0$*) is the plan plus to be modified by a plan plus modification rule after resolution.*

e1 *If $n = 0$, then the plan plus is not modified.*

e2 *If $n \geq 1$, H_1 is the action data of A, and A is neither consumable nor inconsumable for PLAN, then the plan plus is not modified.*

e3 *If $n \geq 1$, H_1 is the action data of A, and A is either consumable or inconsumable for PLAN, then the plan plus is modified to:*

$\quad$ (NEWPLAN, CSET, $[H_2, ..., H_n]$)

where NEWPLAN is made from PLAN by applying a plan modification rule after the execution of A (Defined in Definition 13). If possible, further modify the plan plus in the same way.

Definition 17. *In the dynamic planning framework, the* **plan goal modification rule after resolution** *is as follows where PGOAL is the plan goal to be modified by the plan goal modification rule:*

f1 *Modify each frontier plan plus that occurs in PGOAL by the plan plus modification rule after the execution of A (defined in Definition 16).*

Example 6. Suppose that the agent has decomposed an abstract plan and derived the plan [buy(b),assemble(pc)]. Suppose that the action buy(b) has been executed before deriving [buy(b),assemble(pc)], and that the action data of buy(b) is recorded in the following plan plus in association with the plan [buy(b),assemble(pc)]:

$\quad$ ([buy(b),assemble(pc)],∅,[dataA(buy(b),undo(con,return(b)))])

Following the plan plus modification rule e3 after resolution, which is defined in Definition 16, the plan plus is modified as follows:

$\quad$ ([assemble(pc)],∅,[])

Note that the already executed action buy(b) has been removed from the plan, and that the history of action execution has become empty. In this way, the plan can be modified using the history of action execution.

Similarly, consider the following plan plus:

$\quad$ ([buy(c),assemble(pc)],∅,[dataA(buy(b),undo(con,return(b)))])

This plan plus is modified to the following plan plus:

$\quad$ ({return(b),[buy(c),assemble(pc)]},∅,[])

Note that return(b) has been inserted to the plan using the action data of buy(b), and that the action data of buy(b) has been deleted from the history of action execution.

5   Program Updates and Plan Modification

This section defines how to modify plans when the program is updated. A program update is done by clause addition or clause deletion, which affects the derivation that is based on the program: the addition (or deletion) of a clause adds (respectively, cuts) branches to (respectively, from) the search tree of the

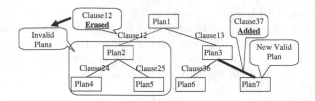

Fig. 9. Modification of a Search Tree

derivation. (See Figure 9.) When adding a clause to the program, we make new valid plans, if possible, using the added clause. When deleting a clause from the program, we delete the invalid plans that are derived using the deleted clause.

Definition 18. *In the dynamic planning framework, the* **plan goal modification rules after a program update** *are as follows where* (PLANS$^+$, SSP$^+$) *is the plan goal to be modified by a plan goal modification rule:*

– *When adding the clause* C, *which defines the literal* LIT, *to the program:*

   g1 *Suppose that*
   (PLAN$_1$, CSET$_1$, HISTORY$_1$), ..., (PLAN$_n$, CSET$_n$, HISTORY$_n$)
   are all the supplementary plan pluses in SSP$^+$ *such that* $n \geq 0$ *and the marked literal in each supplementary plan* PLAN$_k$ *($1 \leq k \leq n$) is unifiable with* LIT. *Let* RPLAN$_i$ *be the resolvent of* PLAN$_i$ *($1 \leq i \leq n$) by* C *where the marked literal in* RPLAN$_i$ *is selected for resolution. The plan goal* (PLANS$^+$, SSP$^+$) *is modified by adding each plan plus:*
   (RPLAN$_i$, {C} $\cup$ CSET$_i$, HISTORY$_i$)
   ($1 \leq i \leq n$) to PLANS$^+$.

– *When deleting the clause* C *from the program:*

   g2 *The plan goal* (PLANS$^+$, SSP$^+$) *is modified by deleting each plan plus that records* C *as a prerequisite clause.*

The clause that might be added to the program defines a dynamic literal. In Figure 9, when resolving Plan 3 by decomposing a dynamic literal L, following the derivation rule p2, we record Plan 3 as a supplementary plan. Therefore, even if Clause 37 that defines L is added to the program after the resolution, we can still make Plan 7 resolving Plan 3 by Clause 37. Note that this resolution corresponds to the addition of a new branch to the search tree.

On the other hand, if a clause is deleted from the program, the plans that were derived using the deleted clause become invalid. In Figure 9, Plan 2, Plan 4, and Plan 5 depend on Clause 12. If Clause 12 defines a dynamic literal, the derivation rule p2 records Clause 12, as a prerequisite clause, in association with Plan 2. In this case, Clause 12 is recorded also in association with Plan 4 and Plan 5 because these plans are made by resolving Plan 2. Therefore, when deleting Clause 12 from the program, we can delete Plan 2, Plan 4, and Plan 5, which are the only plans that have become invalid. Note that this plan deletion corresponds to the deletion of a branch from the search tree.

6   Agent Life Cycle

This section defines an agent life cycle that integrates planning, action execution, program updates, and plan modifications. Given the *initial goal* (a literal), the agent makes plans to obtain the initial goal, selects a plan, and starts the plan execution. After executing an action or updating the program, the agent incrementally modifies its plans. When one of the plans becomes empty and its history of action execution becomes empty, the agent finishes its life cycle as the initial goal has been satisfied.

Definition 19. *In the dynamic planning framework, given a literal* L *as the* **initial goal,** *the* **agent life cycle** *is defined as follows:*

1. *Let* {L} *be the* **initial plan** IPLAN. *Let* (IPLAN, {}, []) *be the* **initial plan plus** IPLAN$^+$. *Let* ({IPLAN$^+$}, {}) *be the* **initial plan goal** IPGOAL. *Set the* **current plan goal** *to* IPGOAL.

2. *Repeat the following procedure until one of the frontier plans in the current plan goal becomes an empty plan and its history of action execution becomes empty:*

   (a) *(Program Updates) Repeat the following procedure if necessary:*

      i. *Add (or delete) a clause[4] C that defines a dynamic literal to (respectively, from) the current program.*

      ii. *After the program update, apply a plan goal modification rule, which is defined in Definition 18, to the current plan goal.*

   (b) *(Action Execution) Repeat the following procedure if necessary:*

      i. *If possible, select a frontier plan which is mentioned in the current plan goal, select an action* A *which is consumable for the selected plan, and execute* A.

      ii. *If the execution of* A *is successful, apply a plan goal modification rule, which is defined in Definition 15, to the current plan goal.*

   (c) *(Plan Decomposition) If possible, make a derivation from the current plan goal to another plan goal* PGOAL, *and update the current plan goal to* PGOAL.

   (d) *(Plan Modification Using History of Action Execution) Apply a plan goal modification rule after resolution, which is defined in Definition 17, to the current plan goal.*

   (e) *(Simplification of Plans) Repeat the following procedure, if possible:*

      i. *Delete empty subplans[5] of a plan that occurs in the current plan goal.*

      ii. *If a subplan* SPLAN *of a plan that occurs in the current plan goal is of the form* {E} *or of the form* [E], *where* E *is a literal or a subplan of* SPLAN, *then replace* SPLAN *with* E.

---

[4] We assume that the agent has the module that decides how to update the program. This module chooses the clause to add or delete at Step 2(a)i.

[5] An empty plan is not deleted if it is not a subplan.

Example 7. In the dynamic planning framework, suppose that good(X) is a dynamic literal, that buy(X) and assemble(X) are actions, and that the program is as follows:

make(X) ⇐ [getPartsFor(X), assemble(X)].
getPartsFor(X) ⇐ {parts(X, Y), get(Y)}.
get([]).
get([H|T]) ⇐ {good(H), buy(H), get(T)}.
parts(pc, [a,b]). parts(pc, [b,c]). parts(pc, [c,a]).
good(a). good(b). good(c).

Note that good(a), good(b), and good(c) are speculatively assumed to be true. (We do not know if those parts are good until we actually buy them.) Given the initial goal make(pc), the agent makes the following three plans:

[{buy(a),buy(b)},assemble(pc)]
[{buy(b),buy(c)},assemble(pc)]
[{buy(c),buy(a)},assemble(pc)]

According to the above plans, the agent is expected to buy some parts and assemble a PC. Note that the execution order of assembling the parts is not specified.

Now, suppose that the agent selects the action buy(a) in the first plan. Suppose that dataA(buy(X),undo(con,return(X))) is the action data of buy(X). After executing buy(a), the plans are modified as follows:

[buy(b),assemble(pc)]
{return(a),[{buy(b),buy(c)},assemble(pc)]}
[buy(c),assemble(pc)]

From the first and third plan, the executed action buy(a) has been removed. In the second plan, return(a), which will undo buy(a), has been inserted. Note that the execution order of return(a) and the rest of the plan is not specified.

At this point, suppose that the agent has got the information that the part "a" is broken and erased good(a) from the program. Because the agent records good(a), as a prerequisite clause, in association with the first plan and the third plan, the agent erases these two plans. As a result, only the valid second plan remains:

{return(a),[{buy(b),buy(c)},assemble(pc)]}

Suppose that the agent has executed buy(b). The agent erases buy(b) from the above plan.

{return(a),[buy(c),assemble(pc)]}

Suppose that the agent has found that the part "a" is not broken and added good(a) again to the program. The agent makes again the two plans that were erased when good(a) was deleted from the program.

[assemble(pc)]
{return(a), [buy(c), assemble(pc)]}
{return(b), [buy(c), assemble(pc)]}

Note that the execution of buy(b) has been reflected in the two revived plans: [assemble(pc)] and {return(b),[buy(c),assemble(pc)]}. This is because the supplementary plan from which [assemble(pc)] and {return(b),[buy(c), assemble(pc)]} are derived records the history of action execution.

7 Experiments

This section evaluates our plan modification method that is described in Section 5 by means of experiments. We compare our plan modification approach with the naive approach of replanning from scratch. We implemented the planning and replanning algorithm in SWI-Prolog, Version 5.3.0. The scenario is as follows:

> The agent wants to cook mochi, which is Japanese sticky rice cake. In order to make mochi, the agent needs to pound steamed mochi rice as many times as possible. Afterwards, the agent gives taste to mochi by spreading either anko paste or kinako paste according to the preference.

First of all, we show the actions, the dynamic literals, and the program, which are used for our experiments. Using Prolog, the actions are declared as follows:

```
action(pound(mochi)).
action(spread(_)).
```

Here, two actions: pound(mochi) and spread(_) are declared. The literals that are unifiable with these actions are also recognized as actions. For example, spread(anko) and spread(kinako) are both actions because they are unifiable with spread(_). We declare the dynamic literal prefer(_) in a similar way:

```
dy(prefer(_)).
```

Because no action is executed in our experiments, we do not need the action data, which describe the side effects of actions. The program is described as follows:

```
axiom(seq,make(mochi,N),[repeatPound(N),giveTaste]).
axiom(con,repeatPound(0),[]).
axiom(con,repeatPound(N),[pound(mochi),repeatPound(M)]):-
    N>0, M is N-1.
axiom(con,giveTaste,[prefer(X),spread(X)]).
axiom(con,prefer(anko),[]).
```

In the above description of the program, the following description of clauses:

```
axiom(seq,H,[B₁,...,Bₙ])
axiom(con,H,[B₁,...,Bₙ])
```

respectively describes the following clauses:

Table 1. Time for Program Updates and Replanning

Replanning Method \ N (Times)	200	400	600	800	1000
Replanning from Scratch (msec)	97	327	688	1215	1790
Replanning by Plan Modification (msec)	0	0	3	0	3

$$H \Leftarrow [B_1, ..., B_n]$$
$$H \Leftarrow \{B_1, ..., B_n\}.$$

Because this description of the program is interpreted by the interpreter that is implemented in Prolog, we can write the condition under which a clause can be used. For example,

```
axiom(con,repeatPound(N),[pound(mochi),repeatPound(M)]):-
    N>0, M is N-1.
```

describes the clause:

$$\text{repeatPound}(N) \Leftarrow \{\text{pound}(\text{mochi}), \text{repeatPound}(M)\}$$

and this clause can be used if "N > 0" and "M is N-1" are true.

Given make(mochi,N) as the initial goal, the agent makes the plan to pound mochi (pound(mochi)) N times and spread anko (spread(anko)). After making this plan, suppose that the agent deletes prefer(anko) from the program and adds prefer(kinako) to the program. Now, the agent needs to replan because the program is updated. If replanned using our plan modification method in Section 5, the modified plan will be to pound mochi (pound(mochi)) N times and spread kinako (spread(kinako)). Because no action is executed, the agent can make the same plan even if it replans from scratch.

Based on this replanning scenario, we conducted the same experiments three times and measured the average time (msec) for updating the program and replanning. We checked both our plan modification approach and the naive re-planning approach. The result is shown in Table 1. If replanned from scratch, the time for updating the program and replanning monotonously increases as the value of N increases. On the other hand, if replanned using the plan modification method in Section 5, the time for updating the program and replanning is almost 0 msec regardless of the value of N. Our plan modification method is faster in this example because it reuses the subplan to pound mochi N times. In general, our plan modification method is more efficient than the naive replanning method as long as it can save much time by reusing already computed subplans. Because plans are modified only partially in a lot of cases, there should be many examples where our plan modification method can save much time. For example, our plan modification method is based on *Dynamic SLDNF* (*DSLDNF*) [7, 8], and DSLDNF succeeded in saving time for recomputing the route for a mobile robot. Especially, DSLDNF saved time when the route is modified partially and many parts of the route are reused.

8   Semantics

It is an important subject of research to prove the soundness of planning algorithms. In fact, soundness is proved in many planning algorithms. Because the agent continuously updates its knowledge and modifies its plans during its life cycle, it is not enough to prove the soundness of a plan when its was made with regard to the initial knowledge of the agent. What we need to prove is that the agent obtains the initial goal, when successfully finishing its life cycle, with regard to the updated knowledge of the agent. In other words, we need to prove the soundness of the agent life cycle. The purpose of this section is to define an independent semantics and prove the soundness of the agent life cycle.

In the semantics we introduce in this section, we use the following predicate of classical logic:

$$hold(\mathsf{L}, [\mathsf{A}_1, ..., \mathsf{A}_n], \mathsf{PLAN})$$

Intuitively, this predicate means that after executing the actions A_1, ..., A_n in this order, the plan for the initial goal L is PLAN. In other words, PLAN takes into account all the actions that have been already executed. After executing the actions A_1, ..., A_n and successfully finishing the agent life cycle, if we can prove

$$hold(\mathsf{L}, [\mathsf{A}_1, ..., \mathsf{A}_n], \emptyset)$$

then we can prove the soundness of the agent life cycle because the empty plan shows that the agent does not have to do anything to obtain the initial goal.

First of all, we define an independent semantics as follows. Note that the connective "←" means the implication of classical logic, which is different from "⇐" that is used to describe clauses.

Definition 20. *In the dynamic planning framework* DPF, *axiom*(DPF) *is defined as follows:*

ax1. *For any literal* L, *the following holds:*

$$\forall hold(\mathsf{L}, [], \{\mathsf{L}\})$$
$$\forall hold(\mathsf{L}, [], [\mathsf{L}])$$

ax2. *Let* L *be any literal. Let* A_1, ..., *and* A_n *be any* n $(n \geq 0)$ *actions. If* PLAN *is the plan that can consume the action* A, *the following holds:*

$$\forall (hold(\mathsf{L}, [\mathsf{A}_1, ..., \mathsf{A}_n, \mathsf{A}], \mathsf{PLAN}^{del(\mathsf{A})}) \leftarrow hold(\mathsf{L}, [\mathsf{A}_1, ..., \mathsf{A}_n], \mathsf{PLAN}))$$

where $\mathsf{PLAN}^{del(\mathsf{A})}$ *is the plan that is made from* PLAN *by removing one of the occurrences of* A *following the plan modification rules after the execution of* A, *which is defined in Definition 13.*

ax3. *Let* L *be any literal. Let* A_1, ..., *and* A_n *be any* n $(n \geq 0)$ *actions. Let* PLAN *be any plan. If* $dataA(\mathsf{A}, noSideEffect)$ *is the action data of the action* A, *then the following holds:*

$$\forall (hold(\mathsf{L}, [\mathsf{A}_1, ..., \mathsf{A}_n, \mathsf{A}], \mathsf{PLAN}) \leftarrow hold(\mathsf{L}, [\mathsf{A}_1, ..., \mathsf{A}_n], \mathsf{PLAN}))$$

ax4. *Let* L *be any literal. Let* A_1, ..., *and* A_n *be any n (n ≥ 0) actions. Let* PLAN *be any plan. If* $dataA(A, undo(seq, A^-))$ *is the action data of the action* A, *then the following holds:*

$$\forall(hold(L, [A_1, ..., A_n, A], [A^-, PLAN]) \leftarrow hold(L, [A_1, ..., A_n], PLAN))$$

ax5. *Let* L *be any literal. Let* A_1, ..., *and* A_n *be any n (n ≥ 0) actions. Let* PLAN *be any plan. If* $dataA(A, undo(con, A^-))$ *is the action data of the action* A, *then the following holds:*

$$\forall(hold(L, [A_1, ..., A_n, A], \{A^-, PLAN\}) \leftarrow hold(L, [A_1, ..., A_n], PLAN))$$

ax6. *For each clause* L ⇐ PLAN *in the program, the following holds:*

$$\forall hold(L, [], PLAN)$$

ax7. *Let* L *and* B *be any literals. Let* A_1, ..., *and* A_n *be any n (n ≥ 0) actions. Let* SPLAN *be any plan. If* PLAN *is the plan in which* B *occurs, then the following holds:*

$$\forall(hold(L, [A_1, ..., A_n], PLAN^{SPLAN/B}) \leftarrow$$
$$hold(L, [A_1, ..., A_n], PLAN) \wedge hold(B, [], SPLAN))$$

where $PLAN^{SPLAN/B}$ *is the plan that is made from* PLAN *by replacing one of the occurrences of* B *with* SPLAN.

ax8. *Let* L *be any literal. Let* A_1, ..., *and* A_n *be any n (n ≥ 0) actions. If* PLAN *be is a plan that has an empty subplan, then the following holds:*

$$\forall(hold(L, [A_1, ..., A_n], PLAN^{del(\emptyset)}) \leftarrow hold(L, [A_1, ..., A_n], PLAN))$$

where $PLAN^{del(\emptyset)}$ *is the plan that is made from* PLAN *by deleting one empty subplan.*

ax9. *Let* L *be any literal. Let* A_1, ..., *and* A_n *be any n (n ≥ 0) actions. Let* E *be any literal or any plan. If* PLAN *is the plan such that* {E} *or* [E] *occurs as a subplan, then the following holds:*

$$\forall(hold(L, [A_1, ..., A_n], PLAN^{nobracket(E)}) \leftarrow hold(L, [A_1, ..., A_n], PLAN))$$

where $PLAN^{nobracket(E)}$ *is the plan that is made from* PLAN *by replacing one occurrence of the subplan of the form* [E] *or* {E} *with* E.

In the above definition, ax1 justifies the initial plan. From ax2, ax3, ax4, and ax5, we can justify the plan modification method after the action execution of A. In ax2, PLAN can consume A. In ax3, A does not have side effects. In ax4 and ax5, A can be undone by A^-. In ax4, A^- need to be executed before PLAN. In ax5, the execution order of A^- and PLAN is not a matter of concern. The meaning of clauses is defined by ax6. Literal decomposition is justified by ax7. Plan simplification is justified by ax8 and ax9. From ax8, we can remove empty subplans. From ax9, we can remove unnecessary brackets.

In order to prove the soundness of the agent life cycle, we need the following lemma:

Lemma 1. *In the dynamic planning framework* DPF, *given the literal* L *as the initial goal, suppose that the agent has started its life cycle, created the initial plan goal, and finished the k-th cycle ($k \geq 0$) of its agent life cycle. Let* $A_1, ... A_n$ *($n \geq 0$) be all the actions that the agent has executed (in this order) since the beginning of its life cycle. Let* PLAN *be any plan mentioned in the current plan goal. If the action data of* $A_{m+1}, ..., A_n$ *($0 \leq m \leq n$) are mentioned in the history of action execution that is recorded in association with* PLAN, *then there exists a substitution* θ *such that the following holds:*

(*1) $axiom(\mathsf{DPF}) \models \forall(\theta(hold(\mathsf{L}, [A_1, ..., A_m], \mathsf{PLAN})))$

Proof. Proof by induction with regard to k. (Sketch of proof)

- *(Base case) When k is 0, the agent has just created the initial plan* {L}, *which is the only plan mentioned in the current plan goal. From ax1 of* $axiom(\mathsf{DPF})$, *the following holds:*

  $axiom(\mathsf{DPF}) \models \forall hold(\mathsf{L}, [], \{\mathsf{L}\})$.
  Since the agent has not executed actions yet, the history of action execution recorded in association with the initial plan {L} *is empty. Therefore, Lemma 1 holds.*
- *(Inductive step) Suppose that Lemma 1 holds when finishing the k-th cycle of the agent life cycle.*

  - *When deleting a clause from the program in the (k + 1)-th cycle, all the invalid plans that were derived using the deleted clause are deleted from the current plan goal. Therefore, for each plan (*PLAN*) that has not been deleted from the current plan goal, (*1) holds.*
  - *When adding a new clause to the program in the (k + 1)-th cycle, some frontier plans might be added to the current plan goal. In this case, each of the added frontier plans is the resolvent of a supplementary plan mentioned in the current plan goal. From the assumption of induction, (*1) holds where* PLAN *is the supplementary plan. Therefore, from ax6 and ax7 of axiom(*DPF*), (*1) holds where* PLAN *is the newly added plan.*
  - *When executing an action in the (k + 1)-th cycle, each plan plus in the current plan goal is modified. When modifying a plan plus after executing an action, either the plan in the plan plus is modified or the history of action execution is updated.*

    * *If the plan in a plan plus has been modified, the history of action execution recorded in the plan plus is empty. From ax2, ax3, ax4, and ax5 of axiom(*DPF*) and from the assumption of induction, (*1) holds where* PLAN *is the modified plan.*
    * *Otherwise, when the history of action execution is updated, the action data of the executed action is just added to the history of action execution. In this case, the plan, with which the updated history of action execution is recorded, is not modified. Therefore, from the assumption of induction, (*1) holds where* PLAN *is the plan with which the updated history of action execution is recorded.*

- *When resolving a frontier plan in the (k + 1)-th cycle, from ax6 and ax7 of axiom(DPF) and from the assumption of induction, (*1) holds where PLAN is the new resolvent.*
- *When modifying a plan using the action data in the history of action execution in the (k + 1)-th cycle, the action data is deleted from the history of action execution. From ax2, ax3, ax4, and ax5 of axiom(DPF) and from the assumption of induction, (*1) holds where PLAN is the modified plan.*
- *When simplifying a plan in the (k + 1)-th cycle, empty subplans and unnecessary pairs of brackets are removed. From ax8 and ax9 of axiom(DPF) and from the assumption of induction, (*1) holds where PLAN is the simplified plan.*

Consequently, after the (k+1)-th cycle of the agent life cycle, Lemma 1 holds.

From the above lemma, the following theorem holds.

Theorem 1. *(Soundness of the agent life cycle) In the dynamic planning framework DPF, given the literal L as the initial goal, suppose that the agent has successfully finished its life cycle. Let $A_1, ... A_n$ $(n \geq 0)$ be all the actions that the agent has executed (in this order) since the beginning of its life cycle. There exists a substitution θ such that the following holds:*

$$axiom(\mathsf{DPF}) \models \forall(\theta(hold(\mathsf{L}, [\mathsf{A}_1, ..., \mathsf{A}_n], \emptyset)))$$

Proof. When the agent has successfully finished its life cycle, there exists an empty frontier plan $\emptyset$ such that its history of action execution is empty. Therefore, from Lemma 1, Theorem 1 holds.

9   Towards Multi-agent Systems

Although the system we have described so far is a single agent system, our incremental plan modification technique is extremely important for making multi-agent systems. This section gives two important examples in which our dynamic planning framework is useful for the implementation of multi-agent systems.

Speculative computation in multi-agent systems is an important subject of research. In multi-agent systems, an agent does not necessarily retrieve information from another agent even if the information is vital to obtain a goal. One way to solve this problem is to speculatively make plans based on assumptions. This is an important subject of multi-agent systems, which is also recognized in [18]. For example, suppose that the user agent needs to reserve a plane ticket and a room in a hotel for the user who wants to stay either in Hawaii or in Guam. At first, the user agent asks an airline agent to reserve a plane ticket to Hawaii. However, the user agent does not have the answer immediately from the airline agent. Because the hotel in Hawaii tends to be very busy, the user

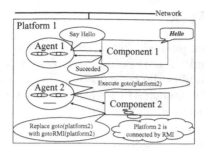

Fig. 10. The picoPlangent Platform

agent wants to reserve a room in the hotel as soon as possible. Therefore, the user agent might reserve a room in the hotel by speculatively assuming that the plane ticket is available before receiving the answer from the airline agent. This is fine as long as the user agent can get the plane ticket. However, when the user agent receives the information that the plane ticket is not available, the user agent might change the destination to Guam. In that case, the agent has to change the plan and cancel the hotel reservation in Hawaii. Note that this scenario includes knowledge updates and action canceling, which can be handled in our dynamic planning framework.

Joint planning in mobile agent systems is another important subject of research. A mobile agent is a kind of software which moves from one computer to another computer through the network. As mentioned in the introduction, we implemented our previous dynamic planning framework on top of our mobile agent system, called picoPlangent [10]. As shown in Figure 10, the picoPlangent mobile agent works on a platform on which some *components* are installed. The mobile agent uses a component on the platform when executing an action. The components on the platform can be regarded as *local agents* that do not move from the platform. Local agents sometimes modify the plans of mobile agents by decomposing a literal into more primitive literals or adding additional goals to the plan. As surveyed in [4], HTN planning is becoming popular in multi-agent systems because an agent can make abstract plans and later another agent can decompose the abstract plans into more concrete plans. This is why HTN planning is important in joint planning in multi-agent systems. Incremental plan modification approach of our planner is very important when plans are partially decomposed or refined by another agent. If replanned from scratch, the agent will forget all those refined plans. In our mobile agent system, the local agent can update the knowledge (program) of mobile agents by adding the "assert" action or the "retract" action to the plans of mobile agents. After executing these knowledge updating actions, the mobile agents modify the plans using our plan modification techniques. This feature is very important because in many cases, a mobile agent does not know the up-to-date information that is available on a remote computer unless the mobile agent actually moves to the computer. Therefore, the mobile agent should be able to modify the plans after moving to a computer and getting the new information from the local agents.

10   Related Work

Our plan modification method after program updates is based on the proof procedure called Dynamic SLDNF(DSLDNF) [7, 8], which incrementally updates
the program and modifies the computation. There is a proof procedure [18] of
abductive logic programming (*ALP*) which is closely related to DSLDNF. This
dynamic ALP procedure is different from the standard ALP procedure [11] because it can handle the abducibles whose truth value dynamically changes. The
similarity of our planner (or DSLDNF) and the dynamic ALP procedure can be
observed as follows:

- While our planner records clauses in association with a plan, the dynamic
  ALP procedure records abducibles in association with a process.
- On the one hand, our planner deletes a plan when a clause recorded in
  association with the plan becomes invalid. On the other hand, the dynamic
  ALP procedure suspends a process when an abducible recorded in association
  with the process becomes invalid.
- On the one hand, our planner makes a new plan from a supplementary plan
  when a new clause becomes valid and the supplementary plan can be resolved
  to the new plan using the new valid clause. On the other hand, the dynamic
  ALP procedure makes the status of a suspended process to active when all
  the abducibles recorded in association with the suspended process become
  true.

From this observation, we can understand that our plan corresponds to the
process of the dynamic ALP procedure, that our clause corresponds to the abducible of the dynamic ALP procedure, that our supplementary plan corresponds
to the suspended process of the dynamic ALP procedure. It is pointed out, in
[18], that DSLDNF is very much related to the dynamic ALP procedure. The
main differences between our planner and the dynamic ALP procedure is as
follows:

- On the one hand, our planner can update the program and incrementally
  modify plans, even after executing actions, by canceling some actions. On the
  other hand, the dynamic ALP procedure cannot modify plans by canceling
  actions after executing some actions.
- On the one hand, our planner updates the validity of clauses. On the other
  hand, the dynamic ALP procedure updates the truth value of abducibles,
  which are literals. Note that clauses can express facts that are literals. In
  this sense, our planner is more general than the dynamic ALP procedure.

Another proof procedure for multi-agent systems, called the *iff proof procedure* [12], modifies the computation after observation. The iff proof procedure is
also based on ALP. When observing a fact, the iff procedure checks the integrity
constrains, and tries to restore the consistency of computation by assuming extra abducibles, if necessary. Once a fact has been observed, however, this proof
procedure cannot delete observed facts from the knowledge base. It keeps adding
abducibles to the knowledge base. (This is not a defect for a system which never

deletes data.) Since our planner does not use integrity constraints, observed facts never affect the validity of derived plans. However, if negation as failure is used, we will have the same problem: the added clauses or observed facts might affect the validity of derived plans. This problem has been solved in the full version [8] of DSLDNF.

In *MINERVA* [13], the agent can assimilate clauses of generalized logic programming, and a special semantics is used to interpret the possibly contradictory programs. We do not have this problem because we do not use generalized logic programs that use explicit negation. We are working on the topic of how to modify computation after program updates, while the challenge of MINERVA is about how to interpret mutually contradictory programs.

Transaction logic programming (*TLP*) [2] is related to our plan modification method after action execution in Section 4. Like Prolog, the procedure in [2] executes literals in the body of a clause from left to right. When backtracking, it undoes actions. There is also a concurrent version [1] of TLP. The action cancellation of our procedure is different from that of TLP in the following points:

- On the one hand, our planner incrementally modifies plans without back-tracking by adding undoing actions to some (not all) of the plans. On the other hand, TLP undoes actions when backtracking.
- One the one hand, in order to avoid unnecessary action cancellation, our planner uses two kinds of undoing actions: sequentially undoing actions and concurrently undoing actions. On the other hand, TLP undoes actions simply in the backtracking order.

The importance of canceling actions is recognized also in the area of web services. For example, according to the specification of *BPEL4WS* [3], which can express the flow of web services, if an activity in a scope is not executed as expected, the activities already executed in the scope will be undone. For example, suppose that the activities A_1, A_2, A_3 in a scope have been executed in this order. When undoing activities in that scope, it first undoes A_3, then undoes A_2, and finally undoes A_1. This is similar to the backtracking of TLP.

The standard replanning method of partial-order planning is explained in such a standard AI textbook as [17]. In the standard partial-order planning algorithm, the plan is made by connecting "preconditions" and "postconditions (effects)" of actions, which is used also for the purpose of replanning. Our planner is different and makes plans by decomposing literals, which is closer to HTN planners such as SHOP [14]. Although SHOP deals with total-order plans only, SHOP2 [15], a new version of SHOP, can handle partial-order plans. Note that we do not use the preconditions and postconditions of actions at all. Although SHOP and SHOP2 use the preconditions and postconditions, they are used for the purpose of task decompostion, which is different from the standard partial-order planning. As mentioned in [5], replanning in dynamic environments is the important future work for SHOP.

11   Conclusion and Future Work

We have shown how to integrate task decomposition of HTN planning, action execution, program updates, and plan modifications. When updating the program or executing an action, our procedure incrementally modifies the plans. Although our procedure does not use the knowledge describing the effects of actions on the state of the world expressed by fluents, it takes into account the side effects of actions when modifying plans after action execution. We have also defined an independent semantics and showed the soundness of the agent life cycle.

Compared with our previous work, we have improved our planning procedure using (restricted) partial-order plans, by which we can further avoid unnecessary cancellation of already executed actions when switching from one plan to another. In addition, we introduced a new type of undoing actions that can be executed anytime, which also contributes to the avoidance of action cancellation.

As mentioned in the previous section, the plan modification method after a program update is based on the proof procedure of DSLDNF. When updating the program, invalid plans are removed and new valid plans are added. In [7, 8], using the robot navigation example, it was shown that DSLDNF generally replans faster than SLDNF. This is because DSLDNF reuses already derived plans while SLDNF has to recompute from scratch. We confirmed the same result by means of experiments in Section 7, using a different scenario.

Finally, we showed two examples where our planning framework plays very important roles in multi-agent systems. From those examples, we can understand that our incremental plan modification is very effective in speculative computation in multi-agent systems and joint planning between mobile agents and local agents in mobile agent systems.

An important subject for future work is the research into the selection strategy of actions and plans. Another subject for future work is handling the interference between subplans. Finally, the most important subject for future work for us is application development although we have tested our new planning algorithm and confirmed it works.

References

1. A. J. Bonner and M. Kifer. Transaction Logic Programming. International Conference on Logic Programming, pp. 257-279, 1993.
2. A. J. Bonner. Workflow, Transactions and Datalog. ACM Symposium on Principles of Database Systems, pp. 294-305, 1999.
3. BPEL4WS v1.1 Specification, 2003.
4. M. E. desJardins, E. H. Durfee, C. L. Ortiz, Jr., and M. J. Wolverton. A Survey of Research in Distributed, Continual Planning. AI Magazine 20(4), pp. 13-22, 1999.
5. J. Dix, H. Munoz-Avila, and D. Nau. IMPACTing SHOP: Putting an AI Planner into a Multi-Agent Environment. Annals of Mathematics and AI 4(37), pp. 381-407, 2003.

6. N. Fukuta, T. Ito, and T. Shintani. MiLog: A Mobile Agent Framework for Implementing Intelligent Information Agents with Logic Programming. Pacific Rim International Workshop on Intelligent Information Agents, 2000.
7. H. Hayashi. Replanning in Robotics by Dynamic SLDNF. IJCAI Workshop "Scheduling and Planning Meet Real-Time Monitoring in a Dynamic and Uncertain World", 1999.
8. H. Hayashi. Computing with Changing Logic Programs. PhD Thesis, Imperial College of Science, Technology and Medicine, University of London, 2001.
9. H. Hayashi, K. Cho, A. Ohsuga. Speculative Computation and Action Execution in Multi-Agent Systems. ICLP Workshop on Computational Logic and Multi-Agent Systems (CLIMA), Electronic Notes in Theoretical Computer Science 70(5), http://www.elsevier.nl/locate/entcs/volume70.html, 2002.
10. H. Hayashi, K. Cho, and A. Ohsuga. Mobile Agents and Logic Programming. IEEE International Conference on Mobile Agents, pp. 32-46, 2002.
11. A. C. Kakas, R. A. Kowalski, and F. Toni. The Role of Abduction in Logic Programming. Handbook of Logic in Artificial Intelligence and Logic Programming 5, pp. 235-324, Oxford University Press, 1998.
12. R. A. Kowalski and F. Sadri. From Logic Programming to Multi-Agent Systems. Annals of Mathematics and Artificial Intelligence 25(3-4), pp. 391-419, 1999.
13. J. A. Leite, J. J. Alferes, and L. M. Pereira. MINERVA-A Dynamic Logic Programming Agent Architecture. Intelligent Agents VIII, LNAI2333, pp. 141-157, Springer-Verlag, 2002.
14. D. Nau, Y. Cao, A. Lotem, and H. Mũnoz-Avila. SHOP: Simple Hierarchical Ordered Planner. International Joint Conference on Artificial Intelligence, pp. 968-975, 1999.
15. D. Nau, H. Mũnoz-Avila, Y. Cao, A. Lotem, and S. Mitchell. Total-Order Planning with Partially Ordered Subtasks. International Joint Conference on Artificial Intelligence, pp. 425-430, 2001.
16. A. Ohsuga, Y. Nagai, Y. Irie, M. Hattori, and S. Honiden. PLANGENT: An Approach to Making Mobile Agents Intelligent. IEEE Internet Computing 1(4), pp. 50-57, 1997.
17. S. Russell and P. Norvig. Artificial Intelligence: A Modern Approach. Prentice-Hall, 1995.
18. K. Satoh, K. Inoue, K. Iwanuma, and C. Sakama. Speculative Computation under Incomplete Communication Environments. International Conference on Multi-Agent Systems, pp. 263-270, 2000.
19. P. Tarau. Jinni: Intelligent Mobile Agent Programming at the Intersection of Java and Prolog. International Conference and Exhibition on the Practical Application of Intelligent Agents and Multi-Agent Technology, 1999.

Revising Knowledge in Multi-agent Systems Using Revision Programming with Preferences

Inna Pivkina, Enrico Pontelli, and Tran Cao Son

Department of Computer Science,
New Mexico State University
{ipivkina, epontell, tson}@cs.nmsu.edu

Abstract. In this paper we extend the *Revision Programming* framework—a logic-based framework to express and maintain constraints on knowledge bases—with different forms of *preferences*. Preferences allow users to introduce a bias in the way agents update their knowledge to meet a given set of constraints. In particular, they provide a way to select one between alternative feasible revisions and they allow for the generation of revisions in presence of conflicting constraints, by relaxing the set of satisfied constraints (*soft constraints*). A methodology for computing preferred revisions using answer set programming is presented.

1 Introduction

Multi-Agents Systems (MAS) require coordination mechanisms to facilitate dynamic collaboration of the intelligent components, with the goal of meeting local and/or global objectives. In the case of MAS, the coordination structure should provide communication protocols to link agents having inter-related objectives and it should facilitate mediation and integration of exchanged knowledge [7]. Centralized coordination architectures (e.g., mediator-based architectures) as well as fully distributed architectures (e.g., distributed knowledge networks) face the problem of non-monotonically updating agent's theories to incorporate knowledge derived from different agents. The problem is compounded by the fact that incoming knowledge could be contradictory—either conflicting with the local knowledge or with other incoming items—incomplete, or unreliable. Recently a number of formalisms have been proposed [16, 4, 2, 20, 8] to support dynamic updates of (propositional) logic programming theories; they provide convenient frameworks for describing knowledge base updates as well as constraints to ensure user-defined principles of consistency. These types of formalisms have been proved effective in the context of MAS (e.g., [12]).

One of such formalisms for knowledge base updates is *Revision Programming*. Revision programming is a formalism to describe and enforce constraints on belief sets, databases, and more generally, on arbitrary knowledge bases. The revision programming formalism was introduced in [15, 16]. In this framework, the *initial database* represents the initial state of a belief set or a knowledge base. A *revision program* is a collection of *revision rules* used to describe constraints on the content of the database. Revision rules could be quite complex and are usually in the form of conditions. For instance, a typical revision rule may express a condition that, if certain elements are present in the database

J. Dix and J. Leite (Eds.): CLIMA IV, LNAI 3259, pp. 134–158, 2004.

and some other elements are absent, then another given element must be absent from (or present in) the database. Revision rules offer a natural way of encoding policies for the integration of agent-generated knowledge (e.g., in a mediator-based architecture) or for the management of inter-agent exchanges.

In addition to being a declarative specification of a constraint on a knowledge base, a revision rule also has a computational interpretation—indicating a way to satisfy the constraint. Justified revisions semantics assigns to any knowledge base a (possibly empty) family of *revisions*. Each revision represents an updated version of the original knowledge base, that satisfies all the constraints provided by the revision program. Revisions are obtained by performing additions and deletions of elements from the original knowledge base, according to the content of the revision rules. Each revision might be chosen as an update of the original knowledge base w.r.t. the revision program.

The mechanisms used by revision programming to handle updates of a knowledge base or belief set may lead to indeterminate situations. The constraints imposed on the knowledge base are interpreted as *hard constraints*, that have to be met at all costs; nevertheless this is rather unnatural in domains where overlapping and conflicting consistency constraints may be present (e.g., legal reasoning [18], suppliers and broker agents in a supply chain [13])—leading to the generation of *no* acceptable revisions. Similarly, situations with under-specified constraints or incomplete knowledge may lead to revision programs that provide *multiple* alternative revisions for the same initial knowledge base. While such situations might be acceptable, there are many cases where a single revision is desired—e.g., agents desire to maintain a unique view of a knowledge base.

Preferences provide a natural way to address these issues; preferences allow the revision programmer to introduce a bias, and focus the generation of revisions towards more desirable directions. Preferences between revisions rules and/or preferences between the components of the revisions can be employed to select the way revisions are computed, ruling out undesirable alternatives and defeating conflicting constraints. The use of preference structures has been gaining relevance in the MAS community as key mechanism in negotiation models for MAS coordination architectures [9, 11].

In this work we propose extensions of revision programming that provide general mechanisms to express different classes of preferences—justified by the needs of knowledge integration in MAS. The basic underlying mechanism common to the extensions presented in this work is the idea of allowing classes of revision rules to be treated as *soft revision rules*. A revision might be allowed even if it does not satisfy all the soft revision rules but only selected subsets of them; user preferences express criteria to select the desired subsets of soft revision rules.

Our first approach (Section 3) is based on the use of *revision programs with preferences*, where dynamic partial orders are established between the revision rules. It provides a natural mechanism to select preferred ways of computing revisions, and to prune revisions that are not deemed interesting. This approach is analogous to the ordered logic program (a.k.a. prioritized logic program) approach explored in the context of logic programming (e.g., [6, 5]). In a labeled revision program, the revision program and the initial knowledge base are enriched by a *control program*, which expresses preferences on rules. The control program may include revision literals as well as conditions on the initial knowledge base. Given an initial knowledge base, the control program and the revision program are translated into a revision program where regular justified revisions semantics is used. This approach provides preference capabilities similar to those supported by the MINERVA agent architecture [12].

The second approach (Section 4) generalizes revision programs through the introduction of *weights* (or *costs*) associated to the components of a revision program (revision rules and/or database atoms). The weights are aimed at providing general criteria for the selection of subsets of the soft revision rules to be considered in the computation of the revisions of the initial database. Different policies in assigning weights are considered, allowing for the encoding of very powerful preference criteria (e.g., revisions that differ from the initial database in the least number of atoms). This level of preference management addresses many of the preference requirements described in the MAS literature (e.g., [11]).

For each of the proposed approaches to the management of preferences, we provide an effective implementation schema based on translation to answer set programming—specifically to the smodels [17] language. This leads to effective ways to compute *preferred* revisions for any initial database w.r.t. a revision program with preferences.

The main contribution of this work is the identification of forms of preferences that are specifically relevant to the revision programming paradigm and justified by the needs of knowledge maintenance and integration in MAS, and the investigation of the semantics and implementation issues deriving from their introduction.

2 Preliminaries: Revision Programming

In this section we present the formal definition of revision programs with justified revision semantics and some of their properties [16, 15, 14].

Elements of some finite universe U are called *atoms*. Subsets of U are called *databases*. Expressions of the form $\textbf{in}(a)$ or $\textbf{out}(a)$, where a is an atom, are called *revision literals*. For a revision literal $\textbf{in}(a)$, its *dual* is the revision literal $\textbf{out}(a)$. Similarly, the *dual* of $\textbf{out}(a)$ is $\textbf{in}(a)$. The dual of a revision literal α is denoted by α^D. A set of revision literals L is *coherent* if it does not contain a pair of dual literals. For any set of atoms $B \subseteq U$, we denote $B^c = \{\textbf{in}(a) : a \in B\} \cup \{\textbf{out}(a) : a \notin B\}$. A *revision rule* is an expression of one of the following two types:

$$\textbf{in}(a) \leftarrow \textbf{in}(a_1), \ldots, \textbf{in}(a_m), \textbf{out}(b_1), \ldots, \textbf{out}(b_n) \qquad \text{or} \qquad (1)$$

$$\textbf{out}(a) \leftarrow \textbf{in}(a_1), \ldots, \textbf{in}(a_m), \textbf{out}(b_1), \ldots, \textbf{out}(b_n), \qquad (2)$$

where a, a_i and b_i are atoms. A *revision program* is a collection of revision rules. Revision rules have a declarative interpretation as constraints on databases. For instance, rule (1) imposes the following condition: a is *in* the database, or at least one a_i, $1 \le i \le m$, is *not* in the database, or at least one b_j, $1 \le j \le n$, is *in* the database.

Revision rules also have a computational (imperative) interpretation that expresses a way to enforce a constraint. Assume that all data items a_i, $1 \le i \le m$, belong to the current database, say I, and none of the data items b_j, $1 \le j \le n$, belongs to I. Then, to enforce the constraint (1), the item a must be added to the database (removed from it, in the case of the constraint (2)), rather than removing (adding) some item a_i (b_j).

Given a revision rule r, by $head(r)$ and $body(r)$ we denote the literal on the left hand side and the set of literals on the right hand side of the $\leftarrow$, respectively.

A set of atoms $B \subseteq U$ is a *model* of (or *satisfies*) a revision literal **in**(a) (resp., **out**(a)), if $a \in B$ (resp., $a \notin B$). A set of atoms B is a *model* of (or *satisfies*) a revision rule r if either B is not a model of at least one revision literal from the body of r, or B is a model of $head(r)$. A set of atoms B is a *model* of a revision program P if B is a model of every rule in P. Let P be a revision program. The *necessary change* of P, $NC(P)$, is the least model of P, when treated as a Horn program built of independent propositional atoms of the form **in**(a) and **out**(b).

The collection of all revision literals describing the elements that do not change their status in the transition from a database I to a database R is called the *inertia set* for I and R, and is defined as follows:

$$Inertia(I, R) = \{\textbf{in}(a): a \in I \cap R\} \cup \{\textbf{out}(a): a \notin I \cup R\}.$$

By the *reduct* of P with respect to a pair of databases (I, R), denoted by $P_{I,R}$, we mean the revision program obtained from P by eliminating from the body of each rule in P all literals in $Inertia(I, R)$. The necessary change of the program $P_{I,R}$ provides a justification for some insertions and deletions. These are exactly the changes that are *a posteriori* justified by P in the context of the initial database I and a putative revised database R.

Given a database I and a coherent set of revision literals L, we define

$$I \oplus L = (I \setminus \{a \in U: \textbf{out}(a) \in L\}) \cup \{a \in U: \textbf{in}(a) \in L\}.$$

Definition 1 ([16]). *A database R is a P-justified revision of database I if the necessary change of $P_{I,R}$ is coherent and if $R = I \oplus NC(P_{I,R})$.*

Basic properties of justified revisions include the following [16]:

1. If a database R is a P-justified revision of I, then R is a model of P.
2. If a database B satisfies a revision program P then B is a unique P-justified revision of itself.
3. If R is a P-justified revision of I, then $R \div I$ is minimal in the family $\{B \div I : B$ is a model of $P\}$—where $R \div I$ denotes the symmetric difference of R and I. In other words, justified revisions of a database differ minimally from the database.

Another important property of revision programs is that certain transformations (*shifts*) preserve justified revisions [14]. For each set $W \subseteq U$, a W-*transformation* is defined as follows ([14]). If α is a literal of the form **in**(a) or **out**(a), then

$$T_W(\alpha) = \begin{cases} \alpha^D, & \text{when } a \in W \\ \alpha, & \text{when } a \notin W. \end{cases}$$

Given a set L of literals, $T_W(L) = \{T_W(\alpha): \alpha \in L\}$. For example, if $W = \{a, b\}$, then $T_W(\{\textbf{in}(a), \textbf{out}(b), \textbf{in}(c)\}) = \{\textbf{out}(a), \textbf{in}(b), \textbf{in}(c)\}$. Given a set A of atoms, $T_W(A) = \{a: \textbf{in}(a) \in T_W(A^c)\}$. In particular, for any database I, $T_I(I) = \emptyset$. Given a revision program P, $T_W(P)$ is obtained from P by applying T_W to every literal in

P. The Shifting Theorem [14] states that for any databases I and J, database R is a P-justified revision of I if and only if $T_{I \div J}(R)$ is a $T_{I \div J}(P)$-justified revision of J. The Shifting Theorem provides a practical way [14] to compute justified revisions using answer set programming engines (e.g., smodels [17]). It can be done by executing the following steps.

1. Given a revision program P and an initial database I, we can apply the transformation T_I to obtain the revision program $T_I(P)$ and the empty initial database.
2. $T_I(P)$ can be converted into a logic program with constraints by replacing revision rules of the type (1) by

$$a \leftarrow a_1, \ldots, a_m, not \ b_1, \ldots, not \ b_n \qquad (3)$$

and replacing revision rules of the type (2) by constraints

$$\leftarrow a, a_1, \ldots, a_m, not \ b_1, \ldots, not \ b_n. \qquad (4)$$

We denote the logic program with constraints obtained from a revision program Q via the above conversion by $lp(Q)$.
3. Given $lp(T_I(P))$ we can compute its answer sets.
4. Finally, the transformation T_I can be applied to the answer sets to obtain the P-justified revisions of I.

3 Revision Programs with Preferences

In this section, we introduce *revision programs with preferences*, that can be used to deal with preferences between rules of a revision program. We begin with an example to motivate the introduction of preferences between revision rules. We then present the syntax and semantics and discuss some properties of revision programs with preferences.

3.1 Motivational Example

Assume that we have a number of agents $a_1, a_2, \ldots, a_n$. The environment is encoded through a set of parameters $p_1, p_2, \ldots, p_k$. The agents perceive parameters of the environment, and provide perceived data (observations) to a controller. The observations are represented using atoms of the form: $observ(Par, Value, Agent)$, where Par is the name of the observed parameter, $Value$ is the value for the parameter, and $Agent$ is the name of the agent providing the observation.

The controller combines the data received from agents to update its view of the world, which includes exactly one value for each parameter. The views of the world are described by atoms: $world(Par, Value, Agent)$, where $Value$ is the current value for the parameter Par, and $Agent$ is the name of the agent that provided the last accepted value for the parameter. The initial database contains a view of the world before the new observations arrive. A revision program, denoted by P, is used to update the view of the world, and is composed of rules of the type:

$$\textbf{in}(observ(Par, Value, Agent)) \leftarrow$$

which describe all new observations; and rules of the following two types:

$$\textbf{in}(world(Par, Value, Agent)) \leftarrow \textbf{in}(observ(Par, Value, Agent)) \tag{a}$$

$$\textbf{out}(world(Par, Value, Agent)) \leftarrow \textbf{in}(world(Par, Value1, Agent1)),$$
$$(where\ Agent \neq Agent1\ or\ Value \neq Value1). \tag{b}$$

Rules of type (a) allow to generate a new value for a parameter of a world view from a new observation. Rules of type (b) are used to enforce the fact that only one observation per parameter can be used to update the view.

It is easy to see that if the value of each parameter is perceived by *exactly one* agent and the initial world view of the controller is coherent, then each P-justified revision reflects the controller's world view that integrates its agent observations whenever they arrive. However, P does not allow any justified revisions when there are two agents which perceive different data for the same parameter at the same time. We illustrate this problem in the following scenario. Let us assume we have two agents a_1 and a_2, both provide observations for the parameter named *temperature* denoting the temperature in the room. Initially, the controller knows that $world(temperature, 76, s_2)$. At a later time, it receives two new observations

$$\textbf{in}(observ(temperature, 74, a_1)) \leftarrow$$

$$\textbf{in}(observ(temperature, 72, a_2)) \leftarrow$$

There is no P-justified revision for this set of observations as the necessary change with respect to it is incoherent, it includes $\textbf{in}(world(temperature, 74, a_1))$ (because of (a) and the first observation) and $\textbf{out}(world(temperature, 74, a_1))$ (because of (a), (b), and the second observation).

The above situation can be resolved by placing a preference between the values provided by the agents. For example, if we know that agent a_2 has a better temperature sensor than agent a_1, then we should tell the controller that observations of a_2 are preferred to those of a_1. This can be described by adding preferences of the form: $prefer(r2, r1)$, where $r1$ and $r2$ are names of rules of type (a) containing a_1 and a_2, respectively. With the above preference, the controller should be able to derive a justified revision which would contain $world(temperature, 72, a_2)$. If the agent a_2 has a broken temperature sensor and does not provide temperature observations, the value of *temperature* will be determined by a_1 and the world view will be updated correctly by P.

The above preference represents a fixed order of rule's application in creating revisions. Sometimes, preferences might be dynamic. As an example, we may prefer the controller to keep using temperature observations from the same agent if available. This can be described by preferences of the form:

$prefer(r1, r2) \leftarrow world(temperature, Value, a_1) \in I,\ \textbf{in}(observ(temperature, NewValue, a_1));$
$prefer(r2, r1) \leftarrow world(temperature, Value, a_2) \in I,\ \textbf{in}(observ(temperature, NewValue, a_2));$

where r1 and r2 are names of rules of type (a) containing a_1 and a_2 respectively, and I is an initial database (a view of the world before the new observations arrive).

3.2   Syntax and Semantics

A *labeled revision program* is a pair $(P, \mathcal{L})$ where P is a revision program and $\mathcal{L}$ is a function which assigns to each revision rule in P a unique name (label). The label of a rule $r \in P$ is denoted $\mathcal{L}(r)$. The rule with a label l is denoted $r(l)$. We will use $head(l)$, $body(l)$ to denote $head(r(l))$ and $body(r(l))$ respectively. The set of labels of all revision rules from P is denoted $\mathcal{L}(P)$. That is, $\mathcal{L}(P) = \{\mathcal{L}(r) : r \in P\}$. For simplicity, for each rule $\alpha_0 \leftarrow \alpha_1, \ldots, \alpha_n$ of P, we will write:

$$l : \alpha_0 \leftarrow \alpha_1, \ldots, \alpha_n$$

to indicate that l is the value assigned to the rule by the function $\mathcal{L}$.

A *preference* on rules in $(P, \mathcal{L})$ is an expression of the following form

$$prefer(l_1, l_2) \leftarrow initially(\alpha_1, \ldots, \alpha_k), \alpha_{k+1}, \ldots, \alpha_n, \tag{5}$$

where l_1, l_2 are labels of rules in P, $\alpha_1 \ldots, \alpha_n$ are revision literals, $k \geq 0, n \geq k$.

Informally, the preference (5) mean that if revision literals $\alpha_1 \ldots, \alpha_k$ are satisfied by the initial database and literals $\alpha_{k+1}, \ldots, \alpha_n$ are satisfied by a revision, then we prefer to use rule $r(l_1)$ over rule $r(l_2)$. More precisely, if the body of rule $r(l_1)$ is satisfied then rule $r(l_2)$ is defeated and ignored. If $body(l_1)$ is not satisfied then rule $r(l_2)$ is used.

A *revision program with preferences* is a triple $(P, \mathcal{L}, S)$, where $(P, \mathcal{L})$ is a labeled revision program and S is a set of preferences on rules in $(P, \mathcal{L})$. We refer to S as the control program since it plays an important role on what rules can be used in constructing the revisions.

A revision program with preferences $(P, \mathcal{L}, S)$ can be translated into an ordinary revision program as follows. Let $U^{\mathcal{L}(P)}$ be the universe obtained from U by adding new atoms of the form $ok(l)$, $defeated(l)$, $prefer(l_1, l_2)$ for all $l, l_1, l_2 \in \mathcal{L}(P)$. Given an initial database I, we define a new revision program $P^{S,I}$ over $U^{\mathcal{L}(P)}$ as the revision program consisting of the following revision rules:

- for each $l \in \mathcal{L}(P)$, the revision program $P^{S,I}$ contains the two rules

$$head(l) \leftarrow body(l), \mathbf{in}(ok(l)) \tag{6}$$

$$\mathbf{in}(ok(l)) \leftarrow \mathbf{out}(defeated(l)) \tag{7}$$

- for each preference $prefer(l_1, l_2) \leftarrow initially(\alpha_1, \ldots, \alpha_k), \alpha_{k+1}, \ldots, \alpha_n$ in S such that $\alpha_1 \ldots, \alpha_k$ are satisfied by I, $P^{S,I}$ contains the rules

$$\mathbf{in}(prefer(l_1, l_2)) \leftarrow \alpha_{k+1}, \ldots, \alpha_n \tag{8}$$

$$\mathbf{in}(defeated(l_2)) \leftarrow body(l_1), \mathbf{in}(prefer(l_1, l_2)) \tag{9}$$

Following the compilation approach in dealing with preferences, we define the notion of $(P, \mathcal{L}, S)$-justified revisions of an initial database I as follows.

Definition 2. *A database R is a $(P, \mathcal{L}, S)$-justified revision of I if there exists $R' \subseteq U^{\mathcal{L}(P)}$ such that R' is a $P^{S,I}$-justified revision of I, and $R = R' \cap U$.*

The next example illustrates the definition of justified revisions with respect to revision programs with preferences.

Example 1. Let P be the program containing the rules

$$r_1 : \textbf{in}(world(temperature, 76, a_1)) \leftarrow \textbf{in}(observ(temperature, 76, a_1)).$$
$$r_2 : \textbf{in}(world(temperature, 77, a_2)) \leftarrow \textbf{in}(observ(temperature, 77, a_2)).$$

and the set S of preferences consists of a single preference $prefer(r_1, r_2)$. Let $I_1 = \{observ(temperature, 76, a_1), observ(temperature, 77, a_2)\}$ be the initial database. The revision program P^{S,I_1} is the following:

$$\textbf{in}(world(temperature, 76, a_1)) \leftarrow \textbf{in}(observ(temperature, 76, a_1)), \textbf{in}(ok(r_1))$$
$$\textbf{in}(world(temperature, 77, a_2)) \leftarrow \textbf{in}(observ(temperature, 77, a_2)), \textbf{in}(ok(r_2))$$
$$\textbf{in}(ok(r_1)) \leftarrow \textbf{out}(defeated(r_1))$$
$$\textbf{in}(ok(r_2)) \leftarrow \textbf{out}(defeated(r_2))$$
$$\textbf{in}(prefer(r_1, r_2)) \leftarrow$$
$$\textbf{in}(defeated(r_2)) \leftarrow \textbf{in}(observ(temperature, 76, a_1)),$$
$$\textbf{in}(prefer(r_1, r_2))$$

Since I_1 has only one P^{S,I_1}-justified revision,

$$R_1 = \left\{ \begin{array}{c} observ(temperature, 76, a_1), observ(temperature, 77, a_2), \\ world(temperature, 76, a_1), prefer(r_1, r_2), ok(r_1), defeated(r_2) \end{array} \right\},$$

then I_1 has only one $(P, \mathcal{L}, S)$-justified revision, $\{world(temperature, 76, a_1)\}$[1].
Now, consider the case where the initial database is

$$I_2 = \{observ(temperature, 77, a_2)\}.$$

The revision program $P^{S,I_2} = P^{S,I_1}$. Since I_2 has only one P^{S,I_2}-justified revision,

$$R_2 = \left\{ \begin{array}{c} world(temperature, 77, a_2), observ(temperature, 77, a_2), \\ prefer(r_1, r_2), ok(r_1), ok(r_2) \end{array} \right\},$$

we can conclude that I_2 has only one $(P, \mathcal{L}, S)$-justified revision,

$$\{world(temperature, 77, a_2)\}[1].$$

Notice the difference in the two cases: in the first case, rule r_2 is defeated and cannot be used in generating the justified revision. In the second case both rules can be used.

---

[1] We omit the observations from the revised database.

3.3 Properties

Justified revision semantics for revision programs with preferences extends justified revision semantics for ordinary revision programs. More precisely:

Theorem 1. *A database R is a $(P, \mathcal{L}, \emptyset)$-justified revision of I if and only if R is a P-justified revision of I.*

Proof. ($\Rightarrow$) Let R be a $(P, \mathcal{L}, \emptyset)$-justified revision of I. By definition, there exists $R' \subseteq U^{\mathcal{L}(P)}$ such that R' is a $P^{\emptyset,I}$-justified revision of I, and $R = R' \cap U$. By definition of a justified revision, $NC((P^{\emptyset,I})_{I,R'})$ is coherent, and $R' = I \oplus NC((P^{\emptyset,I})_{I,R'})$. Revision program $P^{\emptyset,I}$ consists of the rules of the form (6) and (7) only. Therefore, R' does not contain atoms of the form $defeated(l)$ ($l \in \mathcal{L}(P)$). Thus, $(P^{\emptyset,I})_{I,R'}$ consists of rules

$$head(l') \leftarrow body(l'), \mathbf{in}(ok(l')) \qquad \qquad \text{(for all } l' \in P_{I,R})$$
$$\mathbf{in}(ok(l)) \leftarrow \qquad \qquad \text{(for all } l \in \mathcal{L}(P))$$

Hence, $NC((P^{\emptyset,I})_{I,R'}) = NC(P_{I,R}) \cup \{ok(l) : l \in \mathcal{L}(P)\}$. Since $NC((P^{\emptyset,I})_{I,R'})$ is coherent, $NC(P_{I,R})$ is coherent, too. If we take intersection with U of left- and right-hand sides of equation $R' = I \oplus NC((P^{\emptyset,I})_{I,R'})$, we get $R = I \oplus NC(P_{I,R})$. By definition, R is a P-justified revision of I.

($\Leftarrow$) Let R be a P-justified revision of I. Consider $R' = R \cup \{ok(l) : l \in \mathcal{L}(P)\}$. Let us show that R' is a $P^{\emptyset,I}$-justified revision of I. Indeed, $Inertia(I, R')$ contains all revision literals of the form $\mathbf{out}(defeated(l))$. Therefore, $(P^{\emptyset,I})_{I,R'}$ consists of rules

$$head(l') \leftarrow body(l'), \mathbf{in}(ok(l')) \qquad \qquad \text{(for all } l' \in P_{I,R})$$
$$\mathbf{in}(ok(l)) \leftarrow \qquad \qquad \text{(for all } l \in \mathcal{L}(P))$$

Thus, $NC((P^{\emptyset,I})_{I,R'}) = NC(P_{I,R}) \cup \{\mathbf{in}(ok(l)) : l \in \mathcal{L}(P)\}$. Consequently, $I \oplus NC((P^{\emptyset,I})_{I,R'}) = (I \oplus NC(P_{I,R})) \cup \{ok(l) : l \in \mathcal{L}(P)\} = R \cup \{ok(l) : l \in \mathcal{L}(P)\} = R'$. By definition, R' is a $P^{\emptyset,I}$-justified revision of I. Hence, R is a $(P, \mathcal{L}, \emptyset)$-justified revision of I. $\square$

We will now investigate other properties of revision programs with preferences. Because of the presence of preferences, it is expected that not every $(P, \mathcal{L}, S)$-justified revision of I is a model of P. This can be seen in the next example.

Example 2. Let P be the program

$$r_1 : \mathbf{in}(a) \leftarrow \mathbf{out}(b) \qquad \qquad r_2 : \mathbf{in}(b) \leftarrow \mathbf{out}(a)$$

and the set S consists of two preferences: $prefer(r_1, r_2)$ and $prefer(r_2, r_1)$. Then, $\emptyset$ is $(P, \mathcal{L}, S)$-justified revision of $\emptyset$ (both rules are defeated) but not a model of P.

The above example also shows that circular preferences among rules whose bodies can be satisfied simultaneously, may lead to a situation when all such rules will defeat each other, and therefore, none of the rules involved will be used in computing justified revisions. This situation corresponds to a conflict among preferences. For instance, in the above example a conflict is between a preference to use r_1 instead of r_2 and a preference to use r_2 instead of r_1. In order to satisfy the preferences both rules need to be removed.

The next theorem shows that for each $(P, \mathcal{L}, S)$-justified revision R of I, the subset of rules in P that are satisfied by R, is uniquely determined. To formulate the theorem, we need some more notation. Let J be a subset of $U^{\mathcal{L}(P)}$. By $P|_J$ we denote the program consisting of the rules r in P such that

- $ok(\mathcal{L}(r)) \in J$, or
- $ok(\mathcal{L}(r)) \notin J$ and $body(r) \setminus J^c \neq \emptyset$.

Theorem 2. *For every $P^{S,I}$-justified revision R of I, the corresponding $(P, \mathcal{L}, S)$-justified revision $R \cap U$ of I is a model of program $P|_R$.*

Proof. Consider a rule r in $P|_R$. Let us prove that $R \cap U$ is a model of r. If $body(r)$ is not satisfied by $R \cap U$, then r is trivially satisfied by $R \cap U$. Assume that $body(r)$ is satisfied by $R \cap U$. Since all revision literals in $body(r)$ belong to U^c, $body(r)$ is satisfied by R, and $body(r) \setminus R^c = \emptyset$. By definition of $P^{S,I}$, rule r'

$$r' = head(r) \leftarrow body(r), \mathbf{in}(ok(\mathcal{L}(r)))$$

belongs to $P^{S,I}$. By definition of $P|_R$, $ok(\mathcal{L}(r)) \in R$. Hence, $body(r')$ is satisfied by R. By definition of a (P, L, S)-justified revision, R is a model of $P^{S,I}$. Therefore, $head(r') = head(r)$ is satisfied by R. Since $head(r) \in U^c$, it is satisfied by $R \cap U$. Thus, $R \cap U$ is a model r. Consequently, $R \cap U$ is a model of $P|_R$. □

In the rest of this subsection, we discuss some properties that guarantee that each (P, L, S)-justified revision of I is a model of the program P. We concentrate on conditions on the set of preferences S. Obviously, Example 2 suggests that S should not contain a cycle between rules. The next example shows that if preferences are placed on a pair of rules such that the body of one of them is satisfied when the other rule is fired, then this may result in revisions that are not models of the program.

Example 3. Let P be the program

$$r_1 : \mathbf{in}(a) \leftarrow \mathbf{in}(b) \qquad r_2 : \mathbf{in}(d) \leftarrow \mathbf{out}(a)$$

and the set of preferences S consists of $prefer(r_2, r_1)$. Then, $\{b, d\}$ is $(P, \mathcal{L}, S)$-justified revision of $\{b\}$ but is not a model of P.

We now define precisely the conditions that guarantee that justified revisions of revision programs with preferences are models of the revision programs as well. First, we define when two rules are disjoint, i.e., when two rules cannot be used at the same time in creating revisions.

Definition 3. *Let $(P, \mathcal{L}, S)$ be a revision program with preferences. Two rules r, r' of P are disjoint if one of the following conditions is satisfied:*

1. $(head(r))^D \in body(r')$ and $(head(r'))^D \in body(r)$; or
2. $body(r) \cup body(r')$ is incoherent.

We say that a set of preferences is *selecting* if it contains only preferences between disjoint rules.

Definition 4. *Let* $(P, \mathcal{L}, S)$ *be a revision program with preferences.* S *is said to be a set of* selecting preferences *if for every preference*

$$prefer(r, r') \leftarrow l_1, \ldots, l_k$$

in S, *rules* r *and* r' *are disjoint.*

Finally, we say that a set of preferences is cycle-free if the transitive closure of the preference relation *prefer* does not contain a cycle.

Definition 5. *Let* $(P, \mathcal{L}, S)$ *be a revision program with preferences and* $<_S = \{(r_1, r_2) \mid prefer(r_1, r_2)$ *occurs as head of a preference in* S *and* $(body(r_1) \cup body(r_2))$ *is coherent*$\}$. S *is said to be* cycle-free *if for every rule* r *of* P, (r, r) *does not belong to the transitive closure* $<_S^*$ *of* $<_S$.

Lemma 1. *Let* $(P, \mathcal{L}, S)$ *be a revision program with preferences where* S *is a set of selecting preferences. Let* R *be a* $(P, \mathcal{L}, S)$-justified revision of I. For every rule r in P *such that* $head(r) \notin R^c$ *and* $body(r) \subseteq R^c$ *there exists a rule* r' *such that* $(r', r) \in <_S$, $head(r') \notin R^c$, *and* $body(r') \subseteq R^c$.

Proof. Let $R' \subseteq U^{\mathcal{L}(P)}$ be a $P^{S,I}$-justified revision of I such that $R = R' \cap U$ (it exists by definition of a $(P, \mathcal{L}, S)$-justified revision). Because $head(r) \notin R^c$ and $body(r) \subseteq R^c$, we have that $defeated(r) \in R'$. Hence, there exists a rule r' in P and a preference

$$prefer(r', r) \leftarrow l_1, \ldots, l_k$$

in S such that $\{l_1, \ldots, l_k\} \subseteq R^c$ and $body(r') \subseteq R^c$. Since $body(r) \subseteq R^c$ and $body(r') \subseteq R^c$, the set $(body(r') \cup body(r))$ is coherent. Therefore, $(r', r) \in <_S$. Rules r and r' are disjoint because S is a set of selecting preferences. Condition 2 in the definition of disjoint rules for r and r' is not satisfied because $(body(r') \cup body(r))$ is coherent. Hence, condition 1 must be satisfied. Namely, $(head(r))^D \in body(r')$ and $(head(r'))^D \in body(r)$. Because $body(r) \subseteq R^c$ and R^c does not contain a pair of dual literals, we conclude that $head(r') \notin R^c$. This proves the lemma.   □

The next theorem shows that the conditions on the set of preferences S guarantee that preferred justified revisions are models of the original revision program.

Theorem 3. *Let* $(P, \mathcal{L}, S)$ *be a revision program with preferences where* S *is a set of selecting preferences and is cycle-free. For every* $(P, \mathcal{L}, S)$-justified revision R of I, R *is a model of* P.

Proof. Let r be a rule in P. If $body(r)$ is not satisfied by R then rule r is trivially satisfied by R. Assume that $body(r)$ is satisfied by R. That is, $body(r) \subseteq R^c$. We need to prove that in this case $head(r) \in R^c$. Assume the contrary, $head(r) \notin R^c$. By Lemma 1, we know that there exists a rule r_1 such that $(r_1, r) \in <_S$, $body(r_1) \subseteq R^c$, and $head(r_1) \notin R^c$. Applying Lemma 1 one more time, we conclude that there exists a rule r_2 such that $(r_2, r_1) \in <_S$, $body(r_2) \subseteq R^c$, and $head(r_2) \notin R^c$, etc. In other words, this implies that there exists an infinite sequence $r_0 = r, r_1, \ldots, r_k, r_{k+1}, \ldots$ such that $(r_{j+1}, r_j) \in <_S$. Since P is finite, we can conclude that there exists some $t > s$ such that $r_t = r_s$. This implies that $(r_t, r_t) \in <_S^*$, i.e., S is not cycle-free. This contradicts the assumption that S is cycle-free. In other words, our assumption that $head(r) \notin R^c$ is wrong. This proves the theorem. $\square$

The next theorem discusses the shifting property of revision programs with preferences. We extend the definition of W-*transformation* to a set of preferences on rules. Given a preference on rules p of the form (5), its W-transformation is the preference

$$T_W(p) = prefer(l_1, l_2) \leftarrow initially(T_W(\alpha_1), \ldots, T_W(\alpha_k)), T_W(\alpha_{k+1}), \ldots, T_W(\alpha_n).$$

Given a set of preferences S, its W-transformation is $T_W(S) = \{T_W(p) : p \in S\}$.

Theorem 4. *Let $(P, \mathcal{L}, S)$ be a revision program with preferences. For every two databases I_1 and I_2, a database R_1 is a $(P, \mathcal{L}, S)$-justified revision of I_1 if and only if $T_{I_1 \div I_2}(R_1)$ is a $(T_{I_1 \div I_2}(P), \mathcal{L}, T_{I_1 \div I_2}(S))$-justified revision of I_2.*

Proof. Let $W = I_1 \div I_2$.
($\Rightarrow$) Let R_1 be a $(P, \mathcal{L}, S)$-justified revision of I_1. By definition, there exists R_1' such that R_1' is a P^{S, I_1}-justified revision of I and $R_1 = R_1' \cap U$. It is straightforward to see that $T_W(P^{S, I_1}) = T_W(P)^{T_W(S), I_2}$. This together with the Shifting Theorem [14] implies that $T_W(R_1')$ is a $T_W(P)^{T_W(S), I_2}$-justified revision of $T_W(I_1) = I_2$. Notice that $T_W(R_1') \cap U = T_W(R_1)$. Therefore, $T_W(R_1)$ is a $(T_W(P), \mathcal{L}, T_W(S))$-justified revision of I_2.
($\Leftarrow$) The proof in the other direction is similar. $\square$

4   Soft Revision Rules with Weights

Preferences between rules (Section 3) can be useful in at least two ways. They can be used to recover from incoherency when agents provide inconsistent data, as in the example from Section 3.1. They can also be used to eliminate some revisions. The next example shows that in some situations, this type of preferences is rather weak.

Example 4. Consider again the example from Section 3.1, with two agents a_1 and a_2 whose observations are used to determine the value of the parameter *temperature*. Let us assume now that a_1 and a_2 are of the same quality, i.e., *temperature* can be updated by one of the observations yielded by a_1 and a_2. This means that there is no preference between the rule of type (a) (for a_1) and the rule of type (a) (for a_2) and vice versa. Yet, as we can see, allowing both rules to be used in computing the revisions will not allow the controller to update its world view when the observations are inconsistent.

The problem in the above example could be resolved by grouping the rules of the type (a) into a set and allowing only one rule from this set to be used in creating revisions if the presence of all the rules does not allow justified revisions.

Inspired by the research in constraint programming, we propose to address the situation when there are no justified revisions by dividing a revision program P in two parts, HR and SR, i.e., $P = HR \cup SR$. Rules from HR and SR are called *hard rules* and *soft rules*, respectively. The intuition is that rules in HR must be satisfied by each revision, while revisions may satisfy only a subset of SR if it is impossible to satisfy all of them. The subset of soft rules that is satisfied, say S, should be optimal with respect to some comparison criteria. In this section, we investigate several criteria—each one is discussed in a separate subsection.

4.1   Maximal Number of Rules

Let $P = HR \cup SR$. Our goal is to find revisions that satisfy all rules from HR and the most number of rules from SR. Example 4 motivates the search for this type of revisions. In the next definition, we make this precise.

Definition 6. *R is a (HR, SR)-preferred justified revision of I if R is a $(HR \cup S)$ - justified revision of I for some $S \subseteq SR$, and for all $S' \subseteq SR$ such that S' has more rules than S, there are no $(HR \cup S')$-justified revisions of I.*

Preferred justified revision can be computed, under the maximal number of rules criteria, by extending the translation of revision programs to answer set programming, to handle the distinction between hard and soft rules. The objective is to determine $(HR \cup S)$-justified revisions of an initial database I, where S is a subset of SR of maximal size such that $(HR \cup S)$-justified revisions exist.

The idea is to make use of two language extensions proposed by the smodels system: choice rules and maximize statements. Intuitively, each soft rule can be either accepted or rejected in the program used to determine revisions. Let us assume that the rules in $T_I(SR)$ have been uniquely numbered. For each initial database I, we translate $P = HR \cup SR$ into an smodels program $lp(T_I(HR)) \cup lp'(T_I(SR))$ where $lp'(T_I(SR))$ is defined as follows. If the rule number i in $T_I(SR)$ is

$$\mathbf{in}(a) \leftarrow \mathbf{in}(p_1), \dots, \mathbf{in}(p_m), \mathbf{out}(s_1), \dots, \mathbf{out}(s_n)$$

then the following rules are added to $lp'(T_I(SR))$

$$\{rule_i\} : - p_1, \dots, p_m, not\ s_1, \dots, not\ s_n.$$
$$a \qquad : - rule_i$$

where $rule_i$ is a distinct new atom. Similarly, if

$$\mathbf{out}(a) \leftarrow \mathbf{in}(p_1), \dots, \mathbf{in}(p_m), \mathbf{out}(s_1), \dots, \mathbf{out}(s_n)$$

is the rule number i in $T_I(SR)$, then the following rules are added to $lp'(T_I(SR))$

$$\{rule_i\} : - p_1, \dots, p_m, not\ s_1, \dots, not\ s_n.$$
$$: - rule_i, a.$$

where $rule_i$ is a distinct new atom. Finally, we need to enforce the fact that we desire to maximize the number of SR rules that are satisfied. This corresponds to maximizing the number of $rule_i$ that are true in the computed answer sets. This can be directly expressed by the following statement:

$$\mathtt{maximize}\{rule_1, \dots, rule_k\}. \tag{10}$$

where k is the number of rules in SR. The way how `smodels` system processes `maximize` statement is as follows. It first searches a single model and prints it. After that, `smodels` prints only "better" models. The last model that `smodels` prints will correspond to a (HR, SR)-preferred justified revision of I. Notice that this is the only occurrence of `maximize` in the translation which is a requirement for the correct handling of this construct in `smodels`.

4.2   Maximal Subset of Rules

A variation of definition from Section 4.1 can be obtained when instead of satisfying maximal number of soft rules it is desired to satisfy a maximal subset of soft rules. In other words, given $P = HR \cup SR$, the goal is to find revisions that satisfy all rules from HR and a maximal subset (with respect to set inclusion) of rules from SR. The precise definition follows.

Definition 7. *R is a (HR, SR)-preferred$^{\subseteq}$ justified revision of I if R is a $(HR \cup S)$-justified revision of I for some $S \subseteq SR$, and for all S' if $S \subset S' \subseteq SR$, then there are no $(HR \cup S')$-justified revisions of I.*

The procedure described in Section 4.1 allows to compute only one of (HR, SR)-preferred$^{\subseteq}$ justified revisions which has maximal number of soft rules satisfied.

4.3   Weights

An alternative to the maximal subset of soft rules is to assign weights to the revisions and then select those with the maximal (or minimal) weight. In this section, we consider two different ways of assigning weights to revisions. First, we assign weight to rule. Next, we assign weight to atoms. In both cases, the goal is to find a subset S of SR such that the program $HR \cup S$ has revisions whose weight is maximal.

Weighted Rules. Each rule r in SR is assigned a weight (a number), $w(r)$. Intuitively, $w(r)$ represents the importance of r, i.e., the more the weight of a rule the more important it is to satisfy it.

Example 5. Let us reconsider the example from Section 3.1. Rules of the type (a) are treated as soft rules, while the rules of type (b) are treated as hard rules. We can make use of rule weights to select desired revisions. For example, if an observed parameter value falls outside expected value range for the parameter, it may suggest that an agent that provided the observation has a faulty sensor. Thus, we may prefer observations that are closer to the expected range. This can be expressed by associating to each rule r of the type (a) the weight

$$w(r) = min\{0, MaxEV - Value\} + min\{0, Value - MinEV\},$$

where $MaxEV$ and $MinEV$ are maximum and minimum expected values for Par.

Let us define the rule-weighted justified revision of a program with weights for rules.

Definition 8. *R is called a rule-weighted (HR, SR)-justified revision of I if the following two conditions are satisfied:*

1. *there exists a set of rules $S \subseteq SR$ s.t. R is a $(HR \cup S)$-justified revision of I, and*
2. *for any set of rules $S' \subseteq SR$, if R' is a $(HR \cup S')$-justified revision of I, then the sum of weights of rules in S' is less or equal than the sum of weights of rules in S.*

Let us generalize the implementation in the previous sections to consider weighted rules. The underlying principle is similar, with the difference that the selection of soft rules to include is driven by the goal of maximizing the total weight of the soft rules that are satisfied by the justified revision. The only change we need to introduce w.r.t. the implementation is in the `maximize` statement. Let us assume that $w(i)$ denotes the weight associated to the ith SR rule. Then, instead of the rule (10) the following maximize statement is generated:

$$\texttt{maximize}[rule_1 = w(1), rule_2 = w(2), \ldots, rule_k = w(k)].$$

Weighted Atoms. Instead of assigning weights to rules, we can also assign weights to atoms in the universe U. Each atom a in the universe U is assigned a weight $w(a)$ which represented the degree we would like to keep it unchanged, i.e., the more the weight of an atom the less we want to change its status in a database. The next example presents a situation where this type of preferences is desirable.

Example 6. Let us return to the example from Section 3.1 with the same partition of rules in hard and soft rules as in Example 5. Let us assume that the choice of which observation to use to update the view of the world is based on the principle that stronger values for the parameters are preferable, as they denote a stronger signal. This can be encoded by associating weights of the form

$$w(world(Param, Value, Sensor)) = -Value$$

and minimizing the total weight of the revision.

Let us define preferred justified revision for programs with weight atoms.

Definition 9. *R is called an atom-weighted (HR, SR)-justified revision of I if the following two conditions are satisfied:*
1. *there exists a set of rules $S \subseteq SR$ s.t. R is a $(HR \cup S)$-justified revision of I, and*
2. *for any set of rules $S' \subseteq SR$, if Q is a $(HR \cup S')$-justified revision of I, then the sum of weights of atoms in $I \div Q$ is greater than or equal to the sum of weights of atoms in $I \div R$.*

Atom-weighted revisions can be computed using `smodels`. In this case the selection of the SR rules to be included is indirectly driven by the goal of minimizing the total weight of the atoms in $I \div R$, if I is the initial database and R is the justified revision. We make use of the following observation: given a revision program P and an initial database I, if $T_I(R)$ is a $T_I(P)$-justified revision of $\emptyset$, then $T_I(R) = I \div R$. Thanks to this observation, the computation of the weight of the difference between the original database and a P-justified revision can be computed by determining the *total* weight of the true atoms obtained from the answer set generated for the $T_I(P)$ program.

The program used to compute preferred revisions is encoded similarly to what is done for the case of maximal number of rules or weighted rules, i.e., each soft rule is encoded using `smodels`'s' choice rules. The only difference is that instead of making use of a `maximize` statement, we make use of a `minimize` statement of the form:

$$\text{minimize}[a_1 = w(a_1), a_2 = w(a_2), \ldots, a_n = w(a_n)] \tag{11}$$

where $a_1, \ldots, a_n$ are all the atoms in U.

4.4 Minimal Size Difference

In this subsection, we consider justified revisions that have minimal size difference with initial database. The next example shows that this is desirable in different situations.

Example 7. Assume that a department needs to form a committee to work on some problem. Each of the department faculty members has his or her own conditions on the committee members which need to be satisfied. The head of the department provided an initial proposal for members of the committee. The task is to form a committee which will satisfy all conditions imposed by the faculty members and will differ the least from the initial proposal — the size of the symmetric difference between the initial proposal and its revision is minimal.

In this problem we have a set of agents (faculty members) each of which provides its set of requirements (revision rules). The goal is to satisfy all agent's requirements in such a way that the least number of changes is made to the initial database (proposal).

Assume that faculty members are Ann, Bob, Chris, David, Emily and Frank. Conditions that they impose on the committee are the following:

$$
\begin{aligned}
Ann: \quad &\textbf{in}(Bob) \quad \leftarrow \textbf{out}(Chris) \\
&\textbf{in}(Chris) \leftarrow \textbf{out}(Bob) \\
Bob: \ &\textbf{out}(David) \leftarrow \textbf{in}(Bob) \\
Chris: \quad &\textbf{out}(Ann) \quad \leftarrow \textbf{out}(David) \\
David: \quad &\textbf{in}(David) \quad \leftarrow \textbf{in}(Chris), \textbf{out}(Ann)
\end{aligned}
$$

The initial proposal is $I = \{Ann, David\}$. Then, there is one minimal size difference P-justified revisions of I, which is $R_1 = \{Ann, David, Bob\}$. The size of the difference $R_1 \div I$ is 1.

Ordinary P-justified revisions of I also include $R_2 = \{Bob\}$ with size of the difference $R_2 \div I$ equal to 3.

The next definition captures what is a minimal size different justified revision.

Definition 10. *R is called a minimal size difference P-justified revision of I if the following two conditions are satisfied:*

1. R is a P-justified revision of I, and

2. for any P-justified revision R', the number of atoms in $R \div I$ is less than or equal to the number of atoms in $R' \div I$.

Minimal size difference justified revision can be computed in almost the same way as for atom-weighted justified revisions. The intuition is that instead of minimizing the total weight of $I \div R$ (where I is the initial database and R is a P-justified revision), we would like to minimize the size of $I \div R$. This can be accomplished by replacing the `minimize` statement (11) with the following `minimize` statement:

$$\text{minimize}\{a_1, a_2, \ldots, a_n\}$$

where $a_1, \ldots, a_n$ are all the atoms in U.

5 Related Work

Since revision programming is strongly related to the logic programming formalisms [15, 14, 19], our work is related to several works on reasoning with preferences in logic programming. In this section, we discuss the differences and similarities between our approach and some of the research in this area. In logic programming, preferences have been an important source for "correct reasoning". Intuitively, a logic program is developed to represent a problem, with the intention that its semantics (e.g., answer set or well-founded semantics) will yield correct answers to the specific problem instances. Adding preferences between rules is one way to eliminate counter-intuitive (or unwanted) results. Often, this also makes the program easier to understand and more elaboration tolerant. In the literature on logic programming with preferences, we can find at least two distinct ways to handle preferences. The first approach is to compile the preferences into the program (e.g., [10, 6]): given a program P with a set of preferences *pref*, a new program P_{pref} is defined whose answer set semantics is used as the preferred semantics of P with respect to *pref*. The second approach deals with preferences between rules by defining a new semantics for logic programs with preferences (e.g., [5, 21]). The advantage of the first approach is that it does not require the introduction of a new semantics — thus, answer set solvers can be used to compute the preferred semantics. The second approach, on the other hand, provides a more direct treatment of preferences.

Section 3 of this paper follows the first approach. We define a notion of *revision program with preferences*, which is a labeled revision program with preferences between the rules. Given a revision program with preferences, we translate it into an ordinary revision program, and we define justified revisions w.r.t. the revision program with preferences as justified revisions w.r.t. the revision program obtained by translation. Our treatment of preferences is similar to that in [10, 6, 1]. In section 4, we introduce different types of preferences that can be dealt with more appropriately by following the second approach.

We will now discuss the relationship between our approach and others in greater detail. We will compare revision programs with preferences with ordered choice logic programs [21] and preferred answer sets [5]. Both frameworks allow preferences between rules — similar to our *prefer* relation — to be added to programs (choice logic programs [21], and extended logic programs [5]). The main difference between our approach and the approaches in [5, 21] lies in that we adopt the compilation approach while preferences in [5, 21] are dealt with using the second approach.

Ordered choice logic programs are introduced in [21] for modeling decision making with dynamic preferences. An ordered choice logic program (OCLP) P is a pair $(C, \preceq)$ where C is a set of choice logic programs whose rules are of the form $A \leftarrow B$ where

A and B are finite sets of atoms and $\preceq$ is a partial order on C. Intuitively, atoms in A represent alternatives and are assumed to be xor'ed together. Each member of C is called a component of P. Intuitively, $\preceq$ specifies an order in which the components of P are preferred. This ordering is used to select rules that can be applied to generate stable models of P. Given an interpretation I, a rule r is defeated with respect to I if there exist(s) some not less preferred rule(s) that can be applied in I whose head(s) contain(s) alternatives to the literals in the head of r. The stable model semantics of OCLP is defined in the same fashion of the original stable model semantics, i.e., given an interpretation M of P, a reduction of P with respect to M – which is a positive logic program – is defined; and, M is a stable model of P iff M is the stable model of the reduction of P with respect to M. It is worth noticing that in the first step of the reduction, defeated rules with respect to M are removed from P. The syntax difference between OCLP and revision program with preferences does not allow a detailed comparison between the two approaches. However, we note that OCLP follows the second approach to deal with preferences while our revision program with preferences uses the compilation approach. It is also interesting to notice that when the head of every rule in a OCLP program P has exactly one element then the preference order does not make any difference in computing stable models of P since there are no defeated rules. This could lead to a situation where P has a stable model M and P contains two rules, r and r', which belong to two components P_i and P_j, respectively, P_j is more specific than P_i, bodies of both r and r' are satisfied in M, and both r and r' are fired. Our formalization makes sure that this situation never happens (due to (6) and (7)). For example, consider the program $P = (C, \preceq)$ with

$$C = \{P_1, P_2\}, \ P_1 = \{p \leftarrow\}, \ P_2 = \{q \leftarrow\}, \ and \ \preceq = \{P_1 \prec P_2\}.$$

Then, $\{p, q\}$ is a stable model of this program. On the other hand, the corresponding revision program with preferences $(P', \mathcal{L}, S)$ with

$$P' = \{r_1 : \mathbf{in}(p) \leftarrow, \ r_2 : \mathbf{in}(q) \leftarrow\}, \ and \ S = \{prefer(r_1, r_2)\}$$

has only $\{p\}$ as its unique $(P', \mathcal{L}, S)$-justified revision of $\emptyset$.

In [5], preferred answer sets for prioritized logic programs with preferences between rules are defined. A new semantics is introduced that satisfies the two principles for priorities: one represents a meaning postulate for the term "preference" and the other is related to relevance. A detailed discussion on the differences and similarities between preferred answer sets for prioritized logic programs and other approaches to preferences handling in logic programming can be found in [5]. For a prioritized logic programs $(P, <)$, where P is an extended logic program and $<$ is a preference ordering between rules of P, the semantics in [5] requires that if A is a preferred answer set of $(P, <)$ then A is an answer set of P. Furthermore, A is generated by applying the rules in the order specified by $<$. Because this is not a requirement in compilation approach, it is not surprising to see that the approach we have taken to deal with preferences in labeled revision programs yield different results comparing to preferred answer sets. For example, consider the program $(P, <)$ with

$$P = \{r_1 : p \leftarrow not \ q, \ r_2 : q \leftarrow\}, \ and \ < = \{r_1 < r_2\}.$$

Then, $(P, <)$ does not have a preferred answer set because its only answer set $\{q\}$ cannot be generated by first applying the rule r_1 and then the rule r_2. On the other hand, the corresponding labeled program $(P', \mathcal{L}, S)$ with

$$P' = \{r_1 : \mathbf{in}(p) \leftarrow \mathbf{out}(q),\ r_2 : \mathbf{in}(q) \leftarrow\}, \ and \ S = \{prefer(r_1, r_2)\}$$

will have only $\{p\}$ as its unique $(P', \mathcal{L}, S)$-justified revision of $\emptyset$ because rule r_2 is defeated.

We notice that the preferences in the above examples, viewed under the revision program framework, are non-selecting preferences (Definition 4), and justified revisions are not models of the program. Theorem 3 discusses a condition under which $(P, \mathcal{L}, S)$-justified revisions are models of the original program P. We show next that under this condition and when only preferences with empty bodies are used, our framework coincides with preferred answer sets for prioritized logic programs [5].

Before we introduce the theorem about the relationship between revision program with preferences and preferred answer sets for prioritized logic programs, we need some more notation. First, we will assume that for every revision program with preferences $(P, \mathcal{L}, S)$, S is a set of selecting preferences, cycle-free, and the body in each preference of the form (5) in S is empty. We will refer to such programs as *static revision programs with preferences*. For such a program, we define a corresponding prioritized logic program $Q(P) = (lp(P), <)$ where $lp(P)$ is defined as in Section 2 and $<= \{(l_1, l_2) : prefer(l_1, l_2) \in S\}$.

Theorem 5. *Let $(P, \mathcal{L}, S)$ be a static revision program with preferences. Then, R is a $(P, \mathcal{L}, S)$-justified revision of the empty database iff R is a preferred answer set of $Q(P)$ as defined in [5].*

The proof of this property can be found in the appendix.

Our work in this paper is also strongly related to dynamic logic programming (DLP) [4]. DLP is introduced as a mean to update knowledge bases that might contain generalized logic programming rules. Roughly, a DLP is an ordered list of generalized logic programs, where each represents the properties of the knowledge base at a time moment. The semantics of a DLP – taking into consideration a sequence of programs up to a time point t – specifies which rules should be applied to derive the state of the knowledge base at t. It has been shown that DLP generalizes revision programming [4]. DLP has been extended to deal with preferences [3, 1]. A DLP with preferences, or a *prioritized DLP*, is a pair (P, R) of two DLPs; P is a labeled DLP whose language does not contain the binary predicate $<$ and R is a DLP whose language contains the binary predicate $<$ and whose set of constants includes all the rule labels from both programs. Intuitively, (P, R) represents a knowledge at different time moments – the same way a DLP does – with the exception that there are preferences between rules in (P, R). An atom of the form $r_1 < r_2$ represents the fact that rule r_1 is preferred to rule r_2. The semantics of prioritized DLP makes sure that the preference order between rules is reflected in the set of consequences derivable from the knowledge base. More precisely, for two conflicting rules r_1 and r_2, if $r_1 < r_2$ is derived, then the consequence of the rule r_1 should be preferred over the consequence of r_2. Prioritized DLP deals with preferences using the compilation approach. In fact, the approach coincides with that of preferred answer sets for extended logic programs [5] when the DLP consists of a single program as shown in [3]. In this sense, the prioritized DLP approach is similar to the approach described in Section 3, in which we add to a revision program a preference relation between its rules and define the semantics of a revision program with preferences following the compilation approach. It follows from our discussion in the previous paragraph that revision programming with preferences and DLP with preferences will yield different results in certain situations. Other difference between our work and prioritized DLP lies in that we consider other types of preferences (e.g., maximal number of applicable rules, weighted rules, weighted atoms, or minimal size difference) and prioritized DLP does not. We plan to investigate the use of these types of preferences in DLP in the future.

Finally, DLP is also used as the main representation language for a multi-agent architecture in [12]. In this paper, we take the first step towards this direction by using revision programming with preferences to represent and reason about beliefs of multi-agents in a coordinated environment. A detailed comparison with MINERVA is planned in the near future.

6   Conclusions

The notion of preference has found pervasive applications in the context of knowledge representation and commonsense reasoning in MAS. Indeed a large number of approaches have been proposed to improve the knowledge representation capabilities of logic programming by introducing different forms of preferences. In this paper, we presented a novel extension of the revision programming framework which provides the foundations for expressing very general types of preferences. Preferences provide the ability to "defeat" the use of certain revision rules in the computation of the revisions; this allows us to either reduce the number of revisions generated (eventually leading to a single revision), or to generate revisions even in the presence of conflicting revision rules.

We proposed different preference schemes, starting from a relatively dynamic partial order between revision rules (*revision programs with preferences*), and then moving to a more general notion of weights, associated to revision rules and/or database atoms. Soft revision rules can be dynamically included or excluded from the generation of revisions depending on optimization criteria based on the weights of the revision (e.g., minimization of the total weight associated to the revision). We provided motivating examples for the different preference schemes, along with a precise description of how preferred revisions can be computed using the smodels answer set inference engine.

7   Appendix

In this section we give a proof of Theorem 5, that under certain conditions, the justified revisions of labeled revision programs with preferences coincide with the preferred answer sets of prioritized logic programs introduced in [5].

A prioritized logic program[2] is a pair $(P, <)$ where P is a logic program and $<$ is a preference relation among rules of P. The semantics of $(P, <)$ is defined by its *preferred answer set* - answer sets of P satisfying some conditions determined by $<$. We will first recall the notion of preferred answer sets from [5]. A binary relation R on a set S is called *strict partial order* (or *order*) if R is irreflexive and transitive. An order R is *total* if for every pair $a, b \in S$, either $(a, b) \in R$ or $(b, a) \in R$; R is *well-founded* if every set $X \subseteq S$ has a minimal element; R is *well-ordered* if it is total and well-founded.

Let P be a collection of rules of the form

$$r : \qquad l_0 \leftarrow l_1, \ldots, l_m, \; not \; l_{m+1}, \ldots, \; not \; l_n$$

where l_i's are ground literals. Literals $l_1, \ldots, l_m$ are called the *prerequisites* of r. If $m = 0$ then r is said to be *prerequisite free*. A rule r is *defeated* by a literal l if $l = l_i$ for some $i \in \{m+1, \ldots, n\}$; r is defeated by a set of literals X if X contains a literal that defeats r. A program P is *prerequisite free* if every rule in P is prerequisite free. For a program P and a set of literals X, the *reduct of P with respect to X*, denoted by $^X P$, is the program obtained from P by

- deleting all rules with prerequisite l such that $l \notin X$; and
- deleting all prerequisites of the remaining rules.

Definition 11. *[5] Let $(P, <)$ be a prioritized logic program where P is prerequisite free and $<$ is a total order among rules of P. An answer set S of P is a preferred answer set of $(P, <)$ if $C_<(A) = A$ where (i) $C_<(A)$ is the smallest set of ground literals that is logically closed (wrt. P); (ii) $\bigcup_{i=0}^{\infty} S_i \subseteq C_<(A)$; and (iii) the sequence S_i is defined as follows:*

$$S_0 = \emptyset$$

$$S_n = \begin{cases} \bigcup_{i=0}^{n-1} S_i & \text{if} & r_n \text{ is defeated by } \bigcup_{i=0}^{n-1} S_i \\ & \text{or} & r_n \text{ is defeated by } A \text{ and } head(r_n) \in A \\ \\ \bigcup_{i=0}^{n-1} S_i \cup \{head(r_n)\} & \text{otherwise} \end{cases}$$

and r_n is the nth rule in the order $<$.

For an arbitrary prioritized logic program $(P, <)$, a set of literals A is called a *preferred answer set of $(P, <)$ if it is a preferred answer set of $(^A P, <')$) for some total order $<'$ that extends $^A <$ which inherits from $<$ by the map: $f : {}^A P \rightarrow P$, i.e., $r_1' \, {}^A <r_2'$ if and only if $f(r_1') < f(r_2')$ where $f(r')$ is the first rule in P with respect to $<$ such that r' is obtained from r through the reduction ^{A}.*

Now we are ready to give the proof of Theorem 5.

---

[2] In this appendix, by a logic program we mean a propositional logic program. This is because we only work with propositional revision programs.

Theorem 5. *Let $(P, \mathcal{L}, S)$ be a static revision program with preferences. Then, R is a $(P, \mathcal{L}, S)$-justified revision of the empty database if and only if R is a preferred answer set of $Q(P)$.*

Proof. Let U be the set of all atoms that appear in the program P.

($\Rightarrow$) Let R be a $(P, \mathcal{L}, S)$-justified revision of the empty database. We have that R is a model of P (Theorem 3). Hence, R satisfies the rules of $lp(P)$. Furthermore, there exist a $P^{S,\emptyset}$-justified revision R' such that $R' \cap U = R$.

We will first show that R is a minimal set of literals satisfying the rules of $lp(P)$. Assume the contrary, that there exists $M \subset R$ such that M satisfies the rules of $lp(P)$. Consider $a \in R \backslash M$. Since $a \in R$, there exists a rule r of $P^{S,\emptyset}$ such that $head(r) = \mathbf{in}(a)$, $\mathbf{in}(a) \in NC(P^{S,\emptyset}_{\emptyset,R'})$, and $body(r)$ is satisfied by R'. Because $r \in P$, we have that $ok(r) \in R'$. Hence, $lp(r) \in lp(P)$ and the body of r is satisfied by R. This contradicts the fact that M is closed under $lp(P)$. This allows us to conclude that R is an answer set of P.

It remains to be shown that R is a preferred answer set of $(lp(P), <)$. Consider the prioritized program $(^R(lp(P)), <')$ where $^R(lp(P))$ is the reduct of $lp(P)$ with respect to R and $<'$ inherits from $<$ (as defined in Definition 11). It follows from the definition of the reduct that if $r \in ^R (lp(P))$ and r is not defeated by R then $head(r) \in R$.

We need to show that R is a preferred answer set of $(^R(lp(P)), <')$. Let $<^*$ be the transitive closure of $<'$, $RN = \{r \mid r \in (^R(lp(P)), r \text{ is not defeated by } R \text{ and } r \text{ does not occur in } <^*\}$, and $RD = \{r \mid r \in (^R(lp(P)), r \text{ is defeated by } R \text{ and } r \text{ does not occur in } <^*\}$. Let $rn_1, \ldots, rn_{n_1}$ be an enumeration of RN and $rd_1, \ldots, rd_{n_2}$ be an enumeration of RD. We define an ordering $<''$ on the rules of $(^R(lp(P)))$ as follows.

- $r <'' r'$ if $r <^* r'$;
- $rn_i <'' rn_j$ for $1 \le i < j \le n_1$;
- $rn_{n_1} <'' r$ for r occurs in $<^*$;
- $rd_i <'' rd_j$ for $1 \le i < j \le n_2$; and
- $r <'' rd_i$ for r occurs in $<^*$ and $1 \le i \le n_2$;

We have that $<''$ is a total order on the set of rules of $^R(lp(P))$. Let $r_1, \ldots, r_m$ be the sequence of rules of $^R(lp(P))$, ordered by $<''$. Let $S_0, \ldots, S_m$ be the sequence of sets of literals defined for $^R(lp(P))$ with respect to $<''$. It is easy to see that because R is an answer set of P, $\bigcup_{i=0}^{m} S_i \subseteq R$. Thus, we only need to show that for every $a \in R$, there exists $0 \le j \le m$ such that $a \in S_j$.

Consider an arbitrary $a \in R$. It follows from the definition of answer set that there exists some rule r of $lp(P)$ such that $head(r) = a$ and $body(r)$ is satisfied by R. This implies that the reduct r' of r belongs to $^R(lp(P))$. Clearly, r' is not defeated by R. Without the lost of generality, we can assume that $r' = r_l$ is the first rule in the sequence of the rules of $^R(lp(P))$ whose head is a. Together with the fact that $\bigcup_{i=0}^{l-1} S_i \subseteq R$, we can conclude that $head(r) \in S_l$. Thus, we have that $R \subseteq \bigcup_{i=0}^{m} S_i$. This, together with the fact that R is an answer set of $lp(P)$, shows that R is a preferred answer set of $(lp(P), <)$.

($\Leftarrow$) Let R be a preferred answer set of $Q(P)$, i.e., R is a preferred answer set of $(lp(P), <')$ for some total order $<'$ that extends $<$.

First, because R is an answer set of $lp(P)$ we have that R is a P-justified revision of $\emptyset$. Let $IN' = Inertia(\emptyset, R) = \{\mathbf{out}(a) : a \notin R\}$. We have that

$$R = \{a \in U : \mathbf{in}(a) \in NC(P_{\emptyset, R})\}$$

where $P_{\emptyset, R}$ consists of rules of the form

$$head(r) \leftarrow body(r) \setminus IN'$$

where $r \in P$ and where, by definition, $NC(P_{\emptyset, R})$ is the least model of $P_{\emptyset, R}$, when treated as a Horn program built of independent propositional atoms of the form $\mathbf{in}(a)$ and $\mathbf{out}(b)$. Let

$$d(R) = \{defeated(r) \mid r \in P, \exists r'.[r' < r, R \text{ satisfies } body(r')]\},$$
$$ok(R) = \{ok(r) \mid r \in P, \; defeated(r) \notin d(R)\},$$

and

$$R' = R \cup d(R) \cup ok(R) \cup S.$$

We will show that R' is a $P^{S,\emptyset}$-justified revision of $\emptyset$. Because the initial database is empty, we have that

$$Inertia(\emptyset, R') = \{\mathbf{out}(a) : a \in U^{\mathcal{L}(P)} \notin R'\}.$$

To simplify the presentation, let us denote $Inertia(\emptyset, R')$ by IN. From the construction of R', we have that $IN' = IN \cap \{\mathbf{out}(a) : a \in U\}$.

We will now construct the program $P' = P^{S,\emptyset}_{\emptyset, R'}$. We have that P' consists of the following rules:

(a) $head(r) \leftarrow body(r) \setminus IN, \mathbf{in}(ok(r))$ where r is a rule in P, $body(r) \setminus IN$ is the set of literals occurring in $body(r)$ which do not occur in IN.
(b) $\mathbf{in}(ok(r)) \leftarrow \mathbf{out}(defeated(r)) \setminus IN$;
(c) $\mathbf{in}(prefer(r, r')) \leftarrow$ if $prefer(r, r') \in S$;
(d) $\mathbf{in}(defeated(r)) \leftarrow body(r') \setminus IN, \mathbf{in}(prefer(r', r))$ if $prefer(r', r) \in S$.

We will now show that R' is P'-justified revision of the empty database. It follows from Definition 1 that we need to show that $R' = \{a : \mathbf{in}(a) \in NC(P')\}$. Let $a \in R'$. We consider four cases:

- $a = ok(r)$ for some r. By construction of R', we have that $a \in R'$ iff $defeated(r) \notin d(R)$ iff $defeated(r) \notin R'$ iff $\mathbf{out}(defeated(r)) \in IN$ iff $\mathbf{in}(ok(r)) \in NC(P')$;
- $a = prefer(r, r')$. From the construction of R', $a \in R'$ iff $prefer(r, r') \in S$ iff $\mathbf{in}(prefer(r, r')) \leftarrow$ belongs to P' iff $\mathbf{in}(prefer(r, r')) \in NC(P')$.
- $a \in U$. We will show that for every $a \in U$, $\mathbf{in}(a) \in NC(P')$ iff $a \in R'$ and $\mathbf{out}(a) \in NC(P')$ iff $a \notin R'$. Observe that for every rule of the type (a) we have that $head(r) \leftarrow body(r) \setminus IN'$ belongs to the program $P_{\emptyset, R}$. Therefore, $a \in R$ (resp. $a \notin R$) implies that $\mathbf{in}(a) \in NC(P_{\emptyset, R})$ (resp. $\mathbf{out}(a) \in NC(P_{\emptyset, R})$). Let T be the fix point operator that is used in computing the least fix point of the program $P_{\emptyset, R}$. We have that $a \in R$ (resp. $a \notin R$) if and only if there exists a minimal number k such that $\mathbf{in}(a) \in T^k(P_{\emptyset, R})$ and $\mathbf{in}(a) \notin T^i(P_{\emptyset, R})$ for $i < k$ (resp. $\mathbf{out}(a) \in T^k(P_{\emptyset, R})$ and $\mathbf{out}(a) \notin T^i(P_{\emptyset, R})$ for $i < k$). We can prove by induction over k that $\mathbf{in}(a) \in NC(P')$ (resp. $\mathbf{out}(a) \in NC(P')$):

- **Base:** $k = 0$ implies that $\mathbf{in}(a) = head(r)$ is a fact in $P_{\emptyset,R}$. Hence, $\mathbf{in}(a) \leftarrow \mathbf{in}(ok(r))$ is a rule in P'. We would like to show that $ok(r) \in R'$. Assume the contrary, $ok(r) \notin R'$. This implies that there exists a rule r' in P such that $prefer(r',r) \in S$ and R satisfies $body(r')$. Because $(P,\mathcal{L},S)$ is static, we have that (i) $body(r') \cup body(r)$ is incoherent; or (ii) $(head(r))^D \in body(r')$ and $(head(r'))^D \in body(r)$. Since the body of r is empty, (i) cannot happen. If (ii) happens, we have that R cannot satisfy the body of r' due to the fact that R is a P-justified revision of $\emptyset$. This implies that our assumption is incorrect, i.e., $ok(r) \in R'$. From the first item, we have that $ok(r)$ is a fact in P'. Thus, $\mathbf{in}(a) \in NC(P')$. Similar argument allows us to conclude that if $\mathbf{out}(a) \in T^0(\emptyset)$ then $\mathbf{out}(a) \in NC(P')$.
- **Step:** Assume that we have proved the conclusion for k. We need to show that if $\mathbf{in}(a) \in T^{k+1}(P_{\emptyset,R})$, then $\mathbf{in}(a) \in NC(P')$. Similar to the base case, we can show that there exists a rule r or P such that $head(r) = \mathbf{in}(a)$, $body(r)\backslash IN \subseteq NC(P')$ and $\mathbf{in}(ok(r)) \in NC(P')$. This allows us to conclude that $\mathbf{in}(a) \in NC(P')$. The same argument holds for $\mathbf{out}(a) \in T^{k+1}(P_{\emptyset,R})$. This proves the inductive step.
- $a = defeated(r)$ for some r. Then, $a \in R'$ if and only if there exists a rule r', $prefer(r',r) \in S$ such that the body of r' is satisfied by R. Thus, $body(r') \setminus IN$ is satisfied by R', i.e., $\mathbf{in}(defeated(r)) \in NC(P')$.

The above items show that $a \in R'$ if and only if $\{a \mid \mathbf{in}(a) \in NC(P')\}$. This implies that R' is a $P^{S,\emptyset}$-justified revision of $\emptyset$, i.e. R is a $(P,\mathcal{L},S)$-justified revision of $\emptyset$. $\square$

References

1. J.J. Alferes, P. Dell'Acqua, and L.M. Pereira. A compilation of updates plus references. In *Logics in Artificial Intelligence, European Conference*, pages 62–73. Springer, 2002.
2. J.J. Alferes, F. Banti, A. Brogi, J.A. Leite. Semantics for Dynamic Logic Programming: A Principle-Based Approach. In *LPNMR*, pages 8–20. Springer Verlag, 2004.
3. J.J. Alferes and L.M. Pereira. Updates plus preferences. In *Logics in Artificial Intelligence, European Workshop (JELIA)*, pages 345–360. Springer, 2000.
4. J.J. Alferes, J.A. Leite, L.M. Pereira, H. Przymusinska, and T.C. Przymusinski. Dynamic Updates of Non-monotonic Knowledge Bases. *JLP*, 45, 2000.
5. G. Brewka and T. Eiter. Preferred answer sets for extended logic programs. *Artificial Intelligence*, 109(1–2):297–356, 1999.
6. E. Delgrande, T. Schaub, and H. Tompits. A framework for compiling preferences in logic programs. *Theory and Practice of Logic Programming*, 3(2):129–187, March 2003.
7. H.E. Durfee. *Coordination of Distributed Problem Solvers*. Kluwer Academic Press, 1988.
8. T. Eiter, M. Fink, G. Sabbatini, and H. Tompits. Using Methods of Declarative Logic Programming for Intelligent Information Agents. *TPLP*, 2(6), 2002.
9. P. Faratin and B. Van de Walle. Agent Preference Relations: Strict, Indifferent, and Incomparable. In *AAMAS*. ACM, 2002.
10. M. Gelfond and T.C. Son. Prioritized default theory. In *Selected Papers from the Workshop on Logic Programming and Knowledge Representation 1997*, pages 164–223, Springer Verlag, LNAI 1471, 1998.
11. P. La Mura and Y. Shoham. Conditional, Hierarchical, Multi-agent Preferences. In *TARK VII*, 1998.

12. J.A. Leite, J.J. Alferes, and L.M. Pereira. MINERVA: a Dynamic Logic Programming Agent Architecture. In *Intelligent Agents VIII*, pages 141–157. Springer Verlag, 2002.
13. J. Liu and Y. Ye. *E-Commerce Agents*. Lecture Notes in AI, Springer Verlag, 2001.
14. W. Marek, I. Pivkina, and M. Truszczyński. Revision programming = logic programming + integrity constraints. In *Computer Science Logic*, Springer Verlag, 1999.
15. W. Marek and M. Truszczyński. Revision programming, database updates and integrity constraints. In *ICDT*, pages 368–382. Springer Verlag, 1995.
16. W. Marek and M. Truszczyński. Revision programming. *Theoretical Computer Science*, 190(2):241–277, 1998.
17. I. Niemelä and P. Simons. Efficient implementation of the well-founded and stable model semantics. In *JICSLP*, pages 289–303. MIT Press, 1996.
18. H. Prakken. *Logical Tools for Modeling Legal Arguments*. Kluwer Publishers, 1997.
19. T. Przymusinski and H. Turner. Update by means of Inference rules. In *LPNMR*, pages 156–174. Springer Verlag, 1995.
20. C. Sakama and K. Inoue. Updating Extended Logic Programs through Abduction. In *LPNMR*, pages 147–161. Springer Verlag, 1999.
21. M. De Voss and D. Vermeir. A Logic for Modeling Decision Making with Dynamic Preferences, In *Logics in Artificial Intelligence, European Workshop (JELIA)*, pages 391–406. Springer, 2000.

A New Framework for Knowledge Revision of Abductive Agents Through Their Interaction

Andrea Bracciali[1] and Paolo Torroni[2]

[1] Dipartimento di Informatica, Università di Pisa,
Via Buonarroti, 2 - 56127 Pisa, Italy
braccia@di.unipi.it
[2] DEIS, Università di Bologna,
Viale Risorgimento, 2 - 40136 Bologna, Italy
paolo.torroni@unibo.it

Abstract. In this paper we discuss the design of a knowledge revision framework for abductive reasoning agents, based on interaction. This involves issues such as: how to exploit knowledge multiplicity to find solutions to problems that agents may not individually solve, what information must be passed or requested, how agents can take advantage of the answers that they obtain, and how they can revise their reasoning process as a consequence of interacting with each other. We describe a novel negotiation framework in which agents will be able to exchange not only abductive hypotheses but also meta-knowledge, which, in particular in this paper, is understood as agents' integrity constraints. We formalise some aspects of such a framework, by introducing an algebra of integrity constraints, aimed at formally supporting the updating/revising process of the agent knowledge.

1 Multiple-Source Knowledge and Coordinated Reasoning

The agent metaphor has recently become a very popular way to model distributed systems, in many application domains that require a goal directed behaviour of autonomous entities. Thanks also to the recent explosion of the Internet and communication networks, the increased accessibility of knowledge located in different sources at a relatively low cost is opening up interesting scenarios where communication and knowledge sharing can be a constant support to the reasoning activity of agents. In knowledge-intensive applications, the agent paradigm will be able to enhance traditional stand-alone expert systems interacting with end-users, by allowing for inter-agent communication and autonomous revision of knowledge.

Some agent-based solutions can be already found in areas such as information and knowledge integration (see the Sage and Find Future projects by Fujitsu), Business Process Management (Agentis Software), the Oracle Intelligent Agents, not to mention decentralized control and scheduling, and e-procurement (Rock-

J. Dix and J. Leite (Eds.): CLIMA IV, LNAI 3259, pp. 159–177, 2004.
© Springer-Verlag Berlin Heidelberg 2004

well Automation, Whitestein Technologies and formerly Living Systems AG, Lost Wax, iSOCO), just to cite some.[1]

In order to make such solutions reliable, easy to control, to specify and verify, and in order to make their behaviour easy to understand, sound and formal foundations are needed. This reason has recently motivated several Logic Programming based approaches to Multi-Agent Systems. Work done by Kowalski and Sadri [1] on the agent cycle, by Leite et al. [2] on combining several Non-Monotonic Reasoning mechanisms in agents, by Satoh et al. [3] on speculative computation, by Dell'Acqua et al. [4, 5] on agent communication and updates, by Sadri et al. [6] on agent dialogues, and by Ciampolini et al. [7] and by Gavanelli et al. [8] on the coordination of reasoning of abductive logic agents, are only some examples of application of Logic Programming techniques to Multi-Agent Systems. A common characteristic among them is that the agent paradigm brings about the need for dealing with knowledge incompleteness (due to the multiplicity and autonomy of agents), and evolution (due to their interactions).

In this research effort, many proposals have been put forward that consider negotiation and dialogue a suitable way to let agents exchange information and solve problems in a collaborative way, and that consider abduction as a privileged form of reasoning under incomplete information. However, such information exchange is often limited to simple facts that help agents revise their beliefs. In [7], for instance, such facts are modelled as hypotheses made to explain some observation in a coordinated abductive reasoning activity; in [3] the information exchanged takes the form of answers to questions aimed at confirming/disconfirming assumptions; in [6] of communication acts in a negotiation setting aimed at sharing resources. In [4] and previous work, the authors present a combination of abduction and updates in a multi-agent setting, where agents are able to propose updates to the theory of each other in different patterns. In this scenario of collaboration among abductive agents, knowledge exchange, update and revision play a key role. We argue that agents would benefit from the capability of exchanging information in its various forms, like predicates, theories and integrity constraints, and that they should be able to do it as a result of a negotiation process regarding knowledge itself.

Finally, the relevance of abduction in proposing revisions during theory refinements and updates is widely recognised. In [9], for instance, it is shown how to combine abduction with inductive techniques in order to "adapt" a knowledge base to a set of empirical data and examples. Abductive explanations are used to generalise or specify the rules of the knowledge base according to positive and negative information provided. In agreement with the basis of this approach, we discuss knowledge sharing mechanisms for agents based on an abductive framework, where information is provided by the interaction between agents, which exchange not only facts, but also constraints about their knowledge, namely in-

---

[1] A summary about industrial applications of agent technology, including references to the above mentioned projects and applications, can be found at: http://lia.deis.unibo.it/~pt/misc/AIIA03-review.pdf.

tegrity constraints of an abductive theory. Agent knowledge bases can hence be generalised or specialised by relaxing or tightening their integrity constraints.

In this paper we focus on information exchange about integrity constraints, abstracting away from issues such as ontology and communication languages and protocols: we assume that all agents have a common ontology and communicate by using the same language. In this scenario, autonomous agents will actively ask for knowledge, e.g. facts, hypotheses or integrity constraints, and will autonomously decide whether and how to modify their own constraints whenever it is needed. For instance, an agent, which is unable to explain some observation given its current knowledge, will try to collect information from other agents, and possibly decide to relax its own constraints in a way that allows him to explain the observation. Conversely, an agent may find out that some assumptions that he made ought to be inconsistent (for instance, due to "social constraints" [10]), and try to gather information about how to tighten his own constraints or add new ones which prevent him from making such assumptions.

The distinguishing features of the distributed reasoning revision paradigm that we envisage consist of a mix of introspection capabilities and communication capabilities. In the style of abductive reasoning, agents are able to provide conditional explanations about the facts that they prove, they are able to communicate such explanations in order to let others validate them, and they are able to single out and communicate the constraints that prevent from or allow them to explain an observation. The following example informally illustrates such a scenario.

Example 1. Let us consider an interaction among two agents, A and B, having different expertise about a given topic.

(1) $A \not\models^{\mathcal{IC}''} \neg f, b$	Agent A is unable to prove (find an explanation for) the goal (observation) "there is a *bird* that does not *fly*", and he is *able to determine* a set $\mathcal{IC}''$ of integrity constraints which prevent to explain the observation ...
(2) $A \rightarrow B : \neg f, b$	... hence A *asks* B for a possible explanation ...
(3) $B \models^{\mathcal{IC}'}_\Delta \neg f, b$	... B is able to explain the observation $\neg f, b$ (e.g., by assuming a set of hypotheses Δ including p: a *penguin* is a *bird* that does not *fly*), and also to *determine* a *(significant)* set $\mathcal{IC}'$ of integrity constraints involved in the abductive proof;
(4) $B \rightarrow A : \mathcal{IC}'$	B suggests $\mathcal{IC}'$ to A;
(5) $A_{\ominus \mathcal{IC}'' \oplus \mathcal{IC}'} \models_{\Delta'} \neg f, b$	A *revises* his own constraints according to the information provided by B, by means of some *updating operation*, and explains his observation, possibly with a different explanation Δ'.

At step (5), the updating operation has been accepted by A, according to a *conservative policy*, since it *relaxes* the original constraints of A, and in particular those preventing to explain the observation ($\mathcal{IC}''$), with a *more generic constraint* provided by B, e.g. $\{b, \neg f, \neg p \rightarrow false\}$ (a bird does not fly, unless it is a penguin).

This example will be further elaborated later on, once the necessary notation is introduced. The various steps involve, to some extent, deduction, introspection, interaction, and revision, and will be further discussed to illustrate the global picture. Then we will focus on the integrity constraint revision process, as part of the overall framework.

The rest of this paper is organised as follows: Section 2 recalls Abductive Logic Programming, Section 3 discusses the above mentioned general steps. Section 4 presents the formal model we devised to address constraint-based knowledge revision: an algebra of constraints, relevant constraint selection operators, and constraint updating/revising operators. Possible applications of the framework in knowledge negotiation scenarios are illustrated in Section 5. Concluding remarks and future work are summarised in Section 6.

2   Background on Abductive Logic Programming

An Abductive Logic Program (ALP) is a triple $\langle T, \mathcal{A}, \mathcal{IC} \rangle$, where T is a theory, namely a Logic Program, $\mathcal{A}$ is the set of "abducible" predicates, and $\mathcal{IC}$ is a set of integrity constraints. According to [11], negation as default can be recovered into abduction by replacing negated literals of the form $\neg a$ with a new positive, abducible atom not_a and by adding the integrity constraint $\leftarrow a, not\_a$ to $\mathcal{IC}$. In line with [12], along with the abducible (positive) predicates, $\mathcal{A}$ will also contain all negated literals, which will be generally left implicit. Given an ALP and a goal G, or "observation", *abduction* is the process of determining a set Δ of abducibles ($\Delta \subseteq \mathcal{A}$), such that:

$$T \cup \Delta \models G, \text{ and}$$
$$T \cup \mathcal{IC} \cup \Delta \not\models \perp.$$

For the sake of simplicity, we assume that T is ground and stratified. In this case, many of the semantics usually adopted for abduction, like stable model semantics or well-founded semantics, are known to coincide, and hence the symbol $\models$ can be interpreted as denoting entailment according to any of them. If there exists such a set Δ, we call it an *abductive explanation* for G in $\langle T, \mathcal{A}, \mathcal{IC} \rangle$:

$$\langle T, \mathcal{A}, \mathcal{IC} \rangle \overset{abd}{\models}_\Delta G$$

Abduction is reasoning in presence of uncertainty, represented as the possibility to assume the truth or falsity of some predicates (called "abducibles") in order to explain an observation. In this context, the set of integrity constraints $\mathcal{IC}$ of an ALP determines the assumptions which can coherently be made together. Informally speaking, $\mathcal{IC}$ restricts the choice of possible explanations to observations, or in other words, it rules out some hypothetical worlds from those modelled by a given ALP.

Syntax and Semantics of Integrity Constraints. We consider integrity constraints of the form $\perp \leftarrow L_1, \ldots, L_n$, where $L_1, \ldots, L_n$ are literals, i.e. atoms or negations of atoms, whose set is indicated as $body(ic)$. Singleton integrity constraints are indicated as ic, ic_1, ic_2, ic', ic'', ..., sets of integrity constraints as $\mathcal{IC}$, $\mathcal{IC}_1$, $\mathcal{IC}_2$, ..., $\mathcal{IC}'$, $\mathcal{IC}''$, ..., and sets of literals as Δ, Δ_1, Δ_2, ..., Δ', Δ'', ... We will use capital letters to refer specific agents (i.e., A, $\mathcal{IC}_A$, T_A, ... in Example 2) and lower case to denote generic knowledge without referring to a specific agent (i.e., a, $\mathcal{IC}_a$, $\mathcal{IC}_b$, ... in Section 4.3). Finally, in the following, we will adopt the notation $\leftarrow L_1, \ldots, L_n$ as a shorthand for $\perp \leftarrow L_1, \ldots, L_n$.

Intuitively, an integrity constraint $\leftarrow L_1, \ldots, L_n$ represents a restriction, preventing $L_1, \ldots, L_n$ from being all true at the same time. If some of the L_j in the body of ic are abducible atoms, ic constrains the set of possible explanations that can be produced during an abductive derivation process. Constraints of the form $\perp \leftarrow x, \neg x$, with x an atom, which prevent x and $\neg x$ from being true at the same time, are left *implicit* in the agents' abductive logic programs, and they can be used to implement negation by default.

Example 2. Let us consider agent A of Example 1. Its abductive program states that something can be considered a bird if it either *f*lies or it has *fe*athers, while it can be considered a *d*olphin if it *s*wims and has no *ha*ir, or a *m*ammal if it has *ha*ir:

$$T_A = \left\{ \begin{array}{l} b \leftarrow fe. \\ b \leftarrow f. \\ d \leftarrow s, \neg ha. \\ m \leftarrow ha. \end{array} \right\} \qquad \mathcal{A} = \{f, s, fe, ha\} \qquad \mathcal{IC}_A = \left\{ \begin{array}{l} \leftarrow b, \neg f. \\ \leftarrow d, \neg s. \end{array} \right\}$$

In order to explain its observations, agent A can make assumptions according to its set $\mathcal{A}$, and, for instance, classify an animal as a dolphin by assuming that it is able to swim. Note how abducibles have no definitions. $\mathcal{IC}_A$, together with all the implicit integrity constraints, prevents A from considering in their models a bird that does not fly or a dolphin that does not swim. It is clear that there is no $\Delta \subseteq \mathcal{A}$ such that $T_A \cup \Delta \models b, \neg f$ and $T_A \cup \Delta \cup \mathcal{IC}_A \not\models \perp$, and hence, as supposed in point (1) of Example 1 (in its informal language), $A \not\models b, \neg f$.

We consider *abductive agents* to be agents whose knowledge is represented by an abductive logic program, provided with an abductive entailment operator. At this stage, we do not make assumptions on the underlying operational model.

3 Issues in a Constraint Revision Framework

Example 1 has informally introduced some issues which a framework supporting a distributed constraint revision process must address. In this section, we discuss them in more detail. The next section will provide a better technical insight, by presenting some results, specifically about constraint-based knowledge revision.

3.1   Communication

Points (2) and (4) of Example 1 require communication between agents. We are aware that the literature on this topic is huge. There is a large number of existing proposals for agent communication models and languages, several dedicated discussion forums such as the Workshop on Agent Communication Languages and Protocols [13, 14], and several conference tracks and special journal issues on this topic. Here, we do not intend to propose a new communication language or a new interaction model, but we assume that agents are able to communicate according to some language and protocols, and that they have a common ontology. The focus of the present work is rather on the *content* than on the syntax, semantics, or pragmatics of the messages that agents exchange with each other, or on the protocols which support at a lower level the knowledge revision process that we envisage. In this section, we make some remarks about communication in our framework from this perspective.

Assumption and Constraint Exchange. Point (4) requires that agents are able to exchange the sets of assumptions they make. In general, existing abductive agent frameworks deal with assumptions at a semantic level, but do not consider assumptions as a first order object in the content of a message. For instance, in [6], the messages themselves are modelled as abducible predicates, but they do not predicate about assumptions. In the computational model of [7] and [8], when agents cooperatively resolve a query, the computational model is in charge of checking the global consistency of the assumptions made against the integrity constraints of all the agent, but, still, agents can not, for instance, directly ask other agents to check for the consistency of a given set of abducibles.

This enhancement with respect to the previous work done on the subject is necessary in order to exploit assumptions in the process of determining significant sets of constraints, like in points (3) and (5). Moreover, agents could be required to explain an observation, starting from a given set of assumptions, or using them in order to determine sets of integrity constraints that have supported (or denied) a proof yielding those explanations. Similarly, it is also necessary to communicate sets of constraints, point (4), which is not allowed in existing abductive agent frameworks either, to the best of our knowledge, and for which analogous considerations hold.

Identity Discover. Starting from point (2), agent A establishes a conversation with agent B. This requires a mechanism allowing A to select B to speak with. For instance, this could be accomplished by means of access mechanisms to semi-open societies [15], such as facilitators or directory servers which let A meet its possible partners. This kind of problem is not addressed in this paper. Instead, we will restrict ourselves to a two-party setting, where agents are already aware of each other.

Trust and Agent Hierarchies. Almost all interaction described in Example 1 is based on relations of trust or dependency among agents [16], based on some form of reputation or determined by social ties, such as those given by a hierarchy. In particular, in the example, agent A and B expose their assumptions and even their constraints, and agent A revises its knowledge based on the view of the world of B. Similarly to the previous point, we do not discuss here the mechanisms which justify such relations. The hypothesis that cooperating agent will share parts of their knowledge is an assumption that we have in common with other work in literature, such as [4] and [7].

Social Constraints. We would like to make a final remark about the use of communicating constraints within a society. Although integrity constraints and assumptions are specific of abductive agents, in [10] an interaction framework is proposed where integrity constraints are used to model interaction protocols. Such protocols are not inside the agents but in a social infrastructure which is outside the agents. In this setting, a society where certain interaction protocols are defined by way of integrity constraints could notify such constraints to newcomers, in order to help them to behave according to the protocols. Or else, a society could notify protocol updates to its members.

3.2   Proof of Goals and Relevance of Integrity Constraints

Constraint revision, as illustrated in Example 1, requires the capability to determine a set of constraints which are "relevant" for a given computation, either because that they contribute to defining a set of assumptions in a successful proof, or because they make a proof fail. For instance in point (3), B, relatively to the explanation Δ, determines the set $\mathcal{IC}'$ of integrity constraints supporting the explanation of the observation.

From a declarative perspective, relevant sets for a successful proof are formally defined in Section 4.1. This definition is used, for instance, by agent B in determining the set $\mathcal{IC}' = \{\leftarrow b, \neg f, \neg p\}$ which is relevant for the proof of the query, and relaxes (see below) the set $\mathcal{IC}''$, points (3) and (5) of the example. The definition of a proof procedure implementing the declarative definition of relevance is one of our ongoing activities, although we reckon that the problem of determining significant integrity constraints for a given proof may be computationally hard.

In general, there will be several alternative sets of relevant constraints for the same query, e.g., because there are different alternative proofs for it. The existence of a unique minimal set is not guaranteed either. For this reason, we envisage that the knowledge revision process will have to go through a search process for suitable sets. For instance, agents can iterate a cooperative dialog, similar to that of Example 1, in which they propose to each other a number of (minimal) significant sets, until they converge to a successful proof, if there exists any. This is in line with the approach of [7] and [6]. In Section 5, we illustrate a possible cycle which allows for such an interaction in the form of a dialogue.

3.3   Constraint Hierarchies

Point (5) requires the definition of the concept of *relaxation* of a set of constraints, i.e. the capability to determine, given a set $\mathcal{IC}$, another set $\mathcal{IC}'$ that relaxes it. In order to address this issue, we propose in Section 4.2 an algebra of $\mathcal{IC}$s, provided with a relaxation-based partial order.

Intuitively, a set $\mathcal{IC}'$ of integrity constraints *relaxes* a set $\mathcal{IC}$, $\mathcal{IC} <^{IC} \mathcal{IC}'$, if all the goals that can be proved with respect to $\mathcal{IC}$ can be also proven with respect to $\mathcal{IC}'$.

The relaxing relation, in some basic cases, can be checked by means of a simple necessary condition, namely a syntactical comparison. This happens when the relation is the set inclusion partial order. More in general, the relation may fail to be a partial order, in which case it is a pre-order, and checking whether a set relaxes another one according to the definition of relaxing relation may require a more complex analysis, based on the semantics of the corresponding ALP. This point is currently under investigation.

Clearly, the partial order can also be read as a tightening-based partial order, i.e. $\mathcal{IC}'$ *tightens* $\mathcal{IC}$, $\mathcal{IC}' <^{IC} \mathcal{IC}$, when the goals that can be proved with respect to $\mathcal{IC}'$ are a subset of those that can proved with respect to $\mathcal{IC}$. A possible definition of $<^{IC}$ can be found in Section 4.2. Hence, the same formal model can be used to describe interactions, which, possibly depending on the issues discussed in Section 3.1, may lead an agent to restrict his own believes.

Finally, the partially ordered set of integrity constraints can be equipped with operations for relaxing, tightening and more in general revising sets of integrity constraints, as described in the next sections.

3.4   Constraint Revision

Once that a relaxing $\mathcal{IC}'$ has been found, it is necessary to be able to use it in order to revise the constraint set $\mathcal{IC}$ of an agent, as it happens in point (5), where A revises its own integrity constraints.

In general, only a subset of the integrity constraints of an agent will have to be revised according to a relaxing or tightening operation. To this aim, we have defined a relaxation operator which, given two sets of integrity constraints $\mathcal{IC}_a$ and $\mathcal{IC}_b$ returns a third set of integrity constraints, $\mathcal{IC}' = \mathcal{IC}_a \uplus \mathcal{IC}_b$ which relaxes $\mathcal{IC}_a$ in case $\mathcal{IC}_a <^{IC} \mathcal{IC}_b$ (see Section 4.3). We present in this paper a specific operator $\uplus$, but indeed, within our framework, other tightening and revising operations can be defined.

Example 3. After having explained in more detail the steps for constraint revision, let us now possible reconsider Example 1, and let A's program be the one introduced in Example 2.

(1) $A \overset{abd}{\not\models} \neg f, b$	A is not able to prove $\neg f, b$ and $\mathcal{IC}'' = \{\leftarrow b, \neg f\}$ is not satisfied by any possible explanation for the observation, and hence are candidate for a possible revision;
(2) $A \rightarrow B : \neg f, b$	A asks B about its observation;
(3) $B \models_{\Delta^{\mathcal{IC}'}}^{abd} \neg f, b$	$\Delta = \{\neg f, p, \neg ha\}$ is an abductive explanation of B, and $\mathcal{IC}' = \{\leftarrow b, \neg f, \neg p\}$ is a relevant constraint for the proof of B;

(4) $B \rightarrow A : \mathcal{IC}'$	B suggests to A the (singleton) set of integrity constraints $\mathcal{IC}' = \{\leftarrow b, \neg f, \neg p\}$;
(5) $A_{\ominus \mathcal{IC}'' \oplus \mathcal{IC}'} \overset{abd}{\models}_{\Delta'} \neg f, b$	A relaxes its constraints using $\mathcal{IC}'$ and is now able to explain his original observation $\neg f, b$, by using a $\Delta' = \{\neg f, p\}$

4 A Formal Model for Constraint Revision

In this section we illustrate some technical aspects we devised in order to support the model for constraint revision that we informally discussed in the previous sections. First, we define the set of integrity constraints that are significant in a successful or failed proof; second, we present a partial order of constraint sets according to a relaxing relation (that can be dually read as a tightening relation); finally, we introduce an updating operator for revising a (significant) set of constraints, which is based on the partial order presented.

4.1 Determining Significant Sets of Constraints

Definition 1 below characterises a set of the constraints involved in a successful abductive proof, relatively to a (minimal) set of explanations Δ. All the constraints in the set are directly involved in the proof. Indeed, as soon as one of them is removed, a smaller set of assumptions can be produced by a successful proof for the same goal.

Definition 1. *Let $P = \langle T, \mathcal{A}, \mathcal{IC} \rangle$ be an abductive logic program and G a goal, such that $\langle T, \mathcal{A}, \mathcal{IC} \rangle \overset{abd}{\models}_{\Delta} G$ (i.e., Δ is a possible explanation for G in P). Let us assume that Δ is minimal, i.e. $\not\exists \hat{\Delta} \subset \Delta$ such that $\langle T, \mathcal{A}, \mathcal{IC} \rangle \overset{abd}{\models}_{\hat{\Delta}} G$.[2] A set of integrity constraints $\mathcal{IC}' \subseteq \mathcal{IC}$ is* relevant *with respect to P, G and Δ, written $\mathcal{IC}'$* rel $(\langle T, \mathcal{A}, \mathcal{IC} \rangle, G, \Delta)$, $\overset{def}{\Longleftrightarrow}$*

$$\forall \, ic \in \mathcal{IC}' \, \exists \Delta' \subset \Delta \text{ such that } \langle T, \mathcal{A}, \mathcal{IC} \setminus ic \rangle \overset{abd}{\models}_{\Delta'} G. \qquad (i)$$

Example 4. Let us consider agent B of Example 1. Its program T_B says that something can be considered a bird if either it flies or it is a penguin, or in any case if it is not a mammal. Something is a mammal if it has hair. Its constraints in $\mathcal{IC}_B$ say that a bird either flies or is a penguin, and that dolphins swim.

$$T_B = \left\{ \begin{array}{l} b \leftarrow f. \\ b \leftarrow p. \\ b \leftarrow \neg m. \\ m \leftarrow ha. \end{array} \right\} \qquad \mathcal{A} = \{f, p, ha\} \qquad \mathcal{IC}_B = \left\{ \begin{array}{l} \leftarrow b, \neg f, \neg p. \\ \leftarrow d, \neg s. \end{array} \right\}$$

---

[2] One amongst the minimal sets can be freely chosen.

Agent B can assume that something flies or it is a penguin, or it has hair, according to its set $\mathcal{A}$.

It turns out that $\langle T_B, \mathcal{A}, \mathcal{IC}_B \rangle \overset{abd}{\models}_{\{\neg f, p, \neg ha\}} \neg f, b$, and $\{\neg f, p, \neg ha\}$ is minimal. Moreover,

$$\mathcal{IC}' = \{\leftarrow b, \neg f, \neg p\} \textbf{ rel } (\langle T_B, \mathcal{A}, \mathcal{IC}_B \rangle, \ \neg f, b, \ \{\neg f, p, \neg ha\}),$$

since $\langle T_B, \mathcal{A}, \mathcal{IC}_B \setminus \mathcal{IC}' \rangle \overset{abd}{\models}_{\{\neg f, \neg ha\}} \neg f, b$, and $\{\neg f, \neg ha\} \subset \{\neg f, p, \neg ha\}$.

In the following, we will use the simplified notation $\mathcal{IC}'$ **rel** $(\langle T, \mathcal{A}, \mathcal{IC} \rangle, G)$ meaning $\exists \Delta \mid \mathcal{IC}'$ **rel** $(\langle T, \mathcal{A}, \mathcal{IC} \rangle, G, \Delta)$

The previous example shows how Definition 1 characterises the set of constraints that B is able to propose to A in points (3) and (4) of our Example 1. The definition represents a "sufficient" condition to individuate relevant constraints. Even if more general criteria are under investigation, this simple definition allows us to substantiate the approach. We are also studying its computational counterpart.

On the other hand, given a failing derivation $\langle T, \mathcal{A}, \mathcal{IC} \rangle \overset{abd}{\not\models} G$ of an abductive agent, it is also worth giving a characterisation of a (minimal) subset of $\mathcal{IC}$ such that, once relaxed, or removed, allows G to be proved. This is the notion of *minimally relaxing* set defined by Definition 2.

Definition 2. *Let $P = \langle T, \mathcal{A}, \mathcal{IC} \rangle$ be an abductive logic program, and G a goal such that $\langle T, \mathcal{A}, \mathcal{IC} \rangle \overset{abd}{\not\models} G$ (i.e., there is no explanation for G in P). A set of integrity constraints $\mathcal{IC}' \subseteq \mathcal{IC}$ is minimally relaxing P (towards explaining G), written $\mathcal{IC}'$ **min_relax** $(\langle T, \mathcal{A}, \mathcal{IC} \rangle, G)$, $\overset{def}{\Longleftrightarrow}$*

$$\exists \Delta \text{ such that } \langle T, \mathcal{A}, \mathcal{IC} \setminus \mathcal{IC}' \rangle \overset{abd}{\models}_\Delta G, \text{ and} \qquad \text{(ii)}$$

$$(\mathcal{IC}' \text{ is minimal}) \ \not\exists \ \mathcal{IC}'' \subset \mathcal{IC}' \text{ s.t. } \mathcal{IC}'' \textbf{ min\_relax } (\langle T, \mathcal{A}, \mathcal{IC} \rangle, G) \qquad \text{(iii)}$$

Example 5. Let us consider an agent A whose abductive logic program is the one introduced in Example 2. Trivially, it turns out that

$$\mathcal{IC}' = \{\leftarrow b, \neg f\} \textbf{ min\_relax } (\langle T_A, \mathcal{A}, \mathcal{IC}_A \rangle, b, \neg f).$$

4.2   A Relaxing-Tightening Hierarchy of Constraints

In this section, we define a partial ordering relationship among integrity constraints, and then we lift it to sets of integrity constraints. For this purpose, we introduce a symbol $<^{IC}$ (to be read: "more restrictive than", or "less relaxed than"). This (complete, under reasonable hypothesis) partial ordering is a specific instantiation of the general notions of relaxation and tightening applied to set of constraints, and it will be used in the next section to define the revision operators.

Definition 3. *Given a pair of integrity constraints, ic_i and ic_j,*

$$ic_i <^{IC} ic_j \overset{def}{\Longleftrightarrow} \forall \Delta, \Delta \cup \{ic_i\} \not\models \bot \Rightarrow \Delta \cup \{ic_j\} \not\models \bot.$$

Example 6. Let us consider the following constraints:

(ic_1) $\bot \leftarrow a, b,$
(ic_2) $\bot \leftarrow a, b, c,$

Then, $ic_1 <^{IC} ic_2$.

We can generalize the ordering relationship, from pairs of integrity constraints to pairs of sets of integrity constraints.

Definition 4. *Given two sets of integrity constrains, $\mathcal{IC}_i$ and $\mathcal{IC}_j$,*

$$\mathcal{IC}_i <^{IC} \mathcal{IC}_j \overset{def}{\Longleftrightarrow} \forall \Delta, \Delta \cup \mathcal{IC}_i \not\models \bot \Rightarrow \Delta \cup \mathcal{IC}_j \not\models \bot.$$

The ordering initially introduced between pairs of integrity constraints is a special case of the more general ordering relation between pairs of sets. In particular, from Definitions 3 and 4 it follows that:

Lemma 1. *Given a pair of integrity constraints, ic_i and ic_j,*

$$body(ic_i) \subset body(ic_j) \Leftrightarrow ic_i <^{IC} ic_j \qquad (iv)$$
$$\{ic_i\} <^{IC} \{ic_j\} \Leftrightarrow ic_i <^{IC} ic_j \qquad (v)$$

If $\mathcal{IC}_j$ is constituted by a single element, $\mathcal{IC}_j = \{ic_j\}$, we use the notation $\mathcal{IC}_i <^{IC} ic_j$ to denote $\mathcal{IC}_i <^{IC} \{ic_j\}$.

Example 7. By defining the *zero element* of the $<^{IC}$ relation as $ic^0 \overset{def}{\Longleftrightarrow} \bot \leftarrow$, i.e. the integrity constraint which is never satisfied, it is easy to see that

$$\forall ic. \ ic^0 <^{IC} ic.$$

Example 8. Let us consider the following constraints:

(ic_1) $\bot \leftarrow a, b,$
(ic_3) $\bot \leftarrow c, \neg b,$
(ic_4) $\bot \leftarrow a, c,$ and the implicit constraint
(ic_5) $\bot \leftarrow b, \neg b.$

Then, $\{ic_1, ic_3, ic_5\} <^{IC} ic_4$.

4.3   A Constraint Updating Operator

We define an "update with relaxation" operator $\mathcal{IC}_a \uplus \mathcal{IC}_b$, which updates the set of integrity constraints $\mathcal{IC}_a$ with respect to $\mathcal{IC}_b$, relaxing, whenever possible, the constraints in $\mathcal{IC}_a$ that are "less relaxed than" ($<^{IC}$) those in $\mathcal{IC}_b$. More precisely, given two constraints $ic_a \in \mathcal{IC}_a$ and $ic_b \in \mathcal{IC}_b$, if $ic_a <^{IC} ic_b$ then $ic_a \notin \mathcal{IC}_a \uplus \mathcal{IC}_b$. Example 9 illustrates the use of the operator, whose definition is straightforward for the basic cases 1. and 2. of the next definition. Further examples of its usage in Section 5 will hopefully make the rationale of its definition clearer, in particular when the set $\mathcal{IC}_b$ has been proposed by a collaborative agent as a relaxation for explaining some facts. This operator supports the revision step done by A in point (5) of the Example 1.

Definition 5. *Let $\mathcal{IC}_a$ and $\mathcal{IC}_b$ be two sets of integrity constraints. Then, the update with relaxation of $\mathcal{IC}_a$ by $\mathcal{IC}_b$, denoted as $\mathcal{IC}_a \uplus \mathcal{IC}_b$, is defined as follows:*

$$\mathcal{IC}_a \uplus \mathcal{IC}_b \stackrel{def}{\Longleftrightarrow} \mathcal{IC}_a \setminus \mathcal{IC}_a' \cup \mathcal{IC}_b,$$

where $\mathcal{IC}_a' = \bigcup_{\mathcal{IC}_a'' \subseteq \mathcal{IC}_a} \mathcal{IC}_a''$ such that $\mathcal{IC}_a'' <^{IC}_{(min)} ic_b$ for some $ic_b \in \mathcal{IC}_b$. $\mathcal{IC} <^{IC}_{(min)} ic$ is defined as follows:

$$\mathcal{IC} <^{IC}_{(min)} ic \stackrel{def}{\Longleftrightarrow} \begin{cases} \mathcal{IC} <^{IC} ic \\ \not\exists \mathcal{IC}' \subset \mathcal{IC} \text{ such that } \mathcal{IC}' <^{IC} ic \end{cases}$$

We have two special cases of $\mathcal{IC}_a \uplus \mathcal{IC}_b$:

1. given two integrity constraints, ic_a and ic_b,

$$\{ic_a\} \uplus \{ic_b\} \Longleftrightarrow \begin{cases} \{ic_b\}, & \text{if } ic_a <^{IC} ic_b \\ \{ic_a, ic_b\}, & \text{otherwise} \end{cases}$$

2. given an integrity constraint ic_a and a set of integrity constraints $\mathcal{IC}_b$,

$$\{ic_a\} \uplus \mathcal{IC}_b \Longleftrightarrow \begin{cases} \mathcal{IC}_b, & \text{if } \exists ic_b \in \mathcal{IC}_b \text{ such that } ic_a <^{IC} ic_b \\ \{ic_a\} \cup \mathcal{IC}_b, & \text{otherwise} \end{cases}$$

Example 9.
Given the following constraints: The following propositions hold:

$(ic_1) \leftarrow a, b.$

$(ic_3) \leftarrow c, \neg b.$

$(ic_4) \leftarrow a, c.$

$(ic_5) \leftarrow b, \neg b.$

$(ic_6) \leftarrow a, b, \neg c.$

(p_1) $ic_1 <^{IC} ic_6$;

(p_2) $\{ic_1, ic_3, ic_5\} <^{IC}_{(min)} ic_4$;

(p_3) $\{ic_6\} = \{ic_1\} \uplus \{ic_6\}$;

(p_4) $\{ic_1, ic_6\} = \{ic_6\} \uplus \{ic_1\}$;

(p_5) $\{ic_4\} = \{ic_1, ic_3, ic_5\} \uplus \{ic_4\}$;

(p_6) $\{ic_3, ic_4, ic_6\} = \{ic_1, ic_3\} \uplus \{ic_4, ic_6\}$;

(p_7) $\{ic_4, ic_5\} = \{ic_1, ic_3, ic_5\} \uplus \{ic_4, ic_5\}$;

5   An Example of Application of Our Framework

In this section we show a possible instantiation of the general framework. We consider, for the sake of simplicity, a 2-agent setting. Agent a is equipped with the abductive logic program $\langle T_a, \mathcal{A}, \mathcal{IC}_a \rangle$; agent b with $\langle T_b, \mathcal{A}, \mathcal{IC}_b \rangle$. Whenever a fails to explain an observation G within its current abductive logic program, it starts an interaction with b, in order to find a suitable relaxation of its integrity constraints that allows him (a) to explain G. On the other hand, b will have to reply to a's request according to some internal policy.

We distinguish between two phases of the interaction between a and b: (i) the process of (pro-actively) asking for a piece of information, be it a set of assumptions, a set of integrity constraints, a set of definitions, or a combination of them, and (ii) the process of reacting to incoming requests of that kind. As far as the first point, we imagine that agents will act according to certain internal cycles and policies. For the sake of clarity, and in order to keep the two things separate, we will call *cycle* the sequence of steps related to the activity described as (i), *policy* that related to the activity described as (ii).

5.1   Cycle

We define a predicate **request**$(a, b, \mathcal{IC}'_a, G)$ which an agent a will use to request a set of constraints $\mathcal{IC}'_b$ from an agent b.

As we said earlier in Section 3, in general, there will be several alternative sets of relevant constraints for the same query. For this reason, the knowledge revision process will have to go through a trial-and-error search process for suitable minimal sets. For instance, agents can iterate a cooperative dialog, similar to that of Example 1, in which they propose to each other a number of minimal significant sets, until they converge to a successful proof, if any.

In **Cycle 1**, we illustrate a possible cycle which allows for such an interaction in the form of a dialog.

Cycle 1 Agent update cycle for an agent a

To explain an observation G, if $\langle T_a, \mathcal{A}, \mathcal{IC}_a \rangle \not\models_a G$:
1: Find a minimal relaxation, $\mathcal{IC}'_a$ **min_relax** $(\langle T_a, \mathcal{A}, \mathcal{IC}_a \rangle, G)$
2: **repeat**
3:    Send **request**$(a, b, \mathcal{IC}'_a, G)$
4:    Wait for **reply**$(b, a, \mathcal{IC}'_a, G, \mathcal{IC}'_a)$
5:    **repeat**
6:       $\mathcal{IC}''_a = \mathcal{IC}_a \uplus \mathcal{IC}'_a$
7:       **if** $\langle T_a, \mathcal{A}, \mathcal{IC}''_a \rangle \models_a G$ **then**
8:          Update $\mathcal{IC}_a$ by $\mathcal{IC}''_a$
9:       **else**
10:        Send **request**$(a, b, \mathcal{IC}'_a, G)$
11:        Wait for **reply**$(b, a, \mathcal{IC}'_a, G, \mathcal{IC}^1_a)$
12:        $\mathcal{IC}'_a \leftarrow \mathcal{IC}^1_a$
13:       **end if**
14:    **until** $\langle T_a, \mathcal{A}, \mathcal{IC}_a \rangle \models_a G$ or $\mathcal{IC}'_a = \emptyset$
15:    **if** $\langle T_a, \mathcal{A}, \mathcal{IC}_a \rangle \not\models_a G$ **then**
16:       Find a *new* minimal relaxation, $\mathcal{IC}^1_a$ **min_relax** $(\langle T_a, \mathcal{A}, \mathcal{IC}_a \rangle, G)$
17:       $\mathcal{IC}'_a \leftarrow \mathcal{IC}^1_a$
18:    **end if**
19: **until** $\langle T_a, \mathcal{A}, \mathcal{IC}_a \rangle \models_a G$ or $\mathcal{IC}^1_a = \emptyset$

The intuitive reading of **Cycle 1** is the following: whenever a has an observation G that he cannot explain, he will:

1. try and find a minimal relaxation $\mathcal{IC}'_a$ for G (**1:**);
2. ask b (**3:**) whether he can tell him something about it (more details about b's reply are given below);
3. once a receives a **reply** from b (**4:**), **reply**$(b, a, \mathcal{IC}'_a, G, \mathcal{IC}'_b)$, if a is able to relax his own constraints by means of $\mathcal{IC}'_b$ and therefore explain the observation, he will revise his knowledge (**8:**) accordingly;
4. otherwise, a will keep asking for different sets of integrity constraints until either he manages to explain his observation, or b has no other sets of constraints (**14:**) to communicate to him;
5. if a does not succeed with $\mathcal{IC}'_a$) (**15:**), the cycle is repeated until either a has managed to explain his observation, or there are no more "new" possible minimal relaxations (**19:**).

A dialogue initiated by an agent by means of **request**$(a, b, \mathcal{IC}'_a, G)$ terminates when the cycle is terminated. The use of such a cycle to try and achieve an agent's needs is in line with the approach of [7] and [6]. In [7], the object of communication are the hypotheses, in the form of predicates. Groups of agents try to explain an observation consistently with the integrity constraints of each other, and re-iterate the whole computational process by proposing different sets of constraints, until a fixpoint is reached. In [6], agents have a similar cycle when they try to obtain the resources that they are missing. The purpose of defining a cycle in this way is to be able to prove some properties about the outcome of the interaction. We will comment more on this in the following.

5.2   Policy

Upon receipt of a's **request**, b will adopt some policy to put together a set of constraints in reply. We use the predicate: **reply**$(b, a, \mathcal{IC}'_a, G, \mathcal{IC}'_b)$ to indicate b's reply to a's **request**. **Policy 1** is one particular policy, defined for an agent b. Its intuitive reading is the following: whenever b receives a message of kind **request**$(a, b, \mathcal{IC}'_a, G)$ from an agent a, b will do the following:

1. check if he can find an abductive explanation for G (**1:**), and answer back with an empty set in case of failure (**2:**);
2. otherwise single out a minimal subset $\mathcal{IC}'_b$ of integrity constraints (**4:**) in $\mathcal{IC}_b$, which are relevant for such an explanation, and which b has not yet communicated to a by means of **reply**$(b, a, \mathcal{IC}'_a, G, \mathcal{IC}'_b)$;
3. communicate $\mathcal{IC}'_b$ to a (**7:**): **reply**$(b, a, \mathcal{IC}'_a, G, \mathcal{IC}'_b)$

This policy is only one example. Other ones are indeed possible. A reason why we have chosen the combination of **Policy 1** and **Cycle 1** is that they allow for exchanging meta-knowledge (constraints) by way of dialogues of the kind of the one shown in the introduction (see Example 10 below). Another reason is that, under some assumptions (atomicity), this combination guarantees termination of the interaction process. In fact, let us consider two agents, a and b, each

Policy 1 Agent policy of an agent b for replying to a $\mathbf{request}(a, b, \mathcal{IC}'_a, G)$

To reply to a $\mathbf{request}(a, b, \mathcal{IC}'_\square, G)$:

1: **if** $\langle T_\square, \mathcal{A}, \mathcal{IC}_\square \rangle \not\models G$ **then**
2:    $\mathcal{IC}'_\square = \emptyset$
3: **else**
4:    $\mathcal{IC}'_\square$ is a subset of $\mathcal{IC}_\square$ with the following properties:
   (i) $\mathcal{IC}'_\square$ rel $(\langle T_\square, \mathcal{A}, \mathcal{IC}_\square \rangle, G)$;
   (ii) $\exists ic_\square \in \mathcal{IC}'_\square, ic_\square \in \mathcal{IC}'_\square$ such that $ic_\square <^{\square\square} ic_\square$
       (potentially, $\mathcal{IC}'_\square$ could be exploited to relax some constraints);
   (iii) $\mathcal{IC}'_\square$ has not been yet communicated to a as a reply to $\mathbf{request}(a, b, \mathcal{IC}'_\square, G)$
       (to prevent b from proposing he same $\mathcal{IC}'_\square$ twice in reply to the same
       request of a's);
5:    if such a subset cannot be found, then $\mathcal{IC}'_\square = \emptyset$
6: **end if**
7: $\mathbf{reply}(b, a, \mathcal{IC}'_\square, G, \mathcal{IC}'_\square)$

---

of them behaving according to **Cycle 1** and **Policy 1** when they are engaged in a dialogue. Let us assume that the interaction happens "atomically", i.e., once a initiates a dialogue by a **request** to explain a goal G, neither agent will update his knowledge base until a succeeds in explaining G, or the interaction has terminated. Then, an interaction protocol initiated by either agent will terminate in a finite number of steps. Informally, this is the case because, given a set $\mathcal{IC}$, there is a finite number of subsets of $\mathcal{IC}$;[3] at each iteration a different subset of $\mathcal{IC}$ is considered, and the two agents will not revise their knowledge base until the interaction has terminated, either successfully or unsuccessfully. Since no message is exchanged twice, and since there is a finite number of messages that a and b can exchange, the interaction finishes in a finite number of steps.

Another property that we would like to achieve is: given two agents a and b, the former trying to relax his constraints by adopting a specific cycle (such as **Cycle 1**), the latter responding to a's requests by following a specific policy (such as **Policy 1**), either b is unable to explain a certain observation G, or it is possible for a to revise his own integrity constraints based on b's reply, and finally explain G using his revised knowledge. This is subject for current work.

A last remark, before we conclude by giving an example where two agents interact by following **Cycle 1** and **Policy 1**. While in this work we are concerned with the exchange of information about constraints, it could also be the case that b's explanation is not prevented by any constraint of a's, but instead a is unable to explain G only because a is missing some definition which b instead knows. In order to tackle this situation, we will need to consider different introspection and updating operators, which need to reason upon and modify not only the

---

[3] We are considering in this work only propositional abductive logic programs. If we extend it to the non-propositional case, the cycle/policy would also have to be suitably adapted.

agents' integrity constraints, but also their programs, and we would need to find some suitable cycles and policies that support such a process.

Example 10. Let us consider two agents A and B, where the abductive logic program of A is that defined in Example 2, and the abductive logic program of B is that defined in Example 4, as reported below. We assume now that A and B have the same set of abducible predicates $\mathcal{A} = \{f, s, fe, ha, p\}$.

$$T_A = \begin{cases} b \leftarrow fe. \\ b \leftarrow f. \\ d \leftarrow s, \neg ha. \\ m \leftarrow ha. \end{cases} \qquad \mathcal{IC}_A = \left\{ (ic_1) \begin{array}{l} \leftarrow b, \neg f. \\ \leftarrow d, \neg s. \end{array} \right\}$$

$$T_B = \begin{cases} b \leftarrow f. \\ b \leftarrow p. \\ b \leftarrow \neg m. \\ m \leftarrow ha. \end{cases} \qquad \mathcal{IC}_B = \left\{ (ic_2) \begin{array}{l} \leftarrow b, \neg f, \neg p. \\ \leftarrow d, \neg s. \end{array} \right\}$$

Let us assume that both A and B follow **Cycle 1** to request relaxations of constraints and **Policy 1** to answer to incoming requests. Finally, we assume that at some point A makes the observation $G = \{\neg f, b\}$. Then, the behaviour of the system $\{A, B\}$ is the following:

(1) $\langle T_A, \mathcal{A}, \mathcal{IC}_A \rangle \overset{abd}{\not\models} \{\neg f, b\}$. At this point A looks for a minimal relaxation of its constraints towards explaining $\{\neg f, b\}$ (see Example 5), and it finds it in $\{ic_1\} = \{\leftarrow b, \neg f.\}$:

$$\{\leftarrow b, \neg f.\} \ \mathbf{min\_relax} \ (\langle T_A, \mathcal{A}, \mathcal{IC}_A \rangle, G)$$

(2) Following **Cycle 1**, A asks B a set of relevant integrity constraints of his, that are relevant for the explanation of G:

$$\mathbf{request}(a, b, \{\leftarrow b, \neg f\}, \{\neg f, b\});$$

(3) Upon receipt of A's request, according to **Policy 1** B verifies that he is able to prove G: $\langle T_B, \mathcal{A}, \mathcal{IC}_B \rangle \overset{abd}{\models}_{\{\neg f, p, \neg ha\}} \{b, \neg f\}$. B finds a set of integrity constraints $\mathcal{IC}'_B = \{ic_2\}$ that are relevant to A's request (see Example 4):

$$\{\leftarrow b, \neg f, \neg p.\} \ \mathbf{rel} \ (\langle T_B, \mathcal{A}, \mathcal{IC}_B \rangle, \{b, \neg f\}),$$

and indeed $\{\leftarrow b, \neg f\} <^{IC} \{\leftarrow b, \neg f, \neg p\}$. At this point, B replies to A's request by communicating $\mathcal{IC}'_B$:

$$\mathbf{reply}(a, b, \{\leftarrow b, \neg f\}, \{\neg f, b\}, \{\leftarrow b, \neg f, \neg p\});$$

(4) A generates the set $\mathcal{IC}''_A = \left\{ \begin{array}{l} \leftarrow b, \neg f, \neg p. \\ \leftarrow d, \neg s. \end{array} \right\}$ as a revision of its own $\mathcal{IC}_A$ by

$\mathcal{IC}'_B$: $\mathcal{IC}''_A = \mathcal{IC}_A \uplus \mathcal{IC}'_B$. Since $\langle T_A, \mathcal{A}, \mathcal{IC}''_A \rangle \overset{abd}{\models}_{\{b, \neg f, p\}} \{b, \neg f\}$, A updates his own abductive logic program.

6   Concluding Remarks

In this work, we have described a framework for agent interaction where the object of interaction is the agent knowledge at different levels. We have considered the case of abductive agents that are capable to formulate assumptions to explain some observations. The agent knowledge is coded into an abductive logic program, consisting of a theory, a set of abducible predicates, and a set of integrity constraints. Indeed, abduction, which we considered as representing the entire agent knowledge, could be part of a more comprehensive agent architecture, like that of computees [17], which allows for multiple forms of reasoning and knowledge representation within an agent.

In this work, we discuss about the characteristics of an interaction framework that can be used to exploit the abductive reasoning of a possibly more complex agent. Agents exchange information about the assumptions that they make in order to explain observations, and the integrity constraints used during their reasoning. Integrity constraints "shape" the reasoning processes of agents by ruling out the set of explanation which are considered to be inconsistent. Exchanging constraints help revising the reasoning capabilities of agents. The methodology presents some difficulties that we singled out, like understanding the role of sets of constraints in a proof, defining constraint revising mechanisms, or design suitable interaction schemata for the collaboration of agents within a society.

We identified some issues that must be tackled by such a framework, both with respect to the kind of communication required and the kind of agent reasoning involved in the revision process. We instantiated the general framework by choosing a specific syntax for abductive logic programs, defining a partial ordering relation among sets of integrity constraints, and proposing a specific revision operator. In the last section of this paper, we showed a possible application of the framework to specific interaction patterns, and we commented on the kind of properties that we want the framework to exhibit. An issue that will have to be investigated is the computational complexity of such interaction patterns, both for what concerns (i) the computational cost of proceeding in the protocol (i.e., by finding a minimal relaxation), and (ii) the properties related to the protocol itself, such as guaranteed termination and convergence. In doing so, we plan to build on results from literature, such as [18, 19] for (i), and [20] for (ii).

This work represents a proposal for a framework to tackle issues that we consider important in multi-source knowledge-intensive applications, and to the best of our knowledge its approach is original. In the future, we intend to complete the formalisation of the aspects that are not already covered by our model. For instance, it seems interesting to work on the definition of further revision operators and on giving a declarative semantics to some specific patterns of interaction, such as the one suggested in Section 5, and, also, to provide a computational counterpart to it.

Acknowledgments

We would like to thank Luís Pereira and the anonymous referees for their valuable comments and feedback. This work was partially funded by the Information Society Technologies programme of the European Commission, Future and Emerging Technologies under the IST-2001-32530 SOCS project [17], within the Global Computing proactive initiative, and by the MIUR COFIN 40% project *Sviluppo e verifica di sistemi multiagente basati sulla logica*.

References

1. Kowalski, R.A., Sadri, F.: From logic programming towards multi-agent systems. Annals of Mathematics and Artificial Intelligence **25** (1999) 391–419
2. Leite, J.A., Alferes, J.J., Pereira, L.M.: $\mathcal{MINERVA}$: A dynamic logic programming agent architecture. In: Intelligent Agents VIII: 8th International Workshop, ATAL 2001, Seattle, WA, USA, Revised Papers. Lecture Notes in Artificial Intelligence **2333**, Springer-Verlag (2002) 141–157
3. Satoh, K., Inoue, K., Iwanuma, K., Sakama, C.: Speculative computation by abduction under incomplete communication environments. In: Proceedings of the 4th International Conference on Multi-Agent Systems, Boston, USA, IEEE Press (2000) 263–270
4. Dell'Acqua, P., Nilsson, U., Pereira, L.M.: A logic based asynchronous multi-agent system. Electronic Notes in Theoretical Computer Science **70** (2002)
5. Dell'Acqua, P.: Weighted multi dimensional logic programs. In this volume.
6. Sadri, F., Toni, F., Torroni, P.: An abductive logic programming architecture for negotiating agents. In Greco, S., Leone, N., eds.: Proceedings of the 8th European Conference on Logics in Artificial Intelligence (JELIA). Lecture Notes in Artificial Intelligence **2424**, Springer-Verlag (2002) 419–431
7. Ciampolini, A., Lamma, E., Mello, P., Toni, F., Torroni, P.: Co-operation and competition in *ALIAS*: a logic framework for agents that negotiate. Computational Logic in Multi-Agent Systems. Annals of Mathematics and Artificial Intelligence **37** (2003) 65–91
8. Gavanelli, M., Lamma, E., Mello, P., Torroni, P.: An abductive framework for information exchange in multi-agent systems. In this volume.
9. Mooney, R.J.: Integrating abduction and induction in machine learning. In Flach, P.A., Kakas, A.C., eds.: Abductive and Inductive Reasoning. Pure and Applied Logic. Kluwer Academic Publishers (2000) 181–191
10. Alberti, M., Gavanelli, M., Lamma, E., Mello, P., Torroni, P.: Specification and verification of agent interactions using social integrity constraints. Electronic Notes in Theoretical Computer Science **85** (2003)
11. Eshghi, K., Kowalski, R.A.: Abduction compared with negation by failure. In Levi, G., Martelli, M., eds.: Proceedings of the 6th International Conference on Logic Programming, MIT Press (1989) 234–255
12. Kakas, A.C., Mancarella, P.: Generalized stable models: a semantics for abduction. In: Proceedings 9th European Conference on Artificial Intelligence, Pitman Publishing (1990)
13. Dignum, F., Greaves, M., eds.: Issues in Agent Communication. Lecture Notes in Artificial Intelligence **1916**, Springer-Verlag (2000)

14. Huget, M.P., Dignum, F., eds.: Advances in Agent Communication: International Workshop on Agent Communication Languages, ACL 2003, Melbourne, Australia, July 14, 2003. Revised and Invited Papers. Lecture Notes in Artificial Intelligence **2922**, Springer-Verlag (2004)
15. Davidsson, P.: Categories of artificial societies. In Omicini, A., Petta, P., Tolksdorf, R., eds.: Engineering Societies in the Agents World II. Volume 2203 of Lecture Notes in Artificial Intelligence., Springer-Verlag (2001) 1–9
16. Castelfranchi, C., Falcone, R., Firozabadi, B., Tan, Y.H.:, guest eds.: Special Issue on "Trust in Agents", Parts 1 and 2. Applied Artificial Intelligence **14** (2000)
17. Societies Of ComputeeS (SOCS): a computational logic model for the description, analysis and verification of global and open societies of heterogeneous computees. Home Page: `http://lia.deis.unibo.it/Research/SOCS/`.
18. Eiter, T., Makino, K.: On Computing all Abductive Explanations. In: Proceedings of the 18th National Conference on Artificial Intelligence, AAAI'02, Edmonton, Alberta, Canada (2002) 62–67
19. Lin, F., You, J.: Abduction in logic programming: a new definition and an abductive procedure based on rewriting. Artificial Intelligence **140** (2002) 175–205
20. Torroni, P.: A study on the termination of negotiation dialogues. In Castelfranchi, C., Lewis Johnson, W., eds.: Proceedings of the First International Joint Conference on Autonomous Agents and Multiagent Systems (AAMAS-2002), Part III, Bologna, Italy, ACM Press (2002) 1223–1230

Weighted Multi Dimensional Logic Programs

Pierangelo Dell'Acqua

Department of Science and Technology - ITN,
Linköping University, Norrköping, Sweden
`pier@itn.liu.se`
and
Centro de Inteligência Artificial - CENTRIA,
Departamento de Informática, Faculdade de Ciências e Tecnologia,
Universidade Nova de Lisboa, 2829-516 Caparica, Portugal

Abstract. In a previous work we introduced a logical framework suitable to formalize structures of epistemic agents. Such a framework is based on the notion of weighted directed acyclic graphs (WDAGs) that allow one to assign a measure of strength to the knowledge relationships represented by the edges. In this paper we present the declarative and operational semantics of such a framework, and give results of correctness. We illustrate the usage of the framework by formalizing social agent structures.

1 Motivation

In previous papers [5, 7, 9] we presented a logical formalization of a framework for multi-agent systems where we embedded a flexible and powerful kind of epistemic agent. In fact, these agents are rational, reactive, abductive, able to prefer and they can update the knowledge base of other agents (including their own). There we presented a declarative semantics for this kind of agent. In [1] we provided a syntactical transformation that is at the basis for a proof procedure for updating and preferring in agents, and in [6] we presented a framework for handling the communication among epistemic agents asynchronously.

It is advocated, especially in open multi-agent systems (cf. [3, 16]), that there is a need to make the organizational elements as well as the formalization of the agent interactions of a multi-agent system externally visible rather than being embedded in the mental state of each agent, i.e., it is desired to explicitly represent the organizational structure and the agent interactions. Zambonelli [15] states that modelling and engineering interactions in complex and open multi-agent systems cannot simply rely on the agent capabilities for communicating. Rather, there is a need for concepts like organizational rules, social laws and active environments. For the effective engineering of multi-agent systems, high-level, inter-agent concepts, language extensions, and abstractions must be defined to explicitly model the organization, the society in which agents operate, and the associated organizational laws. With this purpose in mind, in [8] we elaborated over the approach proposed in [7], and usher in the more flexible

J. Dix and J. Leite (Eds.): CLIMA IV, LNAI 3259, pp. 178–200, 2004.

notion of weighted directed acyclic graphs (WDAGs), generalizing the notion of directed acyclic graphs (DAGs), and permitting us to address the issues at hand by assigning a measure of strength to the knowledge sharing relationships represented by the edges. In [8] we first introduced the paradigm of weighted multi dimensional logic programing (WMDLP) as a formal tool for knowledge representation and reasoning. WMDLP generalizes the paradigm of multi dimensional logic programming (MDLP) presented in [12] by replacing the path relation over DAGs (on which MDLP is based) with a prevalence relation (over WDAGs) induced by the weights assigned to the edges of the WDAG. The declarative and procedural semantics of WMDLP are similar to the ones of MDLP except for employing the prevalence relation.

Arguably, the use of WMDLPs as a representational tool allows one to formalize in a natural and abstract way agent societies (cf. [8]). In this paper, we illustrate the expressivity and flexibility of the usage of WMDLP by exploring social agent societies. It is worth noting that WMDLP also promotes modularity and information hiding. Consider for example a society comprising two agents, α and β. To express that α is predominant over β, we can associate a weight to α greater than the weight associated to β without having to know the internal representational structure of the agents.

In this paper we (i) refine the prevalence relation (wrt. the original definition given in [8]) and discuss its properties (Section 3); (ii) recall the declarative semantics (Section 4) and illustrate the usage of WMDLP to model social agent structures (Sections 5, 6 and 7); (iii) provide the operational semantics for WMDLP together with results of correctness (Section 8); and finally (iv) formally discuss the relationship between WMDLPs and MDLPs (Section 9).

An implementation of WMDLP is available at http://www.itn.liu.se/~piede.

2   Background

Generalized Logic Programs. To represent negative information we allow default negation $not\,A$ to occur in premises of rules as well as in their heads[1]. By a *generalized logic program* P over a language $\mathcal{L}$ we mean a finite or infinite set of rules of the form $L_0 \leftarrow L_1, \ldots, L_n$, where each L_i is a *literal* (i.e. an atom A or its default negation $not\,A$). We use ';' to separate the rules in a program. For instance, if a program P contains the rule $a \leftarrow b, c$ together with the rule $e \leftarrow f$ and the fact d, we write $P = \{a \leftarrow b, c; e \leftarrow f; d\}$. In the following we syntactically represent generalized logic programs as propositional Horn theories. In particular, we represent default negation $not\,A$ as a propositional variable. Given an arbitrary set $\mathcal{K}$ of propositional variables, whose names do not begin with *not*, the propositional language $\mathcal{L}$ generated by $\mathcal{K}$ is the language whose set of propositional variables consists of:

$$\{A \mid A \in \mathcal{K}\} \cup \{not\,A \mid A \in \mathcal{K}\}.$$

---

[1] For further motivation and intuitive reading of logic programs with default negations in the heads see [2].

If r is a rule of the form $L_0 \leftarrow L_1, \ldots, L_n$, by $head(r)$ we mean L_0, and by $body(r)$ we mean $L_1, \ldots, L_n$. If $head(r) = A$ (resp. $head(r) = not\,A$) then $not\,head(r) = not\,A$ (resp. $not\,head(r) = A$). By a (2-valued) *interpretation* M of $\mathcal{L}$ we mean any set of literals from $\mathcal{L}$ that satisfies the condition that for any atom A, precisely one of the literals A or $not\,A$ belongs to M. Given an interpretation M, we define $M^+ = \{A \mid A \in M\}$ and $M^- = \{not\,A \mid not\,A \in M\}$.

Following established tradition, wherever convenient we omit the default atoms when describing interpretations and models. We say that a (2-valued) interpretation M of $\mathcal{L}$ is a *stable model* of a generalized logic program P if $M = least(P \cup M^-)$. The class of generalized logic programs can be viewed as a special case of yet broader classes of programs, introduced earlier in [13], and, for the special case of normal programs, their semantics coincides with the stable models semantics [10].

Directed Acyclic Graphs. A *directed graph* $D = (V, E)$ is a pair comprised of a finite set V of *vertices* and a finite set E of ordered pairs (v_1, v_2) called *edges*, where v_1 and v_2 are vertices in V with $v_1 \neq v_2$. The vertex v_1 is the *initial vertex* of the edge and v_2 the *terminal vertex*. The *in-valency* of a vertex v is the number of edges with v as their terminal vertex. The *out-valency* of a vertex v is the number of edges with v as their initial vertex. A *source* is a vertex with in-valency 0 and a *sink* a vertex with out-valency 0. A *path* in a directed graph is a sequence of consecutive edges in the graph that begins at an initial vertex and ends at a terminal vertex. If there exists a path from a vertex v_1 to a vertex v_2 we write $v_1 \prec v_2$, otherwise $v_1 \not\prec v_2$. We write $v_1 \preceq v_2$ if $v_1 \prec v_2$ or $v_1 = v_2$. We write $v_1 \not\preceq v_2$ if $v_1 \not\prec v_2$ and $v_1 \neq v_2$. Sometime to make explicit the vertices occurring in a path $v_1 \prec v_n$ we write the sequence $\langle v_1 v_2 \ldots v_n \rangle$ of all vertices occurring in the path. A *cycle* is a path in which the initial vertex of the path is also the terminal vertex. A *directed acyclic graph* (DAG) is a directed graph that does not contain any cycle.

3   Weighted Directed Acyclic Graphs

In this section, we first introduce weighted directed acyclic graphs (WDAGs) that generalize the notion of DAGs to associate weights to their edges, and then we presents a number of notions based on WDAGs. Some of these notions were first introduced in [8].

Definition 1. *A* weighted directed graph *is a tuple* (V, E, w) *where* V *is a set of vertices,* E *a set of edges and* $w : E \rightarrow \mathbb{R}^+$ *a function mapping the edges in* E *to positive real numbers in* $\mathbb{R}^+$. *A* weighted directed acyclic graph *(WDAG) is a weighted directed graph that does not contain any cycle.*

Given two vertices v_1 and v_n in a WDAG, the following definition distinguishes the paths from v_1 to v_n that are dominant.

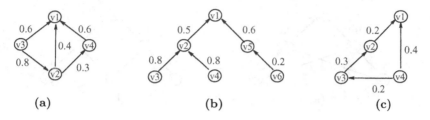

Fig. 1. WDAGs of Example 1, 2 and 3

Definition 2. *Let $D = (V, E, w)$ be a WDAG and $v_1 \prec v_n$ $(1 < n)$ a path with vertices $\langle v_1 v_2 \ldots v_n \rangle$. Then, $v_1 \prec v_n$ is a dominant path iff for every path $\langle a_1 a_2 \ldots a_m \rangle$ $(1 < m)$ such that $a_1 = v_1$, $a_m = v_n$ and $v_i = a_j$ for some i, j with $1 < i \leq n$, $1 < j \leq m$ it holds that $w((v_{i-1}, v_i)) \geq w((a_{j-1}, a_j))$.*

Example 1. Let $D = (V, E, w)$ be the WDAG depicted in Fig. 1a, where $V = \{v_1, v_2, v_3, v_4\}$, E consists of the edges: $e_1 = (v_2, v_1)$, $e_2 = (v_3, v_2)$, $e_3 = (v_3, v_1)$, $e_4 = (v_2, v_4)$ and $e_5 = (v_4, v_1)$. Let $w(e_1) = 0.4$, $w(e_2) = 0.8$, $w(e_4) = 0.3$ and $w(e_3) = w(e_5) = 0.6$. Then there exist two paths from v_3 to v_1 that are dominant: the path $\langle v_3 v_1 \rangle$ and the path $\langle v_3 v_2 v_4 v_1 \rangle$. Note that the path $\langle v_3 v_2 v_1 \rangle$ is not dominant.

Definition 3. *Let $D = (V, E, w)$ be a WDAG and $v_1 \prec v_n$ a dominant path with vertices $\langle v_1 v_2 \ldots v_n \rangle$. Then, the* prevalence relation *is defined as follows:*

- *Every vertex v_i prevails v_1 wrt. v_n, for every $1 < i \leq n$.*
- *If there exists a path $a_1 \prec v_i$ with vertices $\langle a_1 \ldots a_m v_i \rangle$ $(1 \leq m)$, for some $1 < i \leq n$, and $w((v_{i-1}, v_i)) < w((a_m, v_i))$, then every vertex a_j prevails v_1 wrt. v_n, for every $1 \leq j \leq m$.*

In the following, we write $v_1 \underset{v}{\sqsubset} v_2$ to indicate that v_2 prevails v_1 wrt. v, and $v_1 \underset{v}{\not\sqsubset} v_2$ to indicate that v_2 does not prevail v_1 wrt. v.

Example 2. Let $D = (V, E, w)$ be the WDAG depicted in Fig. 1b, where $V = \{v_1, v_2, v_3, v_4, v_5, v_6\}$, E consists of the following edges $e_1 = (v_2, v_1)$, $e_2 = (v_3, v_2)$, $e_3 = (v_4, v_2)$, $e_4 = (v_5, v_1)$ and $e_5 = (v_6, v_5)$. Let $w(e_1) = 0.5$, $w(e_2) = w(e_3) = 0.8$, $w(e_4) = 0.6$ and $w(e_5) = 0.2$. Then, the prevalence relation includes among the others the following: $v_4 \underset{v_1}{\sqsubset} v_1$, $v_2 \underset{v_1}{\sqsubset} v_1$, $v_6 \underset{v_1}{\sqsubset} v_5$, $v_2 \underset{v_1}{\sqsubset} v_5$ and $v_4 \underset{v_1}{\sqsubset} v_6$.

Example 3. Let $D = (V, E, w)$ be the WDAG depicted in Fig. 1c, where $V = \{v_1, v_2, v_3, v_4\}$, E consists of the following edges $e_1 = (v_2, v_1)$, $e_2 = (v_3, v_2)$, $e_3 = (v_4, v_1)$ and $e_4 = (v_4, v_3)$. Let $w(e_1) = 0.2$, $w(e_2) = 0.3$, $w(e_3) = 0.4$ and $w(e_4) = 0.2$. Then, the prevalence relation contains: $v_3 \underset{v_1}{\sqsubset} v_1$, $v_4 \underset{v_1}{\sqsubset} v_1$, $v_2 \underset{v_1}{\sqsubset} v_4$ and $v_3 \underset{v_1}{\sqsubset} v_4$. The vertex v_3 does not prevail v_4 since the unique dominant path from v_4 to v_1 is $\langle v_4 v_1 \rangle$.

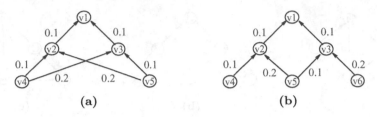

Fig. 2. WDAGs of Example 4 and 5

The next result presents the basic properties of the prevalence relation.

Lemma 1. *Let* $D = (V, E, w)$ *be a WDAG and* $\subseteq_v$ *the prevalence relation wrt. a vertex* $v \in V$ *over* D. *Then, it holds that:*

a) $\subseteq_v$ *is irreflexive, i.e.,* $\forall v_1 \in V.\ v_1 \not\subseteq_v v_1,$

b) $\subseteq_v$ *is not antisymmetric, i.e., it does not hold* $\forall v_1, v_2 \in V.\ v_1 \subseteq_v v_2 \Rightarrow v_2 \not\subseteq_v v_1,$

c) $\subseteq_v$ *is not transitive.*

The next examples illustrate two WDAGs whose prevalence relation is neither antisymmetric nor transitive.

Example 4. Let $D = (V, E, w)$ be the WDAG depicted in Fig. 2a, where $V = \{v_1, v_2, v_3, v_4, v_5\}$, E consists of the edges $e_1 = (v_2, v_1)$, $e_2 = (v_3, v_1)$, $e_3 = (v_4, v_2)$, $e_4 = (v_5, v_3)$, $e_5 = (v_4, v_3)$ and $e_6 = (v_5, v_2)$. Let $w(e_1) = w(e_2) = w(e_3) = w(e_4) = 0.1$ and $w(e_5) = w(e_6) = 0.2$. Then, we have that $v_4 \subseteq_{v_1} v_5$ and $v_5 \subseteq_{v_1} v_4$. Thus, $\subseteq_{v_1}$ is not antisymmetric.

Example 5. Let $D = (V, E, w)$ be the WDAG depicted in Fig. 2b, where $V = \{v_1, v_2, v_3, v_4, v_5, v_6\}$, E consists of the edges $e_1 = (v_2, v_1)$, $e_2 = (v_3, v_1)$, $e_3 = (v_4, v_2)$, $e_4 = (v_5, v_2)$, $e_5 = (v_5, v_3)$ and $e_6 = (v_6, v_3)$. Let $w(e_1) = w(e_2) = w(e_3) = w(e_5) = 0.1$ and $w(e_4) = w(e_6) = 0.2$. Then, we have that $v_4 \subseteq_{v_1} v_5$ and $v_5 \subseteq_{v_1} v_6$. Since $v_4 \not\subseteq_{v_1} v_6$, $\subseteq_{v_1}$ is not transitive.

To avoid cases of vertices that can reciprocally prevail one another, we introduce the notion of strong prevalence.

Definition 4. *Let* $D = (V, E, w)$ *be the WDAG. A vertex* $v_2 \in V$ *strongly prevails a vertex* $v_1 \in V$ *wrt. a vertex* $v \in V$ *iff* $v_1 \subseteq_v v_2$ *and* $v_2 \not\subseteq_v v_1$.

We write $v_1 \triangleleft_v v_2$ to indicate that v_2 strongly prevails v_1 wrt. v. The properties of the strong prevalence relation are summarized by the next result.

Lemma 2. *Let* $D = (V, E, w)$ *be a WDAG and* $\triangleleft_v$ *the strong prevalence relation wrt. a vertex* $v \in V$ *over* D. *Then, it holds that:*

a) $\underset{v}{\lhd}$ *is irreflexive,*

b) $\underset{v}{\lhd}$ *is antisymmetric, and*

c) $\underset{v}{\lhd}$ *is not transitive.*

4   Logic Framework

In this section, we generalize MDLPs (introduced in [12]) to allow for states to be represented by the vertices of WDAGs and their relations by the corresponding weighted edges. This enables us to prioritize the dimensions of a representational updatable system. Such a system is suitable to formalize among others organizational structures for epistemic agents (cf. [8]), and societies of social epistemic agents. In this setting, *WMDLP* assigns semantics to sets of generalized logic programs, depending on how they stand in relation to one another.

The next definition extends the original definition of MDLP to take into consideration WDAGs.

Definition 5. *Let $\mathcal{L}$ be a propositional language. A weighted multi-dimensional dynamic logic program (WMDLP) $\mathcal{P}$ is a pair $(\mathcal{P}_D, D)$, where $D = (V, E, w)$ is a WDAG and $\mathcal{P}_D = \{P_v \mid v \in V\}$ is a set of generalized logic programs over $\mathcal{L}$ indexed by the vertices $v \in V$.*

Following the established terminology of MDLP, we call *states* the vertices of WDAGs. We can now introduce the declarative semantics for WMDLPs.

Definition 6. *Let $\mathcal{P} = (\mathcal{P}_D, D)$ be a WMDLP, where $D = (V, E, w)$ and $\mathcal{P}_D = \{P_v \mid v \in V\}$. Let $s \in V$ be a state and $\underset{s}{\lhd}$ the strong prevalence relation wrt. s over D. An interpretation M is a* stable model *of $\mathcal{P}$ at state s iff*

$$M = least(\,[\,Q(\mathcal{P}, s) - Reject(\mathcal{P}, s, M)\,] \cup Default(Q(\mathcal{P}, s), M)\,)$$

where:

$$Q(\mathcal{P}, s) = \bigcup_{v \preceq s} P_v$$

$$Reject(\mathcal{P}, s, M) = \{r \in P_{v_2} \mid \exists r' \in P_{v_1}, head(r) = not\ head(r'), M \vDash body(r'),$$
$$and\ v_2 \underset{s}{\lhd} v_1\}$$

$$Default(Q(\mathcal{P}, s), M) = \{not\ A \mid \nexists r \in Q(\mathcal{P}, s), head(r) = A\ and\ M \vDash body(r)\}.$$

$Q(\mathcal{P}, s)$ contains all rules of all programs that are indexed by a state along all paths to a state s, i.e. all rules that are potentially relevant to determine the semantics at s. The set $Reject(\mathcal{P}, s, M)$ of rejected rules contains those rules belonging to a program indexed by a state v_2 that are overridden by the head of another rule with true body in state v_1 such that v_1 strongly prevails v_2 wrt. s. Note that we need to use strong prevalence (and not prevalence) otherwise

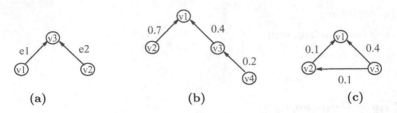

Fig. 3. WDAGs of Example 6, 7 and 8

we can have situations where rules reject each other. For instance, given the two programs $P_{v_2} = \{a\}$ and $P_{v_1} = \{not\,a\}$, if the two states v_1 and v_2 reciprocally prevail one another, then both rules a and $not\,a$ would be rejected. $Default(Q(\mathcal{P}, s), M)$ contains default negations $not\,A$ of all unsupported atoms A, i.e., those atoms A for which there is no rule in $Q(\mathcal{P}, s)$ whose body is true in M.

It is worth noting that MDLP [12] is a special case of WMDLP where all the edges have the same weight (see Appendix 9 for a discussion). In this case, the strong prevalence relation reduces to the path relation over which MDLP is based. Hence, at the semantical level the sets of rejected rules in MDLP and WMDLP are the same.

Example 6. Let $\mathcal{P} = (\mathcal{P}_D, D)$ be the WMDLP depicted in Fig. 3a, where $D = (V, E, w)$ and $V = \{v_1, v_2, v_3\}$. E consists of $e_1 = (v_1, v_3)$ and $e_2 = (v_2, v_3)$. Let $\mathcal{P}_D = \{P_{v_1}, P_{v_2}, P_{v_3}\}$ with $P_{v_1} = \{a\}$, $P_{v_2} = \{not\,a\}$ and $P_{v_3} = \{\}$. If $w(e_1) = w(e_2)$, then there exists no stable model of $\mathcal{P}$ at state v_3. In fact, $Q(\mathcal{P}, v_3) = \{a; not\,a\}$ and $Reject(\mathcal{P}, v_3, M) = \{\}$, $Default(Q(\mathcal{P}, v_3), M) = \{\}$, for any interpretation M. Thus, there exists no interpretation M such that $M = least(Q(\mathcal{P}, v_3))$. If instead $w(e_1) > w(e_2)$, then there exists a unique stable model $M = \{a\}$ of $\mathcal{P}$ at state v_3. In fact, $Reject(\mathcal{P}, v_3, M) = \{not\,a\}$ as $v_2 \underset{v_3}{\lhd} v_1$, $Default(Q(\mathcal{P}, v_3), M) = \{\}$ and $M = least(\{a\})$.

Example 7. Let $\mathcal{P} = (\mathcal{P}_D, D)$ be the WMDLP depicted in Fig. 3b, where $D = (V, E, w)$ and $V = \{v_1, v_2, v_3, v_4\}$. E consists of $e_1 = (v_2, v_1)$, $e_2 = (v_3, v_1)$ and $e_3 = (v_4, v_3)$, and $w(e_1) = 0.7$, $w(e_2) = 0.4$ and $w(e_3) = 0.2$. Let $\mathcal{P}_D = \{P_{v_1}, P_{v_2}, P_{v_3}, P_{v_4}\}$ with $P_{v_1} = \{b\}$, $P_{v_2} = \{a\}$, $P_{v_3} = \{not\,a; d \leftarrow a, b\}$ and $P_{v_4} = \{not\,b\}$. The unique stable model of $\mathcal{P}$ at state v_1 is $M = \{a, b, d\}$. In fact, as it holds that $v_4 \underset{v_1}{\lhd} v_1$ and $v_3 \underset{v_1}{\lhd} v_2$, we have that $Reject(\mathcal{P}, v_1, M) = \{not\,a; not\,b\}$ and $Default(Q(\mathcal{P}, v_1), M) = \{\}$. Thus, $M = least(\{a; b; d \leftarrow a, b\})$.

Example 8. Let $\mathcal{P} = (\mathcal{P}_D, D)$ be the WMDLP depicted in Fig. 3c, where $D = (V, E, w)$ and $V = \{v_1, v_2, v_3\}$. E consists of $e_1 = (v_2, v_1)$, $e_2 = (v_3, v_1)$ and $e_3 = (v_3, v_2)$, and $w(e_1) = 0.1$, $w(e_2) = 0.4$ and $w(e_3) = 0.1$. Let $\mathcal{P}_D = \{P_{v_1}, P_{v_2}, P_{v_3}\}$ with $P_{v_1} = \{c \leftarrow a, b, not\,d\}$, $P_{v_2} = \{b; not\,a\}$ and $P_{v_3} = \{a; not\,c\}$. The unique stable model of $\mathcal{P}$ at state v_1 is $M = \{a, b, c\}$. In fact, as it holds that $v_2 \underset{v_1}{\lhd}$

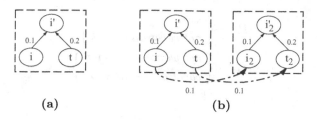

Fig. 4. (a) Ivan's theory (b) Adding temporal dimension to Ivan's theory

v_1, $v_3 \mathrel{\underset{v_1}{\vartriangleleft}} v_1$ and $v_2 \mathrel{\underset{v_1}{\vartriangleleft}} v_3$, we have that $Reject(\mathcal{P}, v_1, M) = \{not\, a; not\, c\}$ and $Default(Q(\mathcal{P}, v_1), M) = \{not\, d\}$. Thus, $M = least(\{a; b; not\, d; c \leftarrow a, b, not\, d\})$.

5 Modelling Epistemic Agents

In this section we consider epistemic agents and show how to formalize them by means of WMDLPs. We consider epistemic agents whose theories are composed by sets of modules. A module for instance can formalize an agent's specific capability (e.g., problem solving, planning, and learning), a view that the agent has of other agents (i.e., an internal representation of another agent's theory), or the normative relations of the agent (i.e., what the agent is obliged, permitted, has the right to do). All the modules that form the theory of an agent are linked together to implement the agent's overall behavior. We assume that each agent has a distinguished module to which the other modules are linked to that represents the query point of the agent. We name such a module *inspection point* of the agent. It is here that the overall "personality" (in terms of knowledge and behavior) of the agent emerges.

An epistemic agent can be directly formalized by a WMDLP by expressing the knowledge of its modules by generalized logic programs, and its module structure by a WDAG.

Example 9. Consider a simple situation where we have an agent, Ivan, whose theory consists of three modules, as depicted in Fig. 4a. The first module (represented by i) expresses Ivan's own knowledge, the second one (represented by t) his view of the theory of his friend Tatiana, and the last (represented by i') is the inspection point of Ivan. The first module expresses that if someone is sick, then he should not go on vacation, and that anyone must work. The second module expresses that anyone must not work during summer, and if someone does not work, then he can go on vacation. Suppose that Ivan gives precedence to what Tatiana believes rather than to his own believes (i.e., he gives precedence to the second module over the first one). This situation can be formalized by a WMDLP $\mathcal{P} = (\mathcal{P}_D, D)$, as follows. Let $D = (V, E, w)$, where $V = \{i, t, i'\}$, E consists of the edges $e_1 = (i, i')$ and $e_2 = (t, i')$, with $w(e_1) = 0.1$ and $w(e_2) = 0.2$. Let $\mathcal{P}_D = \{P_i, P_t, P_{i'}\}$ be the following set of generalized logic programs:

$$P_i = \left\{ \begin{array}{l} work \\ not\ vacation \leftarrow sick \end{array} \right\}$$

$$P_t = \left\{ \begin{array}{l} not\ work \leftarrow summer \\ vacation \leftarrow not\ work \end{array} \right\}$$

$$P_{i'} = \{\}$$

Then, the unique stable model of Ivan at state i' is $M_{i'} = \{work\}$.

To capture the dynamic behavior of the world in which they are situated, epistemic agents must be able to evolve by updating their information. At every time stamp, an agent may receive new information and thereby evolve to the next state. An agent may acquire new information via its sensing actions, communication acts, and so on. When the agent evolve to the next state, he does so by updating some (possibly all) of its modules to take into consideration the new incoming information.

Example 10. Consider the scenario described in Example 9. Assume that at the next state t_2, things change and it becomes summer. This situation can be formalized (as depicted in Fig. 4b) by adding three new vertices indexed by the time stamp 2 to the WDAG of Example 9. Thus, we obtain $\mathcal{P}_2 = (\mathcal{P}_{D_2}, D_2)$, where $D_2 = (V_2, E_2, w_2)$ with $V_2 = \{i, t, i', i_2, t_2, i'_2\}$, E_2 consists of the edges $e_1 = (i, i')$, $e_2 = (t, i')$, $e_3 = (i_2, i'_2)$, $e_4 = (t_2, i'_2)$, $e_5 = (i, i_2)$, and $e_6 = (t, t_2)$, with $w(e_1) = w(e_3) = w(e_5) = w(e_6) = 0.1$ and $w(e_2) = w(e_4) = 0.2$. Let $\mathcal{P}_{D_2} = \{P_i, P_t, P_{i'}, P_{i_2}, P_{t_2}, P_{i'_2}\}$ where P_i, P_t, $P_{i'}$ are as defined in Example 9, $P_{t_2} = P_{i'_2} = \{\}$ and $P_{i_2} = \{summer\}$.

Then, the unique stable model of Ivan at state i'_2 is $M_{i'_2} = \{summer, vacation\}$. In fact, having the module formalizing the theory of Tatiana priority over the module formalizing Ivan's own knowledge, we have that *not work* prevails over *work*.

Note that in the example above the graph structure as well as the weights of the edges remains unchanged when the agent evolves to the successive state. This needs not to be so. One may define a more general scenario where the agent's graph structure changes as well. Furthermore, explicitly encoding the graph structure within the theory of the agent makes it possible to declaratively define the agent self-evolution.

6   Adding Roles to Epistemic Agents

Agents typically operate in the context of multi-agent systems. Most of these systems, like those for electronic auctions, can be best understood as computational societies. It is argued (cf. [4]) that there is a need to make organizational and legal elements of the society externally visible, rather than being embedded into the beliefs of each agent. In literature, there have been several attempts to engineer agent societies based on notions of teams, groups, and institutions [3, 11, 14].

When agents are situated in an environment and therefore they can interact with one another, the problem of determining the kind of interaction arises. This leads to the concept of role. A *role* can be understood as a set of obligations, rights and privileges that governs the behavior of an agent occupying a particular position in the society.

The adoption of roles as a tools for description and modelling in multi-agent systems has several benefits. For example, formal roles allow for generic models of agents with unknown internal states to derive enough information to predict the agent behavior. Furthermore, the use of roles promotes flexibility since different modes of interaction become possible among agents. An agent may fulfill different roles depending on the agents it is interacting with. Finally, roles can adapt and evolve within the course of interactions to reflect the learning process of the agents. This allows for dynamic systems where the modes of interactions change.

We believe WMDLPs is an adequate tool for formalizing social agent societies where the roles as well as the society's structure can evolve. We start by defining what is a role, and what is an agent playing a role.

Typically, roles are associated to a default context that defines the different social relationships, like authority and friendship, and specifies the behavior of the roles between each other. Hence, the default context defines a partial order between roles. Generally, in a society agents may interact in several, different contexts. Therefore, there is a need to consider different abstraction levels of contexts. More specific contexts can overturn the orderings between the roles of more general contexts, and establish a social relation among them. This leads us to define a role as a theory composed of several modules where each module defines the normative relations with respect to a specific context in the society.

When an agent plays a role, the overall behavior of the agent obeys both the "personality" of the agent as well as its role. We call *actor* an agent playing a role:

$$\text{actor} := \langle\ \text{role, agent}\ \rangle$$
$$\text{actor} := \langle\ \text{role, actor}\ \rangle$$

An actor is an agent playing a role, or an actor itself playing a role. The notion of actor is important to define situations where an agent plays a role in virtue of the fact of playing another role. For example, in an organization an employee can be selected to be the manager of his group. Thus, this employee plays the role of group manager. Typically, an organization has the board of directors consisting of the chairman of the organization, together with some selected manager. In such a case, our employee may play the role of director being a manager.

Actors can be expressed in our framework in a modular, flexible way. Let R and A be two WDAGs formalizing a role and an agent, respectively. Then, a WDAG RA formalizing an actor is obtained from R and A by introducing a new vertex i, and by linking the inspection points a and r of A and R with i, as showed in Fig. 5a. The new vertex i is the inspection point of the actor.

By assigning different weights to the edges linking the vertices a and r to i, one can model different types of behavior. For example, by letting $w_1 > w_2$ we can enforce that the actor obeys the norms of its role. On the contrary, if

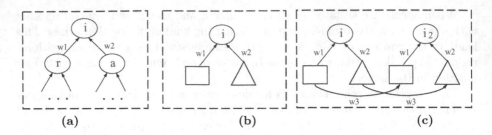

Fig. 5. (a) An actor (b) Graphical representation of an actor (c) Adding a temporal dimension to actors

$w_2 > w_1$ then the personality of the agent will prevail its role. We may also define a situation, by letting $w_1 = w_2$, where the actor will operate in accordance to both its personality and role. As depicted in Fig. 5b, we graphically represent roles and agents by boxes and triangles, respectively.

An actor can fulfill several roles depending on the context. Fig. 6 shows two distinct agents playing the same role, and an agent playing two distinct roles. It is worth noting that the use of WDAGs promotes both modularity and information hiding. In fact, in Fig. 6a for example, one needs not to know the internal structure of the agent and of the role to built up an actor. One simply combines these two modules by assigning weights that reflect the way he wants to combine them. The situation is different in MDLP where one needs to combine these two modules one after the other one (i.e., in sequence) to achieve the desired effect. Hence, one needs to know the DAG of the receiving module to be connected with the inspection point of the incoming module.

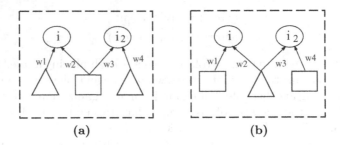

Fig. 6. (a) Two agents playing the same role (b) An agent playing two roles

Fig. 7a shows a role r_2 that overrides another role r_1 and an actor i that plays the second role. Fig. 7b shows two actors: i and i_2. Note that the actor i_2 consists of the actor i playing the role r_2. Fig. 7c shows a hierarchy of two distinct actors i and i_2. Letting w_3 be greater than both w_1 and w_2 will make i predominant over i_2.

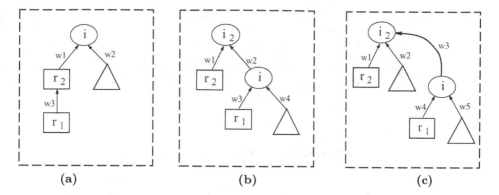

Fig. 7. (a) An actor (b) Two actors (c) Hierarchy of two actors

7   Engineering Social Agent Societies

Having defined some key concepts for epistemic agents, we can now present our conception of an agent society. We consider social agent societies where the behavior of their members is regulated by normative relations describing what an agent is obliged, permitted, and has the right to do. For simplicity, we only consider static societies where the temporal dimension is not present. We start by defining the notion of context, and assume given a corresponding theory defining its normative relations.

Definition 7. *Let Ag be a set of agents and R a set of roles. Then, a context is a pair (Ac, T) where Ac is a set of actors defined over Ag and R, and T is a theory defining the normative relations of the context.*

A context consists of a set of actors together with a theory T expressing the obligations, and rights of its members. A context can be represented by a WMDLP as depicted in Fig. 9a. The basic idea is to link the theory T with the inspection point i of each actor. Letting the weight of the edge (T, i) be greater that any other edge incoming to i will make that actor respect the obligations imposed by the context. The following example illustrates the use of contexts.

Example 11. Consider a group of two actors, A and B. We want to formalize a situation where A is the manager of the group and B is an employee. Suppose that the behavior of both A and B is characterized by the following policy:

$$\text{EmpPolicy} = \left\{ \begin{array}{c} give \leftarrow request,\ not\ need \\ not\ give \leftarrow request,\ need,\ not\ higher\_rank \\ give \leftarrow request,\ need,\ higher\_rank \end{array} \right\}$$

When requested, an employee gives an object to the questioner if the employee does not need it; an employee keeps the object if he needs it and he is not requested by a superior; a request from a superior is stronger than an employee's own need.

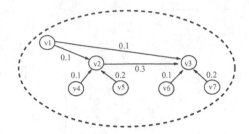

Fig. 8. Context C of Example 11

In addition, we have a theory representing the general behavior of the company's employees:

$$\text{ComPolicy} = \left\{ \begin{array}{l} \textit{need} \leftarrow \textit{urgent\_need} \\ \textit{not give} \leftarrow \textit{urgent\_need} \end{array} \right\}$$

An employee keeps the requested object in case he has an urgent need of it.

Such a group can be represented via a context $C = (Ac, T)$ depicted in Fig. 8 where $Ac = \{A, B\}$ and T is the theory ComPolicy above.

Assume that the own personality of each employee prevails the role he plays. This situation can be formalized as follows.

Let $\mathcal{P}_A$ and $\mathcal{P}_B$ be the WMDLPs formalizing the actors A and B. Let $\mathcal{P}_A = (\mathcal{P}_{D_A}, D_A)$ where $D_A = (\{v_2, v_4, v_5\}, \{(v_4, v_2), (v_5, v_2)\}, w_A)$, $w_A((v_4, v_2)) = 0.1$, $w_A((v_5, v_2)) = 0.2$, $P_{v_4} = \text{EmpPolicy}$, $P_{v_5} = \{\textit{not give} \leftarrow \textit{competitor}\}$, and v_2 is the inspection point of A (hence, $P_{v_2} = \{\}$). Let $\mathcal{P}_B = (\mathcal{P}_{D_B}, D_B)$ where $D_B = (\{v_3, v_6, v_7\}, \{(v_6, v_3), (v_7, v_3)\}, w_B)$, $w_B((v_6, v_3)) = 0.1$, $w_B((v_7, v_3)) = 0.2$, $P_{v_6} = \text{EmpPolicy}$, $P_{v_7} = \{\textit{request; need; higher\_rank; competitor}\}$, and v_3 is the inspection point of B.

The context C is represented by introducing a new vertex v_1 together with the edges (v_1, v_2), (v_1, v_3) whose weight is 0.1. We let $P_{v_1} = \text{ComPolicy}$.

Suppose that B operates (strictly) in accordance with the manager A. To enforce such a constraint we add the edge (v_2, v_3) with weight 0.3.

According to the declarative semantics of WMDLPs, B will not give the object requested by a higher-rank employee that is a competitor. In fact, the semantics of B, whose model is determined at its inspection point v_3, is $M_{v_3} = \{\textit{request; need; higher\_rank; competitor}\}$.

We can now define the notion of agent society.

Definition 8. *An agent society is modelled as a tuple:*

$$\Sigma = (Ag, R, C)$$

where Ag is a set of epistemic agents, R is a set of roles, and C is a set of contexts over Ag and R.

An agent society can be formalized by a WMDLP as depicted in Fig. 9b. Modelling agent societies by means of the notion of contexts is general and flexible. In fact, several organizational structures (see [16]) can be expressed in terms of contexts. For example, agents often forms subgroups inside a greater society of agents. These subgroups usually inherit the constraints of the greater society, override some of them and add their own constraints. Such a situation can be expressed in our framework by simply defining two contexts, C_1 and C_2. C_1 represents the greater society, and C_2 the subgroup. Then, the two new contexts can be linked together by adding an edge from the theory T of C_1 to the theory T of C_2.

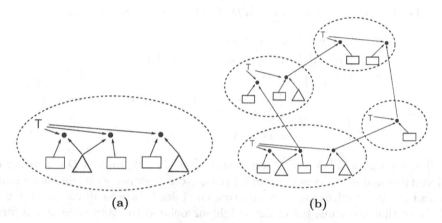

Fig. 9. (a) Context (b) Agent society

In general, we can incorporate a temporal dimension into the modelling of the agent society. Doing so will allow us to capture the dynamic behavior of the contexts and therefore of the entire society. For example, we can formalize situations where the normative relations of the contexts and the roles of the agents change. Thus, by exploiting the use of WMDLP several representational dimensions of the agent society can be formalized in a flexible and uniform manner.

8 Syntactic Transformation for WMDLPs

We next present a syntactical transformation that, given a WMDLP $\mathcal{P}$, produces a generalized logic program whose stable models coincide with the stable models of $\mathcal{P}$. Thus this transformation provides the grounds for implementing WMDLPs. The transformation is established based on the proven correct syntactical transformation for the original definition of MDLP over DAGs given in [12]. The transformation is based on the following definitions.

Given a set $\mathcal{K}$ of propositional variables and a set V of states, we write $\mathcal{K}^*$ to indicate the following set of propositional variables:

$$\mathcal{K}^* = \mathcal{K} \cup \{A^-, A_s, A_s^-, A_{P_s}, A_{P_s}^-, reject(A_s), reject(A_s^-)\}$$

for every atom $A \in \mathcal{K}$ and state $s \in V \cup \{s_0\}$, where $s_0 \notin V$ is a reserved state called *initial state*. Let $\mathcal{L}^*$ be the propositional language generated by $\mathcal{K}^*$. In the remaining of the paper we assume that every WDAG D does not contain the initial state s_0 among its vertices. Instead, s_0 belongs to the relevancy WDAG of D, defined next.

Definition 9. *Let $D = (V, E, w)$ be a WDAG and $s \in V$ a state. The* relevancy WDAG *of D wrt. a state s is the WDAG $D' = (V', E', w')$ where:*

$$X = \{v \mid v \in V \text{ and } v \preceq s\}$$
$$Y = \{(v_1, v_2) \mid (v_1, v_2) \in E \text{ and } v_2 \in X\}$$
$$V' = X \cup \{s_0\}$$
$$E' = Y \cup \{(s_0, v) \mid \text{ for every vertex } v \in X \text{ that is a source}\}$$
$$w'(e) = \begin{cases} w(e) & \text{if } e \in Y \\ 0.1 & \text{if } e \in (E' - Y) \end{cases}$$

The relevancy WDAG of D wrt. a state s is the subgraph of D consisting of all vertices and edges contained in all paths to s together with the initial state s_0 and the set of edges (s_0, v) connecting the initial state to all the sources v in X. Note that the value 0.1 of the weight associated to every edge of the form (s_0, v) is irrelevant since that is the unique edge incoming to v (by construction).

Since the relevancy WDAGs contain the initial state s_0 and new edges outgoing from it, we need to define the prevalence relation for relevancy WDAGs. The idea is to let every vertex of a relevancy WDAG prevail s_0 wrt. any other vertex.

Definition 10. *Let $D = (V, E, w)$ be a WDAG and $\vartriangleleft_s$ the strong prevalence relation wrt. a state $s \in V$ over D. Let $D' = (V', E', w')$ be the relevancy WDAG of D wrt. s. Then, the strong prevalence relation $\diamondsuit_s$ wrt. s over D' is defined as:*

$$\forall v_1, v_2 \in V'. \, v_1 \vartriangleleft_s v_2 \Rightarrow v_1 \diamondsuit_s v_2$$

$$\forall v \in V'. \, s_0 \neq v \Rightarrow s_0 \diamondsuit_s v$$

The following example illustrates the use of relevancy WDAGs.

Example 12. Let $D = (V, E, w)$ be the WDAG of Example 4. The relevancy WDAG D' of D wrt. v_1 is $D' = (V', E', w')$ where $V' = \{s_0, v_1, v_2, v_3, v_4, v_5\}$ and E' consists of the edges $e_1 = (v_2, v_1)$, $e_2 = (v_3, v_1)$, $e_3 = (v_4, v_2)$, $e_4 = (v_5, v_3)$, $e_5 = (v_4, v_3)$, $e_6 = (v_5, v_2)$, $e_7 = (s_0, v_4)$ and $e_8 = (s_0, v_5)$. The weight function is $w'(e_1) = w'(e_2) = w'(e_3) = w'(e_4) = w'(e_7) = w'(e_8) = 0.1$ and $w'(e_5) = w'(e_6) = 0.2$. Thus, the strong prevalence relation $\diamondsuit_{v_1}$ over D' wrt. v_1

is defined as: $v_2 \diamondsuit_{v_1} v_1$, $v_3 \diamondsuit_{v_1} v_1$, $v_4 \diamondsuit_{v_1} v_1$, $v_5 \diamondsuit_{v_1} v_1$, $s_0 \diamondsuit_{v_1} v_1$, $v_4 \diamondsuit_{v_1} v_2$, $v_5 \diamondsuit_{v_1} v_2$, $s_0 \diamondsuit_{v_1} v_2$, $v_4 \diamondsuit_{v_1} v_3$, $v_5 \diamondsuit_{v_1} v_3$, $s_0 \diamondsuit_{v_1} v_3$, $s_0 \diamondsuit_{v_1} v_4$ and $s_0 \diamondsuit_{v_1} v_5$.

The following proposition establishes that when determining the stable models of a WMDLP $\mathcal{P}$ at a state s, we can restrict our attention to the part of $\mathcal{P}$ corresponding to the relevancy WDAG wrt. s.

Proposition 1. *Let $\mathcal{P} = (\mathcal{P}_D, D)$ be a WMDLP. Suppose that $D = (V, E, w)$ and $\mathcal{P}_D = \{P_v \mid v \in V\}$. Let $s \in V$ be a state. Let $\mathcal{P}' = (\mathcal{P}_{D'}, D')$ be a WMDLP such that $D' = (V', E', w')$ is the relevancy WDAG of D wrt. s, and $\mathcal{P}_{D'} = \{P_v \mid v \in V'\}$ where $P_{s_0} = \{\}$. Then, M is a stable model of $\mathcal{P}$ at state s iff M is a stable model of $\mathcal{P}'$ at state s.*

Note that the program P_{s_0} associated to the initial state does not contain any rule.

The following definition presents a syntactic transformation that allows one to map WMDLPs into generalized logic programs. Such a transformation is based on the syntactic transformation for MDLPs [12]. They differ only in the treatment of the rejection rules.

Definition 11 (Mapping Φ). *Let $\mathcal{P} = (\mathcal{P}_D, D)$ be a WMDLP over the propositional language $\mathcal{L}$. Suppose that $D = (V, E, w)$. Given a state $s \in V$, the generalized logic program $\Phi(\mathcal{P}, s)$ consists of the following generalized rules over the language $\mathcal{L}^*$.*

Let $\mathcal{P}' = (\mathcal{P}_{D'}, D')$ be a WMDLP where $D' = (V', E', w')$ is the relevancy WDAG of D wrt. s, and $\mathcal{P}_{D'} = \{P_v \mid v \in V'\}$ where $P_{s_0} = \{\}$.

(RP) Rewritten Program Clauses:

$$A_{P_v} \leftarrow B_1, \ldots, B_m, C_1^-, \ldots, C_n^- \tag{1}$$

or

$$A_{P_v}^- \leftarrow B_1, \ldots, B_m, C_1^-, \ldots, C_n^- \tag{2}$$

for any clause:

$$A \leftarrow B_1, \ldots, B_m, not\, C_1, \ldots, not\, C_n \tag{3}$$

respectively, for any clause:

$$not\, A \leftarrow B_1, \ldots, B_m, not\, C_1, \ldots, not\, C_n \tag{4}$$

in the program $P_v \in \mathcal{P}_{D'}$. The rewritten clauses are obtained from the original ones by replacing atoms A (respectively, the default atoms $not\, A$) occurring in their heads by the atoms A_{P_v} (respectively, $A_{P_v}^-$) and by replacing negative premises $not\, C$ by C^-.

(IR) Inheritance Rules:

$$A_v \leftarrow A_u, not\, reject(A_u) \tag{5}$$

$$A_v^- \leftarrow A_u^-, not\, reject(A_u^-) \tag{6}$$

for every atom $A \in \mathcal{K}$ and every edge $(u, v) \in E'$. The inheritance rules say that an atom A is true (respectively, false) in the state $v \in V'$ if it is true (respectively, false) in any ancestor state u and it is not rejected, i.e., forced to be false (respectively, true).

(RR) Rejection Rules:

$$reject(A_u^-) \leftarrow A_{P_v} \tag{7}$$

$$reject(A_u) \leftarrow A_{P_v}^- \tag{8}$$

for every atom $A \in \mathcal{K}$ and every state $u, v \in V'$ such that $u \diamondsuit_s v$, where $\diamondsuit_s$ is the strong prevalence relation wrt. s over the relevancy $\widehat{WDAG}$ D'. The rejection rules say that if an atom A is true (respectively, false) in the program P_v, then it rejects inheritance of any false (respectively, true) atom of any state u that is strongly prevailed by v wrt. s.

(UR) Update Rules:

$$A_v \leftarrow A_{P_v} \tag{9}$$

$$A_v^- \leftarrow A_{P_v}^- \tag{10}$$

for every atom $A \in \mathcal{K}$ and every state $v \in V'$. The update rules state that an atom A must be true (respectively, false) in the state v if it is true (respectively, false) in the program P_v.

(DR) Default Rules:

$$A_{s_0}^- \tag{11}$$

for every atom $A \in \mathcal{K}$. Default rules describe the initial state s_0 by making all atoms initially false.

(CS_s) Current State Rules:

$$A \leftarrow A_s \tag{12}$$

$$A^- \leftarrow A_s^- \tag{13}$$

$$not\ A \leftarrow A_s^- \tag{14}$$

for every atom $A \in \mathcal{K}$. Current state rules specify the current state s in which the program is being evaluated and determine the values of the atoms A and A^-, and the default atom $not\ A$.

The following result establishes the correctness of the syntactic transformation.

Theorem 1. *Given a WMDLP $\mathcal{P}$ over the language $\mathcal{L}$, the stable models of $\Phi(\mathcal{P}, s)$, restricted to $\mathcal{L}$, coincide with the stable models of $\mathcal{P}$ at state s.*

9   Relationship Between WMDLPs and MDLPs

This section describes the relationship between MDLPs and WMDLPs. We start by showing how to embed MDLPs into WMDLPs.

Definition 12 (WMDLP-Embedding). *Let $n \in \mathbb{R}^+$ be any positive real number. Let $\mathcal{P} = (\mathcal{P}_D, D)$ be an MDLP, where $D = (V, E)$. A WMDLP-embedding of $\mathcal{P}$ is a WMDLP $\mathcal{P}' = (\mathcal{P}_{D'}, D')$ such that $\mathcal{P}_{D'} = \mathcal{P}_D$, $D' = (V, E, w)$ and $w(e) = n$, for every edge $e \in E$.*

By simply assigning the same weight n to every edge, we can embed MDLPs into WMDLPs. The correctness of the embedding is stated by the next result.

Theorem 2. *Let $\mathcal{P}$ be an MDLP and $\mathcal{P}'$ a WMDLP-embedding of $\mathcal{P}$. Then, the stable models of $\mathcal{P}$ at state s coincide with the stable models of $\mathcal{P}'$ at state s.*

In general, it is not possible to embed WMDLPs into MDLPs unless by duplicating states in the DAGs of MDLPs. This is due to the fact that WDAGs are based on the notion of prevalence relation that is not transitive, while DAGs are based on the notion of path relation that is transitive. Thus, by duplicating vertices in DAGs one can rule out tuples in the path relation that are derived by transitivity. For instance, consider the strong prevalence relation $\lhd$ over the WDAG depicted in Fig. 2b. It holds that $v_4 \underset{v_1}{\lhd} v_5$, $v_5 \underset{v_1}{\lhd} v_6$, and $v_4 \underset{v_1}{\not\lhd} v_6$. By embedding $\underset{v_1}{\lhd}$ into the path relation $\prec$, we would obtain three paths $v_4 \prec v_5$, $v_5 \prec v_6$, and by transitivity $v_4 \prec v_6$. Instead, by duplicating the vertex v_5 into a new vertex v_5' and by substituting the edge (v_5, v_3) with (v_5', v_3), we obtain only two paths $v_4 \prec v_5$ and $v_5' \prec v_6$.

However, by restricting the attention to WDAGs whose prevalence relations satisfy certain properties, it is possible to directly embed WDAGs into DAGs without having to duplicate vertices. This result is important because it allows one to relate WMDLPs to MDLPs. We introduce a function mapping WDAGs into directed graphs. Note that this translation is possible only by fixing a state s over D.

Definition 13 (Mapping $\varGamma$). *Let $D = (V, E, w)$ be a WDAG. Given a state $s \in V$, the function $\varGamma(D, s)$ maps D and s into a directed graph $D' = (V', E')$ as follows:*

- $V' = V$, and
- $E' = \{(v_1, v_2) \mid$ for every v_1, v_2 in V such that $v_1 \underset{s}{\lhd} v_2\}$.

The following example illustrates the usage of $\varGamma$.

Example 13. Let D_1, D_2 and D_3 be the WDAGs in Fig. 1a, 1b, and 1c. Then, the DAGs in Fig. 10a, 10b and 10c are the DAGs $\varGamma(D_1, v_1)$, $\varGamma(D_2, v_1)$ and $\varGamma(D_3, v_1)$, respectively.

Not always the directed graph obtained via the mapping $\varGamma$ is a DAG because it can contain cycles. For instance, if it holds that $v_1 \underset{s}{\lhd} v_2$, $v_2 \underset{s}{\lhd} v_3$, and $v_3 \underset{s}{\lhd} v_1$

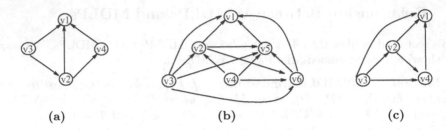

Fig. 10. Mapping WDAGs into DAGs

over D, then there exists a path $\langle v_1\, v_2\, v_3\, v_1\rangle$ over $\Gamma(D,s)$ that is a cycle. As next result shows, cycles can be ruled out provided that some condition holds. Below we write $\vartriangleleft_s^*$ to indicate the transitive closure of $\vartriangleleft$, and we write $\vartriangleleft_s \equiv \vartriangleleft_s^*$ to indicate that the strong prevalence relation and its transitive closure are equal, that is, for every vertex v_1, v_2, it holds that $v_1 \vartriangleleft_s v_2$ iff $v_1 \vartriangleleft_s^* v_2$.

Proposition 2. *Let $D = (V, E, w)$ be a WDAG and $s \in V$ a state. Let $\vartriangleleft_s$ be the strong prevalence relation wrt. s over D. If $\vartriangleleft_s \equiv \vartriangleleft_s^*$, then $\Gamma(D, s)$ is a DAG.*

The following property relates the strong prevalence relation and the path relation.

Proposition 3. *Let $D = (V, E, w)$ be a WDAG and $s \in V$ a state. Let $\vartriangleleft_s$ be the strong prevalence relation wrt. s over D. If $\vartriangleleft_s \equiv \vartriangleleft_s^*$, then it holds that $v_1 \vartriangleleft_s v_2$ over D iff $v_1 \prec v_2 \preceq s$ over $\Gamma(D, s)$, for every state v_1, v_2 in V.*

The following example shows that the mapping Γ is not functional over D. This property prevents us from having an incremental implementation of Γ. Note also that not necessarily it holds that $E' \subseteq E$.

Example 14. Let $D = (V, E, w)$ be a WDAG, where $V = \{v_1, v_2, v_3\}$ and E consists of the edges $e_1 = (v_3, v_2)$ and $e_2 = (v_2, v_1)$ with $w(e_1) = w(e_2) = 0.1$. Then, it holds that $\Gamma(D, v_1) = (V, E)$.

If we add the edge $e_3 = (v_3, v_1)$ to E with $w(e_3) = 0.4$, then $\Gamma(D, v_1) = (V, E')$ where $E' = \{(v_2, v_1), (v_2, v_3), (v_3, v_1)\}$.

Note that $\Gamma(D, v_1)$ of Fig. 11 contains the edge (v_3, v_2), while $\Gamma(D, v_1)$ of Fig. 12 contains the opposite edge (v_2, v_3).

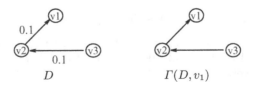

$$D \qquad\qquad \Gamma(D, v_1)$$

Fig. 11.

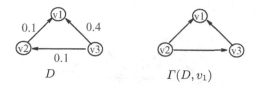

Fig. 12.

Definition 14 (MDLP-Embedding at a state). Let $\mathcal{P} = (\mathcal{P}_D, D)$ be a WMDLP where $D = (V, E, w)$ and $s \in V$ a state. The MDLP-embedding of $\mathcal{P}$ at state s is the MDLP $\mathcal{P}' = (\mathcal{P}_{D'}, D')$ such that $\mathcal{P}_{D'} = \mathcal{P}_D$ and $D' = \Gamma(D, s)$.

The next theorem states the properties of correctness of Γ. This result does not hold in general, but only for those WDAGs whose strong prevalence relation equals its transitive closure.

Theorem 3. Let $\mathcal{P} = (\mathcal{P}_D, D)$ be a WMDLP where $D = (V, E, w)$. Let $s \in V$ be a state and $\mathcal{P}'$ the MDLP-embedding of $\mathcal{P}$ at state s. Let $\lhd$ be the strong prevalence relation wrt. s over D. If $\lhd \underset{s}{\equiv} \lhd^*$, then it holds that the stable models of $\mathcal{P}$ at state s coincide with the stable models of $\mathcal{P}'$ at state s.

Example 15. Let $\mathcal{P} = (\mathcal{P}_D, D)$ be the WMDLP depicted in Fig. 3c of Example 8. Let $\lhd$ be the strong prevalence relation wrt. v_1 over D. Clearly, it holds that $\underset{v_1}{\lhd} \equiv \underset{v_1}{\lhd^*}$. The unique stable model of $\mathcal{P}$ at state v_1 is $M_1 = \{a, b, c\}$. Let $\mathcal{P}' = (\mathcal{P}_{D'}, D')$ be the MDLP-embedding of $\mathcal{P}$ at state v_1. The DAG D' is depicted in Fig. 12. Then, the unique stable model of $\mathcal{P}'$ at state v_1 is $M_2 = \{a, b, c\}$. Thus, we have that the stable models of $\mathcal{P}$ and $\mathcal{P}'$ at state v_1 coincide.

The next example illustrates a situation where the stable models of a WMDLP $\mathcal{P}$ and its MDLP-embedding do not coincide being the property $\lhd \underset{s}{\equiv} \lhd^*$ not satisfied.

Example 16. Let $\mathcal{P} = (\mathcal{P}_D, D)$ be the WMDLP where D is the WDAG of Example 5 and $\mathcal{P} = \{P_{v1}, P_{v2}, P_{v3}, P_{v4}, P_{v5}, P_{v6}, \}$ with $P_{v1} = P_{v2} = P_{v3} = P_{v5} = \{\}$, $P_{v4} = \{not\, a\}$ and $P_{v6} = \{a\}$. Let $\lhd$ be the strong prevalence relation wrt. v_1 over D. Clearly, it holds that $\underset{v_1}{\lhd} \not\equiv \underset{v_1}{\lhd^*}$. Let $\mathcal{P}' = (\mathcal{P}_{D'}, D')$ be the MDLP-embedding of $\mathcal{P}$ at state v_1 where D' is depicted in Fig. 13. Then, $M = \{a\}$ is a stable model of $\mathcal{P}'$ at state v_1, while it is not a stable model of $\mathcal{P}$ at state v_1.

10   Related Work and Concluding Remarks

We have presented a logical framework that allows one to model structures of social agent societies. In doing so, we have first introduced the notion of WDAG that extends directed acyclic graphs to associate weights to every edge of the

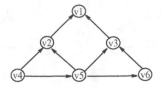

Fig. 13. DAG of Example 16

graph. Then, we have presented our framework WMDLP with the corresponding declarative and operational semantics, and we have given results of correctness. The framework having a formal semantics will allow us to study and prove the properties of social agent societies.

WMDLP is based on and builds upon MDLP [12] by employing WDAGs and by replacing the path relation (used by MDLP) with the prevalence relation between vertices of a WDAG. By exploiting the weights, WMDLP allows to represent the knowledge of a system at a level of abstraction higher than the one of MDLP. Furthermore, WMDLP promotes modularity and information hiding. The relationship between MDLP and WMDLP has been discussed in Section 9.

To illustrate the usage of WMDLP we have formalized social agent societies by introducing the notions of role and context in the same spirit as [11, 14]. However, these two approaches essentially differ from our. Kakas and Moraïtis [11] present a framework based on argumentation with the aim to support the deliberation process of an agent. This framework uses roles and contexts to define dynamic preferences between alternative arguments of the agents fulfilling certain roles. The representation of role and context information is then expressed directly in the framework in terms of priority rules. In turn, these rules form new arguments and are reasoned about in the same way as object level arguments.

Lindemann and Münch [14] focus on the concept of role and discuss the importance of using roles in organizational structures for modelling social actions in multi-agent systems. In situations where agents interact, and communication and observation are insufficient for the agents to draw conclusions, then roles can be used to mimic the expectations of behavior of one agent towards another agent. In contrast to [11, 14] we use contexts and roles to design and model agent societies. In our approach roles are added to epistemic agents to guide their behavior and regulate their interactions with other agents within the same context. We have shown that WMDLPs is a suitable tool to formalize roles and contexts in a modular and flexible way, and it is general in the sense that several representational dimensions of a society can be uniformly represented in the same framework, like a temporal dimension. This would allow the modelling of societies whose roles and contexts evolve.

Our framework builds on the notion of prevalence of vertices. However, other notions of prevalence can be accommodated within it. To do so it is necessary to incorporate these new notions both at the semantical level, that is to modify the definition of $Reject(\mathcal{P}, s, M)$ in Def. 6, and at the syntactical level, that is to modify the Rejection Rules (RR) in Def. 11 to reflect the new relation.

In a previous work [8], we explored how to explicitly represent organizational structures in epistemic multi-agent systems (eMAS), including groups of agents, institutions, and complex organizational structures for agent societies. Here, we have illustrated the usage of WMDLPs to represent social agent societies. For simplicity, we haven't considered the dynamic aspects of the agent knowledge like, for example, when an agent updates its knowledge to incorporate new incoming information (via updates). These aspects are discussed in [7].

An interesting direction for future work is to represent the logical framework within the theory of the agent members of the society. That is, we can code the graph structure of the agents and the links among them into the theory of the agents themselves. Doing so will empower the agents with the ability to reason about and to modify the structure of their own graph together with the general group structure comprising the other agents. At the level of each single agent, declaratively expressing the graph structure enables that agent to reason over it in a declarative way. At the level of the group structure, this ability will permit the managing of open societies where agents can enter/leave the society. This in fact can be achieved by updating the graph structure representing the group by adding/removing vertices and edges. Therefore, encoding the graph structure within the language of the agents makes the system updatable to capture the dynamic aspects of the system, i.e., of the open society.

Acknowledgements

The author acknowledges L. M. Pereira for commenting and reading previous versions of the paper.

References

1. J. J. Alferes, P. Dell'Acqua, and L. M. Pereira. A compilation of updates plus preferences. In S. Flesca, S. Greco, N. Leone, and G. Ianni (eds.), *Logics in Artificial Intelligence*, LNAI 2424, pp. 62–74, Berlin, 2002. Springer-Verlag.
2. J. J. Alferes, J. A. Leite, L. M. Pereira, H. Przymusinska, and T. C. Przymusinski. Dynamic updates of non-monotonic knowledge bases. *The J. of Logic Programming*, 45(1-3):43–70, 2000. A short version titled *Dynamic Logic Programming* appeared in A. Cohn and L. Schubert (eds.), *KR'98*, Morgan Kaufmann.
3. A. Artikis and G. Pitt. A formal model of open agent societies. Proc. of Autonomous Agents, 2001.
4. C. Castelfranchi. Engineering Social Order. In Andrea Omicini, Robert Tolksdorf, and Franco Zambonelli (eds.), *Engineering Societies in the Agents World. 1st Int. Workshop ESAW 2000. Revised Papers*, LNAI 1972, pp. 1–18, Berlin, 2000. Springer-Verlag.
5. P. Dell'Acqua, J. A. Leite, and L. M. Pereira. Evolving multi-agent viewpoints - an architecture. In P. Brazdil and A. Jorge (eds.), *Progress in Artificial Intelligence, 10th Portuguese Int. Conf. on Artificial Intelligence (EPIA'01)*, LNAI 2258, pp. 169–182. Springer-Verlag, 2001.

6. P. Dell'Acqua, U. Nilsson, and L. M. Pereira. A logic based asynchronous multi-agent system. Computational Logic in Multi-Agent Systems (CLIMA02). Electronic Notes in Theoretical Computer Science (ENTCS), Vol. 70, Issue 5, 2002.
7. P. Dell'Acqua and L. M. Pereira. Preferring and updating in abductive multi-agent systems. In A. Omicini, P. Petta, and R. Tolksdorf (eds.), *Engineering Societies in the Agents' World (ESAW 2001)*, LNAI 2203, pp. 57–73. Springer-Verlag, 2001.
8. P. Dell'Acqua and L. M. Pereira. A Logical Framework for Modelling eMAS. In V. Dahl and P. Wadler (eds.), *Fifth Int. Symp. on Practical Aspects of Declarative Languages (PADL03)*, LNCS 2562, pp. 241–255, Berlin, 2003. Springer-Verlag.
9. P. Dell'Acqua and L. M. Pereira. Preferring and updating in logic-based agents. In O. Bartenstein, U. Geske, M. Hannebauer, and O. Yoshie (eds.), *Web-Knowledge Management and Decision Support. Selected Papers from the 14th Int. Conf. on Applications of Prolog (INAP)*, LNAI 2543, pp. 70–85, Berlin, 2003. Springer-Verlag.
10. M. Gelfond and V. Lifschitz. The stable model semantics for logic programming. In R. Kowalski and K. A. Bowen (eds.), *ICLP'88*, pp. 1070–1080. MIT Press, 1988.
11. A. C. Kakas and P. Moraitis. Argumentative agent deliberation, roles and context. Electronic Notes in Theoretical Computer Science (ENTCS), Vol. 70, Issue 5, 2002.
12. J. A. Leite, J. J. Alferes, and L. M. Pereira. Multi-dimensional dynamic logic programming. In F. Sadri and K. Satoh (eds.), *Procs. of the CL-2000 Workshop on Computational Logic in Multi-Agent Systems (CLIMA'00)*, pp. 17–26, 2000.
13. V. Lifschitz and T. Woo. Answer sets in general non-monotonic reasoning (preliminary report). In B. Nebel, C. Rich, and W. Swartout (eds.), *KR'92*. Morgan-Kaufmann, 1992.
14. G. Lindemann and I. Munch. The role concept for agents in multi-agent systems. In G. Lindemann, C. Jonker and C. Castelfranchi (eds.). Proceedings of the KI'2001 Workshop on Modelling Artificial Societies and Hybrid Organizations MASHO'01. 2001.
15. F. Zambonelli. Abstractions and infrastructures for the design and development of mobile agent organizations. In M. J. Wooldridge, G. Weiß, and P. Ciancarini (eds.), *Agent-Oriented Software Engineering II, Second International Workshop, AOSE 2001*, LNCS 2222, pp. 245–262, Berlin, 2001. Springer-Verlag.
16. F. Zambonelli, N. R. Jennings, and M. Wooldridge. Organisational abstractions for the analysis and design of multi-agent systems. In P. Ciancarini and M. Wooldridge (eds.), *Agent-Oriented Software Engineering*, LNCS 1957, pp. 127–141, Berlin, 2001. Springer-Verlag.

(Dis)Belief Change Based on Messages Processing

Laurent Perrussel and Jean-Marc Thévenin

IRIT - Université Toulouse 1, Manufacture des Tabacs,
21, allée de Brienne,
F-31042 Toulouse Cedex - France
{Laurent.Perrussel, Jean-Marc.Thevenin}@univ-tlse1.fr

Abstract. This paper focuses on the features of belief change when agents have to consider information received from other agents. We focus on belief change operators when agents have to process messages about a static world. We propose to consider agents' belief state as a set of pairs ⟨belief, origin of the belief⟩ combined with a preference relation over the agents embedded in the multi-agent system. The belief revision procedure for handling received messages is a safe base revision procedure where messages are considered in their syntactic form. According to the reliability of the sources of the conflicting belief, agents remove the less reliable belief in order to handle the received message. Notice that the less reliable source can be the sender of the message itself. In order not to loose precious information conflicting belief are not removed but considered as *potential* belief. As the agent changes its belief, potential belief is reconsidered and may be reinstated as current belief. In a similar way, messages can concern statements that should not be believed, called *disbelief*. As belief, disbelief can become potential. These different kinds of belief enables us to propose a new semantics for a modal based language for describing (dis)belief. Agents may handle sequences of messages since the proposed belief change operators handle iterated belief change.

1 Introduction

It is quite common to characterize intelligent agents in cognitive terms such as the well known belief, desire, intention mental attitudes [15]. In that context, belief change is a key problem for agents. In a multi-agent system, agents communicate with each other in order to solve a problem such as building a plan or establishing a diagnosis.

In this paper we focus on how an agent should change its beliefs when it receives new information from the other agents, i.e. how its beliefs should look like after interpreting the received message [13]. We focus here on multi agent systems that exchange messages about a world that does not change. In that context, belief change has to be considered as belief revision. In our proposal agents handle iterated belief revision [3] which is a key feature when we consider

J. Dix and J. Leite (Eds.): CLIMA IV, LNAI 3259, pp. 201–217, 2004.

autonomous agents able to take into account sequences of messages. In addition, agents do not always adopt the received messages so that the proposed operators belong to the family of non-prioritized operators [8]. Agents consider the reliability of the senders to select inconsistent beliefs that should be dropped when a change raises inconsistencies in their beliefs.

In this work we focus on the characteristics of information held by agents, i.e. agents do not only maintain beliefs. Instead of dropping inconsistent belief during the process of belief change, agents move them into a *potential belief* set. As new messages come, some potential beliefs become consistent with the new belief set. Agents move them to this new set. This approach enables agents to consider as much as possible of the received messages. In addition, agents maintain a set of statements that should not be believed: these statements, called *disbeliefs*, are justified by messages describing what should not be believed. We show that our belief change operators in that context respect most of the AGM postulates.

This work extends a previous one [11] (i) by removing a strong constraint that was requiring a linear order over the (dis)beliefs for revising them and (ii) by proposing a modal-language for describing epistemic attitudes. The semantics of this language is based on the interpretation of the messages and the notions of belief, disbelief and potential belief. This language allows to describe the opinion of an agent. After it received a message with content ϕ: the agent has an opinion about ϕ and it believes or disbelieves ϕ.

The paper is organized as follows: section 2 presents an intuitive example for justifying our framework. Section 3 presents the formal definitions for describing an agent's belief state, messages and reliability levels of beliefs. Section 4 presents a semantics for describing epistemic attitudes based on the agent's (dis)belief state. In section 5, we present constructive definitions for the change functions. In section 6 we revisit the intuitive example in a formal way. Section 7 concludes the paper by discussing related works and some open issues.

2   An Intuitive Example

Let us consider three agents: Paul, Peter and the police department. Paul tells Peter that *John is a murderer*. Peter adopts this statement and believes it. Paul also says to Peter that *if John is a murderer, John will go to jail*. Thus, Peter believes that John has killed somebody and consequently that John will go to jail. Next, the police department tells Peter that *if John is a murderer then there is evidence* against him. In addition, they say that they do not believe that there is evidence against John. Because Peter considers the police department has a more reliable source of information than Paul, Peter does not believe, i.e. disbelieves, that John has killed somebody and thus he also disbelieves that John will go to jail. This last statement may be considered as a "potential belief" since Peter may adopt it later if the police department tells in a future message that it has been proved that John is a murderer. Suppose that next the police department tells Peter it has found evidence that John has actually killed someone. Thus, Peter both believes that there is evidence and potential belief "John is a murderer" is consistent again with Peter's beliefs. Thus Peter believes again that John is a murderer and that John will go to jail.

As we can see, every message received by an agent triggers a change in its beliefs. Some messages do not concern belief but rather disbelief. A new disbelief may entail inconsistency with the already adopted beliefs. Consequently, the agent has to reconsider some beliefs as potential beliefs. At the same time, the agent may reinstate potential beliefs when it changes its set of beliefs and disbeliefs.

3   Agent Beliefs

We assume that beliefs are expressed in a propositional language $\mathcal{L}_0$. Changes in a belief set are caused by communication. We assume throughout the paper that the external world is *static*; handling changes caused by "physical" actions would require the integration of belief update to our formalism, which we leave for further work. Thus, we are considering cases such as diagnosis. We assume that messages are sent point-to-point. In order to identify the sender of messages we introduce a set of agent id: let $A = \{a, b, c \cdots \}$ be this set. We usually denote by s the sender agent and by r the receiver.

3.1   Describing Messages

In our context, an agent may send two kinds of messages to other agents: agent a informs agent b that ϕ holds or not. These messages may occur after a request sent by b to a and asking if ϕ holds or not. In more formal terms, we get:

Definition 1 (Message). *A message M is defined as a tuple of receiver r, sender s, content ϕ, status st. The receiver and the sender are agent ids, the content is an $\mathcal{L}_0$-formula and the status is one of the two possible status: {*Hold, NotHold*}. Inconsistent statements are not allowed ($\phi \nvdash \bot$). Let $\mathcal{M}$ be the set of all possible messages.*

When the agent r receives a message about ϕ with a status equals to Hold, it will try to insert ϕ in its belief base. Similarly, if the status of ϕ is equal to NotHold, agent r will consider ϕ as a disbelief, i.e. it should not believe ϕ. Thus NotHoldϕ is not equivalent to Hold$\neg\phi$. At each moment one agent sent one message and the receiver changes its beliefs and disbeliefs accordingly.

Definition 2 (Sequence of Messages). *A sequence of messages σ is a function which associates integers and messages: $\sigma : \mathbb{N} \to \mathcal{M}$*

3.2   Describing Agent Beliefs

The key idea is to represent the "belief state" of an agent as three sets:

- a set of labeled statements representing *current beliefs*. The set of current belief changes with respect to the flow of messages about statements which have a status equal to Hold;

- a set of *disbeliefs* representing statements that should not be believed by the agent. The set of disbeliefs changes with respect to the flow of messages including statements that do not hold;
- a set of *potential beliefs*: messages received by the agent which could not be handled since they are in conflict with its current beliefs (respectively disbeliefs). As the current beliefs (disbeliefs) change with respect to the received messages, some potential beliefs may become consistent with the new current beliefs (disbeliefs) and thus will be considered as current beliefs (disbeliefs) in future states.

To represent beliefs of an agent, we define a signed belief as a pair ⟨statement, origin of the statement⟩ (the associated message):

Definition 3 (Signed Belief). *Let σ be a sequence of messages. A signed belief is a pair $\langle \phi, i \rangle$ where ϕ is a $\mathcal{L}_0$-formula and $i \in \mathbb{N}$ s.t. $(\exists r, s, st)(\sigma(i) = \langle r, s, \phi, st \rangle)$. Let S be the set of signed beliefs and let $\mathcal{SB} = 2^S$ be the set of all sets of signed beliefs.*

Example 1. Let a and b be two agents and a message $\sigma(1) = \langle a, b, \neg\phi, \mathtt{Hold} \rangle$. The pair $\langle \neg\phi, 1 \rangle$ is the associated signed belief.

Based on the set of signed beliefs, we define which statements are inferred by an agent:

Definition 4 (Belief Set). *Let Bel be a function which maps a signed belief set S to a set of $\mathcal{L}_0$-formulas: $Bel(S) = \{\psi | \bigwedge_{\langle \phi, i \rangle \in S} \phi \vdash \psi\}$. $Bel(S)$ represents the belief set associated to S.*

Example 2. Suppose two messages $\sigma(1) = \langle a, b, \neg\phi, \mathtt{Hold} \rangle$ and $\sigma(2) = \langle a, b, \neg\phi \rightarrow \phi', \mathtt{Hold} \rangle$. The belief set associated to $S = \{\langle \neg\phi, 1 \rangle, \langle \neg\phi \rightarrow \phi', 2 \rangle\}$ contains all the consequences of $\neg\phi, \neg\phi \rightarrow \phi'$, i.e. $\phi' \subseteq Bel(S)$.

From a set of signed beliefs, we consider the minimal subsets entailing a specific conclusion. Let ϕ be a formula and S a set of signed beliefs. Let *support* be a function returning the set of minimal subsets of S entailing ϕ.

$$support(S, \phi) = \{s' | s' \subseteq S, Bel(s') \vdash \phi \text{ and } \forall s'' \subset s'(Bel(s'') \nvdash \phi)\}$$

In order to describe what is believed by an agent, we introduce the notion of epistemic state. An epistemic state describes what is "currently" believed by the agent, what should not be believed and what could be potentially believed or disbelieved. Let us stress that our definition of epistemic states should not be confused with the epistemic states defined by [3] since we do not consider preferences at this stage.

Definition 5 (Epistemic State). *Let σ be a sequence of messages. The epistemic state of agent r is a structure: $\langle CB, DB, PB \rangle$ where $CB \in \mathcal{SB}$, $DB \in \mathcal{SB}$ and $PB \in \mathcal{SB}$. CB represents the current beliefs, DB represents disbeliefs and PB represents the potential beliefs such that:*

1. $(\forall \langle \phi, i \rangle \in CB)(\exists s)$ *s.t.* $(\sigma(i) = \langle r, s, \phi, \texttt{Hold} \rangle)$ *and* $Bel(CB) \nvdash \bot$;

2. $(\forall \langle \phi, i \rangle \in DB)$ $(\exists s)$ *s.t.* $\sigma(i) = \langle r, s, \phi, \texttt{NotHold} \rangle)$ *and* $(Bel(CB) \nvdash \phi)$;

3. $(\forall \langle \phi, i \rangle \in PB$ *s.t.* $(\exists s) \sigma(i) = \langle r, s, \phi, \texttt{Hold} \rangle)(Bel(CB) \wedge \phi \vdash \bot$ *or* $(\exists \langle \phi', i' \rangle \in DB)(Bel(CB) \wedge \phi \vdash \phi'))$;

4. $(\forall \langle \phi, i \rangle \in PB$ *s.t.* $(\exists s) \sigma(i) = \langle r, s, \phi, \texttt{NotHold} \rangle)$ $(Bel(CB) \vdash \phi)$;

Let $\mathcal{ES}$ be the set of all epistemic states.

According to definition 5, condition (1) states that statements in CB are consistent and have their status equals to Hold; condition (2) states a similar constraint for disbeliefs; condition (3) and (4) states that potential beliefs are signed beliefs in conflict with current beliefs or disbeliefs.

Example 3. Suppose the following messages $\sigma(1) = \langle a, b, \neg\phi, \texttt{Hold} \rangle$, $\sigma(2) = \langle a, b, \neg\phi \rightarrow \phi', \texttt{Hold} \rangle$, $\sigma(3) = \langle a, c, \neg\phi', \texttt{Hold} \rangle$, $\sigma(4) = \langle a, c, \phi'', \texttt{NotHold} \rangle$ and $\sigma(5) = \langle a, d, \phi' \rightarrow \phi'', \texttt{Hold} \rangle$. Assume agent a has adopted messages 1 and 2 as current beliefs and message 4 as a disbelief: let $E = \langle \{ \{ \langle \neg\phi, 1 \rangle, \langle \neg\phi \rightarrow \phi', 2 \rangle \}, \{ \langle \phi'', 4 \rangle \}, \{ \langle \neg\phi', 3 \rangle, \langle \phi' \rightarrow \phi'', 5 \rangle \} \} \rangle$ be its epistemic state. The signed belief $\langle \neg\phi', 3 \rangle$ belongs to PB since $\neg\phi'$ contradicts $Bel(CB)$. The signed belief $\langle \phi' \rightarrow \phi'', 5 \rangle$ also belongs to PB because if it were a member of CB then the disbelief $\langle \phi'', 4 \rangle$ would have been violated.

According to example 5, agent a could have reached another epistemic state by selecting other messages for its current beliefs and disbeliefs. Actually, agents use a procedure for changing their epistemic states. This procedure considers the reliability of the senders in order to state what are current beliefs, disbeliefs and potential beliefs. This procedure will be discussed section 5 after giving a semantics for interpreting messages.

4   A Semantics for Describing Belief and Disbelief

The aim of this section is to propose a modal based language for reasoning about the epistemic states of agents. By considering current beliefs, disbeliefs and potential beliefs we describe the following epistemic attitudes:

- an agent has an opinion about ϕ: the agent believes or disbelieves ϕ;
- an agent believes ϕ: ϕ belongs to its current belief set;
- an agent does not believe ϕ: ϕ belongs to its set of disbeliefs;
- an agent could believe, respectively disbelieve, ϕ: ϕ belongs to its set of potential beliefs. Thus it has no opinion about ϕ.

Notice that we do not define non-beliefs by considering beliefs. The classical approach such as the BDI-based representation, supposes that an agent does not believe a statement if this statement does not belong to its set of beliefs. We propose to re-consider this approach by considering two cases: (i) an agent has an opinion on ϕ (i.e. it previously received a message about ϕ) and it does not believe ϕ; (ii) an agent has no opinion about ϕ since it does not received any message about this statement. This distinction is useful when we consider the context of an investigation: the detectives may explicitly ignore some testimonies.

The proposed logic extends the propositional logic by considering modal operators. Let $\mathcal{L}$ be this language. We limit the agent's belief to propositional sentences. In order to define $\mathcal{L}$, we introduce the following notations: $B_a\phi$ means agent a believes ϕ; $DB_a\phi$ means agent a disbelieves ϕ; $O_a\phi$ means agent a has an opinion about ϕ, $PB_a\phi$ means that ϕ is a potential belief for a; $PDB_a\phi$ means that ϕ is a potential disbelief for a. $\blacklozenge\phi$ means that the $\mathcal{L}$-statement ϕ held in the past.

Definition 6 (Syntax). *A $\mathcal{L}$-formula is defined as follows. Let $\mathcal{PROP}$ be a set of propositional symbols. If $\phi \in \mathcal{L}_0$ and $a \in A$ then $B_a\phi \in \mathcal{L}$, $DB_a\phi \in \mathcal{L}$, $O_a\phi \in \mathcal{L}$, $PB_a\phi \in \mathcal{L}$, $PDB_a\phi \in \mathcal{L}$; if $\phi, \psi \in \mathcal{L}$ then $\phi \vee \psi$, $\phi \wedge \psi$, $\phi \to \psi$, $\neg\phi$, $\blacklozenge\phi$ belong to $\mathcal{L}$.*

Let us consider a function M which associates moment n, agent ids and epistemic states: $M : \mathbb{N} \times A \to \mathcal{ES}$. With respect to a sequence of messages and an interpretation M we define agent's epistemic attitudes:

Definition 7 ($\models$). *Let σ be a sequence of messages, M an interpretation, a an agent id and $n \in \mathbb{N}$ be a moment in time. Let $E_a^n = \langle CB_a^n, DB_a^n, PB_a^n \rangle = M(n, a)$. A model M and a sequence σ satisfy a formula ϕ at n according to the following rules:*

- $M, \sigma, n \models B_a\phi$ *iff* $\phi \in Bel(CB_a^n)$.
- $M, \sigma, n \models DB_a\phi$ *iff* $\exists \langle \phi, k \rangle \in DB_a^n$.
- $M, \sigma, n \models PB_a\phi$ *iff* $M, \sigma, n \not\models B_a\phi$ *and*
  $support(CB_a^n \cup \{\langle \psi, k \rangle \in PB_a^n | \exists s \text{ s.t. } \sigma(k) = \langle a, s, \psi, \text{Hold} \rangle\}, \phi) \neq \emptyset$.
- $M, \sigma, n \models PDB_a\phi$ *iff* $\exists \langle \phi, k \rangle \in PB_a^n$ *s.t.* $\exists s\sigma(k) = \langle a, s, \phi, \text{NotHold} \rangle$.
- $M, \sigma, n \models O_a\phi$ *iff* $M, \sigma, n \models B_a\phi$ *or* $M, \sigma, n \models DB_a\phi$.
- $M, \sigma, n \models \blacklozenge\phi$ *iff* $\exists n' < n$ *s.t.* $M, \sigma, n' \models \phi$.
- $M, \sigma, n \models \neg\phi$ *iff* $M, \sigma, n \not\models \phi$.
- $M, \sigma, n \models \phi \vee \psi$ *iff* $M, \sigma, n \models \phi$ *or* $M, \sigma, n \models \psi$.
- $M, \sigma, n \models \phi \wedge \psi$ *iff* $M, \sigma, n \models \phi$ *and* $M, \sigma, n \models \psi$.
- $M, \sigma, n \models \phi \to \psi$ *iff if* $M, \sigma, n \models \phi$ *then* $M, \sigma, n \models \psi$.

We write $\models \phi$ iff for all σ, M and n, we have $M, \sigma, n \models \phi$

The following formulas characterizing some epistemic attitudes are valid in our framework:

(1) $B_a(\phi \to \psi) \to (B_a\phi \to B_a\psi)$ (2) $\blacklozenge(\phi \to \psi) \to (\blacklozenge\phi \to \blacklozenge\psi)$

(3) $B_a\phi \to \neg B_a\neg\phi$ (4) $DB_a\phi \to \neg B_a\phi$

Formulas (1) and (2) correspond to the K axiom schema. Formula (3) corresponds to the D axiom schema (consistency of current beliefs). The last formula enforces the consistency of current beliefs by linking them to disbeliefs (i.e. none disbelief is believed). Let us mention that the K-like formula, $O_a(\phi \to \psi) \to (O_a\phi \to O_a\psi)$, is not valid. Notice also that the opposite of formula (4): $\neg B_a\phi \to DB_a\phi$, is not valid. This is due to our distinction between belief, disbelief and ignorance.

Example 4. Let us reconsider example 3. According to the sequence of messages σ and the interpretation $M(6, a) = \langle \{\{\langle \neg \phi, 1 \rangle, \langle \neg \phi \rightarrow \phi', 2 \rangle\}, \{\langle \phi'', 4 \rangle\}, \{\langle \neg \phi', 3 \rangle, \langle \phi' \rightarrow \phi'', 5 \rangle\}\rangle$, we get the following epistemic attitudes:

$$M, \sigma, 6 \models \mathsf{O}_a \phi' \wedge \mathsf{B}_a \phi' \wedge \mathsf{O}_a \phi'' \wedge \mathsf{DB}_a \phi'' \wedge \mathsf{PB}_a \phi'$$

In the following of the paper, we mainly focus on the dynamics of epistemic states in presence of disbelief and potential belief. The advantage of the logic proposed here is to help understanding the interest of disbelief and potential belief in terms of describing epistemic states of agents. This logic is closed to the logic presented in [12]. In [12], the proposed logic does not take into account potential beliefs but handles preferences. A detailed study of the behaviour of the modal operators is presented in [12].

5   Epistemic State Change

In order to handle messages, agents need change operators. The proposed operators belong to the family of non-prioritized operators [6, 8] because the main criterion for adopting a message is the reliability of the sender and not the novelty of the message. In our context, the operators have to handle belief, disbelief and potential belief.

The reliability of agents introduces a preference order noted $\leqslant$: each agent considers its own most reliable sources. Agents that could not be distinguished are considered in an equal way which entails a total preorder. This preorder entails a preorder over signed beliefs (since every signed belief is associated to a message through σ and thus to a sender). This latter preorder over signed beliefs will be used (i) to check if a change operation has to occur and (ii) to select (dis)beliefs to be retained in the change operation.

Definition 8 (Agent Preferences). *Let $\mathcal{P}$ be a function associating each agent a with a total preorder $\leqslant_a$, $\mathcal{P} : A \rightarrow 2^{A \times A}$. $\mathcal{P}$ describes the agent preferences.*

Writing $a <_r b$ means that b is a strictly better source than a for agent r: $a \leqslant_r b$ but $b \not\leqslant_r a$. The preorder over agents entails a preorder over signed beliefs also noted $\leqslant_r$.

Definition 9 (Preferences Over Signed Beliefs). *Let us consider two signed beliefs $\langle \phi, i \rangle$ and $\langle \psi, j \rangle$ s.t. $\sigma(i) = \langle r, s, \phi, st \rangle$ and $\sigma(j) = \langle r, s', \psi, st' \rangle$. Let $\leqslant_r$ be the preferences of agent r. Preferences over signed beliefs are determined as follows: $\langle \phi, i \rangle \leqslant_r \langle \psi, j \rangle$ iff $s \leqslant_r s'$.*

Let S be a set of signed beliefs; since $\mathcal{P}(r)$ is total, $min(S)$ is always defined.

According to their current belief base and their preferences, agents change their epistemic state as they interact with other agents. We describe the two main kinds of belief change: contraction and revision. Let us consider a set of agents A where their initial epistemic states is empty: $(\forall a \in A) E_a^0 = \langle \emptyset, \emptyset, \emptyset \rangle$, some preferences $\mathcal{P}$ and a sequence of messages σ. Messages received by agents entail a revision or a contraction action. Let $n \in \mathbb{N}$ and $\sigma(n) = \langle r, s, \phi, status \rangle$ be a message. Suppose $E_a^n = \langle CB, DB, PB \rangle$ be the epistemic state of agent a at n. The epistemic state of a is recursively defined accordingly to $\mathcal{P}(a)$ for any message received by a at $n' < n$. Since only one message is sent at n, only one agent changes its epistemic state.

Definition 10. *Let A be a set of agents, E_a^n be the epistemic state of each agent a at n and $\sigma(n) = \langle r, s, \phi, status \rangle$ be a message.*

$$E_a^{n+1} = \begin{cases} (E_a^n) & \text{if } a \neq r \\ (E_a^n)^*_{\langle \phi, n \rangle} & \text{if } status = \text{Hold } and\ a = r \\ (E_a^n)^-_{\langle \phi, n \rangle} & \text{if } status = \text{NotHold } and\ a = r \end{cases}$$

Agents are autonomous, thus, the change action should not be specific to a belief state but must be appropriate for handling sequences of belief change. Our framework enables agent to handle iterated belief change [3] since preferences are not specific to an epistemic state. When agents determine which beliefs should be dropped they consider beliefs in their syntactic form, i.e. the messages, and thus change will be based on this approach [5, 10].

Agent r *revises* its epistemic state if the status of the received statement is Hold: it inserts in a consistent way the new piece of information and moves some of its current beliefs or disbeliefs into its potential belief set. Agent r *contracts* its epistemic state if the status of the received statement is NotHold: it moves some current beliefs into its set of potential beliefs and expands its set of disbeliefs. In both cases, agent r reconsiders its potential beliefs in order to reinstate some of them if they are consistent with the new epistemic state.

5.1   Contraction

In this section, we describe the contraction operator $-$. Let $\sigma(n) = \langle r, s, \phi, \text{NotHold} \rangle$ be a message, $E^n = \langle CB, DB, PB \rangle$ be the epistemic state of agent r at n and $E^{n+1} = (E^n)^-_{\langle \phi, n \rangle}$ be the resulting epistemic state of the contraction of E^n by the signed belief $\langle \phi, n \rangle$. When we contract the epistemic state of agent r, we check the degree of ϕ according to preferences (see def 11): if s is lower than the highest degree of a conflicting belief of r then ϕ simply goes to the potential belief set; otherwise agent s has to be trusted and we actually performed the contraction.

In order to check the degree of ϕ, we consider the set Γ of minimal subsets of $\mathcal{L}_0$-statements issued from CB entailing ϕ: $\Gamma = support(CB, \phi)$. Then, we employ a complete preorder with maximal elements on the entire set Γ [10] based on $\leqslant_r$: we say that a set γ_1 is preferred to a set γ_2, noted $\gamma_2 \ll_r \gamma_1$, if the maximal element of γ_1 is strictly preferred to the maximal element of γ_2; γ_1 is equally preferred to γ_2, $\gamma_2 =_r \gamma_1$, if the maximal element of γ_1 is equal to the maximal element of γ_2. Note that such maximal elements of γ always exist.

Definition 11 uses the following notions that will be further discussed in the following of the paper: function *esc* gives the new current belief set and it is a safe contraction function [1] based on $\ll_r$. Current beliefs which have been removed by contraction function esc are added to the potential beliefs. If the received message do not entail a contraction then it is considered as a "potential disbelief". The set Π represents the most preferred potential beliefs which are consistent with the contracted current belief set. it has to be added to $esc(CB, \langle \phi, n \rangle)$. Similarly, the set Δ represents the potential disbeliefs that have to be reinstated (since current beliefs have been changed) (definition of Π and Δ are presented definition 13).

Definition 11 (-). *Let* $\sigma(n) = \langle r, s, \phi, \mathtt{NotHold} \rangle$ *be a message and* $E^-_{\langle \phi, n \rangle}$ *be the epistemic state of agent* r *at the moment* $n+1$ *s.t.:*

- *if* $Bel(CB) \vdash \phi$ *and* $\exists \gamma \in support(CB, \phi)$ *s.t.* $\{\langle \phi, n \rangle\} \ll_r \gamma$ *then*

$$E^-_{\langle \phi, n \rangle} = \langle CB, DB, PB \cup \{\langle \phi, n \rangle\}\rangle$$

- *else*

$$E^-_{\langle \phi, n \rangle} = \langle esc(CB, \langle \phi, n \rangle) \cup \Pi, DB \cup \Delta \cup \{\langle \phi, n \rangle\},$$
$$PB - \Pi - \Delta \cup (CB - esc(CB, \langle \phi, n \rangle))\rangle$$

The contraction operator is a two stage operator: firstly the current beliefs are contracted if the sender of the message is sufficiently reliable and secondly, the potential beliefs that are consistent with the resulted current beliefs are added to them.

First Stage, Contracting CB: Here, we use the degree of each conflicting belief. We remove minimal elements in every set $\gamma \in support(CB, \phi)$, one by one, in an iterative way, w.r.t. $\ll_r$. Let $\min(\Gamma)$ be the set of minimal subsets of Γ with respect to $\ll_r$. The contraction function, esc removes from CB the less reliable signed beliefs belonging to $\min(\Gamma)$, i.e. $min(\min(\Gamma))$.

Definition 12 (esc). *The contraction of the current signed beliefs of an epistemic state* E *by a signed belief* $sb = \langle \phi, n \rangle$ *is defined as* $esc(CB, sb) = CB^{|\Gamma|}$ *where* $CB^{|\Gamma|}$ *is defined as follows:*

- $CB^0 = CB$, $\Gamma^0 = support(CB^0, \phi)$;
- $CB^{i+1} = CB^i - min(\cup_{\gamma \in \min(\Gamma^i)} \gamma)$;
- $\Gamma^{i+1} = support(CB^{i+1}, \phi)$.

Before stating the behavior of esc we reformulate the AGM postulates [7] w.r.t. our definitions:

(C1) $esc(CB, \langle \phi, n \rangle)$ is a set of signed beliefs.
(C2) $esc(CB, \langle \phi, n \rangle) \subseteq CB$.
(C3) If $\phi \notin Bel(CB)$ then $esc(CB, \langle \phi, n \rangle) = CB$.
(C4) If $\nvdash \phi$ then $\phi \notin Bel(esc(CB, \langle \phi, n \rangle))$.
(C5) If $\phi \in Bel(CB)$, then $CB \subseteq esc(CB, \langle \phi, n \rangle) \cup \{\langle \phi, n+1 \rangle\}$.

(C6) If $\vdash \phi \leftrightarrow \psi$, then $esc(CB, \langle \phi, n \rangle) = esc(CB, \langle \psi, n \rangle)$.

(C7) $esc(CB, \langle \phi, n \rangle) \cap esc(CB, \langle \psi, n \rangle) \subseteq esc(CB, \langle \phi \rightarrow \psi, n \rangle)$.

(C8) If $\phi \notin Bel(esc(CB, \langle \phi \wedge \psi, n \rangle))$, then $esc(CB, \langle \phi \wedge \psi, n \rangle) \subseteq esc(CB, \langle \phi, n \rangle)$.

We get the following theorem for the contraction function esc:

Theorem 1 ([10]). *Let r be an agent, $\leqslant_r$ be its preferences, $E^n = \langle CB, DB, PB \rangle$ its epistemic state and a message $\sigma(n) = \langle r, s, \phi, \mathtt{NotHold} \rangle$. The contraction function esc determined by E^n, $\leqslant_r$ and $\langle \phi, n \rangle$ satisfies AGM postulates for contraction (C1) through (C5), (C7) and (C8).*

AGM postulate (C6) which states the syntax irrelevance principle is not satisfied since we consider a syntax-based technique.

Second Stage, Adding/Removing Potential Beliefs and Disbeliefs: After contracting its current belief set, agent r has to consider all potential beliefs. Indeed, some potential beliefs may be consistent with new set $esc(CB, sb)$. A potential belief may be reinstated if it does not entail (i) an inconsistency with the current beliefs, (ii) nor with the disbeliefs and (iii) no potential disbelief is more reliable. In order to define which potential beliefs may be reinstated, we introduce two functions, $CBeligible$ and $DBeligible$, which state if a potential belief may be reintroduced in the set of current beliefs or disbeliefs.

Sets Π and Δ represent the sets of potential beliefs that have to be reinstated as current belief and disbelief. For this, we consider the most preferred potential beliefs with the contracted current belief set and we build Π, a set of potential beliefs that should be added to $esc(CB, \langle \phi, n \rangle)$, i.e. to the new set of current beliefs. We proceed in a similar way for the set Δ.

Definition 13 (Π and Δ). *The set Π of potential beliefs to add to the new current belief set and the set Δ of potential beliefs that have to be considered as disbeliefs are defined as follows:*

- $PB^0 = PB$, $\Pi^0 = \emptyset$, $\Delta^0 = \emptyset$;
- *Let $\langle \psi, k \rangle \in PB^i$. If*

    1. $CBeligible((\langle esc(CB, \langle \phi, n \rangle) \cup \Pi^i, DB \cup \Delta^i, PB^i \rangle, \{\langle \psi, k \rangle\}) = \mathsf{true}$ *and;*
    2. $(\forall \langle \psi', k' \rangle \in PB^i) CBeligible((\langle esc(CB, \langle \phi, n \rangle) \cup \Pi^i, DB \cup \Delta^i, PB^i \rangle, \{\langle \psi', k' \rangle\}) = \mathsf{true} \Rightarrow \langle \psi, k \rangle <_r \langle \psi', k' \rangle$.

    then

$$\Pi^{i+1} = \Pi^i \cup \{\langle \psi, k \rangle\} \text{ and } \Delta^{i+1} = \Delta^i$$

- *Let $\langle \psi, k \rangle \in PB^i$. If $DBeligible((\langle esc(CB, \langle \phi, n \rangle) \cup \Pi^i, DB \cup \Delta^i, PB^i \rangle, \{\langle \psi, k \rangle\}) = \mathsf{true}$ then*

$$\Delta^{i+1} = \Delta^i \cup \{\langle \psi, k \rangle\} \text{ and } \Pi^{i+1} = \Pi^i$$

- $PB^{i+1} = PB^i - \{\langle \psi, k \rangle\}$.

    The sets Π, Δ are equal to $\Pi^{|PB|}$ and $\Delta^{|PB|}$.

The sets Π and Δ have to be removed from the potential beliefs. Now, we give the definitions of the functions $CDeligible$ and $DBeligible$ which states if a potential belief can be reinstated.

Definition 14 (CBeligible). *Let $CBeligible$ be a function stating if a signed belief can be added to a set of current beliefs. Let $E_r = \langle CB, DB, PB \rangle$ be the epistemic state of agent r, $\langle \psi, k \rangle$ be a signed belief, $\leqslant_r$ be the preferences of r and σ be a sequence of messages.*

- $CBeligible(E_r, \langle \psi, k \rangle) = \mathsf{true}$ *iff:*
    1. $(\exists s')(\sigma(k) = \langle r, s', \psi, \mathsf{Hold} \rangle)$;
    2. $Bel(CB \cup \{\langle \psi, k \rangle\}) \not\vdash \bot$ *and*
    3. $(\forall \langle \psi', k' \rangle \in DB)$ $((\forall \gamma \in support(CB \cup \{\langle \psi, k \rangle\}, \psi'))(\langle \psi, k \rangle \in \gamma \Rightarrow \{\langle \psi', k' \rangle\} \ll_r \gamma))$.
    4. $(\forall \langle \psi', k' \rangle \in PB)$ $(\exists s'')(\sigma(k') = \langle r, s'', \psi', \mathsf{NotHold} \rangle) \Rightarrow \langle \psi', k' \rangle \leqslant_r \langle \psi, k \rangle$

- $CBeligible(E_r, \langle \psi, k \rangle) = \mathsf{false}$ *otherwise.*

In other words, a signed belief may be chosen for becoming a current belief (w.r.t. to an epistemic state) iff (1) the status of the signed belief is Hold (i.e. the agent has to consider that the statement has to be believed); (2) the statement is consistent with the current beliefs; (3) the statement do not entail the violation of a disbelief or if it entails a violation of a disbelief then the statement is more reliable than the violated disbeliefs; (4) there is no potential disbelief that is more "important" (w.r.t. to the preferences) than this signed belief. In a similar way, $DBeligible$ is a function stating if a potential disbelief has to be considered as a disbelief.

Definition 15 (DBeligible). *Let $DBeligible$ be a function stating if a signed belief can be added to a set of disbeliefs. Let $E_r = \langle CB, DB, PB \rangle$ be the epistemic state of agent r, $\langle \psi, k \rangle$ be a signed belief, $\leqslant$ be the preferences of r and σ be a sequence of messages.*

- $DBeligible(E_r, \langle \psi, k \rangle) = \mathsf{true}$ *iff:*
    1. $(\exists s')(\sigma(k) = \langle r, s', \psi, \mathsf{NotHold} \rangle)$;
    2. $Bel(CB) \not\vdash \psi$ *or* $(\forall \gamma \in support(CB, \psi))(\{\langle \psi, k \rangle\} \ll_r \gamma)$
    3. $(\forall \langle \psi', k' \rangle \in PB)$ $(\exists s'')(\sigma(k') = \langle r, s'', \psi', \mathsf{Hold} \rangle) \Rightarrow \langle \psi', k' \rangle \leqslant_r \langle \psi, k \rangle$

- $DBeligible(E_r, \langle \psi, k \rangle) = \mathsf{false}$ *otherwise.*

A signed belief may be inserted in a set of disbeliefs iff: (1) the status of the signed belief is equal to $\mathsf{NotHold}$; (2) the current beliefs do not entail the statement associated to the signed belief or, if the statement is entailed by the current beliefs, then the statement is more reliable than every minimal subsets issued from the current beliefs entailing it; (3) there is no possible belief that is more reliable than this potential disbelief.

A consequence of the definition of $-$ is that every state has a successor state.

Observation 1. *Let E be an epistemic state and sb a signed belief. E_{sb}^- is an epistemic state.*

Notice that according to the definitions of $CBeligible$ and $DBeligible$ a contracted epistemic state may admit several successor states.

Observation 2. *Let E be an epistemic state and sb a signed belief. There exists at least one epistemic state characterizing E_{sb}^-.*

5.2   Revision

Our revision operation is based on the safe contraction operation previously defined and the Levi identity. In order to contract the epistemic state, we introduce the notion of the negation of a signed belief:

Definition 16 ($\overline{\langle \phi, i \rangle}$). *Let σ be a sequence of messages and $m = \langle r, s, \phi, \mathtt{Hold} \rangle$ be a message s.t. $\sigma(i) = m$. Let $\overline{\langle \phi, i \rangle}$ be a signed belief, called the mirror of $\langle \phi, i \rangle$ s.t. the associated message to $\overline{\langle \phi, i \rangle}$ is equal to $\langle r, s, \neg\phi, \mathtt{NotHold} \rangle$.*

Let $\sigma(n) = \langle r, s, \phi, \mathtt{Hold} \rangle$ be a message, E^n be the epistemic state of agent r at n and $E^{n+1} = (E^n)^*_{\langle \phi, n \rangle}$ be the resulting epistemic state of the revision of E^n by the signed belief $\langle \phi, n \rangle$. Set of current beliefs CB is "contracted" by the mirror of $\langle \phi, n \rangle$:

Definition 17 (*esr*). *Let $E = \langle CB, DB, PB \rangle$ be an epistemic state. The revision of the set CB by a signed belief $\langle \phi, n \rangle$, s.t. $\sigma(n) = \langle r, s, \phi, \mathtt{Hold} \rangle$ is defined as:*

$$esr(CB, \langle \phi, n \rangle) = esc(CB, \overline{\langle \phi, n \rangle}) \cup \{\langle \phi, n \rangle\}$$

As for the contraction function *esc* all the postulates describing revision actions [7] are satisfied except the syntax-independence postulate.

The second stage where we consider potential beliefs that may be reinstated slightly differs from the one previously described. The main difference concerns the disbeliefs since some of them should no longer hold. The disbeliefs that should no longer considered have to be removed from DB and transferred into PB. Definitions of Π is unchanged. Let $\overline{\Delta}$ be this set of this disbeliefs:

$$\overline{\Delta} = \{\langle \psi, k \rangle | \sigma(k) = \langle r, s', \psi, \mathtt{NotHold} \rangle \text{ and}$$
$$Bel(esr(CB, \langle \phi, n \rangle) \cup \Pi) \vdash \psi \text{ and}$$
$$(\exists \gamma \in support(esr(CB, \langle \phi, n \rangle, \psi)))(\{\langle \psi, k \rangle\}) \ll_r \gamma)\}$$

Definition 18 (*). *Let $E^*_{\langle \phi, n \rangle}$ be the epistemic state of agent r at moment $n+1$:*

- *if* $((\exists \langle \psi, k \rangle \in DB) \text{ s.t. } (\forall \gamma \in support(esr(CB, \langle \phi, n \rangle), \psi))(\gamma \ll_r \{\langle \psi, k \rangle\}))$ *or* $((\exists \gamma \in support(CB, \neg\phi)(\{\langle \phi, n \rangle\} \ll_r \gamma))$ *then*

$$E^*_{\langle \phi, n \rangle} = \langle CB, DB, PB \cup \{\langle \phi, n \rangle\}\rangle$$

$- \; else$

$$E^*_{\langle \phi, n \rangle} = \langle esr(CB, \langle \phi, n \rangle) \cup \Pi, DB \cup \Delta - \overline{\Delta}, PB - \Pi - \Delta \cup \overline{\Delta} \rangle$$

As for the contraction function, we can make a similar observation about the successor states.

Observation 3. *Let E be an epistemic state and sb a signed belief. There exists at least one epistemic state characterizing E^*_{sb}.*

Now, we describe the behavior of the function $*$, i.e. how this function respects AGM postulates. We propose here to rephrase the AGM postulates for revision in a way similar to those exhibit by A. Darwiche and J. Pearl in [3] for their epistemic states. Before introducing the modified postulates which are a KM formulation of the AGM postulates [3, 9], let us briefly describe the expansion of an epistemic state. Let sb be a signed belief and E an epistemic state:

$$E^+_{sb} = \langle CB \cup \{sb\}, DB, PB \rangle$$

To simplify notation in the postulates, we use $Bel(E)$ instead of $Bel(CB)$ $(E = \langle CB, DB, PB \rangle)$. The modified AGM postulates are:

$(R * 1)$ $Bel(E^*_{\langle \phi, n \rangle}) \vdash \phi$.
$(R * 2)$ If $Bel(E) \nvdash \neg\phi$ then $E^*_{\langle \phi, n \rangle} = E^+_{\langle \phi, n \rangle}$.
$(R * 3)$ If $\nvdash \neg\phi$ then $Bel(E^*_{\langle \phi, n \rangle}) \nvdash \bot$.
$(R * 4)$ If $E = F$ and $\phi \leftrightarrow \psi$ then $Bel(E^*_{\langle \phi, n \rangle}) \leftrightarrow Bel(F^*_{\langle \psi, n \rangle})$.
$(R * 5)$ $Bel((E^*_{\langle \phi, n \rangle})^+_{\langle \psi, n+1 \rangle}) \vdash Bel(E^*_{\langle \phi \wedge \psi, n \rangle})$.
$(R * 6)$ If $Bel((E^*_{\langle \phi, n \rangle})^+_{\langle \psi, n+1 \rangle}) \nvdash \bot$ then $Bel(E^*_{\langle \phi \wedge \psi, n \rangle}) \vdash Bel((E^*_{\langle \phi, n \rangle})^+_{\langle \psi, n+1 \rangle})$.

We have the following theorem:

Theorem 2. *Let r be an agent, $\leqslant_r$ be its preferences, $E^n = \langle CB, DB, PB \rangle$ its epistemic state and a message $\sigma(n) = \langle r, s, \phi, \mathtt{Hold} \rangle$. The revision function $*$ determined by E^n, $\leqslant_r$ and $\langle \phi, n \rangle$ satisfies modified AGM postulates for revision $(R * 2)$ and $(R * 3)$.*

AGM postulate $(R * 1)$ which states the success principle is not satisfied since cases may occur where input is not inserted in the current beliefs. $(R * 4)$ states syntax irrelevance principle and as previously it is not satisfied since we consider a syntax-based technique (regardless the definition of the equality of two epistemic states). Postulates $(R * 5)$ and $(R * 6)$ are not satisfied since input may be considered in the resulting epistemic state as current or potential belief.

Because function $*$ is non-prioritized, postulates introduced by A. Darwiche and J. Pearl in [3] characterizing iterated revision do not hold.

5.3 Linking Change Action and Models for Epistemic Attitudes

Since we have shown how a sequence of actions is handled for constructing epistemic states, we refine interpretation function M described section 4. Let σ be a sequence of messages, $\mathcal{P}$ be agent preferences. Let $M : \mathbb{N} \times A \to \mathcal{ES}$ be the interpretation function defined as follows:

- for all $a \in A$, $M(0, a) = \langle \emptyset, \emptyset, \emptyset \rangle$
- for all $a \in A$ and $n > 0$ s.t. $\sigma(n-1) = \langle r, s, \phi, status \rangle$:

$$M(n, a) = \begin{cases} M(n-1, a) & \text{if } a \neq r \\ M(n-1, a)^*_{\langle \phi, n \rangle} & \text{if } status = \texttt{Hold} \text{ and } a = r \\ M(n-1, a)^-_{\langle \phi, n \rangle} & \text{if } status = \texttt{NotHold} \text{ and } a = r \end{cases}$$

Actually, the procedure for handling changes, and thus the sequence of messages, justifies the epistemic attitudes section 4.

6   Revisiting the Example

In this section, we revisit the example described at the beginning of the paper. Let us consider three agents $pa(ul)$, $pe(ter)$, $po(lice)$. The preferences of $peter$ are: $\mathcal{P}(pe) = \langle \{(pa < pe, pe < po)\} \rangle$ and the initial state is $E^0_{pe} = \langle \emptyset, \emptyset, \emptyset \rangle$. $murd$, $evid$ and $jail$ stand for $murderer$, $evidence$ and $jail$. Let us consider what $paul$ tells $peter$ about John: we get the following messages $\sigma(0)$ and $\sigma(1)$:

$$\sigma(0) = \langle pe, pa, murd, \texttt{Hold} \rangle$$
$$\sigma(1) = \langle pe, pa, murd \rightarrow jail, \texttt{Hold} \rangle$$

After processing these two messages as revision actions, $peter$ believes all the consequences of $Bel(CB^1_p e) = \{\alpha | murd \wedge (murd \rightarrow jail) \vdash \alpha\}$. The resulting epistemic states are:

$$E^1 = \langle \{\langle murd, 0 \rangle\}, \emptyset, \emptyset \rangle$$
$$E^2 = \langle \{\langle murd, 0 \rangle, \langle murd \rightarrow jail, 1 \rangle\}, \emptyset, \emptyset \rangle$$

Next $peter$ processes the messages sent by the police (john is a murderer iff there is evidence against him; and the police do not believe there is evidence):

$$\sigma(2) = \langle pe, po, murd \rightarrow evid, \texttt{Hold} \rangle$$
$$\sigma(3) = \langle pe, po, evid, \texttt{NotHold} \rangle$$

According to the preferences and the change operators, we get the following epistemic states for $peter$:

$$E^3 = \langle \{\langle murd, 0 \rangle, \langle murd \rightarrow jail, 1 \rangle, \langle murd \rightarrow evid, 2 \rangle\}, \emptyset, \emptyset \rangle$$
$$E^4 = \langle \{\langle murd \rightarrow jail, 1 \rangle, \langle murd \rightarrow evid, 2 \rangle\}, \{\langle evid, 3 \rangle\}, \{\langle murd, 0 \rangle\} \rangle$$

At this moment, $peter$ does no longer believe that John is a murderer and he will go to jail. Indeed $Bel(CB^3_{pe}) \vdash evidence$ and $evidence$ is inserted in DB^4_{pe} (because of the reliability of the police) and thus $murderer$ is moved into PB^4_{pe}. Finally, the $police$ informs $peter$ about proofs against John:

$$\sigma(4) = \langle pe, po, evid, \texttt{Hold} \rangle$$

We get the following epistemic state for *peter*:

$$E^5 = \langle \{\langle murd, 0\rangle, \langle murd \rightarrow jail, 1\rangle, \langle murd \rightarrow evid, 2\rangle, \langle evid, 4\rangle\}, \emptyset, \{\langle evid, 3\rangle\}\}\rangle$$

Messages 0, 1, 2 and 4 entail a revision operation while message 3 entails a contraction operation. Notice that statement "John is a murderer" has been reinstated as a current belief since it is consistent with the new epistemic state. Let us also notice that the last message (*police* informs *peter* that *evidence* holds) entails that *jail* is believed by *peter*. This is due to the fact that agent *police* is more reliable that *paul*. Suppose now, that instead of agent *police*, agent *paul* informs *peter* about evidence against John. We have:

$$\sigma(4b) = \langle pe, pa, evid, \texttt{Hold}\rangle$$

Finally, we get the following epistemic state for *peter*:

$$E^{5b} = \langle \{\langle murd \rightarrow jail, 1\rangle, \langle murd \rightarrow evid, 2\rangle\}, \{\langle evid, 3\rangle\}, \{\langle murd, 0\rangle, \langle evid, 4\rangle\}\}\rangle$$

In other words, disbelief *evid*(*ence*) which is stronger (since it has been send by *po* and *po* is better than *pa*) prevents agent *peter* to adopt the statement *murd*(*erer*). However, *peter* considers that there is potentially evidence against John.

Let M be an interpretation function reflecting the changes, i.e. $M(5, pe) = E^5$. According to the sequence of messages and M, we get the following epistemic attitudes about the content of the messages:

$$M, \sigma, 5 \models \mathsf{B}_{pe} jail \qquad\qquad M, \sigma, 5b \models \mathsf{DB}_{pe} evidence$$
$$M, \sigma, 5 \models \mathsf{O}_{pe} murderer \qquad\qquad M, \sigma, 5b \models \blacklozenge(\mathsf{B}_{pe} murderer)$$
$$M, \sigma, 5 \models \mathsf{PDB}_{pe} evid \wedge murd \qquad\qquad M, \sigma, 5b \models \mathsf{PB}_{pe} jail$$

Next, let us assume a statement γ s.t. γ has nothing in common with ϕ and ψ; a_1 has no opinion about γ and thus does not believe or disbelieve γ:

$$M, \sigma, 5 \models \neg\mathsf{O}_{a_1}\gamma \wedge \neg\mathsf{B}_{a_1}\gamma \wedge \neg\mathsf{DB}_{a_1}\gamma$$

7   Discussion

Our work focusses on belief change when agents exchange information about a static world. The first characteristic of our operators is to enable agents to handle any sequence of messages. The second characteristic of our framework is to keep all the received messages and to reconsider them whenever a change action occurs so that received information is handled as much as possible. The third characteristic of our proposal is a semantics for describing beliefs, disbeliefs, potential beliefs which is explicitly based on messages. Moreover, the proposed semantics enables to represent opinions.

A. Dragoni and P. Giorgini present a similar framework [4]. They propose to apply non-prioritized belief revision in a multi-agent system by considering the origin of information. Based on the reliability of the incoming statements, agents can reject new information. Agents can also reconsider all the previous messages and more specifically discarded beliefs can be reinstated. J.W. Roorda et al. [14] present also a similar work based on modal logics. They propose a function returning the history of messages and a second one to select a subset of messages in a consistent way. Thus, changes are handled only by expansions. The main difference with our work is that they do not consider disbeliefs in an explicit way and thus they do not take into account contraction operations. A second difference is that we consider more fine-grain epistemic attitudes: for instance, we can describe potential belief and thus what could be believed by agents. Our work is also connected to the work of S. Chopra *et al.* [2] which proposed a definition of non-prioritized belief and disbelief change based on the notion of ranked belief state. As [2], we claim that in order to handle iterated contraction, we need a "memory" for these actions and disbelief represents this memory. However, [2] does not consider potential belief which provides a memory for discarded belief or disbelief.

Our approach does have some limitations. In a short term, we would like to generalize our framework in order to handle the limitation about the static world, i.e. handling belief update. In a more longer term, our aim is to enable agents to reason about their different kinds of beliefs so that they can initiate messages for acquiring new information and adopting new epistemic attitudes (knowledge, goals, desires, commitments...). We are currently investigating all these topics.

References

1. C. Alchourrón and D. Makinson. The logic of Theory Change: Safe Contraction. *Studia Logica*, 44:405–422, 1985.
2. S. Chopra, A. Ghose, and T. Meyer. Non-Prioritized Ranked Belief Change. *Journal of Philosophical Logic*, 32(4):417–443, 2003.
3. A. Darwiche and J. Pearl. On the logic of Iterated Belief Revision. *Artificial intelligence*, 89(1):1–29, 1997.
4. A. Dragoni and P. Giorgini. Revising beliefs received from multiple source. In M.A. Williams and H. Rott, editors, *Frontiers of Belief Revision, Applied Logic*. Kluwer, 1999.
5. R. Fagin, J. Ullman, and M. Vardi. On the semantics of Updates in Databases. In *Proceedings of the second ACM SIGACT-SIGMOD Symposium on Principles of Database Systems, Atlanta, Ga., USA*, pages 352–365, 1983.
6. N. Friedman and J. Halpern. Belief revision: a critique. In L. Carlucci Aiello, J. Doyle, and S. Shapiro, editors, *Proceedings of KR'96*, pages 421–431. Morgan Kaufmann, 1996.
7. P. Gärdenfors. *Knowledge in flux: Modeling the Dynamics of Epistemic States*. MIT Press, 1988.
8. S.O. Hansson. A Survey of Non-Prioritized Belief Revision. *Erkenntnis*, 50:413–427, 1999.
9. H. Katsuno and A. Mendelzon. Propositional Knowledge Base Revision and Minimal Change. *Artificial Intelligence*, 3(52):263–294, 1991.

10. B. Nebel. Syntax-based approaches to belief revision. In P. Gärdenfors, editor, *Belief revision*, volume 29 of *Journal of Cambridge Tracts in Theoretical Computer Science*, pages 52–88. Cambridge University Press, 1992.
11. L. Perrussel. Handling sequences of belief change in a multi-agent context. In M. Schillo, M. Klusch, J. Muller, and H. Tianfield, editors, *Multiagent System Technologies. First German Conference, MATES 2003, Erfurt, Germany, September 22-25, 2003, Proceedings*, volume 2831. Springer, 2003.
12. L. Perrussel and J.M. Thvenin. A logical approach for describing (dis)belief change and message processing. In *Proceedings of the AAMAS'04 - New York, USA, July 2004*. ACM, 2004.
13. A. Rao. Dynamics of belief systems: A philosophical, logical, and ai perspective. Technical Report 02, Australian Artificial Intelligence Institute, Melbourne, Australia, 1989.
14. J.W. Roorda, W. van der Hoek, and J.J. Meyer. Iterated belief change in mas. In C. Castelfranchi and W.L. Johnson, editors, *Proceedings of AAMAS'02*, pages 889–896. ACM, July 2002.
15. M. Wooldridge and N. R. Jennings. Intelligent agents: Theory and practice. *The Knowledge Engineering Review*, 10(2):115–152, 1995.

Learning in BDI Multi-agent Systems

Alejandro Guerra-Hernández[1], Amal El Fallah-Seghrouchni[2],
and Henry Soldano[1]

[1] Université Paris 13, Laboratoire d'Informatique de Paris Nord, UMR 7030 - CNRS,
Institut Galilée, Av. Jean-Baptiste Clément, Villetaneuese 93430, France
{agh, soldano}@lipn.univ-paris13.fr
[2] Université Paris 6, Laboratoire d'Informatique de Paris 6, UMR 7606 - CNRS,
8 rue du Capitaine Scott, Paris 75015, France
Amal.Elfallah@lip6.fr

Abstract. This paper deals with the issue of learning in multi-agent systems (MAS). Particularly, we are interested in BDI (Belief, Desire, Intention) agents. Despite the relevance of the BDI model of rational agency, little work has been done to deal with its two main limitations: i) The lack of learning competences; and ii) The lack of explicit multi-agent functionality. From the multi-agent learning perspective, we propose a BDI agent architecture extended with learning competences for MAS context. Induction of Logical Decision Trees, a first order method, is used to enable agents to learn when their plans are successfully executable. Our implementation enables multiple agents executed as parallel functions in a single Lisp image. In addition, our approach maintains consistency between learning and the theory of practical reasoning.

1 Introduction

The relevance of the BDI (Belief, Desire, Intention) model of rational agency can be explained in terms of its philosophical grounds on intentionality [7] and practical reasoning [2], as well as its elegant abstract logical semantics [23, 25, 29]. In addition, different implementations of the model, e.g., IRMA [3], and the PRS-like systems [11], have led to successful applications, including diagnosis for space shuttle, factory process control, and business process management [12]. However, two limitations of the BDI model are well known [13]: Its lack of learning competences; and the lack of explicit multi-agent functionality. Both limitations constitute an issue of what is now known as MAS learning [28, 26], roughly characterized as the intersection of MAS and Machine Learning (ML). MAS learning is justified as follows: Learning seems to be the way to deal with the complexity inherent to agents and MAS, while at the same time, learning on the MAS context could improve our understanding of learning principles in natural and artificial systems.

From the MAS learning perspective, this paper shows how a BDI architecture, based in dMARS specification [15], was extended to conceive a BDI learning architecture. The design of this architecture is inspired by the definition of

J. Dix and J. Leite (Eds.): CLIMA IV, LNAI 3259, pp. 218–233, 2004.
© Springer-Verlag Berlin Heidelberg 2004

a learning agent by Stuart Russell and Peter Norvig [24]. Design choices were constrained by the fact that BDI agents perform practical reasoning to behave. Practical reasoning, together with BDI semantics, pose a hard design problem: Learning methods directed towards action, very popular in MAS learning, use representations less expressive than those used in the BDI model, i.e., basically propositional representations as in classic reinforcement learning [27]; Learning methods with more expressive representations are usually conceived as isolated learning systems, directed towards epistemic reasoning. This may explain why in the abundant MAS learning literature, only Olivia et al. [21] has considered the problem of BDI learning agents, despite the relevance of the model in agency and MAS. The approach we use to solve this problem, applies Inductive Logic Programming (ILP) [20] methods, particularly Induction of Logical Decision Trees [4], to learn when plans are executable, as expressed by the context of plans, i.e., the components of the BDI model behind choices in practical reasoning.

This paper is organized as follows: Section 2 introduces the key BDI concepts that are necessary to explain our approach. Emphasis is set on the aspects of intentional agency and practical reasoning, involved in learning. Section 3 describes our BDI learning architecture and justifies the choices of design and implementation. Justifications include a hierarchy of learning MAS, built on the concept of awareness, to decide when agents should learn either by themselves or in cooperation with other agents. Also, the section briefly describes the learning method used on the architecture – Induction of Logical Decision Trees. Section 4 introduces an example of learning BDI agent at level 1 of the proposed hierarchy, i.e., centralized learning; Details of MAS learning at level 2, i.e., distributed learning, are considered in section 5. Finally, section 6 deals with related work and concludes this paper.

2 BDI Agency

Software agents are usually characterized as computer systems that exhibit flexible autonomous behavior [29], which means that these systems are capable of independent, autonomous action in order to meet their design objectives. BDI models of agency approximate this kind of behavior through two related theories about the philosophical concept of intentionality: Intentional Systems, defined by Daniel Dennett [7] as entities which appear to be subject of s, desires and other propositional attitudes; and the Practical Reasoning theory, proposed by Michael Bratman [2] as a common sense psychological framework to understand ourselves and others, based on beliefs, desires, and intentions conceived as partial plans. These related notions of intentionality provide us with the tools to describe agents at the right level of abstraction, i.e., in terms of beliefs, desires and intentions (BDI), adopting the intentional stance; and to design agents in a compatible way with such intentional description, i.e., as practical reasoning systems. Different aspects of intentionality and practical reasoning have been formally studied, resulting in the so called BDI logics [23]. For a road map of the evolution of these formalisms, see [25, 29]. Implementations make use of refinement techniques, e.g., using specifications in Z language [17].

This section sketches our BDI architecture, based on dMARS [15] specification, using a very simple scenario proposed by Charniak and McDermott [8]. This scenario (Fig. 1) is composed of a robot with two hands, situated in an environment where there is a board, a sander, a paint sprayer, and a vise. Different goals can be proposed to the robot, e.g., sand the board, or even get self painted! this introduces the case of incompatible goals, since once painted the robot is not operational (its state changes from ok to `painted`) for a while. The robot has different options, i.e., plans, to achieve its goals. It is possible to introduce other robots (see agent `r2`) in the environment to experiment social interactions [6], e.g., sharing goals, conflict for resources, etc. This scenario will be used in the examples in the rest of the paper.

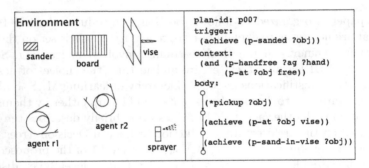

Fig. 1. A simple scenario for the examples in this paper and a simplified BDI plan

2.1   The BDI Model

In general, an architecture built on the BDI model of agency is specified in terms of the following data structures:

Beliefs. They represent information about the world. Each belief is represented as a ground literal of first-order logic. Literals not grounded, known as belief formulae, are used to define plans, but are not considered beliefs. They are updated by the perception of the environment, and the execution of intentions. The scenario shown in Fig. 1 can be represented with the following beliefs: (`p-state r1 ok`), (`p-at sander free`), (`p-at board free`), (`p-handfree r1 left`), (`p-handfree r1 right`), (`p-at sprayer free`). Where `free` is a constant meaning that the object is not at the vise or an agent has it. The rest is self explicative.

Desires. Also known as goals, correspond to the tasks allocated to the agent. Usually, they are considered logically consistent among them. Desires include to achieve a belief, and to test a situation, expressed as a situation formula, i.e., a belief formula or a disjunction and/or a conjunction of them, e.g., (test (and (p-state r1 ok) (p-freehand r1 ?x))). All strings starting by '?' are variables. Those starting by 'p-' are predicate symbols.

Event Queue. Perceptions of the agent are mapped to events stored in a queue. Events include the acquisition or removal of a belief, e.g., (add-bel (p-sand board)), the reception of a message, e.g., (told r2 (achieve (p-sand board))), and the acquisition of a new goal. These examples are simplified, events are implemented as structures keeping track of historical information. What is shown corresponds to a trigger, a component of events, used to identify them. The reception and emission of messages is used to implement MAS competences of our BDI agents. For the moment, no explicit agent communication language (ACL) is considered, but they can easily be included in our architecture since Lisp packages exist for them, at least for FIPA ACL and KQML.

Plans. BDI agents usually have a library of predefined plans. Each plan has several components, the most relevant for us are shown in the simplified plan on Fig. 1. The **plan-id** is used to identify a plan in the plan library. In our example, the plan is identified as **p007**. The trigger works like an invocation condition of a plan, it specifies the event a plan is supposed to deal with. Plan p007 is triggered by an event of the form (achieve (p-sanded ?obj)). Observe that the use of variables is allowed here. If the agent registers an event like (achieve (p-sanded board)) in the event queue, it will consider plan p007 as relevant to deal with such event. The context specifies, as a situation formula, the circumstances under which a plan should be executed. Remember that a situation formula is a belief formula or a conjunction and/or disjunction of them. Plan p007 is applicable if the agent has one hand free and the object to be sanded is free. The plan body represents possible courses of action. It is a tree which nodes are considered as states and arcs are actions or goals of the agent. The body of plan p007 starts with an external action, identified by a symbol starting by '*', (*pickup ?x). External actions are like procedures the agent can execute directly. Then the body continues with two goals. Goals are posted to the event queue when the plan is executed, then other plans that can deal with such events are considered, and so on. Additionally, plans have some maintenance conditions which describe the circumstances that must remain to continue the execution of the plan. A set of internal actions is specified for the cases of success and failure of the plan. Finally, some BDI architectures include some measure of the utility of the plan.

Intentions. They are courses of action an agent has commited to carry out. Each intention is implemented as a stack of plan instances. In our example, as seen above, in response to the event (achieve (p-sanded board)), plan p007 is considered as relevant. If the context of a plan is a consequence of the beliefs of the agent, the plan is considered executable. A plan instance is composed of a plan, as defined in the plan library, and the substitutions that make it relevant and applicable, e.g., *(board/?obj, left/?hand, r1/?ag)*. If the event that triggered the plan is an external one, i.e., no plan has generated it, then an empty stack is created and the plan instance is pushed on it. If the event is internal, i,e., generated by a plan, then the plan instance is pushed on the existing stack containing the plan that generated the event, e.g., imagine that a plan instance p005 deals with the event (`achieve` (`p-at`(`board, vise`))), generated while executing p007, this plan instance will be pushed on the stack containing p007, resulting on (`p005 p007`).

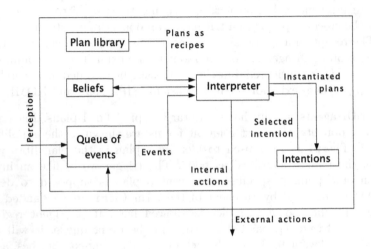

Fig. 2. Our BDI architecture inspired in dMARS specification

These structures interact with an interpreter, as shown in Fig. 2. Different algorithms for the interpreter are possible, the most simple is:

1. Update the event queue by perception and internal actions to reflect the events that have been observed;
2. Select an event, usually the first one in the queue, and generate new possible desires by finding the set of relevant plans in the library for the selected event, i.e., those plans whose trigger condition matches the selected event;
3. Select from the set of relevant plans an executable one, i.e., one plan whose context is a logical consequence of the beliefs of the agent, and create an instance plan for it.
4. Push this instance plan onto an existing or new intention stack, as explained before;
5. While the event queue is empty, select an intention stack, take the top plan, and execute its current step. If this step is an action, execute it, otherwise if it is a subgoal, post it to the event queue.

Michael Wooldridge [29] presents some algorithms for the BDI interpreter, corresponding to different commitment strategies, e.g., single-minded and open-minded commitments. David Kinny and Michael Georgeff [16] present a comparative study of two strategies identified as bold and cautious. Both strategies perform well if the environment is not very dynamic, but if this is not the case, cautious agents out perform bold ones.

2.2   Some Issues on Implementation

Given the nature of the PRS-dMARS approach, we considered using a symbolic programming language to implement our architecture. Since we decided to do our own Lisp implementation of a BDI architecture, some arguments are in place. We knew that different implementations for BDI architectures already existed. For PRS [11], and its re-implementation dMARS [15], we only had access to formal specifications. A PRS-like system, Jam! [14], became available once we had started implementing our interpreter, but its semantics differs from the specification we were using, particularly the context of plans are defined as conjunctions of belief formulae. Most importantly, there is evidence [18] that adapting existing software, even when disposing of low level specifications, to produce a learning agent or to attach one to existing software, is not obvious at all. In addition, sometimes it is even impossible without depth changes in the design of the original software. We found out that the structures and procedures used in the dMARS, fit well the features of Lisp, i.e., uniformity of representation for data and procedures as lists, data an procedure abstraction, etc. Note that PRS was originally developed using Lisp, so that dMARS, at least at the specification level, is pretty much influenced by this language.

Our architecture already provides functions to define primitive actions available to the agents in the system; to define plans that may use these primitive actions; to define and assign different competences to agents, in terms of a plan library; to bootstrap goals for each agent in terms of initial events; and to execute agents under different commitment strategies. These can be considered standard BDI features, together with syntax verification tools for the BDI language used to define agents, and built-in functions to test if BDI formulae are a logical consequence of a set of beliefs. The interface with the OS is provided by Lisp.

Non standard BDI features in our architecture include a set of functions to simulate agents in a MAS, as parallel processes running in the same Lisp image; and an interface to use DTP theorem prover [10] in the case agents need to perform more sophisticated epistemic reasoning, beyond the built-in logical competences. DTP does refutation proofs of queries from databases in First-Order predicate calculus, using a model elimination algorithm and domain independent control reasoning. The use of sub-goaling inference with model elimination reductions, makes the inference of DTP sound and complete.

3   BDI Learning Agents

Based on the definition of a well posed learning problem as proposed in ML [19], Stuart Russell and Peter Norvig [24] have conceptually structured a generic learning agent architecture into four components: i) A learning component responsible for making improvements by executing a learning algorithm; ii) A performance component responsible of taking actions; iii) A critic component responsible for providing feedback; and iv) A problem generator responsible for suggesting actions that will lead to informative experiences. The design of the learning component, and consequently the choice of a particular learning method, is usually affected by five major issues. They are considered here assuming that our BDI architecture, adapted after dMARS specification [15] as described up to here, corresponds to the performance component of a BDI learning architecture.

3.1   Which Elements of the Performance Component Are to be Improved by Learning?

BDI agents perform practical reasoning [2] to behave, i.e., reasoning directed towards action, while no-agent AI systems, may be seen as performing epistemic reasoning, i.e., reasoning directed towards beliefs. From the role of beliefs in the theory of practical reasoning, e.g., the asymmetry thesis, the standard and filter of admissibility, it is clear that even when they justify the behavior of the agent, they do it as a part of a background frame that, together with prior intentions, constrain the adoption of new intentions. In doing so, they are playing a different role that the one they play in epistemic reasoning. Particularly, practical reasons to act sometimes differ from epistemic reasons. This is the case for reasonableness of arbitrary choices in Buridan cases[1], e.g., it is *practical reasonable* to choose any plan in the set of relevant applicable plans to form an intention, even if there is no epistemic reason, no reason purely based on the beliefs of the agent, behind this choice. The context of plans may be seen as encoding practical reasons to act in some way and not in another, that together with the background frame of beliefs and prior intentions, support the rational behavior of intentional agents. Then we decided to extend the BDI architecture, enabling the agents to learn about the context of their plans, i.e., when plans are executable. Properly, our agents are not learning their plans [9], but when to use them.

3.2   What Representation Is Used for These Elements?

As mentioned, representations in our BDI architecture are based on two first-order formulae: Belief formulae and situation formulae. Beliefs are grounded belief formulae, like Prolog facts. Belief formulae are used to define plans. Every belief formula is also a situation formula, but situation formulae also include conjunctions and/or disjunctions of belief formulae. The context of plans are represented as situation formulae. These representation issues have two immediate consequences when considering candidate learning methods: First, given the representation of belief and situation formulae, propositional learning methods are discarded. Second, the fact that the context of plans is represented as situation formulae, demands that the target representation of the learning method, enables disjunctive hypothesis, e.g., decision trees.

---

[1] According to the philosopher Jean Buridan, they are situations equally desirable.

3.3   What Feedback Is Available to Learn?

Getting feedback from our BDI architecture is almost direct, since it already detects and processes success and failure of the execution of plan instances. This is done by executing a set of internal actions, up to now, add and delete beliefs. These internal actions are predefined for each plan in the library. The architecture is then extended with a special internal action, that generates a log file of training examples for the learning task. Items to built these examples include: the beliefs characterizing the moment when the plan was selected, the label of success or failure after the execution of the plan, and the plan-id.

3.4   What Prior Information Is Available to Learn?

There are already two sources of prior information in our BDI architecture. First, the plan library of the agents can be seen as prior information, in the sense that plans state expected effects which, from the perspective of the agent, must hold in the environment, i.e., the event e will be satisfied if the plan p is executed, and this is the case if the context of p is a logical consequence of the beliefs of the agent. Second, our BDI architecture also keeps track of predicates, functions, and their signatures, used to define the plans in the library of each agent. These elements can be used to specify the language for the target concept of the learning process.

3.5   Is It a Centralized or Distributed Learning Case?

We believe that awareness seems to be indicative of a learning MAS hierarchy of increasing complexity. In a certain way, this hierarchy of learning environments corresponds to the scale of intentionality of Daniel Dennett [7]. We intend to perform learning at levels 1 and 2 of this hierarchy. Level 0, i.e., only one agent is there, the true isolated learning case, can be seen as a special case of level 1. Levels in this hierarchy are as follows:

Level 1. At this level, agents act and learn from direct interaction with the environment, without being explicitly aware of other agents in the MAS. However, the changes other agents produce in the environment can be perceived by the learning agent. Consider again the robot scenario with two robots: one specialized in painting objects, the other in sanding objects. It is possible to program the painter robot, without awareness of the other robot in the environment, i.e., all it has to learn is that once an object is sanded, it can be painted.

Level 2. At this level, agents act and learn from direct interaction with other agents, using exchange of messages. For the example above, the sander robot can inform the painter robot, that an object is already sanded. Also, the painter agent can ask the sander robot for this information. Exchange of training examples in learning processes is also considered at level 2.

Level 3. At this level, agents learn from the observation of the actions performed by other agents in the system. It involves a different kind of awareness from that of level 2. Agents are not only aware of the presence of other agents, but are also aware of their competences, hence the painter robot is able to perceive that the sander robot is going to sand the table.

3.6   Top-down Induction of Logical Decision Trees

From the representation of the context of plans, as discussed above, we decided to use decision trees as target representation. Top-down induction of decision trees (TDIDT) is a widely used and efficient machine learning technique. As introduced in the ID3 algorithm [22] it approximates discrete value-target functions. Learned functions are represented as trees, corresponding to a disjunction of conjunctions of constrains on the attribute values of the instances. Each path from the decision tree root to a leaf, corresponds to a conjunction of attribute tests, and the tree itself is the disjunction of these conjunctions, i.e., the kind of representation we need for the plan context. However, training examples are represented as a fixed set of attribute-value pairs, i.e., a propositional representation, which does not fix our requirements. Another limitation of ID3-like algorithms, is that they can not use information beyond the training examples, i.e., other things the agent believes, as their plans. ILP [20] can overcome these two main limitations of classic ML inductive methods.

Logical decision trees upgrade the attribute-value representation to a first-order representation, using the ILP paradigm known as learning from interpretations [4]. In this setting, each training example e is represented by a set of facts that encode all the properties of e. Background knowledge can be given in the form of a Prolog program B. The interpretation that represents the example is the set of all ground facts that are entailed by $e \wedge B$, i.e., its minimal Herbrand model. Observe that instead of using a fixed-length vector to represent e, as the case of attribute-value pairs representation, a set of facts is used. This makes the representation much more flexible. Learning from interpretations can be defined as follows. Given: i) A target variable Y; ii) A set of labelled examples E, each consisting of a a set of definite clauses e labelled with a value y in the domain of Y; iii) A language L; iv) A background theory B. Find a hypothesis $H \in L$ such that for all examples labelled with y: i) $H \wedge e \wedge B \models label(y)$; and ii) $\forall y' \neq y : H \wedge e \wedge B \not\models label(y')$.

Learning from interpretations exploits the local assumption, i.e., all the information that is relevant for a single example is localized in two ways. Information contained in the examples is separated from the information in background knowledge. Information in one example is separated from information in other examples. The learning from interpretations setting can be seen as situated somewhere between the attribute-value and learning from entailment [20] settings. It allows extending attribute-value representation towards ILP, without sacrifying efficiency.

ACE [5] is a learning from interpretations system, building logical decision trees, that is, decision trees where every internal node is a first-order conjunction of literals. It uses the same heuristics that ID3 algorithms (gain-ratio and post-pruning heuristics), but computations of the tests are based on the classical refinement operator under Θ-subsumption, which requires the specification of a language L stating which kind of tests are allowed in the decision tree. This is exemplified in the next section, showing how the agents in our extended architecture, guided by autonomy and intentionality, determine when they should learn, configure its learning set, and execute ACE.

4   Learning at Level 1 (Centralized Learning)

Consider that the agent identified as r1 in figure 1, has selected the plan p007 to deal with the event (achieve (p-sanded board)). Then during the execution phase of the interpreter, this plan will either succeed or fail. If the plan fails, we want the agent trying to learn why the plan failed considering that the agent had practical reasons, expressed in the context of the plan, to adopt it as an intention. So the agent should reconsider after its experience, the situation formula expressing the context of the plan. In order to execute the learning process, the agent needs to generate a set of three files consisting of the training examples, the background theory, and the parameters for ACE, including the specification of the target language L, the desired format output, etc. The plan-id is used to identify these files. Files are as follows: i) The knowledge base, identified by the extension .kb, which contains the examples labelled with the class they belong to; ii) The background theory, identified by the extension .bg; and iii) the language bias, identified by the extension .s. These files are generated automatically by the agent, as follows.

When the success or failure of its intention is detected, the agent r1 tracks these executions in a log file identified as p007.kb to indicate to ACE that it contains the examples associated to this plan. Models for the example are shown in table 1. Each model starts with a label that indicates the success or failure of the plan execution. Then a predicate plan is added to establish that the model is an instance of the execution of a particular plan by a particular agent. The model also contains the beliefs of the agent when the plan was selected to create the plan instance. Partial models are memorized by the agent when the plan is selected as relevant and applicable. The label is added in the execution phase. The knowledege base for the examples is stored in the file p007.kb.

The background theory contains information about the plan being learned. The symbols for the variables and constants are taken from the plan definition. A function of our system translates the original definition of plan p007 to this format. It encodes the plan context of p007:

```
plan_context(Ag,p007) :- p_handfree(Ag,Hand), p_at(Obj,free).
```

Then the configuration file is generated. Following the example, this information is stored in a file called p007.s. The first part of this file is common to all configurations. It specifies the information ACE prints while learning (talking); the minimal number of cases to learn; the format of the output (either a logical decision tree or a logic program); and the classes used for the target concept, i.e., either success or failure.

Table 1. Training examples as models at level 1, examples are generated by a single agent

```
begin(model(1)).      begin(model(2)).       begin(model(3)).
success.              success.               failure.
plan(r1,p007).        plan(r1,p007).         plan(r1,p007).
p_state(r1,ok).       p_state(r1,ok).        p_state(r1,painted).
p_handfree(r1,left).  p_handfree(r1,right).  p_handfree(r1,left).
p_at(board,free).     p_at(board,free).      p_handfree(r1,right).
end(model(1)).        end(model(2)).         p_at(board,free).
                                             end(model(3)).


begin(model(4)).      begin(model(5)).       begin(model(6))
failure.              success.               success.
plan(r1,p007)         plan(r1,p007)          plan(r1,p007)
p_state(r1,painted).  p_state(r1,ok).        p_state(r1,ok).
p_handfree(r1,right). p_handfree(r1,left).   p_handfree(r1,left).
p_at(board,free).     p_at(board,free).      p_at(board,free).
p_at(sander,vise).    end(model(5)).         end(model(6))
end(model(4)).
```

```
talking(0).
load(models).
minimal_cases(1).
output_options([c45,lp]).
classes([success, failure]).
```

The second part of the configuration file specifies the predicates to be considered while generating tests for the nodes of the tree. The way our agent generates this file relies on the agent definition. Every time a plan is defined, the interpreter keeps track of the predicates used to define it, and their signature. In this example, three predicates have been used to define the agent: *(p_state/2, p_freehand/2, p_at/2)*. So the agent asks the learning algorithm to consider these predicates with variables as arguments:

```
rmode(p_state(Ag,State)).
rmode(p_freehand(Ag,Hand)).
rmode(p_at(Obj,Place)).
```

Then the agent asks the learning algorithm to also consider these predicates with arguments instantiated after the examples:

```
rmode(p_state(+Ag,#)).
rmode(p_freehand(+Ag,#)).
rmode(p_at(+Obj,#)).
```

Finally the predicates used in the background theory are considered too. At least the two following forms are common to all configurations:

```
rmode(plan_context(Ag,Plan)).
rmode(plan_context(+Ag,#)).
```

The rmode command is used by ACE to determine the language bias L. The '#' sign may be seen as a variable place holder, that takes its constant values from the examples in the knowledge base. The '+' prefix means the variable must be instantiated after the examples in the knowledge base.

Once the number of examples is greater than a threshold (5 in the example) the agent executes a modified non-interactive version of ACE, and suggests the user to watch the p007.out file, containing the result of the learning process, to accordingly modify the definition of the plan. It is also possible that the agent modifies the definition of the plan itself. The strategy adopted to incorporate the results of learning, depends on the domain of application, i.e., sometimes the supervision of the user is preferable.

Output for our example is:

```
Compact notation of pruned tree:
plan_context(Ag,p007) ?
+--yes: p_state(Ag,painted) ?
|       +--yes: [failure] [2.0/2.0]
|       +--no:  [success] [3.0/3.0]
+--no:  [succes] [1.0/1.0]


Equivalent logic program:
n1:-plan_context(Ag,p007).
n2:-plan_context(Ag,p007),p_state(Ag,painted).
class([failure]):-plan_context(Ag,p007),p_state(Ag,painted).
class([succes]):-not(n1).
class([succes]):-plan_context(Ag,p007),not(n2).
```

Fractions of the $[i/j]$ form indicate that there were i examples in the class, and that j of them were well classified by the test proposed. This example used six models and the time of induction was 0.01 seconds, running on a Linux RedHat 8.0 Pentium 4, at 1.6 GHz.

5   A MAS of BDI Learning Agents (Level 2)

The example of the previous section corresponds to level 1 in our hierarchy of learning MAS. At level 2, agents are supposed to learn while they are aware of other agents. Communication is very important when learning in a MAS, but the design of the agent should determine when, what, and why should an individual agent communicate [1].

There are two situations under which a BDI agent should consider communicating while learning. First, the agent is no able to start the execution of its learning process, i.e., it does not have enough examples to run ACE. In this case the agent can ask other agents in the MAS for training examples. Second, the agent is unable to find out a hypothesis to explain the failure of the plan in question, i.e., after the execution of the learning process, the tree produced by ACE has only the node [failure], or the hypothesis found is the original plan context being learned. This means that the examples used by the BDI agent to learn, were insufficient to find out why the plan has failed. In this case the agent may ask other agents in the MAS for more evidence, before executing ACE again.

The results of a learning process are shared by the agents in the MAS due to the way they are defined in the BDI architecture. If the agent has found a hypothesis for the failure of its plan, it will communicate this result to the user, asking for modifications of the plan definition accordingly to the decision tree found. If the user modifies the plan definition, this change automatically affects all agents having this plan in the library. Observe that this does not imply that all plans are shared by the agents, therefore heterogeneous MAS are possible in our architecture.

The concept of competence is used to address communications. It is defined as the set of all the trigger events an agent can deal with, i.e., the union of all triggers in the agent's plan library. Then two ways of sending messages are possible. The agent broadcasts its message including the trigger and the plan-id of the plan to be learned, The other agents accept and process the message if the trigger event is on their competences. Alternatively, competence is used to build a directory for each agent, where each trigger event in the competence of an agent, is associated to the id of other agents in the system that deal with the same trigger event.

Competence and plans determine what to communicate. If two agents have the same plan for the same event, they can be engaged in a process of distributed data gathering, i.e. they can share the examples they have collected. In this case agents are involved in collecting data, but each agent learns locally. The models obtained from three agents in the scenario of figure 1 are shown in table 2. Agent r2 is the learner agent.

This learning process results in the same decision tree obtained in the previous section, but since the first execution done by the learning agent r2 of plan p007 lead to a failure (model 1), it would not be able to collect success training examples for this plan (the BDI interpreter blocks plans that failed for a given event, to avoid the agent trying to execute them again). It means that outside the MAS, agent r2 is not able to learn for this plan. Also the failure example of agent r3 is important, since without it ACE is not able to induce a tree.

6   Conclusion

We have shown how ILP methods, particularly the induction of logical decision trees, can be used to extend a BDI architecture to endow agents with learning skills. These skills were designed to be compatible with the practical rationality behind the behavior of BDI agents. The result is a BDI learning agent architecture implemented on Lisp. The architecture also includes two non-standard

Table 2. Models at level 2, examples are generated by different agents

```
begin(model(1)).        begin(model(2)).        begin(model(3)).
failure.                success.                success.
p_state(r2,painted).    p_freehand(r1,right).   p_state(r1,ok).
p_freehand(r2,right).   p_at(board,free).       p_at(board,free).
p_freehand(r2,left).    plan(r1,p007).          p_handfree(r1,left).
p_at(board,free).       p_state(r1,ok).         plan(r1,p007).
plan(r2,p007).          end(model(2)).          end(model(3)).
end(model(1)).


begin(model(4)).        begin(model(5)).        begin(model(6)).
success.                success.                failure.
p_state(r3,ok).         p_state(r1,ok).         p_state(r3,painted).
p_freehand(r3,left).    p_freehand(r1,left).    p_freehand(r3,right).
p_at(board,free).       p_at(board,free).       p_freehand(r3,left).
plan(r3,p007).          plan(r1,p007).          p_at(board,free).
end(model(4)).          end(model(5)).          plan(r3,p007).
                                                end(model(6)).
```

BDI features, several options for MAS simulation, and an interface to the DTP theorem prover. The example introduced in the previous section, shows that BDI agents situated in a MAS, increase their chances of learning if they can share training examples. Our research contributes from a MAS learning perspective, to extend the well known and studied BDI model of rational agency, beyond its limitations, i.e., lack of learning competences and MAS functionality.

As mentioned here in, at the moment of submission, only Cindy Olivia et al. [21] are focused on the same problem. They present a mono-agent Case-Based BDI framework applied to intelligent search on the web. Even when agents in this framework are based on BDI representations, they perform case-based reasoning (CBR) to act, instead of practical reasoning. CBR is a learning method directed towards action, which makes it very attractive for learning agents, nevertheless much more work is needed to understand the relationship between CBR and the theory of practical reasoning, i.e., what the meaning of similarity functions in terms of practical reasoning is. Observe that this work is ssituated at level 0 (true isolated agents) of the hierarchy of MAS learning systems proposed here.

Future work includes implementing more MAS features for the architecture, e.g., including an ACL. More interestingly, it is possible to design protocols for sharing information of the learning set in more complex situations, e.g., agents having the same competences, but different plans. This is particularly true if ACE is modified to learn incrementaly with each example it receives. We must also consider the relationship between learning and the multi modal logic theories of intentional agency, e.g., If the learning processes described here, maintain the strong-realism conditions, and other forms or realism.

Acknowledgments

We thank David Kinny and Pablo Noriega for their help in our research. The first author is supported by Mexican scholarships from Conacyt, contract 70354, and Promep, contract UVER-53.

References

1. Bradzil, P., et.al.: Learning in Distributed Systems and Multi-Agent Environments. In: Kodratoff (ed.): Machine Learning - EWSL-91, European Working Session on Learning. Lecture Notes in Computer Science, Vol. 482. Springer-Verlag, Heidelberg, Germany (1991)
2. Bratman, M.: Intention, Plans, and Practical Reasoning. Harvard University Press, Cambridge MA., USA (1987)
3. Bratman, M., Israel, D.J., Pollack, M.E.: Plans and resource-bounded practical reasoning. Computational Intelligence. 4:349–355 (1988)
4. Blockeel, H., De Raedt, L.: Top-down induction of first-order logical decision trees. Artificial Intelligence, 101(1–2):285–297 (1998)
5. Blockeel et al., H.: Executing query packs in ILP. In: Cussens, J. and Frish, A. (eds.): Inductive Logic Programming, 10th International Conference, ILP2000, London, U.K. Lecture Notes in Artificial Intelligence, Vol. 1866, pages 60–77. Springer Verlag, Heidelberg, Germany (2000)
6. Castelfranchi, C.: Modelling Social Action for AI Agents. Artificial Intelligence, 103(1):157–182 (1998)
7. Dennett, D.C.: The Intentional Stance. MIT Press, Cambridge MA., USA (1987)
8. Charniak, E., McDermott D.: Introduction to Artificial Intelligence. Addison-Wesley, USA (1985)
9. García, F.: Apprentissage et Planification. In: Proceedings of JICAA'97 USA (1997) 15–26
10. Geddis, D.F.: Caching and First-Order inference in model elimination theorem provers. Ph.D. Thesis. Stanford University, Stanford, CA., USA (1995)
11. Georgeff M.P., Lansky A.L.: Reactive Reasoning and Planning. In: Proceedings of the Sixth National Conference on Artificial Intelligence (AAAI-87), pages 667–682, Seattle WA., USA (1987)
12. Georgeff, M.P., Rao A.S.: A Profile of the Australian AI Institute. IEEE Expert, 11(6):89–92, December (1996)
13. Georgeff, M.P. et.al.: The Belief-Desire-Intention Model of Agency. In: Müller, J., Singh M.P., and Rao, A.S. (eds.): Proceedings of the 5th International Workshop on Intelligent Agents V : Agent Theories, Architectures, and Languages (ATAL-98). Lecture Notes in Artificial Intelligence, Vol. 1555, pages 1–10. Springer Verlag, Hedelgerg, Germany (1999)
14. Huber, M.: A BDI-theoretic mobile agent architecture. In: Proceedings of the Third Conference on Autonomous Agents (Agents99). Seattle, WA., USA (1999) 236–243
15. D'Inverno, M., Kinny, D., Luck, M., Wooldridge M.: A Formal Specification of dMARS. In: Intelligent Agents IV. Lecture Notes in Artificial Intelligence, Vol. 1365. Springer-Verlag, Berlin Heidelberg New York (1997) 155–176
16. Kinny, D. and Georgeff, M.P., Commitment and effectiveness of situated agents. In: Proceeding of the Twelfth International Conference on Artificial Intelligence IJCAI-91, pages 82–88, Sidney, Australia (1991)

17. Lightfoot, D., Formal Specification Using Z. The Macmillan Press LTD, Macmillan Computer Science Series, London, UK (1991)
18. Metral, M.: A generic learning interface architecture. Massachusetts Institute of Technology. Master's thesis. Cambridge, MA., USA (1992)
19. Mitchell, T.M.: Machine Learning, Mc Graw-Hill International Editions, Singapore (1997)
20. Muggleton, S., de Raed, L.: Inductive Logic Programming: Theory and Methods. Journal of Logic Programming, 19:629–679 (1994)
21. Olivia, C., et.al.: Case-Based BDI agents: An Effective Approach to Intelligent Search on the WWW. In: AAAI Symposium on Intelligent Agents. Stanford University, Stanford CA., USA (1999)
22. Quinlan, J.R.: Induction of Decision Trees. Machine Learning 1:81–106 (1986)
23. Rao A.S., Georgeff, M.P.: Decision procedures of BDI logics. Journal of Logic and Computation, 8(3):293–344 (1998)
24. Russell, S.J., Norvig, P.: Artificial Intelligence, a modern approach. Prentice-Hall, New Jersey NJ, USA (1995)
25. Singh, M., Rao, A.S., Georgeff, M.P.: Formal Methods in DAI: Logic-based representations and reasoning. In: Weiss, G. (ed.): Multiagent Systems, a modern approach to Distributed Artificial Intelligence. MIT Press, Cambridge MA., USA (1999)
26. Stone, P., Veloso, M.: Multiagent Systems: A Survey from a Machine Learning Perspective. Autonomous Robotics, 8(3):345-383 (2000)
27. Sutton, R.S., Barto, A.G.: Reinforcement Learning: An introduction. MIT Press, Cambridge, MA., USA (1998)
28. Weiss, G., Sen, S.: Adaptation and Learning in Multiagent Systems. Lecture Notes in Artificial Intelligence, Vol. 1042. Springer-Verlag, Berlin Heidelberg New York (1996)
29. Wooldridge, M.: Reasoning about Rational Agents. MIT Press, Cambridge MA., USA (2000)

The Apriori Stochastic Dependency Detection (ASDD) Algorithm for Learning Stochastic Logic Rules

Christopher Child* and Kostas Stathis

Department of Computing,
School of Informatics,
City University, London
{c.child, k.stathis}@city.ac.uk

Abstract. *Apriori Stochastic Dependency Detection* (ASDD) is an algorithm for fast induction of stochastic logic rules from a database of observations made by an agent situated in an environment. ASDD is based on features of the Apriori algorithm for mining association rules in large databases of sales transactions [1] and the MSDD algorithm for discovering stochastic dependencies in multiple streams of data [15]. Once these rules have been acquired the *Precedence* algorithm assigns operator precedence when two or more rules matching the input data are applicable to the same output variable. These algorithms currently learn propositional rules, with future extensions aimed towards learning first-order models. We show that stochastic rules produced by this algorithm are capable of reproducing an accurate world model in a simple predator-prey environment.

1 Introduction

This paper introduces the *Apriori Stochastic Dependency Detection* (ASDD) algorithm for fast induction of stochastic logic rules from a database of observations. The focus of our research is on methods by which a logic-based agent can automatically acquire a rule-based model of a stochastic environment in which it is situated from observations and use the acquired model to form plans using decision theoretic methods. Examples in this paper are geared towards this research, but the algorithm is applicable to induction of stochastic logic rules in the general case.

The key feature of this algorithm is that it can eliminate candidate n element rules by reference to n-1 element rules that have already been discounted without the need to for expensive scans of the data set. This is achieved via a breadth first search. Rules are discounted at each level of the search if they do not occur regularly in the data set or the addition of extra constraints has no statistical significance on their performance.

Although research in stochastic rule induction is in its infancy, some previous research includes MSDD [14], ILP [12], and the schema mechanism [2]. For a discussion on the topic see [10].

---

* Corresponding author.

J. Dix and J. Leite (Eds.): CLIMA IV, LNAI 3259, pp. 234–249, 2004.

Our research is motivated by the observation that rule based methods in decision theoretic planning, such as stochastic STRIPS operators (SOPs) promise to be a highly efficient method of representing a world model for an agent in a stochastic environment [2]. The main advantage of SOPs is that they provide a solution to the frame problem which other methods in this area do not address [11].

Previous research in automatic acquisition of stochastic environment models has been focused on either explicit state space models or dynamic Bayesian networks (DBNs). State space models record the relative frequency with which each action available to an agent leads to a next state from an initial state [16]. These methods do not scale up well because each environment state must be explicitly enumerated. Dynamic Bayesian networks are an example of a factored state approach, in which the state space is modeled as a set of nodes representing state variables, and dependencies represented as connections. Although methods exist for modelling DBNs from data [13] the representation must explicitly assert that variables unaffected by an action persist in value and therefore suffers from the frame problem. Variables which are unaffected by an action in the probabilistic STRIPS representation, however, need not be mentioned in the actions description [2].

In order to give context to the ASDD algorithm, an example predator-prey domain and probabilistic strips operators (PSOs) are first introduced, which will form the basis of examples in the remainder of the paper. Section (1) describes the ASDD algorithm for stochastic rule induction. Section (2) describes the Precedence algorithm for operator precedence. Section (3) describes the process of state generation from PSO operators. Section (4) gives results comparing the algorithms performance against MSDD and a state space method. Conclusions and future work are presented in section 6.

1.1 Example Predator Prey Domain

The environment consists of a four by four grid surrounded by a "wall". There is *one* predator and *one* prey. The predator will be assumed to have caught the prey when it lands on the same square. The prey selects a random action at each move. Both predator and prey have four actions: move north, east, south and west. An action has the effect of moving the agent one square in the selected direction, unless there is a wall, in which instance there is no effect. The predator and prey move in simultaneous turns.

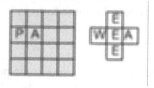

Fig. 1. Simple predator prey scenario. Predator and prey in a 4 by 4 grid. P indicates the predator and A the prey agent. The percept from the predator's perspective is shown to the right

The agent's percept gives the contents of the four squares around it and the square under it. Each square can be in one of three states: empty, wall or agent. For example a predator agent has a wall to the west and a prey to the east would have the percept {EMPTYNORTH, AGENTEAST, EMPTYSOUTH, WALLWEST, EMPTYUNDER}   corresponding to the squares to the north, east, south, west and under respectively (shown in figure 1).

1.2 Probabilistic STRIPS Operators

The STRIPS planning operator representation has, for each action, a set of preconditions, an "add" list, and a "delete" list (Fikes and Nilsson 1971) [6]. The STRIPS planner was designed for deterministic environments, with the assumption that actions taken in a state matching the operator's preconditions would consistently result in the state changes indicated by the operator's add and delete lists. In a non-deterministic environment a less restrictive view is taken, allowing actions to be attempted in any state. The effects of the action then depend on the state in which it was taken and are influenced by some properties external to the agents perception which appear random from the agent's perspective.

The following format for a stochastic STRIPS operator is an adaptation of that used by Oates & Cohen [15] to the form of stochastic logic programs (section 1.3). A stochastic STRIPS operator takes the form: *prob: e ← a, c,* where *a* specifies an action, *c* specifies a context, *e* the effects and *prob* the probability of the effects. If the agent is in a state matching the context *c*, and takes the action *a*, then the agent will observe a state matching the effects *e* with probability *prob*.

The agent is assumed to have a set of *n* possible actions, $A = \{a_1, ..., a_n\}$ and can perceive *m* possible state variables $P = \{p_1, ... p_m\}$, each of which can take on a finite set of possible values. Let $p_i = \{p_{i1}, ..., p_{ik}\}$ be the values associated with the ith variable. The context, *c*, of an operator is specified as a set of variables from P representing the perception of the agent. In order to restrict the number of possible operators, *e* is defined to be a *single* variable for each operator, again taken from the set P. A combination of single variable operators is, however, sufficient to generate a full percept.

In the predator prey domain:

- $A = \{$MOVENORTH, MOVEEAST, MOVESOUTH, MOVEWEST$\}$
- $P = \{$NORTH, EAST, SOUTH, WEST, UNDER$\}$
- $P_{NORTH} = \{$EMPTYNORTH, WALLNORTH, AGENTNORTH$\}$
- $P_{EAST}, P_{SOUTH}, P_{WEST}, P_{UNDER}$ follow the same form as P_{NORTH}

1.3 Stochastic Logic Programs

Stochastic logic programs (SLPs) are first-order logic program extensions of stochastic grammars. Although ASDD is currently not able to learn first-order programs, the full SLP representation is presented, with the eventual goal of this research being to learn programs of this nature. Muggleton [12] defines the syntax of an SLP in as follows:

"An SLP, S, is a set of labelled clauses $p{:}C$ where p is a probability (i.e. a number in the range [0,1] and C is a first-order range-restricted clause. The subset S_p is of clauses in S with predicate symbol p in the head is called the definition of p. For each definition S_p the sum of probability labels π_p must be at most 1. S is said to be complete if $\pi_p = 1$ for each p and incomplete otherwise. $P(S)$ represents the definite program consisting of all the clauses in S, with labels removed."

2 Apriori Stochastic Dependency Detection (ASDD)

ASDD is based on the Apriori algorithm for mining association rules (section (2.1)), and the MSDD algorithm for finding dependencies in multiple streams of data. MSDD has previously been applied to the problem of learning probabilistic STRIPS operators in [15] [4].

2.1 The Apriori Method for Association Rule Mining

The Apriori algorithm was designed to address the problem of discovering association rules between items in a large database of sales transactions. A record in these databases typically consists of a transaction date and the items bought in the transaction (referred to as *basket* data). An example of association rule is that 98% of customers purchasing tyres and auto accessories also purchase automotive services [1]. The form of this rule is similar to a stochastic logic rule of the form: 0.98: Automotive Services ← Tyres, Accessories. The Apriori algorithm and its descendants have been shown to scale up to large databases and methods also exist for incrementally updating the learned rules [3]. For a survey see [7]. These features are highly desirable to probabilistic STRIPS learning with its need to process a large database of perceptions, and incrementally improve these rules as the agent receives new data. The language used to describe ASDD ((2.2)) has been chosen to reflect that used in [1]. The algorithm is largely similar, but has an additional *aprioriFilter* step ((2.2.5)) which removes potential conditions from rules if they are shown to have no significant effect on their probability. There is also a final *filter* step, which is equivalent to that used in MSDD.

2.2 Apriori Stochastic Dependency Detection (ASDD)

The task of learning probabilistic STRIPS operators proceeds as follow: The sets P and A are as defined in section (1.2). Let D be a set of perceptual data items (*PDIs*) from an agent, where each *PDI* is a triplet of the form $\{P_{t-1}, A_{t-1}, P_t\}$ i.e. the percept and action at time t-1 and the percept at time t. The elements of $P \cup A$ are collectively defined as *rule elements*.

A *PDI* contains rule element set X, if $X \subseteq P_{t-1} \cup A_{t-1}$. A *rule* is an implication from a rule element set to an effect, e, of the form $e \leftarrow X$, where $e \in P_t$. In logic programing terms e is the *head* of the rule and X is the *body*.

A *PSO (prob: e ← X)* is a *rule* with an associated probability (*prob*). A *rule* holds in the data set D with *probability prob* if *prob%* of *PDIs* which contain X also contain e.

The *rule e ⟵ X*, has *support s* in the perceptual data set *D* if *s* of PDIs in *D* contain $e \cup X$. *minsup* defines the minimum *support* a PSO has to display before it is admissible to the rule base[1].

The problem of discovering a PSO set can be separated into three sub-problems:

1. *Discover large rule element sets* at level *k* exhibiting *support* above *minsup*. The *support* for a rule element set is the number of *PDIs* that contain the rule element set. The level of a rule element set is defined as the number of rule elements it contains (section 2.2.1).
2. Combine rule element sets at level *k* to form a list of candidate sets for level *k+1* using *aprioriGen*, which removes all candidates that cannot have minimum support (section 2.2.3).
3. After level 3, apply the *AprioriFilter* function to remove stochastic planning operators (rule element sets with a result element) at level *k*, which are *covered* by an operator at level *k-3* (section 2.2.5).
4. Finally, *filter* the remaining rules to remove stochastic planning operators which are *covered* by a rule at any level (section 2.2.4).

2.2.1 Discovering Large Rule Element Sets

Discovering large rule element sets involves making multiple passes over the perceptual data set D. In the first pass (giving level k = 1) the support of individual rule element sets is counted to determine which of them are *large*, i.e. have minimum support. In each subsequent pass, large rule element sets from the previous pass (k-1) are used to create *candidate* rule element sets.

The support for each of these candidate sets is counted in a pass over the data. Candidates that do not have minimum support are removed and the remaining candidates are used to generate candidates for the next level. After the third pass, rule element sets that have an effect element (rule head) can be *filtered* by rules at the k-1th level to see if additional conditions have a significant effect on its probability (section (2.2.5)). This process continues until no new sets of rule elements are found.

The *AprioriGen* algorithm (adapted from [1]) generates the candidate rule element sets to be counted in a pass by considering only the rule element sets found to be large in the previous pass. Candidates with k rule elements are generated by rule element sets at the k-1 level. Any generated candidates containing a k-1 set which does not have minimum support are then removed in a the prune step, because any subset of a large set must also be large. This avoids the need for an expensive pass over the data set when generating candidates.

The notation is used in the following algorithms is:

- L[k]: Set of large k-rule element sets (those with minimum support). Each member of this set has four fields:

---

[1] This definition of support is slightly different from the Apriori algorithm, in which support is defined as a percentage of the data.

1. elements: a set of rule elements.
2. support: the number of times the rule matched the database (if the set of rule elements has an effect (rule head).
3. bodySupp: the number of times the body of the rule matched the database.
4. ruleSet: see section 3.1.
−   C[k]: Set of candidate k-rule element sets (potentially large sets). Fields are identical to L[k].

2.2.2 The ASDD Algorithm

The first part of the Apriori algorithm simply counts occurrences of single rule elements to determine large 1 rule element sets. A subsequent pass consists of the following steps:

1. Large rule element sets L[k-1] found in the pass (k-1) are used to generate the candidate rule element sets C[k], using the *aprioriGen* function (section 2.2.3).
2. The *support* of candidates in C[k] is counted by a database scan using the *subset* function, which returns the subset of C[k] contained in a PDI[2].
3. Rule element sets with below minimum support are removed.
4. If rule element set has no effect (head) bodySupp = support.
5. Rules, which are rule element sets with an effect element (rule head), are filtered against rules that subsume them at the level k-3 by the *aprioriFilter* function (section 2.2.5).

Finally, rules are filtered with a greater test for statistical significance by the *filter* function (section 2.2.4).

```
ASDD(D)
L[1] = {large 1-literalsets};
for (k = 2; L[k-1] ≠ Ø; k++) {
   Ck = AprioriGen(L[k-1]);                    //(1)
   for (pdi ∈ D) {                             //(2)
      Ct = Subset(Ck, pdi)
      for (c ∈ Ct)
         c.support ++;
   }
   L[k] = {c ∈ Ck | c.support ≥ minsup}    //(3)
   for (l ∈ L[k] where not HasEffect(l))
         l.bodySupp = l.support;
   if (k > 3)
      L[k] = AprioriFilter(L[k], L[k-3]);  //(4)
}
ruleSet = ∪ for k of L[k];
return Filter(ruleSet, D, g);
```

2.2.3 AprioriGen

The aprioriGen function generates a set of potentially large k-rule element sets from (k-1) sets.

---

[2] An efficient subset function is described in the original algorithm but is not used in the implementation tested here.

There are two main steps:

1.   The join step joins L[k-1] with L[k-1] to form candidate rule sets C[k].
2.   The prune step deletes generated candidates for which some (k-1) subset is not present in L[k-1].

For the purposes of rule generation, the following steps have been added:

1.   Rules (rule element sets with an effect element) will have a body that is equal to one of the rules used to form them. In this case the bodySupp variable is copied to restrict the number of database passes required.
2.   Effects are restricted to just one variable. If both L[k-1] rules have an effect variable (rule head) they are not combined (the *HasEffect* function will return true).

```
Join(L[k-1])
C[k] = Ø
for (p ∈ L[k-1]) {
    for (q ∈ L[k-1]) {
        generate = true;
        if (p == q) next q;
        if (HasEffect(p) and HasEffect(q)) next q;
        if (p.lastElement > last(q.elements)) {
            generate = false; next q; }
        for (i from 0 to num elements in p-2) {
            if (p.elements[i] ≠ q.elements[i])
                generate = false; next q;
        }
        if (!generate)
            next q;
        newC.elements = p.elements + last(q.elements);
        if (HasEffect(newC) {
            if (body(newC) == body(p)) newC.bodySupp = p.bodySupp;
            if (body(newC) == body(q)) newC.bodySupp = q.bodySupp;
        }
        add(C[k], newCandidate);
}}
return C[k]

Prune(Ck, L[k-1])
for (c ∈ C[k]) {
    forall (k-1 size subsets s of c) {
        if (s ∉ L[k-1]) delete c from C[k]
```

Note: The body function returns all rule elements excluding effect rule elements (rule head).

Example: L[3] rule element sets are (← indicates an effect element):

1.   {MOVENORTH, AGENTNORTH ←, EMPTYEAST},
2.   {MOVENORTH, AGENTNORTH ←, WALLSOUTH},
3.   {MOVENORTH, EMPTYEAST, WALLSOUTH},
4.   {MOVENORTH, EMPTYEAST, WALLNORTH},
5.   {AGENTNORTH ←, EMPTYEAST, WALLSOUTH}.

The join step creates the C[4] rule element sets as follows: From a combination of 1 and 2: {MOVENORTH, AGENTNORTH ←, EMPTYEAST, WALLSOUTH). From a combination of 3 and 4: {MOVENORTH, EMPTYEAST, WALLSOUTH, WALLNORTH}.

The prune step will delete the rule element set {MOVENORTH, EMPTYEAST, WALLSOUTH, WALLNORTH } because the subset {MOVENORTH, WALLSOUTH, WALLNORTH } is not contained in L[3]. In the full data set this behaviour is observed because the agent cannot perceive the conditions WALLSOUTH and WALLNORTH simultaneously. The algorithm is able to draw this conclusion without a further pass through the data.

2.2.4 Filter

The *filter* function was presented in (Oates and Coen) [15] as an extension to the MSDD algorithm. It removes rules that are *covered* and *subsumed* by more general ones. For example, the rule {Prob 1.0: WALLNORTH ← MOVENORTH, WALLNORTH, WALLEAST } is a more specific version of {Prob 1.0: WALLNORTH ← MOVENORTH, WALLNORTH, } and therefore *subsumes* it. If the extra condition has no significant effect on the probability of the rule then it is *covered* by the more general rule (and therefore unnecessary). In this example the additional condition WALLEAST has no significant effect.

More general operators are preferred because they are more likely to apply to rules outside the original data set and a reduced number of rules can cover the same information. The test determines whether *Prob* ($e| c_1, c_2, a$) and *Prob* ($e | c_1, a$) are significantly different. If not, the general operator is kept the specific one discarded.

```
Filter (R, D, g)
sort R in non-increasing order of generality
S = {}
while NotEmpty(R)
    s = Pop(R)
    Push (s, S)
    for (r ∈ R)
        if (Subsumes(s, r) and G(s, r, D) < g)
            remove r from R
Return S
```

R is a set of stochastic rules. D is the set of PDIs observed by the agent. *Subsumes*(d_1, d_2) is a Boolean function defined to return true if dependency operator d_1 is a generalisation of d_2. $G(d_1, d_2, H)$ returns the G statistic to determine whether the conditional probability of d_1's effects given its conditions is significantly different from d_2's effects given its conditions. The parameter g is used as a threshold, which the G statistic must exceed before d_1 and d_2 are considered different[3]. For an explanation of calculation of the G statistic see [14].

2.2.5 AprioriFilter

The AprioriFilter function is similar to filter, but checks candidate rules at level k against rules at level k-3.

---

[3] A value of 3.84 for g tests for statistical significance at the 5% level.

```
AprioriFilter(Ck, L[k-3], significant)
RulesL[k-3] = {l ∈ L[k-3] | HasEffect(l)}
for (c ∈ Ck where HasEffect(c))
    for (lr ∈ RulesL[k-3])
        if (Subsumes(lr,c) and G(c,lr) < significant) {
            remove c from Ck;
            next c;
        }
return Ck
```

The significant parameter defines the g statistic level at which we filter. Rules filtered by this function are removed in the same way as pruned rules, and therefore take no further part in rule generation. For example, if the rule: a ← b is removed by this method no further rules will be generated with head *a* and body *b* (e.g. {a ← b,c}, {a ← b,d}). This can cause a problem when the effect of *b* as a condition for *a* is not immediately apparent (e.g. the XOR function in which the output is determined by a combination of each input, with the observation of a single input appearing to have no bearing on the output).

The problem was resolved by setting the significant parameter to 0.1 (3.84 would be 95% significance), by not filtering until rules at level 4 (i.e. the rule {a ← b,c,d} can be filtered by {a ← b,c}, and by filtering against rules with three less conditions (k-3). Further experimentation is required in this area.

The *aprioriFilter* function alters the stopping criteria through removing rules that do not appear significant at each level. Apriori halts when there are no further rules that can be generated above minimum support. ASDD halts with the additional criteria that there are likely to be no further significant rules.

2.2.6 Generating Rule Probabilities

The rule probability (*prob*), which is the probability of the effect (rule head) being true if the body (conditions) is true is derived empirically as *prob = support/bodySupp*. This is called rule *confidence* in association rule literature.

2.2.7 Add Rule Complements

The *Filter* function often filters rules and not their complements. For example, the variable, NORTH, can take the values: EMPTYNORTH, AGENTNORTH and WALLNORTH. The filter process could filter rule 2 below, but leave 1 and 3.

1.   0.6: EMPTYNORTH   ← MOVENORTH, EMPTYWEST
2.   0.1: AGENTNORTH   ← MOVENORTH, EMPTYWEST
3.   0.3: WALLNORTH   ← MOVENORTH, EMPTYWEST

This would cause a problem in the state generation (section (4)), because the set of rules will not generate states with AGENTNORTH present. The algorithm iterates through all rules in the learned dependencies, *R*, checking that all possible values of its effect fluent are either present in *R* already or do not match any observations in the data *D*. If a missing rule is found it is added to *R*.

```
AddRuleComplements(R, D)
for (r ∈ R) do
    f = r.head;
    for (fValue ∈ possibleValues(f))
```

```
if (fValue ≠ f.value)
    newRule = copy of f with f.head set to fValue
        if (newRule ∉ R)
            if (newRule matches a PDI in D)
                add newRule to R
```

3 The Precedence Algorithm

The *Precedence* algorithm provides a method of resolving conflicts when more than one *rule set* is applicable to the same state. A *rule set* is defined as a set of rules that apply to the same output variable and has the same body.

Example: The percept at time t-1 is {EMPTYNORTH, WALLEAST, AGENTSOUTH, EMPTYUNDER } and the action at time t-1 is MOVENORTH . The conflicting rule sets in Table 1 and Table 2 apply to the same output variable, NORTH, which can take values WALLNORTH, EMPTYNORTH, AGENTNORTH   . The *Precedence* algorithm defines how conflicts of this nature are resolved.

Table 1. Rule set with body: action = MOVENORTH   and percept contains EMPTYNORTH

Effect	Conditions
0.6: EMPTY_NORTH	← MOVE_NORTH, EMPTY_NORTH
0.1: AGENT_NORTH	← MOVE_NORTH, EMPTY_NORTH
0.3: WALL_NORTH	← MOVE_NORTH, EMPTY_NORTH

Table 2. Rule set with body: action = MOVENORTH   and percept contains AGENTSOUTH

Effect	Conditions
0.7: EMPTY_NORTH	← MOVE_NORTH, AGENT_SOUTH
0.3: WALL_NORTH	← MOVE_NORTH, AGENT_SOUTH

The precedence algorithm evaluates the precedence of a generated set of rules *R*, over a set of PDIs, *D*, and proceeds in the following 2 steps:

1. Categorise all rules into *rule sets*. A *rule set* is a group of rules with the same output variable and the same body (section 3.1).
2. For all PDIs in the database, if two rule sets apply to the same PDI and have same output variable, define which one has precedence using the *FirstRuleSetSuperior* function. This function finds the subset of PDIs for which both rule sets apply and uses an error measure to check which set performs best on the subset (section 3.2).

```
Precedence(R, D)
ruleSets = FormRuleSets(R, D)
for (p ∈ D){
    matchedRules = MatchingRules(ruleSets, p);
    for (rSet1 ∈ RuleSetsIn(matchedRules)) {
        for (rSet2 ∈ RuleSetsIn(matchedRules)) {
            if (rSet1 == rSet2) next rSet2;
            if (OutputVar(rSet1) ≠ OutputVar(rSet2)) next rSet2;
            if (PrecedenceSet(rSet1, rSet2) next rSet2;
            if (FirstRuleSetSuperior(set1, set2))
```

```
                    SetPrecedenceOver(set2, set1);
             else
                    SetPrecedenceOver(set1, set2);
   }   }   }
```

The *MatchingRules* function returns the subset of rule sets with a body matching the percept and action from the PDI. The *RuleSetsIn* function returns the rule sets contained in the matching rules. The *OutputVar* function returns the variable that forms the head of a rule (rather than it's actual value). If the head of a rule is EMPTYNORTH then the variable is NORTH.

Note that D can be either the same set of data used to learn the rules, or a separate set used purely to test the rules. If the same data set is used, the speed of the algorithm can be increased by the observation that a specific rule set (one with more conditions) will always have precedence over a general one (section 3.2).

3.1 FormRuleSets

Rule sets are sets of rules with the same conditions (rule body) which apply to the same output variable. E.g. {Prob: 0.5: EMPTYNORTH ← MOVENORTH, Prob: 0.5: AGENTNORTH ← MOVENORTH } is a rule set for the variable NORTH.

```
FormRuleSets(R)
for (r ∈ R) {
    if (NotEmpty(r.ruleSet) next r;
    for (c ∈ R) {
        if (Body(r) ≠ Body(c)) next c;
        if (OutputVar(r) ≠ OutputVar(c)) next c;
        if (r ∈ c.ruleSet)) {
            copy(r.ruleSet, c.ruleSet)); next r; }
        r.ruleSet += c;
}} return R;
```

3.2 FirstRuleSetSuperior

The *FirstRuleSetSuperior* function returns true if the first rule set should have precedence in situations where the two rule sets conflict. This is achieved by comparing the probability values for the output variable of the rule sets with a new rule set generated by combining their conditions. The probabilities for the new rule set are generated empirically in the same manner as all other rules (section 2.2.6) *prob = support/bodySupp*.

Example: The rule sets in Table 1 and Table 2 have the conditions {MOVENORTH, EMPTYNORTH } and {MOVENORTH, AGENTSOUTH } respectively. If the two sets of conditions are combined and the effects (rule heads) added the new rule set shown in Table 3 is generated.

Table 3. Rule set formed from the combination of rule sets in Table 1 and Table 2

0.75: EMPTY_NORTH	← MOVE_NORTH, EMPTY_NORTH, AGENT_NORTH
0.0: AGENT_NORTH	← MOVE_NORTH, EMPTY_NORTH, AGENT_SOUTH
0.25: WALL_NORTH	← MOVE_NORTH, EMPTY_NORTH, AGENT_SOUTH

The rule set that has the least error when compared to the combined rule set is given precedence over the other. In the implementation used for this paper, an error of +0.5 was given for each non-matching output and the difference otherwise. The rule set in Table 1 would therefore have an error of 0.5 (for AGENTNORTH) + (0.75 -0.6 = 0.15) for EMPTYNORTH + (0.3 -0.25 = 0.05) for WALLNORTH . The total error is therefore 0.7. This error measure is somewhat arbitrary, but was defined in order to penalise rules which failed to generate all values for a variable, however infrequently that value occurs.

Note 1: A rule set which is *subsumed* by a more general rule will always have precedence over a general one, if we are using the same data set to test rule sets as to create them. This is because the combined rule set will be equal to the more specific rule set. For example, if we have a rule with conditions {a,b} and a rule with conditions {a}, the combined rule has conditions {a,b}.

Note 2: If the combined rule set applies to a limited number of examples from the data this method is likely to produce spurious results.

4   Generating States from Learned Rules

The state generator function generates all possible next states (with associated probabilities) for an action that the agent could take in a given state. These states are generated using the rules learned by ASDD from the history of observations. The generated states can then be used as a model by a reinforcement learning algorithm such as value learning to generate a policy. This method has been applied previously in [4].

Our implementation of the ASDD algorithm generates a set of rules with only one fluent in the effects in order to reduce substantially the number of rules that must be evaluated. States are generated as follows:

1. Find all rules matching the current state and selected action. This is the subset of rules with conditions matching the state and action.
2. Remove rules that defer to other matching rules. For each rule in the rule set from step 1, remove it if another rule has precedence over it.
3. Generate possible states and probabilities (section 4.1).
4. Remove impossible states using constraints and normalise the state probabilities (section 4.2).

4.1   Generate Possible States

The possible states are generated as follows:

1. Create a new state from each combination of effect fluent values in the rules remaining after steps 1 and 2 above.
2. Multiply the probability of each effect rule to generate the probability of each state.

In order to demonstrate this process, we refer back to the predator-prey scenario, introduced in section 4, which forms the basis of the experiments in section 0 and shows how the predator generates states from the learned rules.

After steps 1 and 2 from section 0, we are left with the rules in **Table 4** for the initial percept {WALL_NORTH, EMPTY_EAST, EMPTY_SOUTH, AGENT_WEST, EMPTY_UNDER} and action MOVE_NORTH .

Table 4. Rules generated by the ASDD algorithm for the predator prey scenario matching the initial percept WALL_NORTH, EMPTY_EAST, EMPTY_SOUTH, AGENT_WEST, EMPTY_UNDER and action MOVE_NORTH, after removal of rules by precedence

Prob:	Effect	Conditions
1.0	WALL_NORTH	MOVE_NORTH, WALL_NORTH
1.0	EMPTY_EAST	MOVE_NORTH, EMPTY_EAST, AGENT_WEST
1.0	EMPTY_SOUTH	MOVE_NORTH, WALL_NORTH, AGENT_WEST
0.59	EMPTY_WEST	MOVE_NORTH, EMPTY_EAST, AGENT_WEST
0.41	AGENT_WEST	MOVE_NORTH, EMPTY_EAST, AGENT_WEST
0.63	EMPTY_UNDER	MOVE_NORTH, WALL_NORTH, AGENT_WEST
0.37	AGENT_UNDER	MOVE_NORTH, WALL_NORTH, AGENT_WEST

The states generated from the rules in Table 4 are shown in Table 5. The probabilities for each state are generated by multiplying the probabilities of each rule that generated the state.

Table 5. Generated states and associated probabilites from the rules in Table 4

WALL_NORTH	EMPT_EAST	EMPT_SOUTH	EMPT_WEST	EMPT_UNDER	Pr: 0.37
WALL_NORTH	EMPT_EAST	EMPT_SOUTH	EMPT_WEST	AGEN_UNDER	Pr: 0.22
WALL_NORTH	EMPT_EAST	EMPT_SOUTH	AGEN_WEST	EMPT_UNDER	Pr: 0.25
WALL_NORTH	EMPT_EAST	EMPT_SOUTH	AGEN_WEST	AGEN_UNDER	Pr: 0.15

There were two rules for the *west* variable with results EMPTY and AGENT, and two rules for the *under* fluent with results EMPTY and AGENT. The other rules had one result each resulting in a total of: 2 *1 *1 *2 *1 = 4 possible states.

4.2   Removing Impossible States with Constraints

Some of the states generated could not occur in the domain area. For example in the predator-prey scenario, the operators may generate a percept with two agents when there is only one agent in the world (e.g. the rule in Italics in Table 5). Ultimately, the agent should automatically generate constraints that define impossible world states. A rule such as IMPOSSIBLE (AGENT_NORTH, AGENT_SOUTH) allows elimination of the impossible world states generated. If we do not use these constraints, the erroneous generated states will propagate (e.g. predator agents, three walls etc.), and the model becomes meaningless, as it is too far detached from the real world states. Currently our system removes impossible states by checking that each generated state contains only one agent, and does not have walls opposite each other, but the *impossible* function should be simple to create by observing rule element sets eliminated in the *prune* step of the ASDD algorithm.

After elimination of illegal states, the probabilities of remaining states are normalised by dividing the probability of each state by the total probability of all generated states to give the final states.

Despite the addition of the two constraints mentioned, the state generator is still able to generate erroneous states as is demonstrated below. Removing states of this type is a complex problem as the states themselves are not impossible.

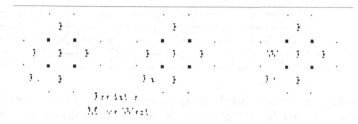

Fig. 2. Generation of erroneous states. From the initial state P1 in which the prey (P) is immediately to the west, the state generator generates the states Pa and Pb after a move west action. Situation Pa is in fact not possible, because the predator and prey take simultaneous moves. For the predator to be on top of the prey after a move west, the prey would have to have stayed still. This is only possible if it moved into a wall, which it cannot have done as all the square around it are empty

Results

Table 6 compares the speed of ASDD against the MSDD algorithm. Timings were taken on learning rules from data sets of 100 to 20000 observations of random moves. Performance was measured on a 350MHz Pentium with 256MB RAM. Although these are only preliminary tests, we found that ASDD displayed roughly equal performance to MSDD initially, and that the time taken to learn rules increased roughly in proportion to the size of the data set for MSDD. On larger data sets time taken by ASDD starts to level and thus shows a dramatic performance increase against MSDD for 20000 observations. ASDD minimum support was set to 1 (any occurrence means a rule set is not discarded), and significant in AprioriFilter to 0.1. For both ASDD and MSDD g in *Filter* was set to 1.17.

Table 7 gives an error measure of the state generation ability of ASDD, MSDD and a state map against an empirical measure of the state transition probabilities taken from a state map of 200,000 trials (a "correct" state map). The state map records, for each percept and action, the relative frequencies of each next percept. The error measure is defined as follows: For each state generated which is not present in the "correct" state map add 0.5 to the error. For each in the "correct" state map which is not in the generated set, add 0.5 to the error. If both state sets contain the same state add the absolute difference in probability for the two states. The total number of state-action pairs in the "correct" map was 168 and total state-action following states was 852.

Table 6. Time taken (in seconds) to learn rules with data collected from 100, 1000, 2000, 5000, 10000 and 20000 random moves

	100	1000	2000	5000	10000	20000
ASDD	36	227	303	471	641	828
MSDD	12	213	442	1151	2363	4930

Table 7. Error measure of generated states generated from rules learned from data collected over 100, 1000, 2000, 5000, 10000 and 20000 random moves

	100	1000	2000	5000	10000	20000
State Map	415.9	355.2	261.8	135.1	40.5	15.3
ASDD	480.0	335.1	274.6	220.4	197.9	108.9
MSDD	482.7	333.5	280.5	198.7	137.6	92.18

The performance of both rule-learning methods is poor against a state map generated from the same number of trials except in the case where there is a limited amount of data. The performance of the rule sets generated by ASDD and MSDD are, however, approximately equal in generating states. This indicates that the error lies in our state generation process, rather than the rules themselves. Further investigation is required to discern why the error rate is high for both rule sets. A possible reason for the error is the removal of impossible states problem outlined in section 4.2.

6   Conclusions

This paper presents the ASDD algorithm, which is the first step in the development of an efficient algorithm for learning stochastic logic rules from data. Results in our preliminary tests are extremely encouraging in that the algorithm is able to learn rules accurately and at over twice the speed of MSDD. Future extensions to the method are expected to greatly increase the performance and application of the algorithm. Some initial areas to examine are:

– Increasing the performance of the algorithm by use of efficient subset function and transaction ID approaches from Apriori.
– Testing the algorithm on a wide variety of data sets to give a better performance measure.
– Implementing incremental updating of rules using methods from association rule mining.
– Generating first-order rules from data through the inclusion of background knowledge.

Acknowledgements

Chris Child would like to acknowledge the support of EPSRC, grant number 00318484 and gratefully acknowledges the contribution of Fabrizio R. Guzzi.

References

1. Agrawal, R. and Srikant, R.: Fast Algorithms for Mining Association Rules. In: *Proc. 20th Int. Conf. Very Large Data Bases {VLDB}*, 12-15, Bocca, J.B., Jarke, M., Zaniolo, C. (eds.), Morgan Kaufmann, (1994).
2. Boutilier, C. and Dean, T. and Hanks, S. Decision-Theoretic Planning: Structural Assumptions and Computational Leverage. *Journal of Artificial Intelligence Research* 11: 1-94. (1999).
3. Cheung, D.W. and Han, J., Ng, V., and Wong, C.Y., Maintenance of discovered association rules in large databases: An incremental updating technique. In Proc. 1996 Int. Conf. Data Engineering, pages 106--114, New Orleans, Louisiana, Feb. (1996)
4. Child, C. and Stathis, K. 2003. SMART (Stochastic Model Acquisition with ReinforcemenT) Learning Agents: A Preliminary Report. Adaptive Agents and Multi-Agent Systems AAMAS-3. AISB 2003 Convention., Dimitar Kazakov. Aberystwyth, University of Wales. ISBN 1 902956 31 5. (2003).
5. Drescher, G.L. *Made-Up Minds, A Constructivist Approach to Artificial Intelligence*. The MIT Press. (1991)
6. Fikes, R.E. and Nilsson, N.J. STRIPS: a new approach to the application of theorem proving to problem-solving. *Artificial Intelligence* 2(3-4): 189-208 (1971).
7. Hidber C., Online Association Rule Mining. SIGMOD Conf., 1999. http://citeseer.nj.nec.com/hidber98online.html (1999).
8. Hipp, J. and Gunter, U. and Nakhaeizadeh, G., Algorithms for Association Rule Mining - A General Survey and Comparison, *SIGKDD Explorations*, 2000, vol. 2, no. 1, 58-64, July. (2000).
9. Kaelbling, L.P. and Littman, H.L. and Moore, A.P. Reinforcement Learning: A Survey. *Journal of Artificial Intelligence Research* 4: 237-285. (1996)
10. Kaelbling, L. P., and Oates, T. and Hernandez, N. and Finney, S. Learning in Worlds with Objects, citeseer.nj.nec.com/kaelbling01learning.html.
11. McCarthy, J. and Hayes, P.J. Some philosophical problems from the standpoint of artificial intelligence. *Machine Intelligence*, 4: 463-502. (1969).
12. Muggleton, S.H. Learning Stochastic Logic Programs. *Proceedings of the AAAI2000 Workshop on Learning Statistical Models from Relational Data*, L. Getoor and D. Jensen, AAAI. (2000).
13. Murphy, K.P. Dynamic Bayesian Networks: Representation, Inference and Learning. Ph.D. Thesis, University of California, Berkeley. (2002).
14. Oates T., Schmill, M.D., Gregory, D.E. and Cohen P.R. Detecting complex dependencies in categorical data. Chap. in *Finding Structure in Data: Artificial Intelligence and Statistics V*. Springer Verlag. (1995).
15. Oates, T. and Cohen, P. R.Learning Planning Operators with Conditional and Probabilistic Effects. *AAAI-96 Spring Symposium on Planning with Incomplete Information for Robot Problems*, AAAI. (1996).
16. Sutton, R.S., and A.G. Barto. *Reinforcement Learning: An Introduction*. A Bradford Book, MIT Press. (1998).

Author Index

Lecture Notes in Artificial Intelligence (LNAI)